HISTORY

OF

THE COMMONWEALTH

AND

PROTECTORATE

VOLUME III.—1653–1655

HISTORY

OF

THE COMMONWEALTH

AND

PROTECTORATE

1649—1656

BY

SAMUEL RAWSON GARDINER

HON. D.C.L. OXFORD ; LITT.D. CAMBRIDGE ; LL.D. EDINBURGH ; PH.D. GÖTTINGEN;
FELLOW OF MERTON COLLEGE ; HONORARY STUDENT OF CHRISTCHURCH ;
FELLOW OF KING'S COLLEGE, LONDON

IN FOUR VOLUMES

VOLUME III.—1653-1655

THE
WINDRUSH
PRESS
GLOUCESTERSHIRE · ENGLAND

History of the Commonwealth and Protectorate
Volume Three
was first published by
Longmans, Green and Co.
in 1903

This edition first published by
The Windrush Press
Windrush House
Main Street, Adlestrop
Gloucestershire GL56 0YN
in 1989

ISBN 0 900075 85 6 (cased)
ISBN 0 900075 90 2 (paperback)

British Library Cataloguing in Publication Data

Gardiner, Samuel Rawson
    History of the Commonwealth and Protectorate: 1649–
    1656: in four volumes.
    Vol. 3, 1653–1655
    1. England, 1625–1660
    I. Title
    942.06′2

    ISBN 0-900075-85-6 (cased)
    ISBN 0-900075-90-2 (paperback)

The publishers regret that it has been impossible to include
the coloured pull-out maps of the original edition.

Printed and bound in Great Britain by
Biddles Ltd, Guildford and King's Lynn

CONTENTS

OF

THE THIRD VOLUME

CHAPTER XXIX

THE FIRST MONTHS OF THE PROTECTORATE

CHAPTER XXX

THE STRUGGLE FOR THE NORTH SEA

CHAPTER XXXII

GLENCAIRN'S RISING

CHAPTER XXXIII

A DOUBLE NEGOTIATION

CHAPTER XXXIV

THE WESTERN DESIGN

CHAPTER XXXV

PROTECTOR AND PARLIAMENT

CHAPTER XXXVI

DRIFTING ASUNDER

CHAPTER XXXIX

PENRUDDOCK'S RISING

CHAPTER XL

THE MAJOR-GENERALS

MAPS

THE COMMONWEALTH

AND

PROTECTORATE

CHAPTER XXIX

THE FIRST MONTHS OF THE PROTECTORATE

On December 16 Cromwell, attired not in military uniform but in 'a plain black suit and cloak,' took the oath required in the Instrument in the Court of Chancery in Westminster Hall. Around him as he seated himself on a chair of State were the chief officers of the army, as well as the representatives of the civilian government—the judges and State officials, including the Lord Mayor and Aldermen of the City of London. Having received their obeisance, after the fashion of the former kings, his Highness, Oliver, the Lord Protector of the Commonwealth of England, was reconducted to Whitehall, assigned to him as the residence of the head of the State.[1] The Protector's passage through the streets was guarded by soldiers, and the acclamations raised were almost entirely confined to them and to Cromwell's own special partisans. The population of London, which had applauded his expulsion of the Long Parliament, accepted, for the most part, with submission the new master imposed on England by the soldiery. If the spectators

1653.
Dec. 16.
Cromwell
installed as
Protector.

[1] *Several Proceedings*, E, 222, 29.

ventured on any remark at all, it bore for the most part on the cleverness with which the new Protector had played his cards.[1]

To bear down the spirit of opposition it was necessary, while accepting the Instrument as a sufficient working theory of politics, to win over the masses by a continuance in well-doing. In the formation of the Council named in the Instrument, Cromwell and the officers had contented themselves with nominating fifteen members, leaving six vacancies to be filled as later adhesions to the new Government came in. The events of the preceding year made it hopeless to expect the concurrence of such men as Vane or Bradshaw, or indeed of any one who had taken an active part in the Long Parliament. The fifteen named consisted of seven officers : Cromwell, Lambert, Fleetwood,[2] Skippon, Desborough, Montague,[3] and Sydenham, with eight civilians : Lord Lisle, the elder brother of Algernon Sidney, Sir Anthony Ashley Cooper,

Formation of the Council.

---

[1] " Le peuple n'a donné aucune demonstration de joye, mais les soldats par des salves et le canon de la Tour s'ont solennisé, et devant les maisons publiques il s'est faict les feux." Bordeaux to Brienne, Dec. $\frac{19}{29}$, *R.O. Transcripts.* The Venetian agent tells the same story at greater length. " In quest' occorenza son stato osservando questi popoli più confusi et attoniti che consolati senza che si sia inteso uscire alcun grido di publico e particolare contento. Ogn' uno si stringe nelle spalle ; di tutti viene ammirata l' avveduta e destra maniera di questo soggetto, con cui è arrivato egli a questo segno di vedersi il disponitore assoluto in questo paese et di dar la legge a questi popoli ; chi pentiti del passato et intimoriti della forza, et può dirsi avilliti, non mostrano più ardire per grandi rissolutioni, et si sottomettono a quella obbedienza et a quegl' aggravii che per l' adietro non potevano fare ne anco con l' immaginatione, per così dire." Pauluzzi to Morosini, Dec. $\frac{14}{24}$, *Letter Book R.O.* There must, however, have been some exceptions to the general silence, as Salvetti (*Add. MSS.* 27,962 O. fol. 177b) writes that the proclamation of the Protectorate was received with applause, the people preferring one master to many, and being alarmed at the proceedings of the late Parliament. If Salvetti was standing anywhere where lawyers were congregated, the discrepancy can be easily explained.

[2] Fleetwood was, for some time to come, absent in Ireland.

[3] Edward Montague, afterwards the Earl of Sandwich of Pepys and the Restoration.

Sir Charles Wolseley, Sir Gilbert Pickering, Henry Lawrence, Francis Rous,[1] Richard Major, and Walter Strickland.

With one possible exception, the members of the new Council were of the type of the men who usually rise to ascend-

Character-
istics of the
members.

ency after a revolution has run its course—men of practical efficiency opposed to further changes in the State, and, above all, to anything savouring of fanati-

cism. Such men are usually content to devote themselves to the task of carrying on government without taking into account the theories on which any special government is founded. Such were the instruments of Napoleon, and such too were the councillors of Oliver.

The one member who does not quite fit into this description is Cooper. He had indeed gained Oliver's confidence by

Sir Anthony
Ashley
Cooper.

his steady application to business as a member of the three Councils which had rapidly succeeded one another since the forcible dissolution in April, and

also as a member of the nominated Parliament, whilst it is moreover possible that his advice was in some measure taken in the arrangements for the new Protectorate, though, as a civilian, he had no place in those meetings in which the Instrument was concocted by the officers.[2] Yet there were distinctive features in Cooper's character which single him out from his colleagues. To the end of his life he was distinguished by the shrewdness with which he anticipated the course of public opinion—a shrewdness which would have profited him little if it had been placed at the service of personal ambition,

---

[1] Mrs. Green, in the list of attendances prefixed to the *Calendar of Domestic State Papers* for 1653-4, calls him Colonel Anthony Rous. The name in the Instrument of Government is, however, Francis Rous, and it stands as 'Mr. Rous' in the Order Book of the Council, from which Mrs. Everett Green derived her information.

[2] Burnet (ed. 1823, i. 165) says of Oliver that Cooper was 'one of those who pressed him most to accept of the kingship, because, as he said afterwards, he was sure it would ruin him.' The evidence is not worth much, but it seems likely that Cromwell would consult Cooper when the proposal was made to him by the officers, and that, if he did, Cooper would recommend its acceptance.

instead of being itself the result of sympathy with the main tendencies of the day. Little as is known of Cooper's opinions at this conjuncture, he may fairly be credited with the principles which formed a thread of continuity in his devious career, a dislike of clerical domination, and a belief that the forces of a State are increased rather than diminished by the practice of toleration.

When the Council met on December 19, it selected Henry Lawrence as its President for the first month. Lawrence had

Dec. 19. Lawrence Lord President.

entered Parliament as a recruiter in 1646, and had done useful work on commissions, but had never risen to eminence as a politician. Before the month expired he was empowered by a warrant from the Protector [1] to retain his post permanently with the title of Lord President of the Council. He was a distant connection of Oliver's, and had at one time been his landlord at St. Ives. Four other members of the Council were more or less nearly connected by marriage with the Protector, Desborough being his brother-in-law, Mayor the father-in-law of his son Richard, whilst Pickering and Montague were more distantly connected with him.[2] Thurloe,

Thurloe secretary.

who had been secretary to successive Councils since the spring of 1652, retained his office, having under his control the Intelligence Department which the Long Parlia-

Milton and Meadows.

ment had confided to Scot. Milton remained at the disposition of the Council, but his blindness incapacitated him from active official work, and Philip Meadows, who had for some time acted as Latin translator, was given the full title of Latin Secretary.[3]

For the present, the efforts of the Protector and his Council were directed to the repression of the fanatical preachers who had been the backbone of the Advanced party in the late Parliament. These were not long in giving cause for the intervention of the Government. On the 18th either Feake or

[1] On Jan. 16, 1654. Council Order Book, *Interr.* I, 75, p. 53.

[2] See a note in Masson's *Life of Milton,* iv. 545.

[3] Order Book of the C. of St., *Interr.* I, 71, p. 118; Council Warrants, *ib.* xliv. 6.

Vavasor Powell openly styled the Protector 'the dissemblingest

Dec. 18.
The Fifth-
Monarchy
preachers
assail
Cromwell.
perjured villain in the world,' adjuring any of his friends who might be present to report the words to him, and to add 'that his reign was but short, and that he should be served worse than that great tyrant the last Lord Protector.' [1]   On the following day Feake, without mentioning Oliver's name, referred to him as the Little Horn of Daniel's prophecy, who was to make war against the saints, and afterwards to perish at their hands.   Powell, who followed him, dwelt with greater emphasis on the same prophecy, averring that Charles I. was the King of the North, in whose place was to stand up 'a raiser of taxes in the glory of the kingdom ; but within a few days he shall be destroyed neither in anger nor in battle.'   "A small matter," cried the preacher, "would fetch him down with little noise."   Then pressing into his service another prophecy relating to 'a vile person to whom they shall not give the honour of the kingdom ; but he shall come in peaceably and obtain the kingdom by flatteries,' Powell drew attention to the prediction that 'arms shall stand on his part.' [2]   The great army men, and swordsmen, the preacher explained, should side with him.   Yet for all that there was a Fifth Monarchy now being set up by Christ for the destruction of all anti-christian churches and clergy.   "Lord," cried Powell in conclusion, "have our army men all apostatised from their principles ?   What is become of all their declarations, protestations, and professions ?   Are they choked with lands, parks, and manors ?   Let us go home and pray, and say, 'Lord, wilt Thou have Oliver Cromwell or Jesus Christ to reign over us ?'" [3]

---

[1] Intercepted letter, Dec. 22, *Thurloe*, i. 641.   The last Protector had been the Duke of Somerset.

[2] Daniel xi. 20, 21, 28, 31.

[3] Information of Marchamount Needham, Dec. 20, *S. P. Dom.* xlii. 59.   On the day on which these sermons were preached appeared a pamphlet under the title of *The Temple's Foundation* (E, 724, 13).   It contained a Bill, ostensibly intended to have been presented to Parliament, authorising juries of saints to punish sinners.   As, apart from the nature

Feake and Powell were summoned before the Council, kept in custody for four nights, and then liberated with a caution to offend no more.[1] Oliver might have regarded their proceedings with equanimity, but for the danger that a soldiery steeped in biblical language might take their predictions as a voice from Heaven. Nor was it less necessary to remove from a position of authority over the soldiers the one man amongst all who sympathised with the rabid utterances at Blackfriars, who was capable of setting an army in array. On the 21st, the day on which the two preachers were sent for, Harrison was asked whether he was prepared to act under the new government, and, giving a negative answer, was deprived of his commission.[2] He was a brave and single-minded soldier, but, with his opinions on the relations between the civil and the ecclesiastical power, he was not one in whose hands any government, careful of the welfare of the State, could safely leave a sword. His position in the army was the more dangerous if there was truth in the rumour that his adherents in the nominated Parliament had thought, in the height of the recent crisis, of substituting him for Oliver as commander of the forces.[3]

It soon appeared that nothing short of actual compulsion would silence the exuberant rhetoric of the Fifth-Monarchy preachers. Early in the new year strong language was again used in the pulpit, and on January 10 orders were given to examine witnesses in the case of the offenders.[4] The legal difficulty that no

Dec. 21-24.
Feake and Powell before the Council.

Dec. 21.
Harrison deprived of his commission.

1654. Jan.
A fresh attack by the preachers.

of its contents, the publisher was George Calvert, who also published *An Answer to . . . a True Narrative* in the interests of the Moderate party, it may be taken as a mere political skit.

[1] Council Order Book, *Interr.* I, 75, pp. 7, 11 ; *Several Proceedings*, E, 2,233.

[2] *Thurloe*, i. 641.

[3] Salvetti's Newsletter, $\frac{\text{Dec. 30}}{\text{Jan. 9}}$, *Add. MSS.* 27,962 O. fol. 183. Harrison though not named is clearly referred to. Compare *An Answer to . . . a True Narrative*, E, 725, 20.

[4] Council Order Book, *Interr.* I, 75, p. 44.

existing law constituted an attack on the authority of the Protector an act of treason was easily surmounted by a
temporary ordinance issued in accordance with the
provisions of the Instrument.[1]

Jan. 19.
The treason
ordinance.

The Fifth-Monarchy preachers were not the men to take
warning. Powell, indeed, had sufficient prudence to escape
to Wales, where for some months he continued to
preach sedition with impunity.[2] Feake and another
minister, John Simpson, set the ordinance at defiance
in London. They were consequently arrested, and on
January 28 committed prisoners to Windsor Castle.[3]
Whatever an ordinance might say, it was not in
Oliver's nature to bring misguided fanatics to the
gallows. Harrison was treated with equal consideration. On
February 3 he was ordered to retire to his father's house in
Staffordshire.[4] Though at first he refused obedience, he submitted in the end, preaching an eloquent sermon to his followers
before his departure.[5] " Surely, sir," wrote Roger Williams to
a friend, " he is a very gallant, very deserving, heavenly man,
but most highflown for the kingdom of the saints and the
Fifth-Monarchy now risen, and their sun never to set." [6]

Powell
escapes to
Wales.

Jan. 28.
Feake and
Simpson
imprisoned.

If there were dangerous elements in the army of England,
it was suspected that there were no less dangerous elements in
the army in Ireland. The sympathy of Fleetwood
and of most of the Irish Commissioners with the
Baptists, amongst whom the Fifth-Monarchy move-

Anxiety
about the
Irish army.

---

[1] *Ordinance on Treason*, E, 1,063, No. 41. It was declared treason
'if any person or persons maliciously or advisedly either by writing,
printing, openly declaring, preaching, teaching, or otherwise, publish'
that the Protector and people in Parliament are not supreme, or that the
administration was not in the Protector and Council, or that their authority
is tyrannical, usurped, or unlawful.

[2] *Thurloe*, ii. 44, 93, 116.

[3] Council Order Book, *Interr.* I, 75, p. 77.

[4] C. of St. Order Book, *Interr.* I, 85, p. 92.

[5] Bordeaux to Brienne, Feb. $\frac{6}{16}$, *R.O. Transcripts*.

[6] Williams to Winthrop, July 12, Knowles, *Life of R. Williams*,
p. 263.

ment had taken its origin, was undeniable.   On January 2, when

Jan. 2.
The Com-
missioners
call a prayer
meeting.

the news of the abdication of the nominated Parliament reached Dublin, the Commissioners issued a
circular lamenting the end of an assembly on which
their hopes had been fixed, and calling on all
Christian people to join in prayer appropriate to the melancholy
occasion.[1]   Yet when it became known that a Protectorate had
been established, the opposition arising from religious animosity

Reception of
the Pro-
tectorate at
Dublin.

died away.   Fleetwood, by no means a strong
character, was as Oliver's son-in-law bound by personal
ties to the new system, and was restrained by habits
of military subordination from offering resistance to the
general under whom he served, especially as the most respected
of the London Baptists wrote to disclaim all participation in
the views of the Fifth Monarchists.   When the proclamation
of the new authority was offered to the Commissioners for

Ludlow's
opposition.

signature, the only refusal came from Ludlow, who
stood in no relationship with the Baptist community.

Jan. 30.
The Pro-
tectorate
proclaimed.

As his scruples were not to be overcome, the
proclamation was ultimately, on January 30, sent out,
in transparent neglect of the usual custom, with the
signature of the secretary alone.[2]

Ludlow's opposition was based on grounds diametrically

Fifth
Monarchist
and Com-
monwealth
men.

opposite to those of the Fifth Monarchists.   Those
who held that the saints ought to rule the world were
as little likely to bow before an elected Parliament
as to accept a King or a Protector.[3]   Yet, trouble-

---

[1] The Commissioners to the Commanders-in-Chief, Jan. 2, *Ludlow*,
i. 540.

[2] *Ib.* i. 373-375.

[3] The Fifth-Monarchy position is well put in a letter from the London
Baptists to those in Ireland.   They say that the substance of the preach-
ings at Blackfriars might be summed up under two heads : ' First that it
was the duty of the magistrates to own their power to be received immediately from Jesus Christ.   From this the consequence would unavoidably
have followed that they were only accountable to Christ for their actions,
and not to men ; and would not this have been the same with the late

some as they were to any settled government, these men had no future before them. The most dangerous enemies of the Protectorate were the Royalists and the Commonwealth's men, because they both anchored themselves on principles which had their roots in the past, and which had still a part to play in the future. Of the Commonwealth's men Ludlow was perhaps the most striking figure. Unimaginative and self-possessed, he had the advantage of grimly holding on to the doctrine which had once gained possession of his mind, all the more because he failed to see it in relation to other doctrines equally important. To the political thinker Ludlow is naturally the object of scorn. Why, it is asked, did he sacrifice himself for the supremacy of Parliament without asking whether such a Parliament as existed after Pride's Purge, or still more the one nominated by the army, was representative or not? It seemed almost as if Parliament was to him a fetish to be worshipped irrespectively of the sources from which it is drawn or the benefits it conferred. Yet, after all, Ludlow's view, broadly regarded, was not unreasonable. Between the two Parliaments which sat in 1653 and the one which in our own day sways the destinies of the nation, the gulf is no doubt profound ; but a yet deeper gulf separated even the Parliament of nominees from the rule of the sword, and it was in protesting against this rule of the sword that Ludlow became the mouthpiece of future generations, whilst he also anticipated them in rejecting the opinion of the Levellers that no Parliament should be entrusted with power unless it were chosen by manhood suffrage.

King, who, being persuaded by his prelates that he received his power immediately from God, was not accountable to the people's representatives? But the second thing held forth with great zeal by those friends was that the great rule by which they were to act in their proceeds towards the making of war or peace with the nations should arise from a spirit stirred up, as they say, by God to throw down potentates and powers rather than these prudential rules of justice and righteousness in the doing to all men as they would men should do to them.' Letter from Kiffen and others, Jan. 20, *Milton State Papers*, 159, 160.

When Henry Cromwell, who was sent in March by his father to report on the feelings of the Irish army, and to calm

March.
Ludlow
and Henry
Cromwell.

the excitement which prevailed in it, arrived in Ireland, a characteristic conversation between him and Ludlow throws light upon the divergence of the parties to which the two men had respectively given in their adhesion. Henry Cromwell urged the practical necessities of the time. Ludlow asked why his father had left ' his former station wherein his power was as great, and his wealth as much as any rational man could wish, to procure to himself nothing but envy and trouble.' " You that are here," replied the younger man, "may think he had power, but they made a very kickshaw of him at London." After hearing this description of Cromwell's position whilst the nominees were sitting, Ludlow fell back on the real strength of his position by arguing, ' that all things ought for the future to run in their proper and genuine channel ; for as the extraordinary remedy is not to be used till the ordinary fail to work its proper effect, so ought it to be continued no longer than the necessity of using it subsists ; whereas this that they call a government had no other means to preserve itself but such as were violent, which not being natural could not be lasting.' "Would you, then," answered Henry Cromwell, " have the sword laid down ? I cannot but think you believe it to be as much your interest to have it kept up as any man."

Each of the two interlocutors saw one side of the position. Without the sword, argued Cromwell's son in effect, No protection of the interests and ideas which have grown up with the Revolution. With the sword, was the equally true reply, No permanent protection for anything. It was hopeless to attempt to bridge over this gulf. Ludlow refused to act as Civil Commissioner under the Protectorate whilst he consented to perform the duties of the military position which he had received from Parliament till the order arrived to supersede him, an order which, as he rightly foresaw, could not be long delayed. Before Henry Cromwell left Ireland, he strongly recommended that the unbending opponent of military interference in civil government should be excluded from the army.[1]

In the City of London, though Royalist and Presbyterian sentiments prevailed in the community at large, regard for order might be expected to have the upper hand, at least amongst the merchants and wealthier shop-keepers. The Fifth Monarchists and the nominated Parliament were not likely to find much support in commercial circles, and the Lord Mayor and Aldermen invited the Protector and his principal supporters to a banquet to take place on February 8, in Grocers' Hall.

Feeling in London.

Cromwell invited to a banquet.

On the appointed morning Cromwell was received at Temple Bar with all the ceremonies formerly paid to kings. As he passed along Fleet Street, Ludgate Hill, and the Poultry, the sides of the way were lined with the members of the City Companies sitting bareheaded on the benches provided for them. Yet, though the Protector doffed his hat repeatedly, neither by them nor by the crowd behind them was a shout of applause raised. In his own person, indeed, he had once more taken care to display the civilian character which he had assumed. He was dressed in a musk-coloured suit richly embroidered with gold. The order of the procession which followed told a tale of military pre-dominance. First came ' about three-score colonels, and other superior officers in very rich habits.' Only after they had passed, appeared the coaches of the members of the Council. Arrived at Grocers' Hall, there was a sumptuous entertainment[2] accompanied by music and the thunder of the Tower guns, and enlivened by the recitation of the best verses of which the City poet was capable.[3] In the end the Protector received a gift of plate valued at 2,000*l.*, and knighted the Lord Mayor, now

Feb. 8. Cromwell in the City.

---

[1] *Ludlow.* i. 380–383.

[2] A dinner followed by a banquet—*i.e.* a dessert—in another room. The practice at the universities of leaving the hall for dessert in the common room is a survival of this custom.

[3] There was also a song prepared, but it seems in great haste :—

         Come away, blest soul, no more
         Feed your eyes with what is poor ;

Sir Thomas Viner, in return. He did not leave till after dark, when he moved back to Whitehall amidst the blaze of three hundred torches. As in the morning, the crowds which thronged the streets preserved a sullen silence, and from the upper window of one house a large stone was aimed at his coach. It fell wide of the mark, and every attempt to discover the offender proved unsuccessful.[1]

That the dissatisfaction with military government should take the shape of a desire for a restoration of the old monarchy, Royalist sentiments in the City. coupled with a sense of the hopelessness of resistance, was perfectly natural. There were signs, it was thought sent by heaven, to warn men that the present tyranny would soon be overpassed. The Thames had flowed and ebbed two hours before the proper time, as it had done in anticipation of King Charles's execution. Part of the wall of St. Paul's had come down with a crash. A comet had appeared in the sky, and, above all, the ghost of the late King had been The True State of the Case of the Commonwealth. descried flitting through Whitehall.[2] It was probably not without design that, on the very day on which the Protector visited the City, a pamphlet— *The True State of the Case of the Commonwealth*— was issued to win public opinion to the side of the new Government, not only by imputing blame freely to the nominated

> It is enough that you have blest
> What was rude, what was undressed.
> Come away and cast your eyes
> On this humble sacrifice ;
> We no golden apples give,
> Here's no Adam, here's no Eve,
> Not a serpent dares appear,
> Whilst your Highness stayeth here.
> O then sit, and take your due,
> Those the firstfruits are that grew.
>
> *The Weekly Intelligencer*, E, 729, 9.

[1] *Ib.* ; *Merc. Pol.* E, 729, 1 ; *A Perf. Account*, E, 729, 12. Pauluzzi to Morosini, Feb. $\frac{11}{21}$, $\frac{18}{28}$, *Venetian Transcripts R.O.*

[2] All this is given in Pauluzzi's letter of Feb. $\frac{11}{21}$. A little later, on March 9, we hear that the great south gate of St. Paul's had fallen down in the course of the week (*Merc. Pol.* E, 731, 21).

Parliament, but by emphasising and even exaggerating the part to be played by the people and their representatives under the Instrument.

"Let us ruminate then, a little," was the conclusion drawn . . . "and behold the great hopes and blessed benefits of security and freedom that we have and may shortly enjoy under the Government as it is now established. The quarrel for hereafter is not between two persons contesting both for a crown; it is not the interest or grandeur of any single person or particular family that is contended for on our part; but, if ever the enemy should, for our sins, arise to the possibility of a future contest, remember what it is he fights for, and what must be the wretched consequence of his prevailing; remember also what we of this nation are to stand for, the preservation of our religion, our liberties, and all that is dear and precious among men, which appear plainly to be embarked in the great bottom of this present establishment. If we falter, or be misled through fantasy, or if that fail through our default, we are immediately swallowed up by tyranny, and have nothing left to do but to put our mouths in the dust, and sit down in sorrow and silence for the glory of our nation. . . . Having therefore a fair and noble way of administration provided, under which men may live in a plenary enjoyment of their liberty as Christians and their rights as men; we do not, we cannot in any measure doubt . . . but that we shall find a ready and cheerful concurrence from all sober persons, and have ground chiefly to expect it for all the people of God, though of different judgments, seeing equal liberty is given to them all . . . and the principal care is for preserving true religion, and the countenance of its professors. . . . When we look back upon what is done, we find nothing that stares in our faces; and if there could have been imagined any better way of settlement, we should have embraced it with the same spirit of submission; but here we see our friends have taken in the good of all the three sorts of government and bound them all in one. If war be, here is the unitive virtue—but nothing else—of monarchy to encounter it; and here is the admirable

An appeal for support.

counsel of aristocracy to manage it. If peace be, here is the industry and courage of democracy to improve it. And whereas in the present constitution the legislative and executive powers are separated ; the former being vested in a constant succession of Parliaments elective by the people, the latter in an elective Lord Protector and his successors assisted by a council ; we conceive the state of this Commonwealth is thereby reduced to so just a temper that the ills either of successive Parliaments furnished with powers both of executing and making laws, or of a perpetual Parliament—which are division, faction and confusion—being avoided on the one side, and the inconveniences of absolute lordly power on the other ; the frame of Government appears so well bounded on all sides against anarchy and tyranny that we hope it may now, through the blessing of God, prove a seasonable mean, as for the better defending these dominions against enemies abroad, and promoting our interests in foreign parts, so also of peace and settlement to this distracted nation ; and be of a durable continuance to succeeding ages for the glory of the most high God, the advancement of His gospel, the protection of His people, and the benefit of posterity." [1]

In haranguing Oliver as he passed through Temple Bar, the Recorder of the City had reminded him that it might be left to other nations ' to salute their rulers and victorious commanders with the name of *Cæsares* and *Imperatores*.' [2] The irrepressible verse-writers of the day would not have it so. One of the fraternity who composed a poem in honour of the Protector's visit to the City, addressed him as a greater than Cæsar, because he had refused to be a Cæsar. Yet a Cæsar he should be when he had burnt Rome, the profane seat of idolatry. [3] Meanwhile, it

Was Oliver a Cæsar?

Oliver declared greater than Cæsar.

---

[1] *The True State of the Case of the Commonwealth*, E, 728, 5.
[2] *Mr. Recorder's Speech*, E, 729, 2.
[3] ' Cæsare major adest, quia noluit esse : coronam
  Accipiant alii : se potuisse sat est.
 Cæsar et alter erit, si quid præsagia possint,
  Cum petet igne tuos, Roma profana, deos.'
         Merc. Pol. E, 729, 14.

was his task to maintain the sovereignty of the sea. He had already beaten down the tyrant, and had converted subjects into citizens, and had taught the soldiers to put on the garb of civil life. By him chaos had been reduced into an orderly world. It was a fascinating picture, if only because it sketched

Object of Oliver Cromwell's policy. out the two leading features of Cromwell's foreign policy : the mastery of the sea and the overthrow, or at least the weakening, of the Papacy.

In handling the ordinary concerns of government, the Protector appeared to be inspired by a desire to avoid all appearance of arbitrary rule. In his choice of judges, at least,

Cromwell's dispositions on the Bench. he consulted the interests of the nation as a whole. Ten of those already on the Bench were retained in their places. Two, Chief Baron Wilde and Puleston, a puisne judge of the Common Pleas, were discontinued, both of whom had made themselves notorious, in the opinion of Royalists, for their violence and unfairness to prisoners who

Wilde and Puleston not reappointed. had served the King—Wilde especially, in the case of Captain Burley, and Puleston in the case of Captain Morris.[1] If it is inferred from the passing over of these two judges that Cromwell desired to conciliate the Royalists, that inference is strengthened by his appoint-

Jan. 25. Hale on the Bench. ment of Matthew Hale as Puleston's successor.[2] Cromwell's attention had been drawn to that eminent lawyer by his services as one of the Law Commissioners appointed by the Long Parliament, and Hale consented—upon strong instances from his Royalist friends—to take part in the administration of justice, though only on the condition that he should be excused from taking part in the trial of political prisoners. The compromise was creditable to both parties.[3]

[1] See vol. i. p. 41, and *Great Civil War*, iv. 54.

[2] Wilde's post remained vacant for some time.

[3] The information on these changes is collected in Foss's *Lives of the Judges*, under the respective headings. Foss was doubtful of the date at which Puleston ceased to be a judge, but it is strongly probable that his supersession was at this time.

It was not long before the judges of the Upper Bench had occasion to give a decision which at least testified to their entire independence of the Government. On September 12 a certain Captain Streeter had been imprisoned by the then exisiting Council of State for publishing seditious pamphlets.[1] On his application for a writ of *habeas corpus*, Parliament on November 21 recommitted him, and no argument on behalf of the prisoner could shake the judges in their opinion that no committal by Parliament—despite the anomalous character of the assembly which then styled itself by that august name—could be questioned in any court of law. With the abdication of Parliament, however, the whole legal aspect of the case was changed. The only warrant for Streeter's committal retaining any semblance of validity was that from the late Council of State, and when, on January 23, Streeter once more took out his writ of *habeas corpus*, the judges, though reluctant to give a hasty decision, pronounced ultimately on February 7 that an Order of Parliament ceased to be of force after a dissolution. As even the Attorney-General, who appeared for the Government, did not venture to suggest that the Council could lawfully imprison, except as a preliminary to a trial in the Upper Bench, the decision in favour of the liberation of the prisoner was a foregone conclusion, and on February 11 he stepped forth into the world as a free man.[2]

Neither directly nor indirectly were the Protector and his Council compromised by this judgment. Yet it certainly deprived them of a weapon which past governments had been in the habit of using freely. A practical point, which they were called on to decide at once, was whether they should allow the prison doors to be thrown open to Lilburne,

Marginal notes:

1653.
Sept. 12.
Streeter's imprisonment by the Council.

Nov. 21.
He is recommitted by Parliament.

The judges refuse to bail him.

1654.
Jan. 23.
After the dissolution he again applies to the Upper Bench,

Feb. 11.
and is liberated.

The Protector not compromised.

Is Lilburne to be set free?

[1] C. of St. Order Book, *Interr.* I, 20, p. 363.

[2] *Clavis ad aperienda Carceris Ostia* (E, 731, 18) contains a full report of the case.

who was certain, unless means were taken to prevent him, to make the application which had proved successful in Streeter's case. On consideration, they resolved to evade the operation of the law. On March 16 the Council ordered the transportation of Lilburne to Mount Orgueil Castle in Jersey, where the writ of the Keepers of the Liberties of England did not run.[1] Nevertheless, on an application on Lilburne's behalf, a writ of *habeas corpus* was issued,[2] to Heane, the governor of the island, but was disregarded by that officer,[3] whose conduct was unhesitatingly sustained by the Council.

March 16. Lilburne sent to Jersey

May. Writ of habeas corpus issued,

June. but not acted on.

Lilburne's case may fairly be regarded as exceptional, and in all matters in which the safety of the State was not directly concerned, the anxiety of the Protector to keep within the measure of the law was beyond dispute. His desire to calm down the agitation to which the proceedings of the nominated Parliament had given rise is best manifested by the character of the eighty-two ordinances which he and his Council issued, in accordance with the permission given by the Instrument up to September 3—the day on which Parliament was to meet. Many of these, indeed, were of an administrative character, or at least of purely temporary interest. Not a few rise into the atmosphere of statesmanship.[4]

Moderation of the Protector's policy.

The eighty-two ordinances.

[1] C. Order Book, *Interr.* I, 75, p. 171.

[2] *A Declaration of the Freeborn People of England*, E, 735, 18, published on May 23.

[3] C. Order Book, *Interr.* I, 75, p. 336; *Perf. Diurnal*, E, 229, 11. This is the beginning of the evasions of the law which, when imitated by the Restoration Government, led to the *Habeas Corpus* Act of 1679. Prynne and his fellows were sent out of England by order of the Court of Star Chamber, at that time a legal court, against the decisions of which no writ of *habeas corpus* would be available. These cases therefore differed in this respect from that of Lilburne, though they may very likely have suggested the line taken by the Council of the Protectorate.

[4] The Treason Ordinance has already been mentioned (see p. 7, note 3). Those relating to Scotland and Ireland will receive treatment in their proper place.

The nominated Parliament had deprived the Engagement of its most tyrannical consequences by directing that those who refused it should no longer be debarred from seeking a remedy in the law courts for wrongs to which they had been subjected.[1] On January 19 the whole of the ordinance enforcing it was repealed by the Protector, and no one was any longer obliged to promise, even as a test for office, that he would be faithful to the Commonwealth 'without king or House of Lords.' For the first time since the Covenant had been imposed in 1643, there was an entire absence of any formula to which men were required to give their assent on pain of being regarded as bad citizens amenable to the justice of the State. Such 'general and promissory oaths and engagements,' the Protector declared, had 'proved burdens and snares to tender consciences.' From henceforth no man was to be counted disloyal to the existing Government who did not assail it by his acts.[2]

Jan. 19. The ordinance for taking the Engagement repealed.

Tolerant of opinion as he was, Oliver was not tolerant of practices tending to immorality of any kind, especially when they proceeded from a class of persons instinctively hostile to a Puritan Government. On March 31 he prohibited public cock-fights on much the same grounds as those on which bear-baitings had been condemned by the nominated Parliament. Such meetings, he declared, 'are by experience found to tend many times to the disturbance of the public peace, and are commonly accompanied with gaming, drinking, swearing, quarrelling, and other dissolute practices to the dishonour of God, and do often produce the ruin of persons and their families.'[3] Yet he took care to emphasise his view that it was the disorderly result of the amusement, and not the amusement itself, that he condemned, by attending a hurling-match in Hyde Park on May Day, where fifty Cornish gentlemen a side contended for the silver ball used in the game, and which was followed by a display of Cornish wrestling.[4]

March 31. Cock-fighting prohibited.

May 1. Cornish games in Hyde Park.

[1] See vol. i. p. 310.   [2] *Scobell,* ii. 277.   [3] *Ib.* ii. 283.
[4] *The Weekly Intelligencer,* E, 734, 3.

The capacity of the new Government for dealing with complicated problems would be best illustrated by its attitude

Aug. 21.
Chancery
reform. towards the two burning questions of Chancery Reform and Church Reform. As to the former, a long ordinance was issued on August 21 with the intention of making access to the Court easier and less expensive than it had hitherto been.[1] Such an attempt was necessarily open to criticism, and it might safely be predicted that the criticism which it would meet with at the hands of lawyers accustomed to the old system would be peculiarly searching.

In dealing with the Court of Chancery, the Protector and his Council had shown themselves conservative reformers,

Church
reform. anxious to retain as much of the existing system as could be left untouched without doing positive evil. In dealing with the Church, or rather with the Churches, they were actuated by precisely the same spirit. With the limits of toleration, indeed, they did not profess to meddle. That point had been settled by the Instrument itself. The questions at issue in the late Parliament had revolved round the appointment and payment of ministers. The advanced party—though every member of Parliament who voted in the majority on the fateful December 12 [2] by no means belonged to it—had aimed at establishing a purely voluntary system, under which ministers were to receive no support whatever from the State or any source under the control of the State, and were to be appointed by their congregations, patronage being thus entirely abolished.

An Es-
tablished
Church
to be main-
tained. Against this the framers of *The Instrument of Government* had set their faces. There was to be an Established Church surrounded by voluntary congregations. The only questions now before the Protector

---

[1] *Scobell*, ii. 324. Mr. Inderwick discusses the ordinance in *The Interregnum*, 224-229. The general result of his opinion is that though it embodied great and useful reforms, it did not sufficiently take into account the evil likely to ensue from substituting 'hard-and-fast rules for the flexibility necessary to a due administration of equity,' but reminds his readers (p. 222) that there was good ground for the attack on Chancery, as there was then no definite system of equity law in existence.   ² See vol. ii. p. 324.

and Council were how the ministers of that Church should be appointed and dismissed, how far they should be restrained to teach any definite doctrine, and from what sources they should be paid. The question of appointment was settled by an ordinance of March 20, that of dismissal and, incidentally, that of restrictions on teaching, by an ordinance of August 28.[1] The question of maintenance was not touched at all.

Questions still unsolved.

The omission was the more noticeable as *The Instrument of Government* had held out a prospect, if not of the complete abolition of tithes, at least of their commutation to some 'provision less subject to scruple and contention, and more certain than the present,' especially as Oliver himself was believed to be favourable to the change. The explanation given by himself, that he was outvoted by his Council, though not in accordance with modern ideas as to his relationship with that body, is quite consistent with the glimpses vouchsafed to us into the inner workings of the Government, and may safely be accepted as true. The members of the Council had been selected as the opponents of headlong and unpopular reform, and it was only in accordance with the mental habits of mankind, that they should set themselves against a reform which, though it might be neither headlong nor unpopular, would certainly have entailed a great amount of trouble on those who originated it, and would have aroused a strong opposition from those who were interested in the maintenance of long-standing abuses.[2]

Question of tithe.

Oliver outvoted in the Council.

[1] *Scobell*, ii. 279, 335.

[2] In a conversation held in December 1654 Oliver was charged with having broken his word 'in his promise about tithes to be taken away before September 3.' He replied 'he wist not whether he had said so or no ; but he heard Mr. Jessey should report it of him, in which he had not done well ; and for his part he could not do it, for he was but one, and his Council allege it not fit to take them away.' (B. T. to —— (?) December 21, *Clarke Papers*, ii. Pref. xxxvi.) If Oliver had expressed his wish—or perhaps his expectation—that the half-promise given in the Instrument might be carried out by an ordinance before September 3, the whole story acquires consistency. Jessey may have exaggerated the words into a

Whatever might be done or left undone in the matter of tithe, it was absolutely necessary to face the question of Church organisation. It was no more than was to be ex-pected that the Protector should take as a basis the propositions which had been developed by Owen and his co-signatories from a clause in *The Agreement of the People*, and had been accepted on February 11, 1653, by the Propaga-tion Committee of the Long Parliament in an amended form.[1] He had also before him the report of the Committee on Tithes in the nominated Parliament.[2] In none of these schemes was a word said about ordination. The State, from the point of view of their authors, had nothing to do with the forms by which a man was set apart for the ministry, or whether he had submitted himself to any forms at all. All that it was con-cerned with was his right to the payment of a settled main-tenance if he desired to place himself in a position in which such maintenance was secured to him, under certain conditions, by the law.

Former proposals on Church organisation.

By an ordinance issued on March 20, provision was made for the appointment of ministers to benefices. In this ordinance the recommendations of the Propagation Committee were followed in the main. The right of patronage was to remain intact, but the minister after he had been presented to a benefice was to submit himself to inquiry by a body of commissioners authorised to act as triers in his case. According to the scheme accepted by the Propagation Committee these triers were to form a separate board in each county, and were to found their action on a certificate from 'six godly ministers and Christians.' The report of the Com-mittee on Tithes merely suggested that counties should be grouped, and that the commissioners appointed for the different circuits should be empowered ' to settle godly and able persons to preach the Gospel in all void places.' The Protector's

March 20. Commission of Triers.

personal engagement. That the phrase ' take away tithes' means no more than the commutation in Oliver's mouth cannot be proved ; but see vol. ii. p. 102.

[1] See vol. ii. p. 98. [2] See vol. ii. p. 323.

ordinance appointed a general Commission of Triers for the whole of England and Wales, meeting in London or Westminster, composed of ministers and laymen ; and contented itself with requiring the certificate of three persons of known godliness and integrity, one of whom was to be a settled minister, testifying to the holy and good conversation of the person to be admitted to the benefice, after which the commissioners were to approve of him ' to be a person for the grace of God in him, his holy and unblamable conversation, as also for his knowledge and utterance, able and fit to preach the gospel.' In other words he was to be religious, moral, and capable. Further limitations, if any there were to be, were left to be dealt with in the future ordinance on ejection. This scheme was to come into force on March 25, but was to apply to all appointments made from April 1, 1653. A further determination of the ordinance settled a question not touched upon by the earlier schemers. Owen's proposal had left the question of patronage out of account. The nominated Parliament had loudly called attention to the abuses of that system,[1] but its complaints, however well founded, had only served to provoke a reaction which the Protector was bound to take into account, and with which he probably sympathised. The right of patrons to present to benefices was therefore fully accepted in the ordinance ; its object being to check their power of making unfit appointments, not to abolish it altogether. The conservative instinct of the country protesting against further change than is necessary to promote efficiency was abundantly satisfied.

On the question of the ejection of scandalous or unfit ministers, the plan of the Propagation Committee had been to give power to a general commission to divide itself into sections for the purpose of visiting a special group of counties, and to associate with its own members persons with local knowledge in each county, and this system was substantially identical with that recommended by the Committee of Tithes. The ordinance of the Protectorate, on the other hand—perhaps on the ground that commissioners

Aug. 28.
Commission
of Ejectors.

---

[1] See vol. ii. p. 322.

coming from headquarters must necessarily be dependent on local knowledge—appointed a separate body of commissioners drawn from the county itself, or, in the case of the more thinly populated districts, one body for a group of counties. These commissioners were to have the power of ejecting, upon charges brought before them, all ministers and schoolmasters 'scandalous in their lives and conversations,' or those who 'shall be proved guilty of holding or maintaining such blasphemous and atheistical opinions as are punishable by' the Blasphemy Act of 1650,[1] 'or guilty of profane cursing or swearing, perjury, subornation of perjury,' together with 'such as shall hold, teach, or maintain any of those Popish opinions required in the oath of abjuration[2] mentioned in an ordinance of Parliament of the 19th of August, 1643, to be abjured, or be guilty of adultery, fornication, drunkenness, common haunting of taverns or ale-houses, frequent quarrelling or fighting, frequent playing at cards or dice, profaning of the Sabbath day, and such as do or shall allow the same in their families, or countenance the same in their parishioners or scholars ; such as have publicly and frequently read or used the Common Prayer-book since the first of January last, or shall at any time hereafter do the same ; such as do publicly and profanely scoff at or revile the strict professors of religion or godliness, or do encourage and countenance by word or practice any Whitsun-ales, wakes, morris-dances, may-poles, stage-plays, or suchlike licentious practices, by which men are encouraged in a loose and profane conversation ; such as have declared or shall declare by writing, preaching, or otherwise publishing their disaffection to the present Government. Such ministers shall be accounted negligent as omit the public exercises of preaching and praying upon the Lord's Day—not being hindered by necessary absence or infirmity of body—or that are or shall be non-resident ; such

[1] See vol. ii. p. 2.

[2] This oath renounces the Pope's authority, the doctrine of transubstantiation, and disclaims belief in the existence of purgatory, in worship being due to the consecrated host, crucifixes or images, and in salvation merited by works (*Scobell*, i. 50).

schoolmasters shall be accounted negligent as absent themselves from their schools, and do wilfully neglect their duties in teaching their scholars.' In the case of an ejected minister leaving his benefice without resistance, the commissioners were empowered to set aside for the benefit of his wife and children a fifth of his successor's income from the benefice vacated.

Such were the foundations of the Established Church conceived in the mind of John Owen, and reduced to practical shape by Oliver. With the exception of the condemnation of the use of the Common Prayer, the scheme was in the highest degree broad and generous, and it is well to remember that those who strove to revive the use of the Common Prayer were a political as well as an ecclesiastical party, and that the weight and activity of that party, except so far as it appealed to the indifferent in religion, were out of all proportion to its numbers.[1] The great bulk of the religious population had attached

The Church of the Protectorate.

---

[1] Baxter's description of the influence of a gentleman at Kidderminster is worth quoting : " One knight — Sir R[alph] C[lare] — which lived amongst us, did more to hinder any great successes than a multitude of others could have done : though he was an old man of great courtship and civility and very temperate as to diet, apparel and sports, and seldom would swear any louder than 'by his troth, &c.' and shewed me much personal reverence and respect, beyond my desert, and we conversed together with love and familiarity ; yet—having no relish of this preciseness and extemporary praying, and making so much ado for heaven ; nor liking that which went beyond the pace of saying the Common Prayer, and also the interest of himself and his civil and ecclesiastical parties leading him to be ruled by Dr. Hammond ; his coming but once a day to church on the Lord's days, and his abstaining from the sacraments, &c. as if we kept not sufficiently to the old way, and because we used not the Common Prayer Book when it would have caused us to be sequestered ; did cause a great part of the parish to follow him, and do as he did, when else our success and concord would have been much more happy than it was. And yet civility and yielding much beyond others of his party—sending his family to be catechised and personally instructed, did sway with the worst almost among us to do the like." *Rel. Baxterianæ,* 94. This lifelike picture probably gives a fair idea of what occurred in other parts of England. A certain number of landowners are attached heart and soul to Episcopacy ;

themselves to one of the three great sections—the Presbyterians, the Independents, and the Baptists. All three preached much the same Gospel, though they differed on special points—the Presbyterian from the other two on organisation, the Baptist from the other two on the age at which baptism should fitly be administered. To Oliver it seemed indifferent whether a preacher took one view or another on these special points. The blot on the system was, no doubt, that it was left to the patron to decide whether the minister of a parish should hold one or the other opinion on these points, but the members of a recalcitrant congregation were at least able—as they had not been able in the days of Laud—to. desert the parish church, and to gather round a minister whose teaching was more to their taste.

No doubt the working of the institution thus launched depended mainly on the character and wisdom of the com-

No minute inquiries justified by the ordinance. missioners. Puritan clergy were apt to push their inquiries into minute phases of doctrine [1] and practice, but there was nothing in the ordinance itself to encourage them to do more than convince themselves of the spiritual earnestness of the candidate presented to a benefice.

With these provisions for the appointment of fit ministers

No provision for internal discipline. and for the elimination of unfit ones, the interference of the State ended. Whether any discipline was to be exercised in the parishes was a question to be

others are mildly dissatisfied with the strictness of Puritanism, and stay away from church more than their minister approves of. The latter class especially have a strong influence on their dependents, who are quite ready to follow the example of staying away from church. Baxter's story of his own life may be sought in vain for evidence of any strong popular movement in favour of Episcopacy and the Prayer-book, though people like the imitators of R. C. would be quite ready to support them both—probably with no little violence—if the old ecclesiastical institutions got the upper hand by reason of a political revolution.

[1] For a bad instance—if the report can be accepted as correct—see *Inquisitio Anglicana*, 698, g. 12, No. 4. See, too, the case of O. Pordage, *State Trials*, v. 539.

settled by the ministers themselves, with the concurrence of their congregations. By the Presbyterian clergy, whose whole system of compulsory discipline had fallen into disuse,[1] the want was specially felt. One of their number, Richard Baxter, who was as distinguished for his charity towards those from whom he differed in non-essentials, as for the controversial vigour with which he assailed extreme opponents, conceived the idea of substituting a voluntary for a coercive jurisdiction. In his own parish of Kidderminster he won over a considerable number of persons—600 out of the 1,600 who were of age entitling them to become communicants—to bind themselves to accept a system which authorised the minister to investigate charges brought against any member of his congregation, though the refusal of communion had to be ratified by the congregation itself.

The Presbyterian discipline in disuse.

Baxter's system of voluntary discipline.

Nor was it only by the establishment of congregational discipline that Baxter showed an appreciation of the needs of his age. Why, he asked, should not the ministers of the county of Worcester form an association for mutual encouragement in their work, and for discussion on their parochial action, irrespective of their differences of opinion? The idea was not long in taking root in the county, and on December 22, 1652, a Worcestershire petition was presented to the Long Parliament asking, amongst other things, that the peaceable divines of each party might be called together to report on 'a meet way for accommodation and unity.'[2] What Parliament could not do, Baxter carried out by his own energy. Before long the Worcestershire Association was well known as a school of charitable helpfulness in which Presbyterian, Independent, and even partisans of moderate Episcopacy united together, without derogation to their individual opinions on church government, in order to assist one another in the ministerial

He proposes an association.

1652. Dec. 22. The Worcestershire petition.

---

[1] See vol. ii. p. 86.

[2] *The Humble Petition of the County of Worcester*, E, 684, 13.

work common to all.[1] In due time the example set was followed by the clergy in other counties. Baxter, indeed, counted Oliver as a traitor and a rebel; but there was no man in England whose action commended itself more highly to the heart of the Protector.

[1] *The Worcestershire Petition Defended*, E, 693, 18; *Church Concord*, T, 749, 4; *Rel. Baxterianæ*, 84–98, 146–140.

CHAPTER XXX

THE STRUGGLE FOR THE NORTH SEA

THE problems of domestic legislation were far from being the most difficult with which the Protector had to cope. In his
1654.
Foreign relations of the Protectorate.
relations with foreign powers he had inherited a situation of extreme complexity. Not only did the war with the Dutch Republic continue, but the Government was entangled in a double negotiation with both France and Spain, from which it could hardly escape with credit. Nor could Oliver with any semblance of justice throw the whole of the blame on his predecessors. If they had engaged the country against his wishes in the Dutch war, it was with his full consent, and partly at his direct instigation, that plans had been laid for an alliance, at one time with France against Spain, at another time with Spain against France.

In March 1653, during the closing days of the Long Parliament, Cromwell's leanings were towards an agreement
1653.
March.
Danger of Bordeaux.
with Spain, to be followed by action on behalf of the French Protestants and the City of Bordeaux. Yet by this time the resistance of Bordeaux was breaking down. Conti's Government was unpopular with all classes, whilst the democrats of the Ormée irritated the lawyers and traders. Vendôme blockaded the Gironde with the King's fleet, and on land one fortified post after another fell into the hands of the royal army. Piteous appeals were despatched to Madrid, and Philip was told that unless his fleet now gathering at Passages were speedily despatched, the cause of Spain and

Condé was lost in Guienne.[1] When at last the fleet was ready, the defection of Le Daugnon, whose port of Brouage was to have afforded a base of operations against Vendôme,

March 25.
Doubts of
Spanish
aid. made new counsels necessary, and on March 25, though this event had not as yet been publicly announced, doubts were expressed at Bordeaux on the efficacy of Spanish aid.

The party of the Ormée accordingly resolved to appeal to England for assistance in money, ships, and men. Three

Commis-
sioners
sent to
England commissioners, of whom the principal was a lawyer named Trancas, were instructed to lay before Parliament the case of the Bordelais. In return for a promise of help they were to offer possession of a port on the Gironde, or, if the English Government preferred it, of Arcachon or Rochelle. The towers which formed the only remaining fortification of the latter place were, however, still held by the King's troops, and it would be necessary to dislodge them.[2]

Before the commissioners reached England the Long Parliament had fallen, and their credentials were presented to the

May.
The com-
missioners
in
England. Lord General. Barrière, as might have been expected, did his best to support their prayer, and Cardenas was no less urgent.[3] So hopeful was the Spanish party on the Continent of winning Cromwell to its side, that Condé drank his health at Antwerp as 'the wisest, greatest and ablest commander in Europe.'[4] Yet, though Cromwell was by no means disinclined to the adventure, it was impossible for him to incur its risk until the Dutch war had been brought to an end. All, therefore, that Cardenas

---

[1] Lenet to Watteville, March 4; Lenet to Condé, March 4; Longchamps to Lenet, March 9, *Bibl. Nat. Fr.* 6714, fol. 33, 39, 57.

[2] Powers given to the commissioners, $\frac{\text{March 25}}{\text{April 4}}$. Instructions to the commissioners, $\frac{\text{March 29}}{\text{April 8}}$, Cosnac, *Souvenirs du Règne de Louis XIV*, vii. 3, 478. Guizot mistakenly, as M. Cosnac points out, says that Oléron was offered to England; it had previously been offered to Spain.

[3] Barrière to Condé, May $\frac{20}{30}$, *Chantilly Transcripts*.

[4] Nicholas to Hyde, May $\frac{19}{29}$, *Nicholas Papers*, ii. 14.

could secure was the permission to hire six or eight ships from

Ships hired
by Car-
denas.

English merchants to be employed in the succour of Bordeaux.   Yet even this limited assistance came to nothing, because, after ships had been hired, the

July.
They
cannot be
manned.

Spanish ambassador found it impossible to man them, all available mariners having been pressed into the navy to fight the Dutch.[1]   In the meanwhile the Spanish squadron had put to sea, but, ill-manned and ill-

June 25.

found, it did not venture to attack the enemy, and,

July 5.
Failure of
the Span-
iards to
relieve
Bordeaux.

though remaining some months longer in the Gironde, it made no serious attempt to relieve Bordeaux.   At the same time 4,000 Irish in the Spanish service, who were intended to break up the

July $\frac{10}{20}$.
Surrender
of Bordeaux.

French Royalist forces by land, deserted in a body.[2] On July 20 Bordeaux surrendered, and resistance to the King in the south of France came to an end.

That the Dutch war was still raging was mainly attributable to the persistency with which the English Council of State

Continu-
ance of the
Dutch war.

continued to press for conditions of peace to which no self-respecting government would submit except under the direst necessity.   When, therefore, on

April 6,

the letter of Parliament[3] offering to take up the

The Eng-
lish terms
unaccept-
able at the
Hague.

negotiation at the stage at which it had been dropped by Pauw reached the Hague, De Witt—who although not formally appointed Pensionary of Holland till July, had for some time been fulfilling the duties of

that office—was eager that his countrymen should accept the hand held out to them.   Yet, anxious as he was to see peace restored, he could not recommend the acceptance of any proposal which implied the acknowledgment that Tromp had maliciously brought about the war, or which derogated from the national independence of the Republic.   If no other reason had weighed with the young statesman, it would have

[1] Bordeaux to Brienne, July $\frac{7}{17}$, $\frac{11}{21}$, *R.O. Transcripts.*

[2] Baradouna to the Doge, July $\frac{6}{16}$, Aug. $\frac{10}{20}$, *Venetian Archives, Spagna.*

[3] *Aitzema*, iii. 805 ; see vol. ii. p. 239.

been enough that merely to entertain such a proposal would have inevitably resulted in an Orange revolution in the Netherlands.

With these rocks ahead, De Witt contented himself with asking the States General to agree to the opening of a fresh negotiation in some neutral town. Even for this he secured no more than the votes of four provinces. Though it was constitutionally doubtful whether any further step could be taken without the approval of those Provincial States by which the recalcitrant deputies had been appointed, the States of Holland, whose commerce was bleeding at every pore, passed on the resolution of the majority to England.[1] On May 6 it was summarily rejected by the new Council of State appointed immediately on the dissolution of the Long Parliament, but assurances were at the same time given that there was no wish to press the Dutch hardly in the interpretation of the offensive articles[2] in the treaty which had been under discussion before the outbreak of the war.

April 28/30.
A new proposal from the Hague.

May 6.
Its rejection in England.

Cromwell, at least, did not regard this answer as final. Yet he was not the man to relax the warlike preparations which he had inherited from the former Government. It was in his favour that a few days before the dissolution Penn had safely brought the long-delayed coalships[3] into the Thames. Not only were the Londoners pacified by the prospect of being able to fill their cellars, but the officials, whose task it was to get the fleet ready for sea, were able to press the mariners who had brought the coals. No such gleam of prosperity enlivened Amsterdam. In that once busy

Continuance of preparations for war.

April 15.
Arrival of the coalships.

Distress in Amsterdam.

---

[1] The States General to Parliament, April $\frac{20}{30}$, *Aitzema*, iii. 806; De Witt to Van Beuningen, $\frac{\text{April 25}}{\text{May 5}}$; Verbael, in De Witt's *Brieven*, v. 121; compare *Geddes*, i. 292–297.

[2] A Declaration of the Council of State, May 6, *Thurloe*, i. 239; The Council of State to the States General, May 6, *Aitzema*, iii. 812; De Witt to Van Beuningen, May $\frac{10}{20}$, *Brieven*, v. 138.

[3] See vol. ii. p. 248.

mart three thousand houses were to let, and the grass was growing in many of the streets.   A glover who had employed forty-eight hands was now working as a journeyman ; whilst a manufacturer of silk bonelace, who in better times had found employment for three or four hundred girls, had been com-

Anxiety for the safety of the mer- chant fleet.

pelled to dismiss all but three.[1]   The only hope of the traders lay in the fleet of merchantmen making its slow way round the north of Scotland, now that it had been found impossible to protect it in the Channel.   It was admitted that if that fleet were to fall into the hands of the enemy, the bankruptcies would be beyond counting.[2]

In order to avert so dire a calamity, Tromp left the Hague on April 22 to resume his command.   Two days later he

April 22.

May 2.

Tromp sets out from the Hague.

warned the States General of the weakness of their navy, ' and how impossible it was for him with such small vessels to do anything against the English, being for the most part all great ships, so as he

April 24.

May 4.

His fore- bodings.

should bring not only himself and many other honest men, but the whole State into inevitable danger ; desiring, therefore, to be dismissed of his charge, which he had far rather another should have than go to sea with such a fleet.'   The States could but refuse to accept his

He offers his resigna- tion.

resignation,[3] on which Tromp, making the best of his position, put out to sea, followed by 200 merchant- men which he conducted in safety as far as Shet-

May 29/30.

Convoys the merchant fleet safely.

land.   There he fell in with a part of the homeward- bound fleet, which he convoyed to Holland without any considerable loss.[4]   Monk and Deane, who had

Monk and Deane miss him.

been in pursuit,[5] had missed him, though they made havoc of the fishing-boats on the Dutch coast.

---

[1] Newsletter, April 29, *Clarendon MSS.* ii. No. 1,121.

[2] *Aitzema*, iii. 813.

[3] News from the Hague, April 28/May 8, *Clarendon MSS.* ii. No. 1,118.

[4] *Aitzema*, iii. 814.

[5] Letter from the fleet, in *The Moderate Intelligencer*, E. 697, 4 ; *Several Proceedings*, E. 213, 14.   Mr. Geddes (i. 311) incorrectly speaks of Blake as pursuing Tromp.

Blake, now to a certain extent recovered from his wound, had

May. 18. regained his good humour, and betook himself to
Blake at Portsmouth to look after the equipment of the ships
Portsmouth.
under orders for active service. These, as well as
others then fitting out in the Thames, were placed at his disposal, either to scour the Channel or to be carried to the help

Keeping of his colleagues in the North Sea.[1] If the words
foreigners traditionally assigned to him : "It is not for us to
from fool-
ing us. mind State affairs, but to keep foreigners from fooling
us," were ever really uttered, they may conjecturally be assigned
to this period of his life, when he finally resolved, much against
the grain, to throw in his lot with a Government whose political principles he detested.[2]

On May 27, Monk and Deane, who had been plying off the

May 27. Texel since their return from a fruitless chase, on
Monk and
Deane put hearing that Tromp was now in command of a fleet—
back to Yar-
mouth. according to report—of 120 ships, put back to Yarmouth

June 1. to collect reinforcements.[3] On June 1 they sailed in
The fleet off
the Gabbard. search of the enemy with 115 sail, five of which were
fireships,[4] anchoring for the night about two miles off the

[1] Newsletter, May 12, *Clarendon MSS.* ii. No. 1,149 ; *Perf. Diurnal*, E,
213, 18 ; *The Weekly Intelligencer*, E, 698, 2 ; *Perfect Account*, E, 698, 3.

[2] That Blake cannot have used this expression at the time of the
expulsion of the Long Parliament appears from the conduct attributed to
him at the time (see vol. ii. p. 270, note 2). In the nominated Parliament, as
has been shown (vol. ii. p. 309, note), he sided with Cromwell. The words
would be in place if they were spoken to some member of the expelled
Long Parliament, remonstrating with him for deserting his colours.

[3] *Several Proceedings*, E, 213, 24.

[4] [The number of ships is slightly overstated in the text. A list
published on July 25 (669, f. 17, No. 34), and reprinted in Penn's *Mem.
of Sir W. Penn*, i. 490, gives a total number of 105, including 5 fireships.
Appended to the list is a note saying : 'Besides this, there have come to
the fleet, and with General Blake, and other ships, above 20 since the
draft of this list.' According to a letter from Penn (*ib.* i. 495), there
were 126 men-of-war after the battle was over. Of these, 13 joined under
Blake in the course of the second day's action, so that there cannot have
been more than 113 present when the battle began. It is possible that there
were fewer, for Dutch accounts describe the English fleet as 95 or 100
sail. Brandt, *Vie du l'Amiral de Ruiter*, ed. 1698, p. 35.]

southern end of the Gabbard shoal.[1]   On the morning of the
2nd they descried Tromp—who had visited the Downs and
found them empty—beating up towards them, not
indeed with 120, but with 104 sail, six being fireships;[2] somewhat, therefore, inferior in the number
and still more inferior in the size of his ships.

June 2.
Approach of
the Dutch.

On the approach of the enemy, the English fleet weighed
anchor, and bore down upon him as quickly as a light wind
somewhat to the eastward of north would allow.[3]   Both fleets
were divided into three squadrons, Monk and Deane commanding the main body of the English, with Penn on the starboard and Lawson on the port side.[4]   In the centre
of the enemy's fleet was Tromp himself, whilst De
Ruyter was at the head of, and De With astern of
the line as it beat up against the wind.   So light was the wind,
that the two fleets only came within range about eleven.   Deane
himself was struck dead by one of the first shots, and Monk,
throwing a cloak over the body of his fallen colleague, found
himself left in sole command.[5]   For about three hours there

The battle
off the
Gabbard.

----

[1] See vol. ii., map facing p. 195.

[2] Tromp to the States General, *Aitzema*, iii. 817.

[3] Tromp's official narrative is quite clear that the English were right
in the wind, and that the wind was N. by E.   Admiral Jordan's journal,
however (*Mem. of Sir W. Penn*, i. 553), gives the wind for the whole day
as N.N.W., N. and N.E.   Probably it was N.N.W. before dawn.

[4] This is nowhere stated, but the battle is unintelligible on any other
supposition.

[5] The only two accounts of the battle at any length are Tromp's
narrative and a letter from Richard Lyons, Monk's chaplain.   According
to Tromp : "We caught sight of the enemy's fleet right in the wind,
which was N. by E.   The enemy for a long time drove down upon us, we
doing our best to beat up towards them.   Finally the enemy separated into
three squadrons, one in the centre and the other two on the wings, sailing
free at a good distance apart, apparently to enclose us in a half-moon.
They, perceiving that we awaited them in good order, again approached
one another, just coming within shot at eleven in the morning.   General
Deane then prepared to attack us, as he did furiously, and we defended
ourselves according to our duty.   In the midst of the fight it fell calm,
and the enemy's Blue Squadron " (*i.e.* Lawson's) " was somewhat separated

was a hot cannonade, without any attempt on the part of Monk to break into the enemy's fleet according to the practice of former actions, probably because the lightness of the wind

from the main body, and the wind changed a little, so that our ships were turned round to catch the wind, in order to cut off the squadron. The enemy perceiving this, took all pains to join one another, but, before that could be well accomplished, we were strongly engaged with the Blue Squadron, and whilst we were still fighting, we fell off into the middle of their main body and passed through it, so that both the fleets were fighting very hard, and surrounded by a cloud of smoke." *Aitzema*, iii. 821.

"But on Thursday," writes Lyons, "at day dawning, we saw the enemy's fleet to the leeward of us ; and weighing all hands, we stood with them, but the wind failed us. By that time we drew near them, and the enemy stood lashing" (*i.e.* lasking) "away ; yet did the 'George'" (Lawson's ship) "and his squadron very hotly engage the enemy for some hours ; so Tromp declines engagement with our main body and flag, but bears up to relieve Ruyter that was hotly engaged by Rear-Admiral Lawson, who, with his second came very well off, and all his squadron, being the Blue, both with safety and honour. And now, the wind bearing about to the eastward, the enemy takes the advantage, and comes with his whole power and engages sharply for two hours, till ours had recovered the weather gage again, and then he endeavoured to keep all as close together as he could that he might make the best of his way without loss, dreading our great ships." *Mem. of Sir W. Penn*, i. 496. Lyons' statement that the Dutch were 'lasking away,' that is to say, were not close-hauled, is inconsistent with Tromp's assertion that he was beating up towards them.

Of shorter accounts we have Monk's despatch : "Early in the morning we discovered the Dutch fleet about two leagues to the leeward. We made sail towards them, and between eleven and twelve at noon we were engaged, and for three hours the dispute was very sharp on both sides, which continued from three to six in the evening." *Ib.* i. 491. "At daylight," writes Rear-Admiral Jordan in his journal, "espied the enemy's fleet, consisting of about ninety sail ; they kept the wind ; we made all haste by getting anchors up, and sailing to them. Proving little wind, it was eleven in the morning ere we came to engagement at a distance ; two or three hours later more closely. My Admiral—the Blue—Lawson, with myself and Rear-Admiral were closely engaged with some others. After that the General and Admiral of the White " (*i.e.* Penn) "came to a close engagement ; sunk three or four. All the night little wind ; we kept fair by them." *Ib.* i. 530. "About mid-day," writes De Ruyter in his journal, "we began the fight, and about three o'clock we turned upon them and drove them to flight." *Hague Archives*.

D 2

would have prolonged the approach of the windward fleet, and would consequently have exposed it in a comparatively defenceless position to the enemy's broadsides.[1]   Tromp on his side fell off from the wind, doubtless that he too might have the full use of all his guns.   Gradually, however, Lawson edged down upon De Ruyter, either driven by the current or prompted by his own impetuosity, and Tromp, seeing his colleague's danger, forsook his own immediate antagonist to push on to his succour. Before anything decisive had been accomplished the wind dropped entirely, and when again a light breeze sprang up it blew from a more easterly quarter than before.   As the wind headed his ships, Tromp, with a promptitude which the soldier-admiral opposed to him could hardly be expected to imitate, ordered out the boats to tow round his ships that they might catch the wind on the starboard tack.   Whilst De Ruyter thus gained the wind of Lawson, Tromp drove his squadron into the gap left between that Admiral and Monk, thus placing Lawson between two fires and anticipating in a rough and imperfect fashion the manœuvre familiar to seamen of a later date as the breaking of the line.   If the movement failed in the success which it achieved in the hands of Rodney and Nelson, this was partly because, in consequence of Lawson's advanced position, Monk was not so much to leeward of him as he would have been if the change of wind had occurred earlier in the battle, and was therefore able to come to his aid without any long delay ; and partly because the gunnery of that day was insufficient to crush even a weaker adversary in what would now be considered a reasonable time.[2]   The battle ended in a general *mêlée*, in which

[1] Not only is there absolutely no mention of the ordinary ' passing through' the Dutch fleet, but the broadside fighting is implied in Jordan's words relating to this part of the fight.

[2] Probably on account of the greater windage as compared with that allowed at the present day :—" With the degree of windage formerly established in the British service, no less than one third or one fourth of the powder escaped and was lost, and as balls are often less than the regulated size, it frequently happened that half the force of the powder was lost by unnecessary windage." Sir Howard Douglas's *Treatise on Naval Gunnery* (3rd ed. 1851), p. 582.

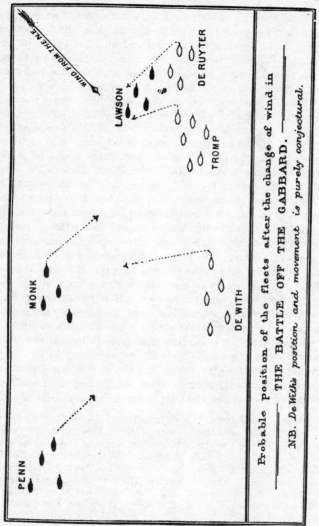

WIND FROM THE NE.

DE RUYTER

LAWSON

TROMP

MONK

DE WITH

PENN

Probable position of the fleets after the change of wind in

THE BATTLE OFF THE GABBARD.

NB. De With's position and movement is purely conjectural.

E. S. Weller.

the English ships by their superior weatherliness forced themselves through the mass of the enemy and regained the weather gage. In this desperate struggle the Dutch lost two ships, the one blown up and the other sunk.[1] Night put an end to the strife, and drifting southwards by wind and tide the two fleets found themselves at nightfall not far from Dunkirk.[2]

With the morning Tromp discovered that, as on that sad day when he had found himself helpless off Cape Grisnez,[3] his powder was running short. De With announced that he had no more than would suffice him for three hours. De Ruyter had even less. Once more the wretched administration of the Republic had provided disaster for her fleet.[4] Yet the old hero could not be content to retreat till he had once more tried a fall with his country's foes. By this time the wind had shifted to the westward, and the English lying to the north-west opened the attack. Just as Tromp was hard-pressed Blake came up with thirteen fresh ships and rendered his position hopeless. Yet even so he kept up the struggle to the close of the day. Towards the end of the fight his ship was boarded by Penn's crew, and seeing no other resource, he set fire to a barrel of powder underneath the part of the deck which had been mastered by the enemy, and blew the assailants into the air. For all that it would have gone hard with him if De Ruyter and De With had not come to their admiral's relief. So well had the struggle been kept up that at sunset a great part of the Dutch fleet was still to the westward of Ostend, though many of their ships had made off to the entrance of the Maes for shelter. Tromp's best ally was

(marginal note: June 3. Tromp short of powder.)

[1] Tromp to the States General, June ³⁄₁₃, *Aitzema*, iii. 817.

[2] The English authorities represent Tromp as flying, but the southward movement is more probably to be ascribed to natural causes, accentuated perhaps in the end by a sense of failure. The fight is usually styled the battle of Nieuport, and is supposed to have been fought off that place. The mistake seems to have arisen from Tromp's expression that it began in the meridian of Nieuport. A letter from Bernard to Strickland (*Thurloe*, i. 272) shows that the first day's fight was not visible from the shore.

[3] See vol. ii. p. 219.   [4] Tromp to the States General, *Aitzema*, iii. 817.

the wind, which was now blowing hard and deterred the English commanders from venturing with their large vessels amongst the sands which fringed the Flemish coast. When

June 4.
Retreat of
the Dutch. the sun rose on the 4th the Dutch were descried in full retreat for the Wielings, to which it was impossible to follow them. In the two days' fight the Dutch had lost, according to the English account, twenty men-of-war, of which eleven were brought in as prizes.[1]

The victory was attributable mainly to superior administration on the English side. The ships of the victors were

Causes of
the
victory. not only larger, but better built, better supplied, and better manned. The division into three squadrons which had been first displayed in the battle off Portland, was imitated from the Dutch practice. If there was superiority in tactics it was on the Dutch side, as no single action of any one of the English commanders can be compared to the promptness with which Tromp took immediate advantage of the change of wind in the midst of the first day's fight. What the Dutch admiral lacked was a fleet equal to his merits.

After his return home, Tromp spoke his mind freely to the government—if government it could be called—under which he served. More than thirty of his remaining ships, he said, were too weak to be of any service against the powerful

Statement
by De
Ruyter. armament of the enemy. De Ruyter added that, for his part, he had made up his mind that unless the fleet were strengthened he would go to sea no more. In the late battle, he added, more than half the ships were mere hindrances to action, as those that were better armed had to defend the weaker ones instead of putting forth all their strength against the enemy. " Why should I be silent ? "

[1] Penn's *Mem. of Sir W. Penn*, i. 491–498 ; Tromp's despatch and narration are in *Aitzema*, iii. 817, 821. The story of Tromp's blowing up his deck is from *Hollandsche Mercurius* (1653), p. 68. That Tromp himself should not have mentioned it is in accordance with his usual modesty, and is an additional reason for doubting the theatrical exhibition of the broom at the masthead.

burst out the impetuous De With. "I stand before my sove-
Indigna-
tion of
De With. reigns: I must speak out. The English are our
masters, and consequently masters of the sea."[1]
The fact was undeniable. The English fleet was
ranging along the coast and blockading the ports. Those who
sent it out aimed at even more than this. There were on
The
English
propose to
occupy a
town in
Holland. board 5,000 soldiers under Goffe who had received
instructions to occupy, if possible, one of the forti-
fied towns of Holland. The scheme, however,
proved impracticable, and Goffe returned without
making the attempt. To the Dutch the mere existence of the
blockade was sufficiently grievous without this culmination of
misfortunes. Trade was at a standstill. Starvation was
followed by tumult, and loud cries were raised for the re-
establishment of the Stadtholderate as the only means of
rescuing the Republic from its misfortunes.

The outcries of the population stimulated De Witt to
search once again for some course which might satisfy England
De Witt
anxious to
negotiate. without rousing the just susceptibilities of his own
countrymen. With this object in view he persuaded
the States General to appoint four commissioners,
Com-
missioners
appointed. not to negotiate a treaty in England, but to ascertain
whether there was any prospect of negotiating on a
reasonable basis. The four were Beverning—a
confidant of De Witt—Nieuport, Van de Perre, and Jongestal.
The first two were Hollanders, the third a Zealander, and the
fourth a native of Friesland who, being a devoted servant of
the House of Orange, was prepared to balk De Witt and the
Hollanders in any endeavour to make peace on unfavourable
conditions. Beverning arrived in London on June 17, and
his fellow-commissioners were not long behind.

The reception of the commissioners was unpromising.
Though the nominated Parliament had not yet met, and the
Reception
of the
com-
missioners. Council of State was therefore one of Cromwell's
own choosing, its members were as stiff in their
demands as if they were utterly indifferent to the

[1] *Aitzema*, iii. 821.

attainment of peace. The attack by Tromp off Folkestone still rankled in their minds, and on June 29 they refused to

June 29. Harsh demands of the Council of State. treat at all unless the Dutch commissioners were prepared to acknowledge in some practical fashion that their great admiral had been in the wrong and to give security that the offence would not be repeated.[1] To Cromwell, then at the height of the religious fervour which expressed itself a few days later in the speech with which he greeted the nominees, this cold treatment of a

June 30. A private communication from Cromwell. Protestant nation was unbearable. On the 30th he sent a private communication to Nieuport, in the hope that it might clear the way for a better understanding. Might not the States General, he suggested, give the required satisfaction by dismissing Tromp temporarily from his command, on the understanding that he was to be reappointed after five or six months? As to security, it would be enough if two or three Dutchmen were appointed to seats in the English Council of State, and the same number of Englishmen to seats either in the Dutch Council of State or in the States General.[2] If these conditions were accepted, a truce would probably be granted and the Dutch would be allowed liberty of fishing in the British seas, and of trading in the West Indies.

That Cromwell foresaw no difficulties in the way of amalgamation in this modified form is probable enough. The

Cromwell's views on amalgamation. grandiose conception of a union between the nations had originated with his ally St. John, and had taken hold on his own mind. "You have appealed," he now argued with the commissioners, "to the judgment of Heaven. The Lord has declared against you. After the defeats you have undergone, your only resource is to associate yourselves with your formidable neighbour to work together for the propagation of the kingdom of Christ, and the

[1] *Verbael*, p. 21.

[2] The idea was probably derived from the arrangement by which Elizabeth and James I., till he abandoned the cautionary towns, were represented by the English ambassador in the Dutch Council of State.

deliverance of the people groaning under oppression." [1]   Nevertheless, Cromwell being firmly convinced that Tromp had been
the real aggressor at the commencement of the war, saw
nothing offensive in demanding some acknowledgment of the
fault.

Though from a Dutch point of view Cromwell's overtures
were absolutely inadmissible, the commissioners were well
aware that he would take umbrage at their rejection ; and it was without surprise that they heard
that he was closeted with Lambert and Harrison, and
had given vent to a suspicion that the only object of their
embassy was to gain time for a fresh development of their naval
power.[2]

July 1.
Cromwell
takes
offence.

Yet it was not in Cromwell's nature to confine himself to
mere distrust.   It is true that at a conference held on the 13th
he reiterated his belief that the Dutch had maliciously
contrived the war, but he was now in the full fervour
of that religious conviction which manifested itself in
him in the early days of the nominated Parliament,
and he not only refrained from repeating his proposal for the
supersession of Tromp, but pleaded long and persuasively for
the closest possible union short of amalgamation.   He told the
commissioners that ' God had wonderfully delivered them out
of the Spanish slavery, and revealed to them the truth of His
word ; that the English therefore honoured and loved them ;
but that people sometimes became careless and did not
sufficiently apprehend the intrigues which were used against
them ; that in England, God be thanked, the work was better
understood than in the United Netherlands, and that, above all
—what must be first thought of—were the essential points
tending to the preservation of freedom, and the outspreading
of the kingdom of Christ, not for themselves only, but also for
posterity, in order that the treaty built on such a foundation—

July 13.
Cromwell
makes a
fresh
suggestion.

---

[1] Sirtema de Grovenstin, *Hist. des Luttes . . . entre les Puissances
Maritimes et la France*, i. 204.   The words are taken from a diary of
Beverning in the Hague archives.

[2] *Verbael*, pp. 84, 85.

yet according to the form and character of the respective governments —might be permanent and inviolable ; that it had often happened that, after a quarrel, friendship became stronger and faster than before ; and that neither of them knew what God the Lord, for the magnifying of His holy name and the delivery of so many oppressed nations, who now more than ever groaned under insufferable tyranny, might intend to accomplish by the two republics in His own good time.' [1]

Such language was a sufficient indication of that zeal for the triumph of his religion which was never far from Cromwell's heart. His practical sense was embodied in a conversation which he held with two of the Dutch commissioners as he was walking in the evening in St. James's Park. 'The interests of both nations,' he said, ' consisted in the welfare of commerce and navigation; and no lasting peace could be established between them unless binding rules were made. He knew well that the industry of the Dutch ought not to be prevented, but that the English having received so many advantages from nature in the way of good havens and geographical situation, could not be deprived of them. The world was wide enough for both ; if the two peoples could only thoroughly well understand each other their countries would become the markets of the world, would dictate their will to Europe, and put everything as regards commerce on a good footing. . . . It would be necessary to adjust and regulate the common interests of commerce and navigation, if the two nations were to live together in harmony.' [2]

July 14. A conversation between Cromwell and the commissioners.

A close union for religious and commercial objects was, in short, the aim of Cromwell's policy, a union which he now dissociated from any conditions degrading to either party. The Dutch would have to abandon the special advantages secured to them in the Sound by their treaty with the King of Denmark.[3] From England they

Cromwell's generous policy.

---

[1] *Verbael,* pp. 42, 43. The translation above is borrowed from Mr. Geddes.

[2] *Ibid.* pp. 45, 46. The translation is again Mr. Geddes's, with one verbal change.   [3] See vol. ii. p. 146.

would at least gain the opening of the colonial trade, if not the repeal of the Navigation Act itself. Not a word was on this occasion uttered by Cromwell as to the payment of money in reparation for the attack on Blake :—still less as to the wild scheme for the political fusion of the two nations which was still in the thoughts of his colleagues, as not long ago it had been in his own.

Unfortunately the decision lay with the new Council of State, of which Cromwell was an influential member, but by no means an absolute master, and a Council of State appointed by the nominated Parliament in its early days was too fully under the influence of abstract ideas to recognise, as Cromwell was always prepared to do, that a position had ceased to be tenable.[1] Though the Dutch commissioners were perfectly ready to treat on the commercial union—it was hardly likely that they would be enthusiastic for the religious crusade—they were flatly told that the Council expected payment, not indeed of any large sum, but of sufficient to imply an acknowledgment of wrong-doing in the past and also security for the future, ' by uniting both States together in such manner as they may become one people and commonwealth.' [2] The remonstrances of the commissioners only drew down on them a repetition of the demand in plainer terms. "The Council," they were told, "did in express terms propose not the establishing of a league and union between two sovereign States and neighbours, but the making of two sovereign States one ; which although it doth not necessitate the alteration of the municipal laws of either, yet it cannot but intend the whole so united to be under one supreme power to consist of persons of both nations, according as shall be agreed upon ; and to have and enjoy the like privileges and freedom in respect of habitations, possessions, trade, ports, fishing, and all

July 21.
The Council of State insists on a political union.

July 25.
The proposal insisted on.

A complete amalgamation demanded.

---

[1] Cromwell took care to put this on record by sending a message on the 20th to the commissioners, begging them to address themselves to the Council of State, not to his Excellency and the Council of State.

[2] Proposal by the Council of State, July $\frac{21}{31}$, *Verbael*, p. 53.

other advantages whatsoever in each other's countries as natives without any difference or distinction." [1]

This outrageous demand having been courteously but decisively rejected,[2] the English Council doggedly repeated its summons. In order to avert an absolute rupture, the Dutch commissioners despatched two of their number, Nieuport and Jongestal, to the Hague, on the pretext that it was desirable that they should personally report to their masters, whilst the other two, Beverning and Van de Perre, remained behind to keep up the semblance of a negotiation in England. If they had any hope left it must have been based on their knowledge that they had Cromwell on their side, and that the difference of opinion between the Lord General and the Council of State was almost as great as that which separated themselves from the English negotiators. Even before the two commissioners left England events had occurred which might well have given pause to all who desired to prolong the conflict between the nations.

July 27. It is rejected by the Dutch.

Aug. 1. The English insist.

Aug. 3. Two commissioners return to the Hague.

Since Tromp's defeat in the North Sea, the Dutch authorities had been putting forth all their strength to cope with the victorious enemy and to free their ports from blockade. Volunteers pressed forward to share in the defence, and before the end of July Tromp, having been strongly re-enforced, was enabled to put out from the Wielings and to hasten to the assistance of De With who was cooped up in the Texel by a superior English force. That force was under the sole command of Monk, Blake having been compelled by the recrudescence of his wound to return to shore.

Dutch preparations.

July. Tromp again at sea.

On July 29, by a feigned retreat, Tromp decoyed his soldier antagonist from his station, and some cannon-shots were exchanged, before night put an end to the fighting. Under cover of the darkness, De With made his

July 29. He decoys Monk away from the Texel,

[1] Answer by the C. of St. $\frac{July\ 25}{Aug.\ 4}$, *Verbael*, p. 62.

[2] Answer by the Dutch commissioners, $\frac{July\ 27}{Aug.\ 6}$; Reply of the C. of St. Aug. $\frac{1}{11}$, *ib.* pp. 66, 70.

way out and joined the Admiral on the following day.
By this time it was blowing a westerly gale, and
neither commander was in a mood to risk a combat
off a lee shore. On the 31st the storm died away,
and Tromp who was lying to windward bore down
upon the enemy. As the fleets were entering into
action, the Dutch Admiral was struck down by a bullet. "It is
all over," he murmured. "O Lord, be merciful to me and Thy
poor people." Tender friends carried him below, but he died
as soon as he reached the cabin. The fight raged on.
Monk, with the ruthlessness which characterised him,
gave orders that the enemy's ships should be sunk or burnt,
but not captured lest his fleet should be weakened by the
necessity of detaching ships to guard the prizes. By one
o'clock the Dutch began to give way, and before long the
English knew that their victory was complete. Yet
so stubborn had the resistance been, that the victors
were compelled to abandon the blockade, and to
take refuge in their own ports to refit their shattered fleet.[1]

*July 30.
and is joined
by De With.*

*July 31.
Battle of the
Texel.*

*Tromp's
death.*

*Victory
of the
English.*

---

[1] *Hollandsche Mercurius* (1653), p. 86; *Aitzema*, iii. 831; Sacheverell to the Navy Commissioners, Aug. 2; Cox to Cromwell, Aug. 2; Cubitt to Blackborne, Aug. 2, *S. P. Dom.* xxxix. 9, 10, 11. Sacheverell's letter confirms Gumble's statement (*Life of Monk*, p. 62) about the order not to take prizes. Monk's despatches are in Penn's *Mem. of Sir W. Penn*, i. 501-504. In the latter work (p. 509) is reprinted from Hoste, *L'Art des Armées Navales*, a narrative of the battle by a French gentleman, who professes himself to have been an eyewitness. "Here," writes Granville Penn, "we find the fleet formed in line, twelve years before the date assigned by Macpherson to the first example of that order of battle in an English fleet." I am sceptical as to the genuineness of this narrative. In it the French gentleman is said to have embarked in a corvette in order to witness the battle, not a very likely story. He says that he caught sight of Tromp's fleet on $\frac{\text{July 28}}{\text{Aug. 7}}$, which is a day too soon, and that $\frac{\text{July 29}}{\text{Aug. 8}}$ and $\frac{30}{9}$ 'se passèrent en escarmouches,' apparently knowing nothing of the gale of $\frac{\text{July 30}}{\text{Aug. 9}}$. He then talks of Tromp's directing the battle in various ways, after which we arrive at his death; not, as in fact happened, early in the battle, but as he was about to board Monk's ship. The fight then comes to an end. It is certain that, however the fleets

Tromp was, in every sense, the hero of the war. If tactical skill could have wrested victory from an enemy greatly superior

Tromp the hero of the war. in force, he would have made the battle off the Gabbard as glorious for his countrymen as had been the fight in the Downs in 1639. Fighting for the liberty of his country's trade, he was borne down by official incompetence and by the defects of a complicated administrative machinery, even more than by the material superiority of the English navy. A partisan of the House of Orange, as every fighting man must of necessity have been, he never allowed his feelings in this respect to interfere with his services to a government which appeared to him in the highest degree ineffectual. Yet he never shrank from pointing out to his masters without exaggeration, but also without diminution, the errors which he and his sailors expiated with their blood. If it had been possible to create a maritime stadtholderate in Tromp's favour, and thus to give unity of direction to the war against England, as William the Silent had given unity of direction to the war against Spain, it is probable that the result would have been less markedly unfavourable to his countrymen.

The Dutch loss was calculated at twenty-six men-of-war. Of their crews it is said there were 2,700 drowned or killed, 2,500 wounded, and 1,000 left as prisoners in the hands of the enemy.[1] The English confessed to the loss of two ships. Seven of their captains, however, perished, and five were wounded. The slain were set down at 250, and the wounded at 800.[2]

Indisputable as had been the victory of the English fleet, the conquerors were no longer in a condition to maintain the

may have been drawn up before the battle, the English did not fight in line. " In the fight," writes Monk (*Penn*, i. 503), "the ' Resolution' with the ' Worcester' frigate led the English fleet, in a desperate and gallant charge, through the whole Dutch fleet."

[1] A communication from Holland, Aug. $\frac{12}{22}$, Penn's *Mem. of Sir W. Penn*, i. 506.

[2] *Ibid*. i. 506.

blockade, and with the sea again open before them, not a man
in any one of the seven Provinces would give ear to
the haughty summons to amalgamate with England
which was all that the returning commissioners could
officially communicate. It cost De Witt many a week of
patient diplomacy before he was able to induce his countrymen
even to offer their alliance to the nation under whose blows they
were staggering.[1]

The blockade broken up.

If the way to an understanding was not made plain the fault
did not lie with Cromwell. His position was now that of an
opposition leader aiming at peace, whilst the recognised authorities were aiming at the continuance of
war, and it was only by underhand methods that he
could communicate with the two Dutch commissioners still remaining at Westminster. Yet he was conscious of force behind
him, and it was as one who had been master of the State and
who might soon be its master again that on August 6,
after Tromp's defeat and the capitulation of Bordeaux
were known in England, he addressed soothing words
to Beverning. There was no wish in England, he
assured the Dutchman, to derogate from the sovereignty of the
United Provinces. It would be sufficient if the two nations were
to form an alliance having the same friends and the same
enemies.[2] After some further discussion by word of mouth and
on paper, this informal negotiation appeared to have fallen asleep,
when, on September 23, one of Cromwell's confidants
—probably Sir Cornelius Vermuyden, the drainer of
the Fens—carried to Van de Perre the most astounding proposal ever made by an Englishman to the minister of a
foreign State.

Cromwell as an opposi- tion leader.

Aug. 6. Cromwell's conversation with Bever- ning.

Sept. 23. An astounding proposal.

What was now asked was that the two nations, abandoning
all thought of amalgamation, should bind themselves in a
perpetual alliance, each being ready to undertake
war—offensive as well as defensive—against the
enemies of the other. With this object in view each

An offensive and defen- sive alliance proposed.

[1] *Geddes*, pp. 355-359.   [2] *Verbael*, pp. 143-149.

was to keep on foot a competent army, whilst England was to furnish sixty ships and the United Provinces forty, to make up a formidable fleet. The alliance was to be distinctly Protestant in its colour, including Denmark, Sweden, and such of the German princes who were not 'Papists' and who did not employ the services of the Inquisition. Even the Crown of France might be admitted if the Reformed Churches in its dominions were secured of complete liberty of conscience. On the other hand, all princes and States maintaining the Inquisition, forcing the consciences of men, and being entirely dependent on the Pope, were to be treated as enemies by both States. Though there was to be no political amalgamation, there was to be a mutual admission to civil rights, the citizens of one State being capable of holding land and offices in the other. In matters of trade the same spirit was to prevail. The fisheries were to be open to Englishmen and Dutchmen without hindrance, and Englishmen and Dutchmen might also carry on trade in either country on the same footing as the inhabitants, thus sweeping away the Navigation Act at a single blow. In Europe and Africa trade was to be open to both, the possession of ports established by the Dutch in Africa being specially recognised.

It is to be joined by the Protestant States and France.

All this, however, startling as it might be, was as nothing to that which followed. England and the United Provinces were to partition the remainder of the globe between them. The whole of Asia was to fall to the share of the Dutch, who were to compensate the English East India Company for the entire loss of its trade. America, on the other hand, with the exception of Brazil, over a corner of which the Dutch still maintained a precarious hold, was to be assigned to the English. Nor was it to be a mere league for opening commerce with those regions. Though neither Spain nor Portugal was mentioned by name, there was to be a war of conquest against both Spain and Portugal. The Dutch were to furnish twenty-five ships to assist the English in making themselves masters of all ports, rivers, towns, and castles which they had a mind to occupy

Character of the proposal.

A partition of the globe.

outside Brazil.   It was not stated, but was probably intended
that England should render similar assistance to the Dutch
within the limits assigned to them in Brazil. To remove all
difficulties which might arise out of this far-reaching agreement,
Commis-   two bodies of commissioners, each composed of four
sioners to   Englishmen and four Dutchmen, were to be esta-
uphold the
agreement.   blished respectively in the two countries, with power
to decide all disputes between Englishmen and Dutchmen.
Finally, missionaries were to be sent to all peoples willing to
receive them, to inculcate the truth of Jesus Christ and the
Holy Gospel.[1]

It scarcely needed this last touch to blast the whole project
in the eyes of later generations.   To evoke a Protestant alliance,
not for the purpose of defending oppressed Protestants, but to
wrest America from Spain and Portugal for the benefit of two
Protestant nations, involves the utilising of religion for purposes of self-interest, of which the modern world has learnt to
be ashamed—at least, in its public professions.   Yet the con-

---

[1] *Verbael*, p. 149.   These propositions are evidently founded on a set
of articles without a date, entitled ' A paper delivered by Sir Cornelius
Vermuyden, relating to a treaty between England and the States General,'
and printed in *Thurloe's Collection* (ii. 125).   There are some alterations
in detail, the changes having been apparently introduced in order to enlarge
the concessions to the Dutch.   For instance, in Vermuyden's project the
trade of Asia Minor is left free to all, and the southern limits of Dutch
Brazil are placed at the Tropic of Capricorn—*i.e.* a little south of Rio de
Janeiro.   In the articles presented to Van de Perre the trade of Asia
Minor is given over to the Dutch, and the southern limit of Brazil fixed
at the Rio de la Plata.   Cromwell's connection with the plan can hardly be
exactly defined.   In the Dutch narrative emphasis is laid on the confidential relations existing between him and the bearer of the articles, and when
they were subsequently modified they were altered with the approval of
the best qualified of the Council and of Cromwell himself.   I think it may
be taken that the proposal as Van de Perre received it was adopted by
Cromwell with the approval of his partisans in the Council.   The connection of Cromwell with the secret negotiation appears from a statement
in a letter from the Hague, written on $\frac{\text{Sep. 27}}{\text{Oct. 7}}$, about the commissioners,
that, ' having gained Cromwell, they conclude the matter done, notwith-
standing the multitude that is against it.'   *Thurloe*, i. 559.

viction that religious zeal might rightly lead to national aggrandisement and personal enrichment had been a dominant note with the Elizabethan adventurers whose exploits held so large a place in Cromwell's mind. The scheme had indeed originated in the brain of a Dutchman, the greater part of whose life had been passed on English soil ; but in Cromwell's mind it found a congenial home. No one living was more eager to make the best of both worlds, and the tragedy of his career lies in the inevitable result that his efforts to establish religion and morality melted away as the morning mist, whilst his abiding influence was built upon the vigour with which he promoted the material aims of his countrymen.

From this confusion the Dutch commissioners kept their minds free. They evidently thought that a common Protestantism was insufficient to induce their countrymen to form an alliance with England in order to renew the long war against Spain from which they had rejoiced to escape five years before, and they at once declared that the utmost to be expected was a defensive league against the assailants of either nation. It was out of the question that they should enter upon an unprovoked quarrel with all States supporting the Inquisition.[1]

The Dutch shrink from the scheme.

The result of these objections appeared in a modified scheme which received the approval of Cromwell and of certain unnamed councillors. It was now left open to either State to form treaties of commerce, even with States maintaining the Inquisition. The article about sending missionaries was omitted, and the partition of the globe postponed to a more convenient season. For the present it would be enough that the commerce of Europe and the Mediterranean should be restored to the footing on which it had stood before the war—a stipulation which implied the maintenance of the Navigation Act, perhaps because the English negotiators wished to keep such a valuable asset in hand to barter for the aid which they still hoped to receive from the Dutch in their

A modified proposal.

---

[1] *Verbael*, 153.

projected attack on Spanish America.[1] To this the commissioners were unable to give any positive answer, and on October 4 Cromwell signed a pass to Van de Perre's son that he might continue the secret negotiations at the Hague. With tears in his eyes he declared to Stockar, who had been charged by the Swiss Protestant cantons to counsel peace, that nothing in the world troubled him so much as this war.[2]

Of Cromwell's eagerness for peace with a Protestant State there can be no doubt, but his sudden reversion to the idea of a war with Spain, which he had entertained in the spring of

Causes of Cromwell's temporary hostility to Spain.

1652, and which he was again to entertain in the autumn of 1654, calls for explanation. Something, perhaps, may be set down to the revelation of the weakness of the Spanish monarchy, derived from its failure to relieve Bordeaux in July. Yet, on the whole, it is perhaps safe to attribute Cromwell's revulsion of feeling partly to his irritation at the attempt of Cardenas to throw obstacles in the way of a peace with the Dutch,[3] but still more to the failure of any response to the overtures which had been made for a toleration to English Protestants in Spain. It is true that after the fall of Bordeaux in July, Thurloe, who, probably more than any other civilian, was deep in Cromwell's confidence, had

July. An overture to Cardenas.

urged Cardenas to proceed with his negotiation and not to lose so good an opportunity of coming to terms with England. At Madrid, however, the Inquisition had given a decided opposition to any attempt to extend the article on toleration further than it stood in the treaty with Charles I., and month after month passed away before any answer was vouchsafed.[4]

---

[1] *Verbael*, 155. The explanation suggested above seems more probable than that, as Mr. Geddes thinks (i. 364) the reference to the Navigation Act was omitted by an oversight.

[2] *Ib.* 160, 161.

[3] Consulta, July $\frac{11}{21}$, *Simancas MSS.* 2,079.

[4] On Sept. $\frac{1}{11}$ the Archduke Leopold wrote to Philip IV., recommending him to form an alliance with England, on the understanding

Yet if Cromwell was beginning to despair of Spain, he had not lost his sympathy with the French Protestants, and towards the end of September, just at the time when the Lord General learnt that his grand scheme for partitioning the globe found no favour in the eyes of the sober Dutchmen, Sexby and Arundel returned from their mission,[1] the last-named of the two having made an excursion to Brussels to confer with Condé. How Sexby had occupied his time we do not know, but as Conan reappeared in England about this time, and the question of an English occupation of Rochelle was again mooted, it is not unlikely that he had been making inquiries on the spot as to the disposition of the Rochellese.

September. Sexby and Arundel in England.

However this may have been, Sexby and Conan were able to bring pressure on the side of Cromwell's mind most accessible to persuasion. They could point to the signs of Mazarin's ill-will—not very strange after the prolonged coolness of the reception of the French ambassador in England—in continued retention of the English prize taken by Rupert, and the favour shown to Charles's privateers. Troubles, too, had arisen amongst the Protestants of the south, especially in the Vivarais where there had been armed resistance to the closure of Protestant churches by the Seigneur of Vals. It is true that these churches had been subsequently reopened by superior authority, but, as was but natural, the disturbance viewed from a distance assumed a

Cromwell urged to war with France.

that Spain was not to break with the Dutch. In November, however, the question was still under consideration at Madrid. *Simancas MSS.* 2,079, 2,569.

[1] Dyer, who accompanied Sexby as his servant, said in 1658 that they returned 'about August' (*Thurloe*, vi. 829). After such a lapse of time, this may easily cover September, and as Sexby claimed payment for his services during an absence of twenty-three months (*S. P. Dom.* lxxi. 49), and cannot have left before Conan's first interview with Cromwell on Oct. 16, 1651, whilst he almost certainly left soon after that, we may safely put down his return as taking place towards the end of September. Arundel's visit to Brussels is implied in Barrière's letter to Lenet of Oct. $\frac{14}{24}$, *Chantilly Transcripts*.

blacker appearance than it did on the spot.[1] To desert the French Protestants in their hour of need was in Cromwell's eyes a betrayal of the most sacred obligation.[2] It was pro-

Oct.
Offers to help the French Protestants if Spain will bear the expense.

bably at this time, setting at nought the advice of the prudent Thurloe, that he offered to Sexby to send 6,000 men and a certain number of ships to re-awaken the war in Guienne, on the condition that the King of Spain would bear the expense.[3]

---

[1] Benoît, *Hist. de l'Edit de Nantes*, III. 158–170. The affair of the Vivarais is mentioned by Bordeaux in his despatches of $\frac{\text{Aug. 29}}{\text{Sept. 8}}$, Sept. $\frac{19}{29}$, *R.O. Transcripts*.

[2] "To Cromwell," writes Mr. Firth, "as to most of his party, one of the worst sins of Charles I. was that he had induced the Huguenots to revolt against Louis XIII., and then left them to be crushed by his force. Englishmen abroad were accustomed to be taunted with their desertion of their co-religionists. 'I have heard,' wrote John Cook, 'fearful exclamations from the French Protestants against the King and the late Duke of Buckingham for the betraying Rochelle.' One of the arguments which the agents of the Huguenots of Guienne used when they appealed to Cromwell was 'that the churches of these parts have endured a very great brunt by the deceitful promises which have been made to them by the former supreme powers of Great Britain.' To this argument Cromwell was particularly accessible." *Journal of Joachim Hane*, Intr. xviii.

[3] "M. de Conan vient tout présentement de parler à Cromwel, qui l'a fort questionné sur les moyens de faire réussir l'affaire dont est question et a tesmoigné desirer avec passion qu'elle se peut exécuter, mais pourtant luy a dit qu'il ne se pourroit enguager à rien jusques à ce que l'on eust des nouvelles d'Espagne, et que lorsqu'il i auret de l'argent, on fourniroit toutes les choses nessessaires, luy a recommandé de revenir le plustost qu'il pourret, et que peut estre à son retour les afaires auroyent changé de face, et que, sela estant, luy, Cromwel, et tout ce qui gouverne en Angleterre estoyent entièrement portés a sela pour le soulagement du peuple et pour le service de son Altesse, pour qui il tesmoigne une grande passion. Je crès bien que si on a d'Espagne ce que on en atend, on pourra peu a peu engager l'Angleterre. Mais jusqu'à ce que nous ayons responce d'Espagne, il ne faut rien esperer." In a later despatch to Condé, written on Nov. $\frac{11}{21}$, Barrière says that the news of the retreat of the Spanish fleet from the Gironde had then reached England (it took place on Oct. $\frac{20}{30}$, Chéruel, *Ministère de Mazarin*, ii. 85), but that Cromwell 'n'a point changé de volonté pour sela, et si V. A. a dessèin que l'on entreprenne l'afaire de Conan, on aura isi pour de l'argent les gens de guerre.'

Till an answer arrived from Madrid all that could be done

A report
wanted on
the French
ports.

was to despatch a competent person to report on the condition of Havre and Rochelle, two ports which in the event of war it might be convenient to occupy, perhaps also on the condition of Bordeaux itself.

For this purpose Cromwell selected Joachim Hane, a German engineer officer, to whose skill it had been mainly

Mission of
Joachim
Hane.

due that the castles of Edinburgh and Stirling had fallen as rapidly as they did, and whose services had been in request after the reduction of Scotland wherever fortifications were planned to hold the country in subjection. On October 11, scarcely more than a fortnight after Cromwell's astonishing proposal for a war against Spain had been made to the Dutch ambassadors, Hane was despatched on the perilous mission of reporting on the state of the French maritime fortresses in view of a possible war against France in alliance with Spain.[1] It was not levity that was at the root of this revulsion of feeling in Cromwell's mind, but sheer inability to formulate a consistent foreign policy, which would find room for an energetic display of the strength of England, and would at the same time in one way or another strike a blow for that which he conceived to be the cause of God upon earth.

In reverting, at least as a contingency, to the Spanish alliance, Cromwell was once more in harmony with the fanatics

Cromwell
differs from
Parliament
on the
subject
of the
Dutch war.

who were beginning to dominate the Parliament which owed its origin to himself. On the subject of the Dutch war there was no such agreement. To Cromwell, as a man of sense, it appeared reasonable that the existing hostilities should be brought to a conclusion before entering on new ones. To the nominated Parliament it seemed advisable that the Dutch should be crushed, or driven to accept the proposed amalgamation as a preliminary to a war against France, lest Mazarin

---

[1] *Journal of Joachim Hane*, ed. Firth, Intr. vi. vii.

should find supporters in a people which had been irritated past endurance by England.[1]

The need of peace was indeed brought home to all who had ears to hear by the financial strain upon the resources of the Commonwealth. The necessity of providing some extraordinary supply had been long under discussion. On September 5 Parliament was informed that there would be a deficit of 515,000*l.* on the estimates for the navy.[2] It was at once proposed to meet the difficulty by calling to account the members of the Long Parliament suspected of malversation.[3] Lenthall, it was said, would be the first to suffer. The scheme was, however, abandoned in favour of a financial operation on the lands of recusants. Every recusant was to be called on to free himself from the annual payment due by him to the State, by the immediate advance of a sum equal to four years' purchase in the case of rentals, and of one-third of the personal property liable to forfeiture. In the event of his being unable or unwilling to enter into this arrangement, any other person, by making over the same amount to the Government, might purchase the right of levying during the lifetime of the recusant the fines and forfeitures hitherto paid to the Commonwealth. An Act giving effect to this scheme was passed on October 21, Praise-God Barebone acting as teller against

The financial strain.

Sept. 5. Deficit on the navy.

Oct. 21. Act for levying money on recusants' lands.

---

[1] That the Fifth Monarchists were for prolonging the war is well established. Harrison, write the Dutch commissioners, ' ende de factie der Anabaptisten . . . altydt gelooft wierdt onse negotiatie meest te traverseren ' (*Verbael*, p. 160). An intercepted letter in *Thurloe*, i. 621, tells the same story : " The Anabaptistical party, who are very prevalent in the House, oppose it "—*i.e.* the peace—" most furiously." Compare Salvetti's Newsletter, Dec. $\frac{16}{26}$, *Add. MSS.* 27,962 O. fol. 176, and News from the Hague, Jan. $\frac{13}{23}$, *Clarendon MSS.* ii. No. 1,684. John Rogers, the Fifth-Monarchy preacher, calls for a war against the Dutch as preferable to one against the French (*Sagrir*, pp. 14, 79, E, 716, 11).

[2] *C.J.* vii. 314.

[3] Newsletter, Sept. 16, *Clarendon MSS.* ii. No. 1,390.

it, apparently on the ground that it implied a toleration of
'popery.'[1]

In the long run this plan might possibly be efficacious, but
it would do little to meet the immediate wants of the navy.
The fleet after the battle of the Texel. It was indeed of no great importance that by the
confession of Monk himself the fleet had been 'very
much shattered in the battle of the Texel.' As
much might have been said after Trafalgar. The real
difficulty lay in the failure of Parliament to meet the expenses
incurred in its service. It was not that good will was lacking.
After the fight in the North Sea, the sick and wounded were
distributed amongst the towns and villages of the east coast,
and not only were surgeons sent down to attend to their ne-
Parliament Joan. cessities, but a kindly widow, Elizabeth Alkin—
familiarly known as Parliament Joan—had volun-
teered to tend them on their sick beds, anticipating the devotion of the nineteenth century. Yet it was easier to organise
help than to find the money needed to support it. On July 10,
before the last battle, there were bitter complaints that the
householders on whom the sufferers were quartered were left
unpaid, so that they began to weary of their guests, and it was
only on Monk's personal engagement that the assistance was
continued.[2] Parliament Joan herself could get no advance
upon the 5*l*. given her when she came down to Harwich,
beyond 20*s*. from the mayor, and 10*l*. from Major Bourne,
who had charge of the maritime district. The whole of the
latter sum she spent not only on the English sick and
wounded, but on the Dutch prisoners as well. Seeing,
as she wrote, 'their wants and misery were so great, I
could not but have pity upon them, although our enemies.'
The constant strain on her strength bore her down, and
she was compelled to return to London, her life wrecked

---

[1] *Act for Recusants*, E, 1,062, No. 20; *C.J.* vii. 337; An Exact
Relation, *Somers Tracts*, vi. 274.

[2] Monk to the Admiralty Committee, July 10, *S. P. Dom.* xxxviii.
34.

by her lonely strivings to assuage the sufferings of the seamen.[1]

The complaints of individuals might be passed over in silence. It was less easy to meet the complaints of a numerous class. The sailors as a body were left

Complaints of the sailors. unpaid. It is true that the Government made most satisfactory arrangements on the subject, and were able to announce that no ship's crew would be sent ashore without its earnings. It was none the less a fact that ships were kept long in commission in order to avoid payment of wages, and that the wives and children of seamen were left to starve till the time came when their husbands or fathers were re-

Oct.
A mutinous spirit. stored to them.[2] In October a mutinous spirit was widely diffused. On the 5th, 200 of the ' Unicorn's ' company at Chatham refused to go on board without pay. Later in the day two other ships' crews joined in the protest, and declared that they would go to London to seek redress.[3] On the 21st, 400 seamen at Harwich refused to do duty unless they were paid. They wandered about the fields pulling up the gates and stiles.[4] It was more serious when,

Oct. 26.
Mutineers in London. on October 26, the crews of the ships in the river poured themselves over the streets of London, clamouring for pay and prize money. A party of three or four hundred, some of whom were armed,[5] betook themselves to Whitehall. As they were pushing through the

Monk drives back the mutineers. streets they were met by Cromwell and Monk. Their roughly expressed demand for justice so exasperated the latter that he drew his sword and, striking the most forward, half persuaded, half compelled them to retire. Enough of the spirit of discipline still prevailed

[1] The story has been collected from the State Papers by Mrs. Everett Green, *Calendar*, 1653–4, xxxi. xxxii.

[2] Bourne to the Navy Commissioners, Oct. 21, *S. P. Dom.* xli. 60.

[3] Pett to the Admiralty Committee, Oct. 5, *ib.* xli. 21, 22.

[4] Bourne to the Navy Commissioners, Oct. 21, *ib.* xli. 60, 61.

[5] According to Bordeaux, they were unarmed, but Pauluzzi says ' that many of them had swords and halberts, and some firearms.'

amongst the malcontents to make them unwilling to use force against their general.

Monk's personal intervention, however, had no more than a temporary effect. Next morning a far larger crowd appeared

Oct. 27.
A second
mutiny

to require satisfaction. When they approached Whitehall they found the street blocked by a regiment of infantry, supported by four troops of cavalry. Exasperated at the sight, the sailors pushed amongst the soldiers, and began snatching their guns out of their hands, whilst one of the mutineers pointed a musket at Cromwell himself. A

suppressed
by soldiers.

cavalry charge soon put a stop to their violence. Of the ringleaders one was hanged and another flogged. A proclamation assured the mariners that whilst any further attempt at mutiny would be punished with severity, every means would be taken to secure the due payment of their wages and prize money. Not a word was said of the grievance which lay at the bottom of the sailors' complaints—the postponement of payment till the crews were dismissed the service.[1]

On the other side of the North Sea there was no confession of defeat, no thought of bowing the necks of the free Provinces

Sept. 11.
Opdam to
succeed
Tromp.

under the detested yoke of amalgamation. Opdam— like Monk a land officer, and therefore less likely to excite the jealousy of the sea-commanders—was appointed the successor of Tromp. New taxes were raised [2]

Oct.
Naval pre-
parations in
Holland.

and men-of-war which were being built large enough to cope with the English ships were sufficiently forward if not to put to sea at once, at least to be

Oct. 23.
De With
brings a con-
voy into the
Texel.

ready for the next naval campaign.[3] On October 23 De With sailed into the Texel followed by a fleet of four or five hundred merchantmen safely convoyed

[1] Pauluzzi to Morosini, Nov. $\frac{3}{13}$, *Letter Book R.O.* ; Bordeaux to Brienne, $\frac{Oct. 30}{Nov. 9}$, *R.O. Transcripts* ; Newsletter, Nov. 4, *Clarendon MSS.* ii. No. 1,502 ; Proclamation by the Council of State in *The Moderate Publisher*, E, 222, 3.

[2] *Aitzema*, iii. 827, 828.

[3] Letter of Intelligence, Oct. $\frac{14}{24}$, *Thurloe*, i. 539.

from the Sound and the coasts of Norway. A day or two later English sailors were tramping through the streets of London as mutineers, and the English fleet was in no condition to make its former mastery felt. It was only lack of

Proposal to make a dash at the Thames.

provisions which prevented the ships of the States from making a dash at the mouth of the Thames, and sinking vessels to block up the entrance to the river in support of the negotiations for peace.[1] The struggle for the command of the North Sea had certainly not resulted in its complete domination by the English fleet.

---

[1] Letters of Intelligence, $\frac{\text{Oct. 28}}{\text{Nov. 7}}$, *Thurloe*, i. 557, 560.

CHAPTER XXXI

THE DUTCH PEACE

So far as foreign affairs were concerned, the election of the new Council of State on November 1 gave Cromwell a freer

1653.
Nov. 1.
Cromwell
has a freer
hand in
foreign
affairs. hand,[1] a change especially grateful to him because the time had now arrived when the negotiations with the Dutch commissioners must be seriously resumed. The two who had gone back to the Hague to

Oct. 25.
Return of
the Dutch
com-
missioners. report on the situation[2] were once more in England, having brought instructions to propose 'a firm alliance and close union' without any reference

Oct. 28.
They pro-
pose a
league. to the coalition which had been pressed on them at Westminster. On October 28, when they made their final proposal, they showed some inclination to gratify Cromwell, at least in words, by offering a league— purely defensive, it is true—with France and the Protestant States, of which an alliance between England and the United Provinces was to be the corner-stone. This alliance, as they

Oct. 31.
Their ex-
planation. subsequently explained, implied joint action in behalf of the freedom and interests of both States. If this principle were accepted it would be easy, they imagined, to come to an understanding.[3]

It was not till November 17, when the new Council was settled in office, that Cromwell, who had been appointed one

Nov. 17.
Cromwell's
reply. of the commissioners for carrying on the negotiation, replied in the name of his colleagues, arguing that, if the coalition had been accepted, the rights and interests of the two nations would have been fused together,

[1] See vol. ii. p. 307.　　　[2] See p. 45.　　　[3] *Verbael*, pp. 165–173.

but that, the situation being changed by the rejection of the English proposal, it was necessary to define the rights possessed by each as a preliminary to the consideration of concessions which each might be disposed to make. On the following morning, to bring matters to a crisis, he produced a draft treaty as a basis of discussion. It was to be stipulated that neither side should assist or even give shelter to the enemies or rebels of the other. If either nation were about to conclude a treaty, it was—upon a demand being made to that effect—to insist that the other should be included in it. There was moreover to be freedom of trade between the two republics, provided that the existing laws were observed —a stipulation which indirectly upheld the Navigation Act. Natives of the United Provinces being Protestants might settle and even hold land in the British Isles.

Nov. 18.
His draft treaty,

Other requirements were likely to rouse greater opposition. In the first place satisfaction was to be made to England for the charges of the war, though the ships and goods captured were to be reckoned as forming part of the compensation. In the second place neither the States General nor any single province should ever appoint the young Prince of Orange to any place of civil or military command. In the third place no Dutch ships of war beyond a certain number, to be fixed by the treaty, should pass through the British seas without the consent of the Commonwealth of England, and that too only upon three months' notice previously given. In the fourth place, all ships of the United Provinces meeting any ships of the Commonwealth were to strike their flag and lower their topsail, and submit to be visited, if required, as well as to 'perform all other respects' due to the said Commonwealth of England to whom the dominion and sovereignty of the British seas belonged. Lastly, the right of fishery in these seas was to be permitted to the Dutch for twenty-one years only on payment being made of a sum hereafter to be determined. It was impossible that such articles could lead to mutual respect and good will. They were terms imposed by a conqueror on a vanquished nation.

and demands.

No wonder that peace was regarded in the Netherlands as desperate, and that De Witt urged the States General to per-

Peace despaired of. sistent efforts and to alliance with the powers, such as France and Denmark, which had most to fear from the ambition of England.[1] Though the extreme demand for the limitation of the numbers of the Dutch men-of-war had been promptly dropped, Cromwell showed no sign of being prepared to make further concessions, and on Decem-

Dec. 5.
The Dutch com-
missioners
ask for
passports. ber 5 the three surviving representatives of the United Provinces—Van de Perre had died on the preceding day—demanded their passports.[2] Two days before this Desborough and Penn were appointed Generals of the Sea in addition to Blake and Monk,[3] whilst every care was taken to strengthen the fleet in order that it might be ready for all emergencies.[4]

It is by no means unlikely that Cromwell's insistence upon demands so harsh was, in part at least, the effect of his wish to conciliate the nominated Parliament, which was notoriously disinclined to make peace except on terms most humiliating to

Effect of
the estab-
lishment of
the Pro-
tectorate. the enemy.[5] At all events his establishment in the Protectorate was followed by the adoption of a more considerate policy. On December 22, when the conferences were resumed, Oliver agreed to drop the

Dec. 22.
Resump-
tion of the
conferences. requirement that the Dutch should pay a sum of money in acknowledgment that the war had originated with them; as well as the demand that they should lease the fishery in the North Sea from the English Government and acknowledge the right of search. He continued, however, to insist that Dutch ships should strike their flags and lower their topsails in the 'British Sea,' and that the Prince of Orange should be excluded from office, though he

---

[1] *Aitzema*, iii. 880 ; *Geddes*, 374 ; *Verbael*, p. 188.

[2] *Verbael*, p. 243.

[3] *C.J.* vii. 361.

[4] Monk to the Admiralty Committee, Nov. 28, Dec. 3, *S. P. Dom.* xli. 118.

[5] See p. 56.

agreed that this should be done by a secret article. The King
of Denmark was to have no benefit by the treaty, and a fresh
demand was made for compensation for the murder of Englishmen
in Amboyna. To provide for the future, commissioners were to
be appointed to settle the East India trade to the advantage of
both States, and to examine the wrongs alleged to have been done
to the English, not only in the East by the seizure of Pularoon
and Puloway, but also in other parts of the world. Further, in
International arbitration proposed. notable anticipation of modern procedure, Cromwell
asked that if within three months the commissioners
failed to agree, the differences between them should
be referred to the arbitration of the Protestant cantons of
Switzerland.[1]

On the far greater number of the points still at issue, an agreement, if not actually reached, might, at least, be reasonably
expected. Two only stood out as the subject of prolonged
Question of the King of Denmark's exclusion from the treaty. antagonism—the exclusion of the King of Denmark
from the benefits of the treaty and the exclusion of
the Prince of Orange from office. On the first head
the Dutch, naturally, showed themselves irrecon-
cilably hostile. Angry as Cromwell may have been with the
King for his seizure of the twenty-two English ships detained
at Elsinore,[2] the United Provinces were bound by all considerations of honour to see that a Prince, who had damaged English
commerce on their behalf, suffered no loss thereby. Though
Cromwell was driven to agree to an arrangement for the
restitution of the ships and the payment of a compensation to
their owners,[3] he persistently refused to include the King in the
treaty. As, however, he acknowledged that he had other
grievances against the King, the Dutch commissioners came to
the conclusion that he wished to isolate Denmark, and declare
war against her nominally on the ground of these further complaints, but, in reality, in consequence of the seizure of the

---

[1] *S. P. Dom.* xli. pp. 198–274. For the seizure of Pularoon and
Puloway, see *Hist. of Engl.* 1603–1642, iii. 167 ; iv. 407.

[2] See vol. ii. p. 199.

[3] See *Thurloe Papers*, ii. 401–404.

ships.   They, accordingly, prepared to return home to seek

1654.
Jan. 3.
The com-
missioners
leave
London.

further instructions rather than yield.   On January 3 they left London, but on the following morning, whilst they were at Gravesend preparing to embark, they received an intimation from Thurloe that the Pro-

Jan. ¹¹⁄₂₁.
An
agreement
arrived at.

tector had at last given way, and that the King of Denmark, on making restitution and satisfaction, should be admitted to the treaty.   One stumbling-block in the way of peace was thus removed.[1]

The question of the Prince of Orange's exclusion from office was, if Cromwell persisted in requiring a vote of the

Is the
Prince of
Orange to
be excluded
from office ?

States General, certain to wreck the treaty.   It was notorious that the States General would never accept a proposal hostile to the House of Orange, and that they would have, in their refusal, the support of the majority of the provinces and of the population.   On the other hand, in the prospect of a Prince of Orange again filling the Stadtholderate or any other post giving him the control of the land and sea forces of the Republic Cromwell foresaw a renewal of the hostile action of William II., which would afford to the Stuart princes a basis of operation against the English Commonwealth with the avowed or secret assistance of their nephew.   There seems to be no reason to doubt that it was to Cromwell that the suggestion of a practical way out of the difficulty was owing, and even that this solution had been dis-cussed by him in privacy with one or more of the Dutch

Secret
diplomacy.

commissioners before they set sail from England.[2]   It was notorious that the Provincial States of Holland were strongly opposed to the pretensions of the House of Orange, and it was hardly conceivable that, without the consent of that influential province, the States General would venture to revive the Stadtholderate in favour of the Prince when he came to years of discretion.   Why therefore might not Holland be asked to engage to resist his nomination, whilst the States

[1] *Verbael*, pp. 275-292.

[2] The indications—they are hardly more—are discussed by Mr. Geddes, pp. 381-393.

General were no longer invited to make any such promise?
In that case it might be enough to ask the States General to
engage that any future Captain-General should be bound to
swear to the observance of the treaty.

When, therefore, the returning commissioners reached their
destination they imparted only the second of these two proposals to the States General. The first they reserved for the
ear of De Witt. Strange as it may seem, De Witt had kept the
most important part of his diplomacy secret, not only from the

De Witt's
shifts.

States General, but even from his own immediate
masters, the States of Holland. If ruling bodies
insist upon conducting a negotiation in a glass house, subjecting
it to reference to several provinces, or to the component parts
of each province, the minister who has the primary management of the affair is compelled to have recourse to shifts from
which the servant of an absolute sovereign, or even the minister
who possesses the full confidence of Parliament in a constitutional State, is altogether free. He is driven to hoodwink
his superiors, to keep them from knowing what is being done
in order that they may not oppose it or delay it, and even, as
was the case with De Witt, to employ deceit and subterfuge to
drive them into doing that which they have no mind to do, but
which seems to himself to be necessary for the salvation of the
State.[1]

There can be little doubt that De Witt earnestly hoped that
Cromwell would content himself with the clause which had

Jan. 25.
Return of
Beverning.

been laid before the States General. Beverning was
hurriedly sent back to London to keep the Protector
in good humour, and on his arrival on January 25
learnt that Cromwell had expressed himself highly satisfied that
there was once more a Dutch representative in England. Yet

His treat-
ment in
England.

when Beverning sought an audience it was not only
refused, but he was himself treated with studied
rudeness. The explanation was not far to seek.
The States General had given him no credentials to the

---

[1] On all this see Mr. Geddes, who goes into the story in great detail.

Protector, nor had in any way authorised him to recognise the new Government.[1]

The success or failure of the negotiation now evidently depended on the States General, and on February 9 that body sufficiently accommodated itself to the urgency of De Witt as to vote that Nieuport and Jongestal should rejoin Beverning, the three together bearing the titles of Extraordinary Ambassadors to the Lord Protector, whose title was thus recognised without qualification. They were to attempt to amend the treaty sent over from England, and to accept the proposal that any future Captain-General should be required to make oath to maintain it.[2]

Feb. 9.
Vote of the States General.

Beverning was rejoined by his colleagues on February 28. When, four days later, they were conducted through the streets of London to their lodgings, they were not only treated with every mark of official courtesy, but were greeted with the loud and hearty acclamations of the crowd. Peace—a necessity for the United Provinces —was welcomed in England as a relief from the burdens and anxieties of war.

Feb. 28.
Beverning joined by his colleagues.

March 1/11.
Their reception in London.

Under these circumstances a satisfactory conclusion could with difficulty be avoided. A month was still spent in diplomatic contention, but on April 5 the treaty was signed by six English commissioners and the three ambassadors. Not much was left of the original scheme for an actual amalgamation or at least for a close union. A conjunction for the defence of the liberties of either people was announced, and a stipulation that each State should lend aid when required by the other at the expense of the party making the demand, and should expel from its borders the enemies or rebels of the other. This last clause virtually amounted to an engagement by the Dutch to keep the Stuart princes at a distance. The further requirements of the English Government had been equally winnowed down. What re-

April 5.
Signature of the treaty.

[1] Beverning to De Witt, $\frac{\text{Jan. 27}}{\text{Feb. 6}}$, *Nijhoff's Bijdragen voor Vaderlandsche Geschiedenis*, X. 301 ; *Verbael*, p 294.   [2] *Ib.* 297-304.

mained was the acknowledgment of the salute owing to its flag
'in the British seas,' and the engagement to do justice on the
Amboyna murderers, 'as the English Commonwealth,' say the
Dutchmen, 'thought fit to style them.' Not merely the wrongs
alleged to have been suffered by the English in
the Eastern seas and elsewhere, but those alleged to
have been suffered by the Dutch were to be referred
to arbitrators equally selected from the two nations. Questions left open at the end of three months were
to be submitted, according to Cromwell's suggestion,
to the Protestant Cantons of Switzerland.[1] In the
end the arbitrators, without the necessity of referring to the
Swiss Cantons, adjudged Pularoon to England, and ordered
the Dutch East India Company to pay to the English Company
85,000*l.*, and 3,615*l.* to the representatives of the Amboyna
victims.[2] After this nothing further was heard of prosecuting
the authors of the outrage, if indeed any of them were still
living. Moreover, the Dutch having undertaken to make
good the losses of the owners of the English merchantmen
detained in the Sound, another body of arbitrators was appointed to assess the damages in this
case ; an early decision having been secured by a
stipulation that if they had not come to an agreement by
August 1 they should be shut up without fire, candles, food or
drink till they had made up their differences. On July 31, just
as their term of grace was about to expire, they awarded
97,973*l. os. 10d.* to the aggrieved shipowners.

The diplomatic battle between the Protector and the States
was, however, by no means at an end with the signature of the
treaty on April 5. Oliver held De Witt responsible
for the procurement from the States of Holland of an
Act excluding the Prince of Orange from office under
the States General. All De Witt's pleadings could
not alter his resolution. The Protector informed the

Marginal notes:
Arbitration on losses in the East,

Aug. 30. on maritime losses,

July 31. and on those in the Sound.

April 5. Oliver expects the exclusion of the Prince of Orange by Holland.

---

[1] *Verbael*, 357. The treaty is also printed in Dumont's *Corps Diplomatique*, vi. 2, 74.

[2] *Ib.* vi. 2, 83.

two Hollanders, Beverning and Nieuport, that if he was to ratify the treaty, it must be upon their giving their word that their province would carry out his wishes within two or three months at the latest.[1] This was the message which reached De Witt together with the treaty.

That provident statesman had already taken measures to bring about a result which, however much he might regret it, *De Witt's manœuvre.* he now regarded as inevitable. To gain time he had persuaded the Provincial States to give themselves a short holiday.[2] In their absence he urged the States General *April 12. The treaty ratified by the States General.* to ratify the treaty, and they, utterly ignorant of De Witt's secret intentions, and overjoyed at finding that the treaty contained no clause prohibiting the future appointment of the Prince, ratified it on April 12, the very day after its delivery at the Hague.[3]

When the States of Holland met again on the 18th, De Witt, after an oath of secrecy had been taken, revealed the *April ⅛. A debate in the States of Holland.* nature of the demand made upon them by the Protector. Hostile as they were to the House of Orange, there were some who hesitated to take on their shoulders the burden of an act constitutionally so questionable as the giving of an undertaking to a foreign power without consultation with the other provinces. The matter was therefore referred to the towns by their delegates. On April 21, *April 21. Another debate.* when the answers were returned, it was found that a large majority of the towns and all the nobles were in favour of granting the required Act, a concession which De Witt knew was more urgent than ever, as Oliver now protested that, though he was still willing to ratify on the promise of the ambassadors, he should not hold the treaty to be binding on

---

[1] Beverning and Nieuport to the States of Holland, April 5/15. *Nijhoff's Bijdragen*, X. ii. 234. Mr. Geddes (407) says that Oliver proposed to ratify 'under a protest that it would be null and void unless an Act of Exclusion were delivered to him by Holland within two or three months.' I can, however, find nothing of this in the ambassador's letter, which agrees with the account in *Thurloe*, ii. 238.

[2] *Geddes*, 405.

[3] *Verbael*, 392.

him unless the required Act were delivered within a few days.
De Witt therefore put forth all his influence, with the result

April 24.
The
Exclusion
Act passed.

that, on April 24, the Exclusion Act was passed by a
majority of thirteen towns to five. It was at once
despatched to England. A sham letter accompanied
it, to be shown to the Frieslander Jongestal, in order to keep
him in the dark.[1]

Oliver had not waited for the passage of the Exclusion Act
to do his part. Satisfied with the assurances given him by the

April 19.
Oliver
ratifies the
treaty.

April 26.
Its pro-
clamation.

April 27.
The am-
bassadors
enter-
tained at
Whitehall.

two Hollanders, he ratified the treaty on the 19th,
and caused it to be proclaimed with all solemnity
on the 26th. Not for many years, it was said, had
any proclamation been so enthusiastically received.
On the following day the Protector entertained the
ambassadors at dinner at Whitehall, whilst the wives
of the two married ones were received at dinner by
the Lady Protectress. Afterwards the whole company
was conducted into a music-room, where, after an
instrumental performance, Oliver took from Pickering a copy
in some metrical version of the Hundred and Twenty-third
Psalm: "Behold how good and how pleasant it is for
brethren to dwell together in unity." "We have," said Oliver
as he handed it to the ambassadors, "exchanged many papers,
but I think that this is the best of them." After the Psalm
had been sung by four voices, the company dispersed.[2]

Some time was to elapse before the Act of Exclusion, so
hardly won, reached the hands of the Protector. De Witt,

Delay in
delivering
the Act of
Exclusion.

May 27.
The
delivery of
the Act
ordered.

hoping against hope that Oliver would yet relent,
instructed the two ambassadors to draw him, if
possible, from his purpose. Oliver was, however,
obdurate, and in the meanwhile such a storm had
arisen in the Netherlands that it was impossible to
prolong the delay. Hearing on May 27 that the
States General had resolved to demand a copy of the Act

[1] *Geddes*, 415–420.

[2] *Verbael*, 407, 419; Jongestal to Count William of Nassau, *Thurloe*,
ii. 257.

from their ambassadors in England, De Witt, who did not know but that the States General might proceed to a positive order to keep it back, contrived, partly by resolutions of the Provincial States of Holland, partly by private letters of his own, to give the two Holland ambassadors reason to understand that its delivery would be taken well by their masters, and the Act was therefore placed by them in the hands of the Protector.[1]

The Act delivered.

Oliver had thus obtained a peace with the Dutch accompanied by what he expected to prove a permanent bar to the advancement of the young Prince of Orange to a position in which he might become dangerous, if not to England, at least to the system of government which at that time prevailed in England. It might indeed be objected to Oliver's diplomacy that, if he had known the Continent as he had known England in the days of the Civil War, he would not at the commencement of the negotiations have taken up ground from which, if Dutch patriotism was not a quality to be left out of account, he would certainly be compelled to recede. To some extent, no doubt, his mistake was attributable to the necessity of conciliating the nominated Parliament; but a great part of the blame lies at Oliver's own door. He had an overweening confidence in the power of England to accomplish great things, which sometimes prompted him to believe that she could obtain anything for which she chose to ask. At all events, after he had the game in his own hands by the establishment of the Protectorate, he conducted his retreat from an untenable position without loss of dignity, and the final bargain which he struck was, as far as money payments were concerned, no more than a requirement that positive losses unfairly suffered should be made good.[2] The

Oliver's diplomacy.

---

[1] The whole story of the shifts to which De Witt was put to gain his ends is told by Mr. Geddes (*John de Witt*, 422–429). De Witt's letters on the subject are printed in Sypesteyn, *Geschiedkundige Bijdragen*, ii. Bijlagen, p. 74.

[2] This is true even of the compensation for the losses incurred by the Danish seizure of English ships. If the Dutch hindered England from

demand for the striking of the flag, monstrous as it appears at the present day, was one which every Englishman in the seventeenth century—Oliver himself most of all—would have pressed as essential to the honour of the country.

On the other hand, it may reasonably be questioned whether, even from his own point of view, Oliver gained anything by insisting on the Exclusion Act. The real obstacle to the restoration of the Stadtholderate was to be found in the grasp of the oligarchy over the province of Holland. As long as that grasp remained unloosed, no restitution of the House of Orange to its old authority was likely to be brought about. If, under any circumstances, that grasp should fail, the Stadtholderate would indubitably be restored, whatever laws and treaties might say to the contrary. Nor was it the only defect in Oliver's policy in this matter that the Act of Exclusion was useless. It set up an irritation against Holland in the other States which, if only the young Prince had reached years of discretion, would, in all probability, have raised a storm powerful enough to sweep De Witt and his colleagues—the only allies on whom the Protectorate could count in the Netherlands—from the political field.

Was it wise to insist on the Act of Exclusion?

Of Oliver's more ideal aim, that of establishing a Protestant league on the basis of an alliance with the Dutch Republic, nothing but words remained. It is true that on April 5, the day on which the Dutch treaty was signed, he despatched John Dury—an enthusiast who had worked for the religious union of all Protestant sects under the auspices of Laud—to pursue the same enterprise with the full support of a Puritan government. Dury was everywhere received with the respect to which his transparent honesty of purpose entitled him ; but though good words in plenty were addressed to him, not a step was taken to give effect to his entreaties.[1]

April 5. Dury's mission.

seeking redress from the King of Denmark, they must take on themselves the consequences of his acts.

[1] *A Summary Account of Mr. John Dury's . . . Negotiation*, 698, g. 12, No. 10.

It was no peculiarity of Dutchmen that they were bent on the pursuit of material rather than spiritual aims. In every
No Protestant league to be had.
part of Europe Oliver was confronted by the difficulty of finding any one who cared for the defence of a Protestantism which, except in occasional circumstances, was by this time able to take care of itself. Even before the dissolution of the Long Parliament, there had
1653. Proposed embassy to Sweden.
been talk of sending an embassy to Sweden, and Lord Lisle had been selected as ambassador. Lisle, however, from time to time postponed his departure,
Lord Lisle will not go.
and ultimately, in the autumn of 1653, declined to go, on the plea of ill-health. At Cromwell's
Whitelocke selected.
suggestion, the Council of State pitched on Whitelocke to take his place. Cromwell was no mean judge of men, and he had a good opportunity to judge of Whitelocke's business capacity, when they were associated in the negotiation for the cession of Dunkirk.[1] That Whitelocke was no religious enthusiast, and that he was timorous in domestic politics formed—as the event showed—no hindrance to success in the work given him to do ; that work
Oct. 28. His instructions.
being in the main a matter of business. The instructions he received from the Council of State were confined to directions to arrive at an understanding in matters of trade, and especially to urge the Queen of Sweden to join England in opening the Sound to the free passage of commerce, 'that it may not depend upon the will of the King of Denmark or the United Provinces of the Netherlands.'[2]

Oct. 29. Swedish mediation refused.
Though Lagerfeldt, the Queen's ambassador in England, had been for some time offering the mediation of his mistress in the war which was still raging, the Council of State would not hear of the intervention of a

[1] The suggestion that Cromwell sent Whitelocke to Sweden to get him out of the way whilst he seized the Protectorate is inadmissible. He was at that time working in close agreement with the nominated Parliament, and he can hardly have thought of a revolution against it. The idea that Cromwell was afraid of Whitelocke is simply ludicrous. He had faced him with impunity when he turned the Long Parliament out of doors.

[2] Whitelocke's *Swedish Embassy*, i. 89.

third power, telling the ambassador that God, in His own good time, would influence the Dutch to respond to their own heartfelt desire for peace.[1]   To Cromwell the material claims he himself put forward were not all that his heart desired. Neither he, nor even Whitelocke, would be satisfied unless an

Cromwell takes leave of White-locke.

agreement with Sweden brought some accession of strength to Protestantism.   " Bring us back a Protestant alliance ! " were his last words as he took leave of the ambassador.[2]

Whitelocke well knew that his journey was not unaccompanied with danger.   To preserve himself from the fate which

Whitelocke provides for his safety.

had befallen Dorislaus and Ascham, he took with him a retinue of a hundred persons, choosing eight lacqueys out of the General's regiment of foot, ' proper, stout, and civil men.'   To us the most interesting part

Queen Christina.

of his embassy is the picture he drew of the young Queen, spirited and eccentric, with a keen intellect and a richly stored mind, who, with no political task in Sweden the accomplishment of which seemed to come within the range of possibility, found herself ill at ease amongst her subjects. She shrank, as Elizabeth had shrunk, from the bonds of marriage, which would place her in the hands of a man who would use her for his own ends, but, unlike Elizabeth, having first declared her successor to be her mother's nephew, Charles Gustavus, of the Palatine family of Zweibrücken, she was now contemplating an abdication which would set her free from the trammels of royalty.   Add to this that Christina was wearied to death by the long sermons and dry theology of the Lutheran divines, and it becomes intelligible that she had made up her mind to submit to the Papal religion, partly because she admired it for placing the dignity of the unmarried

[1] Lagerfeldt to the C. of St., Oct. 26 ; the C. of St. to Lagerfeldt, Oct. 29, *Portland MSS.*, *Hist. Com*. Rep. xiii. App. i. 1.

[2] Whitelocke's feeling about the Protestant cause may be gathered from the account he gives in his *Swedish Embassy* of his motives for going. Cromwell's words are reported in a letter from Ellis Leighton. See note 1, p 119, *post.*

above that of the married life—partly because she expected to find in it free scope for her intellectual imaginations.

Of this latter possibility neither Whitelocke nor those who sent him had any conception. The ambassador soon found delight in the information and mental accomplishments of the little lady who was dressed, in sheer defiance of the canons of fashion, in a plain. grey petticoat sweeping the ground and a jacket of the same colour, such as men wore, reaching to her knees. On her neck was a black scarf tied with a black ribbon, like that usually worn by soldiers or sailors, and on her head a black velvet fur cap, lined with sable, which she used to put off and on as men did theirs. Her only condescension to the feminine love of brightness was a crimson ribbon fastening the jewel of the order of Amaranta which she had herself invented.

Dec. 23. Christina's reception of Whitelocke.

Whitelocke found Christina by no means inclined to reject the idea of a conjunction between the English fleet and her own to open the Sound to foreign commerce. Though she was now at peace with Frederick III. of Denmark, and had secured by the Treaty of Brömsebro in 1645 the exemption of her own subjects from the Sound dues, there had been a long rivalry between the two countries, which from time to time had broken out into open war, and there was something attractive in the prospect of seeing the Swedish ports in the Baltic open without hindrance to the shipping and commerce of other nations. Moreover, no Swede could be otherwise than pleased with the thought of breaking up the hold of the Danish king on the shores on either side of the Sound. Yet in spite of all these influences in his favour Whitelocke did not find his business progressing. It may be that the Swedes, much as they disliked the Danes, disliked still more the prospect of an English fleet commanding the Baltic by the occupation of fortresses on the shores of the Sound.[1] It is certain that both the Queen and the aged chan-

1654. Question of opening the Sound.

---

[1] On November $\frac{11}{21}$, 1653, the Dutch commissioners write that the Swedish agent Lagerfeldt had assured them that the Queen 'Danum semper quam Anglum vicinum mallet' (*Verbael*, 181, 182).

cellor Oxenstjerna thought it more prudent to await the issue of the English negotiations with the Dutch Republic before coming to a decision. When it was known that a treaty in which the King of Denmark was comprised had been agreed on at Westminster, there was no longer any motive for Whitelocke to press for an armed alliance against Denmark.

April 11.
A commercial treaty. He therefore contented himself with a treaty for the friendly regulation of commercial intercourse between the two nations. This treaty was signed on April 11,[1]

June 6.
Christina's abdication. and Whitelocke left Sweden too soon to be a witness of the Queen's abdication on June 6, or the subsequent coronation of her cousin and successor as Charles X.[2]

The question of the Sound dues now had to be settled, if settled at all, by a direct negotiation between England and Denmark.

Sept. 15.
A treaty with Denmark. On September 15, accordingly, a commercial treaty[3] was signed between the Protector and Frederick III., in which it was stipulated that English vessels should pay no dues higher than those charged on other nations, except the Swedes who were exempted from payment. Practically, the result of this treaty was to place English commerce on an equality with that of the Dutch in the Baltic, as the peculiar arrangement by which the Dutch had redeemed the Sound dues[4] had fallen through, and vessels of that nationality had since been required to pay according to a tariff fixed at an earlier date.[5]

July.
English ships lading for Antwerp. But for Oliver's prudence another question would have been opened, not altogether dissimilar from that of the Sound dues. As Denmark held both coasts of the opening into the Baltic, so did the United Provinces hold both coasts of the opening into the

---

[1] Dumont, *Corps Diplomatique*, vi ii. 80.

[2] Whitelocke's *Journal of the Swedish Embassy.*

[3] Dumont, *Corps Diplomatique*, vi. ii. 92.

[4] See vol. ii. p. 146.

[5] For a sketch of the history of the Sound dues, see Wheaton, *Hist. of the Modern Law of Nations* (ed. 1845), p. 160.

Scheldt. In the latter case, however, the treaty of 1648 between the Provinces and Spain acknowledged that the river was to be closed—that is to say, not that all commerce was forbidden, but that every ship, whether Dutch or foreign, bringing goods for the Spanish territory on the Scheldt was to pay all the dues required by the province of Zealand, and to transfer the goods to vessels belonging to that province, by which they would be carried up the stream,[1] whilst no vessel from the Spanish Netherlands would be allowed to pass down the river to the sea.[2] Obviously, no trade could be successfully carried on on such conditions. When, therefore, the States General heard that English merchants were proposing to send cargoes direct to Antwerp, on the ground that the treaty gave them the right to trade in or through any places within the jurisdiction of the United Provinces, they at once protested that this permission was stated to be subject to the laws of the country, and that those laws prohibited trade with Antwerp except on the conditions named. Oliver had no mind to provoke a new war on a point on which the Dutch were so sensitive, and the permission sought by the English merchants was never accorded.

The Dutch protest.

---

[1] The Dutch ambassadors to the States General, July $\frac{3}{13}$; the States General to the ambassadors, July $\frac{14}{24}$, *Verbael*, pp. 482, 513. The last letter incloses (p. 514) an arrangement based on diplomatic papers exchanged when the treaty with Spain was under discussion, the effect of which is given above.

[2] This is not mentioned in the passages referred to in the last note, but is implied in the phrase 'the closing of the Scheldt.' In 1784, when Joseph II. attempted to set this arrangement at naught, he sent down a vessel with orders to reach the sea. The Dutch stopped it on the ground that it was bound to obtain a passport and pay duties at Fort Lillo. (Martens, *Causes célèbres du droit des gens*, 2ᵐᵉ édition, iii. 338.) This must mean that the vessel had the right of taking goods to the territory of Zealand on paying duty, but not of putting to sea. Mirabeau, in his *Lettres Historiques* (p. 103), only states part of the purport of the clause in the treaty. The agreement, he says, was 'que la navigation de l'Escaut, d'Anvers à la mer, seroit fermée à tous autres qu'aux possesseurs de ses embouchures.'

So far the outcome of Oliver's negotiations was that he had

entered upon advantageous commercial relationships with the chief Protestant States—Sweden and Denmark, the Swiss Protestant Cantons, and certain princes and cities of the empire which had asked to be included in the Dutch peace.[1]

Not, indeed, that Oliver was so wedded to a sectional Protestantism as to be unwilling to contract friendship with a

Catholic power if he could thereby secure commercial advantages for Englishmen, and some modified toleration for the exercise of their religion. It was with this aim in view that a treaty with Portugal had been for some time under negotiation. Early in December 1652

her ambassador, the Count of Peneguiaõ, had agreed to pay 50,000*l.* in compensation for the losses of English merchants at the time of Rupert's visit to Lisbon,[2] and before the breaking up of the Long

Parliament a treaty had been drafted which accorded considerable commercial advantages to English merchants, and granted those very concessions in favour

of religious liberty which Spain had refused to grant.[3] The only difficulty remaining was to secure the payment of the money. Month after month, however, passed without any attempt being made to satisfy the English demands on this score, and Peneguiaõ was compelled to prolong ineffectually his stay in England.

The wearisome delay was likely enough to have produced

[1] *Verbael*, pp. 502–504.

[2] Bordeaux to Brienne, Dec. $\frac{12}{22}$, *R.O. Transcripts*. Bordeaux merely says that at this time the ambassador had agreed to pay the compensation required. The amount can be gathered from later information. The claim made on Guimaraes had been for 180,000*l.* Of this 115,000*l.* were taken off as being the value of prizes captured from the Portuguese. 15,000*l.* more were now remitted, the sum to be paid being 50,000*l.* Cardenas to Philip IV. Dec. $\frac{21}{31}$, 1652, *Simancas MSS.* 2,528. Writing on July $\frac{10}{20}$, 1654, Cardenas says (*ib.* 2,569) that the treaty had been agreed on fifteen months before, consequently the agreement must have been reached about April 1653.   [3] See vol. ii. p. 239.

a nervous irritation on the members of the Portuguese embassy, which may to some extent account for an unfortunate occurrence which justifiably roused an angry feeling against them. The New Exchange on the south side of the Strand, and more especially the arcades in the upper story, fringed with rows of stalls for the sale of haberdashery and other articles of attire, was at that time much frequented in the evening as a fashionable lounge.[1] After nightfall on November 21, the ambassador's brother, Dom Pantaleon Sa, a youth of nineteen, was amusing

Nov. 21.
Scuffle in
the New
Exchange. himself on the promenade when he conceived himself to have been insulted by a Colonel Gerard, a young Royalist of some note. In the scuffle which followed Gerard as well as one of Dom Pantaleon's attendants was slightly wounded. The fiery young Portuguese cherished designs of vengeance, and on the following evening returned to the spot to wipe off the stain upon the honour of his nation. As he entered the building with fifty armed companions, the frightened stall-keepers naturally put up their shutters, whilst the few English who were on the spot did their best to keep

Nov. 22.
Murder of
Greenway. out of the way. Amongst those who were alarmed was a young man named Greenway, who had brought his sister and his affianced bride to make purchases with a view to the wedding which was to take place in two days. After conducting the ladies to a place of safety, he stepped out to learn the cause of the disturbance when he was shot through the head by one of Dom Pantaleon's attendants.[2]

[1] There, writes Pauluzzi, 'suole rittrovarsi molti Signori e Dame di condizione a passar l'ore noiose della notte.' Pauluzzi to Morosini, $\frac{Nov. 25}{Dec. 5}$, *Letter Book*, *R.O.* For its position, see Mr. Wheatley's *London Past and Present*, ii. 58, where it is stated that Messrs. Coutts' Bank occupies nearly the centre of the site.

[2] *State Trials*, v. 462; *The Weekly Intelligencer*, E, 721, 6; Pauluzzi to Morosini, $\frac{Nov. 25}{Dec. 5}$, *Letter Book*, *R.O.*; Bordeaux to Brienne, $\frac{Nov. 26}{Dec. 6}$, *R.O. Transcripts*. It is clear that the shot was not fired by Dom Pantaleon himself, not only from his own statement in *A Narrative of the late Accident*, E, 723, 14, but from the answer by Greenway's sister, Mrs. Clarke, *A Brief Reply*, E, 724, 9.

The Portuguese company at once took refuge in the house of the ambassador. As soon as the news reached Cromwell,

Arrest of Dom Pantaleon Sa. he directed Whalley to surround the embassy, and compelled Peneguiaŏ to deliver up the culprits, including his own brother. Dom Pantaleon was

Nov. 23. Committal to Newgate. committed to Newgate, and when, after a short interval, Oliver assumed the Protectorate, he was confronted with the question whether the prisoner was

Question of privilege raised. exempted from the operation of the law by any privileges attached to the dwelling of an ambassador. The question was put to a committee of civilian lawyers summoned for the purpose, and on their report [1] that

July 5. Dom Pantaleon sentenced to death. no such privilege had ever been recognised in England, the Protector resolved that the law must take its course. Accordingly Dom Pantaleon together with four of his associates was tried on July 5 by a special commission, by which they were all five sentenced to death.

At once the foreign embassies were astir, and even Cardenas, to whom Peneguiaŏ's master was no more than the tyrant of

Intercession of the ambassadors. Portugal, interceded warmly for one whose sentence was a blow aimed at the privileges of all ambassadors. In an interview accorded to Peneguiaŏ himself, the Protector was so far melted by human pity as to allow words to drop from his mouth which the grief-stricken brother interpreted as a promise of pardon. Whatever these words may have been, Oliver did not leave the ambassador long under his mistake. Peneguiaŏ scarcely reached his house when he was followed by a messenger who informed him that no pardon could be granted. [2] On July 10 Dom Pantaleon was beheaded

July 10. Execution of Dom Pantaleon. on Tower Hill, and an English servant who had taken part in the outrage was hanged at Tyburn. The three Portuguese who had been condemned at

---

[1] A justification of the proceedings against the Portuguese, *Thurloe*, ii. 428.

[2] Cardenas, who is the most explicit of the reporters of this scene, does not go beyond this. " Yendo el Conde à pedir la vida de su hermano y

the same time were reprieved till the pleasure of Parliament was known, a delay which in their case was equivalent to a pardon. Whether it would have been so in the case of their master may reasonably be doubted. The popular voice called loudly for justice on the stranger who was responsible for a deliberate murder, and there can be little doubt that the Protector's firmness gained the respect of many an Englishman who had hitherto stood aloof.

Rather than remain to be a witness of his brother's death, Peneguiaõ signed the long-delayed treaty on the morning of the execution, and then betook himself to Gravesend that he might there embark for his native country. The delay in the signature of the treaty had been caused partly by the fact that when Peneguiaõ recognised the Protectorate, he presented the treaty in an altered form,[1] but still more by his inability to lay down a penny of the 50,000*l.* which his master was expected to pay. It was comparatively easy to restore the treaty, except in one or two unimportant particulars, to its original shape—by rejecting, for instance, the insertion of words implying that toleration should be refused to Englishmen who gave scandal, thus practically leaving them, so far as the exercise of their religion was concerned, at the mercy of Portuguese officials. It was a far harder problem to draw 50,000*l.* out of an impecunious king. The difficulty was at last solved by an agreement that a mixed commission of

Signature of the Portuguese treaty.

echandose a sus pies—todo en lagrimas—el protector le consolò con palabras que el interpretò significaban el perdon, y asì le pidiò las manos por él, y cuando saliò de la audiencia dijo à mucho numero de mercadores ingleses que commercian en Portugal y habian ydo à interceder por la vida de este caballero que ya no tenian necesidad de hacer aquella diligencia porque el protector se la habia concedido—pero poco despues que el Conde llegò à su casa tuvo aviso contrario." Cardenas to Philip IV., July $\frac{9}{19}$, *Simancas MSS.* 2,529. Strictly speaking, the Protector could not, according to the *Instrument of Government*, pardon for treason or murder ; but, as is seen above, he could reprieve.

[1] Compare the remarks made on the alterations of the treaty on April 22 (*Thurloe*, ii. 248) with the treaty itself. Dumont, *Corps Diplomatique*, VI. part ii. 82.

Portuguese and Englishmen should meet to determine the sum
to be paid, and that half the duties paid by English merchants
in Portugal should be kept in pledge till the whole of the
amount awarded by the arbitrators had been covered.[1]

The treaty thus signed gave to English merchants the right
of commercial intercourse with Portugal, coupled with the
Nature of   assurance that they would never be called on to pay
the treaty.   duties higher than those which had been authorised
on March 10 in the current year.   It also freed them from the
interference of the Inquisition in their ships and houses, and
opened to them the trade of all the Portuguese territories
beyond the sea :—Brazil, from which the last Dutch garrisons
were in this year cleared away, St. Thomas in the West Indies,
Guinea in Africa, and the dwindling remains of Portuguese
sovereignty in the East Indies were specifically mentioned.
The two points of religion and trade were precisely those which
Oliver had attempted in vain to secure from Spain.[2]

Taking all these treaties together, it might look as if Oliver
were aspiring to the position occupied by Richelieu at the
Oliver's   beginning of the century, and which for a brief
foreign   moment was held by England in the days of the
policy.   Triple Alliance in 1668, and for a longer period in
the days of William III. and Anne.   He would thus have taken
up the leadership of the weaker States of Europe against the

---

[1] Cardenas to Philip IV., July $\frac{9}{19}$, *Simancas MSS.* 2,529.   Pauluzzi,
in his despatch of July $\frac{15}{25}$, attributes the signature by the ambassador,
without waiting to hear whether the King of Portugal approved of the
treaty—*i.e.* without the required alterations—to his expectation 'che la
rissolutione potesse valere alla salvatione del fratello, onde può dirsi che
da questa parte si sia usato sempre dell' arti e d' inganno delle buone
parole per arrivare a questo fine.'   Such a charge was certain to be made,
but the dates refute it.   Peneguiaõ knew that his brother was to die two
days before the treaty was signed.   His signature was probably affixed on
the 10th, because he wished to leave London in the morning before the
execution.   If, as is extremely likely, he had instructions to agree to the
original terms if no better could be had, there would be nothing to wonder
at in the matter.

[2] Dumont, *Corps Diplomatique*, VI. part ii. 82.

greater and more powerful irrespective of their religion. That he did not do so is not to be attributed to him as a fault. A great statesman does not create a foreign policy. It finds him out and tests his quality. Richelieu put himself at the head of the weaker powers because he needed them to overthrow the House of Austria ; William III. because he needed them to overthrow Louis XIV. In Oliver's time there was no apparent danger from any one predominant power. If France and Spain did not weigh equally in the balance, neither of them decidedly kicked the beam. No other power—and England least of all—was much afraid of either. There was therefore no room for a policy directed against an overwhelming predominance. There was however room for a policy of aggression calculated on the weakness of one or the other of the leading States, and it remains to be seen how far Oliver could succeed in persuading himself or others that a war of aggression might be based on the highest motives.

CHAPTER XXXII

GLENCAIRN'S RISING

WHATEVER Oliver's course might be, it would be useless for him to embark on a stirring foreign policy unless he could secure at least the passive obedience of the whole of the British Isles. From Ireland, indeed, crushed down under the iron heel of a victorious soldiery, there was nothing to be feared ; but Scotland, weakened though she had been by her reverses, found it hard to accept her destiny without yet another attempt to shake off the galling yoke of her conquerors. In the early summer of 1652, less than a year after the ruin of Scottish hopes at Worcester, the eyes of the depressed nobility and gentry were turned towards their exiled king. In the course of June, Charles, who was at that time hopefully watching the strife between the Commonwealth of England and the Republic of the United Provinces, received an intimation from a body of Royalists, comprising on the one hand several noblemen, and on the other a certain number of Highland chieftains, that they were prepared to strike another blow for their king and country. On June 15, in response to this request, he appointed Middleton to the military command in Scotland with the title of lieutenant-general, instructing him on August 9 to betake himself to Holland, where he was to collect money from Scottish and other Royalists in those parts in order that he might start for Scotland with some prospect of success. Middleton, however, fell ill soon after his arrival in Holland, and even if he had been in good

1654. Ireland and Scotland.

1652.

June.

June 15. Middleton appointed to command in Scotland.

Aug. 9. Instructions for Middleton.

health, the petty contributions which reached him in driblets would have been altogether insufficient to maintain a war.[1]

In the meantime the Highland chiefs were growing impatient. In October a messenger who came from the most notable

Oct.
A fresh
message
from the
Highlands.

amongst them, Macdonald of Glengarry, was urging Charles to send commissions and some slight assistance and stores, so that the chieftains might be able to place their clans in the field without delay. On

Dec. 20.
Commissions
sent to the
chiefs.

December 20, after much consideration, an instrument was drawn up appointing six of the leading personages to serve as commissioners for the King, and authorising them to select a commander-in-chief in Middleton's absence.[2] Yet as there was slight chance that Highland chiefs and Lowland nobles, impatient of control—especially impatient of control by a neighbour and rival—would combine in nominating a commander Charles contented himself with forwarding the commission to Middleton at the Hague, bidding him to keep it with him or send it to Scotland as he

1653.
Glencairn's
offer.

thought fit.[3] Middleton objected to this ill-concocted proposal;[4] and before long a message from the Earl of Glencairn offered what appeared a better alternative. Glencairn, a Cunningham from the South, had been a member of the Hamiltonian party, and, as a supporter of the engagement for the rescue of Charles I., was in 1649 deprived of his earldom by Argyle and his followers. In 1651 he was one of the Royalists admitted to the reformed Committee of Estates, and he now announced his readiness again to do service to the King. In March 1653 Charles sent him a commission appointing him commander-in-chief till Middle-

[1] Charles to the noblemen and gentlemen of Scotland, June $\frac{15}{25}$; Instructions to Middleton, Aug. $\frac{9}{19}$; Charles to Middleton, Nov. $\frac{6}{16}$; Firth's *Scotland and the Commonwealth*, 46, 50, 60.

[2] *Nicholas Papers*, i. 314; Commission to Macdonald of Sleat and others, Firth's *Scotland and the Commonwealth*, 65.

[3] Hyde to Nicholas, Nov. $\frac{12}{22}$, *Clar. St. P.* iii. 117.

[4] Hyde to Middleton, March $\frac{11}{41}$, Firth's *Scotland and the Commonwealth*, 103.

ton arrived, and at the same time suggested to him that if
there was any likelihood that the Highlanders would
voluntarily place him at their head, he need say
nothing about his nomination, but hand over to them
the earlier commission in which the right of election
was conferred upon themselves.[1] So much diplomacy was hardly likely to result in efficient generalship.

Mar. 4.
Charles
appoints
Glencairn
to the com-
mand in
Middleton's
absence.

In the Highlands the confederates were increasing in
number. Young Seaforth, the son of the vacillating earl who
had played fast and loose with Montrose, had joined
the insurgents towards the end of May and laid
hands on a party of English sailors who had landed
in Lewis.[2] Early in June there were meetings held
secretly at which those who appeared promised to
take part in the coming enterprise.[3] On the 16th
Lord Balcarres announced to Robert Lilburne—who had been
left in command of the Parliamentary forces in Scotland—that
as engagements made to him had been broken, he had retired
'somewhat further out of the way.' Two days later Sir Arthur
Forbes renounced the benefit of his former capitulation. In
the cases of both hostility to the English Government was
intensified by the fear of a sequestration of their estates.[4]

May 29.
English
sailors
captured.

June.
Meetings
of the con-
federates.

This declaration of war—for such it virtually was[5]—received
at least the tacit support of the other confederates. In Scotland, as in England, sweeping confiscations made the
quarrel between the new government and the great
landed proprietors irreconcilable. The only possible
counter-weight lay in the efforts of the English authorities to win
over the people to their side against the lords. Yet—even leaving
out of consideration the natural abhorrence of an alien yoke—

Effect of
the confisca-
tions.

[1] Instructions to Glencairn, March $\frac{4}{14}$, Firth's *Scotland and the Commonwealth*, 99.

[2] Summons to the Captain of the ' Fortune,' May 29 ; Lilburne to
Cromwell, June 18, *ib.* 140, 147.   [3] *Ib.* 144, note 2.

[4] Balcarres to Lilburne, June 16 ; Forbes to Lilburne, June 18, *ib.* 146,
147.

[5] " This was practically a declaration of war." *Ib.* Introduction, xlvi.

there were causes enough to render this solution hopeless. The
The assessment. assessment of 8,500*l.* a month [1] for the partial support
of the army of occupation was a heavy burden on a poor
country. Nor did the confiscations go in relief of public taxation.
Employment of the confiscated estates. Part of them were employed for the expenses of building the fortresses at Inverness, Ayr, and in other
places by which Scotland was to be held in a vice ;
part went in the form of estates conferred upon English officers.
Land valued at 1,000*l.* a year was assigned to Lambert. Monk,
together with three colonels, secured a rental of 500*l.* apiece,
whilst other commanders contented them with smaller but not
inconsiderable estates. Against these sums is to be set 1,000*l.*
voted by Parliament to be paid to the poor of Glasgow, whose
houses had been destroyed by a recent fire. [2]

The chasm which separated the English military government from the people of Scotland was widened by the growing
hostility of the clergy. It is true that the Kirk no longer
Divisions in the Kirk. possessed the united force which had swayed the
national destinies in the days of the Covenant. The
nobility, her close ally in 1638, was slipping out of her hands,
and her own ministers were divided into two bitterly antagonistic
parties, each filling the air with recriminations against the other.
The Government hopes to win over the Remon-strants. For some time, indeed, the Government had hoped
to gain the support of the Remonstrants, who had
vigorously protested against trusting to an un-
covenanted king. With this end commissioners
appointed in February by Parliament to visit the Universities
forced Patrick Gillespie upon the reluctant college of Glasgow
Hopeless-ness of the attempt. as its principal. [3] Yet a government which allowed
soldiers to dispute publicly with ministers in churches,
and sheltered the few Independent and Anabaptist
congregations which defied the sacred authority of the Presbytery, could hardly long retain the good-will of ministers to
whom submission to the Presbyterian order was a matter of

[1] The Valuation of Scotland, Firth's *Scotland and the Commonwealth*, 170.

[2] *Ib.* Introduction, xxxi, xxxii. 　　　　[3] *Baillie*, iii. 212.

Divine obligation. Lilburne, indeed, who, like his brother, was of a sanguine nature, was able to hope that he would find support in 'the people in the West, who have been always accounted most precise.'[1] The knowledge that a movement was preparing in the Western Highlands had been gradually growing upon him during the spring and early summer and made him, much as he was inclined to minimise the danger,[2] shrink from the risk of leaving an organised opposition in the rear if he should, after all, be called on to march into the North.

Even as late as July 12 Lilburne imagined that the confederates in the North would be unable to induce their

July 12. Lilburne fears the meeting of the General Assembly

dependents to rise, the people being 'more apt to be quiet than they are able to provoke new troubles.' Yet, hopeful as he was, the approaching meeting of the General Assembly, which was to take place on the 21st, filled him with anxiety 'in regard of the fickleness of the times and present designs that are amongst many.' Accordingly, he begged Cromwell to direct him what to do.[3] Cromwell, however, made no response,[4] and Lilburne, having received intimation, true or false, that the assembled ministers

---

[1] A letter from Lilburne, April 19, Firth's *Scotland and the Commonwealth*, 127.

[2] On Feb. 5 Lilburne writes slightingly of Glengarry's movements. On April 16 he thinks that in consequence of the English success at sea against the Dutch, 'at present we are in a very peaceable posture, and, I hope, our adversaries at their wits' end.' On June 18 he thinks that 'their chief design that I can learn' is 'to gain some reputation abroad that there is yet the face of an army in the Highlands, that young Charles by that means may gain some assistance.' *Ib.* 79, 122, 147.

[3] *Ib.* 160.

[4] Lilburne's own account is clearly that of a man who was not acting under orders :—" Having some intimation that the present meeting of the ministers of the General Assembly at Edinburgh tended to a further correspondence with those met in the Highlands, I thought it my duty, for the prevention of anything that might be to the disturbance of the public peace, to dissolve their Assembly." Lilburne to Cromwell, July 21, *ib.* 162.

were likely to open a correspondence with the Royalists in the Highlands, resolved to act on his own responsibility. On the morning of the 21st, after two sermons had been preached, before each of which the preachers offered a prayer for the King, Lieutenant-Colonel Cotterell, supported by Captain Hope, summoned the Assembly to disperse on the ground that it had no warrant to sit 'either from the Parliament of England or the Commander-in-chief in Scotland.' In vain the Mode-

July 21.
The
Assembly
dissolved.

rator, David Dickson, appealed to the law of the land and to the 'power and warrant' which the Kirk had received from Jesus Christ. Cotterell did but call in his soldiers, and the ministers, guarded by horse and foot, were marched out to Bruntsfield Links and bidden to go home with all speed. It was only as a matter of favour that they were allowed to remain in Edinburgh till the next morning on condition that no more than three should remain in company.[1]

In defiance of this order the Remonstrant party, whom the popular voice charged with having concerted the dissolution

July 22.
Protest of
the
Remon-
strants.

Both parties
joined
against the
English.

with Lilburne, drew up a protestation against his act of violence.[2] From this moment the weight of both the clerical factions would be thrown into the scale against the English Government. Baillie's complaint to a correspondent in London doubtless found an echo in the heart of many a Remonstrant: "Thus our General Assembly—the glory and strength of our Church upon earth—is by your soldiery crushed and trod under foot without the least provocation from us at this time either in word or deed. For this our hearts are sad, our eyes run down with water, we sigh to God against whom we have sinned, and wait for the help of His hand, but from those who

---

[1] Compare with Lilburne's letter, *An Account of the late Violence*, E, 708, 23 ; *Life of Blair*, 307 ; *Baillie*, iii. 225.

[2] Lilburne to Cromwell, July 21, Firth's *Scotland and the Common-wealth*, 163 ; *Life of Blair*, 308, where a note by David Laing calls attention to the evidence on the part played by the Remonstrants, and criticises Baillie's innuendo that they were favourable to the dissolution.

oppressed us we deserved no evil." [1]   Lilburne had no doubt
of the rectitude of his course.   It was only from fear of popular
indignation that he refrained from doing his work thoroughly
and dissolving the local Presbyteries as well. [2]   A man of his
character, slow to suspect danger, is apt to plunge into in-
temperate action when at last aroused.   Cromwell, as far as
is known, made no sign of approbation or disapprobation.   The
nominated Parliament was by this time in session, and it is
likely enough that any action against the Presbyterian clergy
would be welcomed on its benches.

The breach between the English Government and the
General Assembly could hardly in any case have been long
averted.   The Divine Right of Presbytery, in alliance with
Scottish nationalism, must sooner or later have come into
collision with the principles of individual religious liberty
upheld by an alien soldiery.   Yet it may be doubted whether
the immediate danger was so great as Lilburne imagined.
There was a gulf between the Presbyterian clergy and the
Royalist gentry which would be hard to bridge over, and it
would be difficult to convince a pious minister of either party
that Middleton—rough soldier as he was—was exactly the man
to be trusted with the championship of the Kirk. [3]

By this time the insurrection in the North appeared even to
Lilburne to be worthy of his attention.   Either towards the
end of June or early in July Glencairn appeared
amongst the assembled chiefs, and produced the
King's letter authorising them to elect a commander
till Middleton arrived.   He was himself promptly chosen, probably on a notification that the King wished it to be so. [4]   On
August 3, at a meeting held in Lochaber, the confederacy

June?
Glencairn
chosen to the
command.

---

[1] *Baillie*, iii. 225.

[2] Lilburne to Cromwell, Aug. 6, Firth's *Scotland and the Commonwealth*, 191, 192.

[3] " I fear you are not Presbyterian enough, for I do not find any of
that tribe who are there have any confidence in you." Hyde to Middleton, March $\frac{18}{28}$, *ib.* 106.

[4] Letter of Intelligence, *ib.* 183.

received a notable addition. Lord Lorne, revolting from his
Aug. 3.
Arrival of
Lorne and of
Kenmure. father who pronounced his curse on him for his dis-
obedience,[1] rode in to offer his services to the King.[2]
Kenmure, too, whose estates had been seized by
the English Government,[3] came in about the same time.
Balcarres and his brother-in-law, Sir Robert Moray, had already
vowed themselves to the cause. Yet amongst these there was
no preponderating personality to keep in check the private
jealousies which had tasked Montrose's skill to the utmost.
Glencairn, though personally brave, had no other claim to the
commanding position in which he had been placed by the
favour of the King, and the Highlanders were even less likely
than the Lowland nobles to look up to him as a predestined
leader.

For some months, however, the danger of internal dissen-
sion inherent in the composition of this motley host was
The con-
federates re-
solve not to
risk a battle
till Middle-
ton's arrival. averted by the resolution taken to avoid active
hostilities till Middleton arrived. Middleton, it was
fondly hoped, would bring with him large stores of
arms and ammunition, of which the Royalists were
sadly in need—perhaps even the active co-operation of a Dutch
fleet. In the meantime it would be enough if they could transfer to their own military chest the cess which Lilburne claimed
to levy in the Highlands, make forays in the Lowlands with the
object of collecting horses on which to mount their men, and
exact money from friend or foe. During the remainder of the
year a few skirmishes only were reported, in which the English
veterans invariably gained the advantage on open ground, but
were no less invariably driven to retreat when they ventured
to advance into the hills. This mode of action had the additional advantage for the Royalists that it enabled them to divide
their forces, and for the most part to keep personages who

---

[1] Lorne left his father on July 17, Firth's *Scotland and the Commonwealth,* 165–169.

[2] Lilburne to Cromwell, Aug. 11, *ib.* 191. Baillie (iii. 250) says that
Lorne was 'but coarsely used by his father.'

[3] *Ib.*

might otherwise have come to blows at a distance from one another.

Nor was Lilburne, on the other side, in a condition to precipitate matters even if he had been by nature capable of hardy
Lilburne's position.
resolutions. His conviction that being without a fleet to search the sea-lochs of the rugged western coast, and to cut off communication with the Dutch fleets on the eastern, it was impossible for him to subdue the enemy's
Cobbet's success in the West.
forces, ministered to his inaction. In August indeed Colonel Cobbet, who was despatched with three vessels for the purpose, succeeded in reducing Lewis, and in occupying Eilandonan in Ross-shire and Duart Castle in the Isle of Mull. Cobbet's force, however, was but small, and later in the year his three vessels were wrecked, and he and his men were compelled to return by land to their quarters.[1]

On land Lilburne felt himself unequal to any considerable movement. In all Scotland he had about 12,000 foot and
Forces at Lilburne's command.
but 2,200 horse.[2] These forces indeed compared favourably even in point of numbers with those which the Scottish Government had from time to time launched against Montrose, and were incomparably superior in every military quality. The Scottish Government, however, had had behind it the population of the Lowlands, whilst Lilburne was well aware that there, as well as in the Highlands, his enemies were many and his supporters few. He therefore contented himself with placing small garrisons at the mouths of the glens opening into the Highlands, a policy which would surely have led to disaster if Montrose and not Glencairn had been in command of the enemy. The constant burden of his letters to England was the necessity of sending ships and horse. As long, however, as the nominated Parliament was in existence and the war with the Dutch continued, scarcely any notice was taken of his cry for help.

---

[1] Cobbet's progress can be traced in *Scotland and the Commonwealth*.
[2] *Ib.* Introd. p. xxxiii.

The war, therefore—if war it can be called—resolved itself into a vain effort to parry the movements of an enemy determined to avoid an engagement. Within a week after the meeting in Lochaber, Kenmure had made a dash into Fife, almost up to the gates of Burntisland.[1] Then, accompanied by Lorne, he betook himself to the land of the Campbells to test the loyalty of the clansmen now that the son was at odds with his father. Argyle himself had a difficult part to play. No one could expect him to throw himself heart and soul into the cause of the alien government, and Sir Robert Moray, writing some months earlier, had assured Charles that nothing but prudence kept him from rallying to the King.[2] Whether it was prudence or conviction that held him back, he loyally carried out his engagements to Lilburne. He did not indeed offer armed support—the prevalent temper of the Campbells rendered it impracticable—but he furnished the information which enabled Cobbet to seize Duart Castle, and later on he provided the escort which conducted Cobbet's shipwrecked soldiers through a hostile country.[3] When, therefore, Lorne broke into Argyleshire, he was far from being able to carry with him the whole strength of the Campbells. Yet considerable numbers came forward to support him with men and money. His failure was owing not so much to external resistance, as to internal disputes between the leaders of the expedition. When Kintyre was reached, Kenmure was resolute to deal harshly with a body of settlers from Ayrshire and Renfrew, who were steadfast in their loyalty to Argyle and consequently to the English Government.

Margin notes: Kenmure and Lorne in the Campbell country. — Argyle's position. — Sept. Oct. — Lorne in Argyle. — He quarrels with Kenmure,

---

[1] Nicoll's *Diary*, 112.

[2] "All I shall say of my Lord Argyle [is] that . . . the course he takes is merely for self-preservation. . . . He thinks things are not yet ripe enough to appear here in arms, alleging that it will come to nothing but the ruin of the Lowlands, and the Highlands are to be destroyed by sea." *Scotland and the Commonwealth*, 134.

[3] Lilburne to Cromwell, Sept. 13, *ib.* 221 ; Campbell of Auchenbreck sided with Lorne, Campbell of Glenorchy with Argyle.

Lorne refused to allow him to inflict punishment on his father's tenants, and a bitter quarrel was the result.[1] At an earlier stage of the expedition Lorne had fallen in with Glengarry, who, as a Macdonald, regarded the heir of the Campbells as an

Sept.
and with
Glengarry.

hereditary foe. As might have been expected, they 'fell out, and drew each upon the other,' but ' were prevented of fighting by some there present; however, they parted great enemies.' [2] There was bad blood, too, between Balcarres and Glencairn, the former having even proposed that the command of the army should be transferred to a committee, a proposal which Glencairn was only able to set aside by producing the warrant in which the King had directly given him the post.[3] In the absence of Lorne and Kenmure

Glencairn
at
Falkland.

in the west, Glencairn swooped down on Falkland, whence he carried off an officer and four or five soldiers, who only recovered their liberty on Lilburne's consenting to pay 80l. for their release.

Lilburne indeed had much to complain of. Many of his officers had taken advantage of quiet times to betake themselves to England. Not a single cavalry regiment

Oct.
State of the
army.

had a colonel at his post, and only one had even a major.[4] What made matters worse was, that Lilburne had well-nigh the whole of Scotland against him. "Glen-

Nov.
The people
of Scotland
hostile to
the English.

cairn and Glengarry," he wrote on November 5, "are also busy up and down, and many small parties fall down into the Lowlands in the night-time and steal horses: indeed, the people do many of them voluntarily give them, and will not give us any intelligence of them." [5] A few days later he heard that Kenmure had returned from Argyleshire. "There are parties of horse and foot," he wrote, " fall down every night in one place or other and steal horses,

---

[1] Lilburne to Cromwell, Oct. 16, *Scotland and the Commonwealth*, 242; *Baillie*, iii. 250.

[2] Letter of Intelligence, Firth's *Scotland and the Commonwealth*, 220.

[3] Instructions to Drummond, Oct. 23, *ib.* 246; *Baillie*, iii. 250.

[4] Lilburne to Cromwell, Oct. 6, *ib.* 240.

[5] Lilburne to Cromwell, Nov. 5, *ib.* 262.

and cannot be prevented. The country is so false to us and complies so with them that though at present there is not so visible an enemy that speaks much danger, yet their daily actions and growing strength may—together with what ill-spirit is generally found in the ministers and people, who doubtless are ready to rise if any visible strength appear—give reason to believe they have some notable design in hand." Yet what could he do? His cavalry were few in number, and it often happened that he could not find a field officer to give him counsel. If Lilburne could hope to find friends in Scotland, it was amongst the Remonstrants of the west, yet he now learnt that the Presbytery of Hamilton had discussed the question whether Kenmure or the English were the greater enemies of the Kirk, and had decided that Kenmure was the less formidable of the two.[1]

By the middle of November the danger had spread to parts of the Lowlands far away from the hills. On the 15th Lilburne informed Cromwell that Falkland had again been set upon in the night, and two officers carried off ; that two soldiers had been seized at Kilsyth, and that houses, one of them being that of Johnston of Warriston, had been plundered in the immediate neighbourhood of Edinburgh.[2] "Hardly any part of the country," he declared, " is free from the night-walkers who continue preying on gentlemen's horses, and by their secret ways convey them to the hills where they have riders in readiness, and beside many younger brothers and desperate persons that privately steal to them, well-mounted, and fitted for service ; but yet all these signify but little in comparison of those secret contrivements and encouragements the generality of the people affords them, and are bringing forth to ripeness, if their dark and wicked designs may take effect. . . . . I have been advising—for the better preventing this inundation—to seize the horses in countrymen's hands, but find these people so ticklish to deal withal at this time—out of that strange expectation they have

Danger in the Lowlands.

[1] Lilburne to Cromwell, Nov. 12, *Scotland and the Commonwealth*, 264.
[2] *Ib.* 270.

of a change—and so ready to take the wing, that it's feared we shall not only lose the horses, but drive many to the hills who seem to be peaceable, rather than part with them to us, and without we could seize all together, which is impossible, it is doubted we shall do more hurt than good." [1]

Before the end of November the very gates of Edinburgh had to be shut at nightfall lest insurgent parties should slip

Nov.-Dec.
Disturbed condition of the south.

into the town.[2]   In December the disorders had spread even further south.   Parties of armed men were roving over Dumfriesshire and Galloway, and horses were seized within four miles of Berwick.   An exploit which testified to the unpopularity of the government in England as well as in Scotland was recorded by Lilburne

Wogan's march.

without any sign of astonishment.   Captain Wogan, who had carried his troop with him when in 1648 he deserted the Parliamentary service to join Hamilton's invading forces, and had in 1649 held bravely out in Ireland as governor of Duncannon,[3] now started from Paris with a few chosen companions to make his way through England to the scene of action.   In London they all disguised themselves in the uniform of Cromwell's cavalry,[4] and then, having increased the number of his companions, set out for Scotland, avoiding the high roads, enlisting men on the route, and making their way by twos and threes together.[5]   When they reached the

Dec. 3.
Dec. 8.

north they appear to have been less careful.   Wogan, when he passed through Durham, had some twenty-two companions with him.   On the 8th he reached Peebles with the same number.[6]   He seems to have gathered

---

[1] Lilburne to Cromwell, Nov. ? , Firth's *Scotland and the Commonwealth*, 272.

[2] Nicoll's *Diary*, 116.

[3] *Clarke Papers*, i. App. A.

[4] So much, I suppose, one may take from *Clarendon* (xiv. 61), though his account is grossly inaccurate.

[5] News from London, Dec. 9, *Clarendon MSS*. ii. No. 1,581.

[6] On Dec. 3 Wogan writes from Durham under the assumed name of Thomas Young, *Thurloe*, i. 623; compare a letter to Lilburne, Dec. 12, Firth's *Scotland and the Commonwealth*, 296.   "You may remember they

strength as he passed through the Lowlands, as he ultimately presented little short of a hundred followers to Glencairn.[1]

Difficult as the situation was, it is impossible to avoid the conclusion that Lilburne was far from being a resourceful com-
Lilburne not a resourceful commander. mander. Sanguine in the spring, he was in despair in the winter. His counsels as a statesman were,
His political advice. however, far more worthy of attention than his military schemes—if indeed he can be said to have formed any. He did not indeed, and in fact he could not, propose any plan for removing the main difficulty with which the Commonwealth would have permanently to contend—the rooted hostility of the Scottish people—but he had much that was valuable to suggest as to the best mode of dealing with the discontented nobility and gentry. Knowing well how much material causes had contributed to drive them into the arms of the insurgents, he advised that with the exception of 'five or six grand offenders for example's sake,' all sequestrations and forfeitures should be taken off, and that the Act of Union so long discussed should be finally passed, accompanied by an Act of Oblivion, and a free pardon to all in arms if they would agree to keep quiet. These generous proposals are marred, in the eyes of later generations, by a suggestion that rewards should be offered to those who would 'bring in any of the present rebels dead or alive.' At the same time, in order to avoid danger from the large numbers of persons without means of subsistence, Lilburne advanced the concession of licenses to levy regiments for foreign princes in amity with the Commonwealth to such Scotsmen as made application for them. Further, he would have a check placed on the rigour with which the new Courts of Justice issued processes for the recovery of debts—amounting it is said at one time to 35,000

were represented a full troop at least, and that they took hundreds on their way, which no man, I believe, would think possible to be acted by twenty-two men, for they were no more when they entered this country." Mews to Hyde, June 4, 1654, Firth's *Scotland and the Protectorate.*

[1] Account of Glencairn's expedition appended to Gwynn's *Memoirs,* 166.

—by granting time to those who had it not in their power to satisfy their creditors at once.[1]

To these wise recommendations was added the inevitable demand for reinforcements and for ships of war to guard against

Men and ships needed.

Middleton's landing.[2] If reinforcements were not sent, Lilburne wrote to Lambert before the end of the year, it would be necessary for him to concentrate his troops in the south of Scotland, giving 'the enemy all beyond Dundee, except Inverness.' Needless to say, the abdication of the nominated Parliament was regarded by the army in

Dec. 20. Reception of the Protectorate by the army in Scotland.

Lilburne's troubles.

Scotland with the highest satisfaction. At last there was a probability that adequate supplies would be despatched, and that dispositions would be taken to ward off the impending danger. "I thought it my duty," wrote Lilburne to Cromwell when the good news arrived, "to let your lordship know that, by all the observation I can make, I find nothing but union amongst us here, and a resolution to stand by your lordship in the management of those weighty affairs that Providence hath cast upon you." He had wondered, he added, that his earnest pleadings for supplies had hitherto received no answer, but he now imputed the neglect 'to the late inconsistency in the Parliament.' The troops, he wrote a few days later, were two months in arrear, and the cess on which they partly relied could not be collected in the disturbed condition of the country.[3] Nor was Lilburne unconscious of his own deficiencies ; "being jealous of my own weakness," he assured the Protector, "I am doubtful so great affairs as are here to be managed may suffer for the want of one more fit to wrestle with them than your Excellency's most humble servant." "I hear," he candidly as-

Wishes to be superseded by Monk.

sured Lambert, "that a commander-in-chief is to be sent down hither, I only wish such a one as may pay these people for their knavery. Methinks Monk's

[1] Lilburne to Cromwell, Dec. ? ; Lilburne's proposals, Dec. ? ; Firth's *Scotland and the Commonwealth*, 289, 295.   [2] *Ib*.

[3] Lilburne to the Protector, Dec. 20 ; Lilburne to [Lambert], Dec. 29, *ib.* 301, 306.

spirit would do well amongst them." [1]　　There was no touch of jealousy in that noble heart.

Yet, as Lilburne knew well, there was no hope of Monk's presence in Scotland, or of any decline in the energy of his adversaries, until a peace with the Dutch had put an end to their hopes of succour from abroad.[2]　A few weeks later Lilburne knew that the Protector had taken his advice, and that Monk, as soon as he could be spared, would be sent down to take the command.[3] Yet how could he be spared as long as a hostile Dutch fleet might at any moment put to sea?

*1654.
Jan.
Monk to come when he can be spared.*

Others besides the soldiers of the Commonwealth had been watching with interest the progress of the negotiation.　For some months Middleton had been tarrying in Holland, hoping, almost against hope, that some monstrous demand on the English side would sting the States General into a determination to prolong the war, and to turn failure into success by sending shipping and warlike stores to the Royalists of the north of Scotland.　When Charles instructed him on January 27 to wait no longer, he took this step partly because there was little prospect of Dutch aid, but still more because the noblemen and Highland chiefs were quarrelling with one another, and it was thought that they would bow their heads in submission to a professional soldier.[4]

Middleton in Holland.

*Jan. 27.
Middleton's instructions.*

Middleton accordingly landed with a very deficient stock of supplies on Tarbatness before the end of February.[5]　At his first rendezvous he was surrounded by ' two or three thousand, of which there were 500 serviceable horse.' At a subsequent meeting at Dornoch he opened his commission to command in chief.　To this Glencairn,

*Feb.
Middleton lands on Tarbatness.*

---

[1]　Lilburne to the Protector, Dec. 20 ; Lilburne to [Lambert], Dec. 29, Firth's *Scotland and the Commonwealth*, 301, 306.

[2]　"I hope a happy conclusion with the Dutch will put an end to these unhappy people's distempers, and things may come to a settlement again." Lilburne to the Protector, Dec. 20, *ib.* i. 302.

[3]　Lilburne to Monk, Jan. 21, Firth's *Scotland and the Protectorate*.

[4]　Instructions for Middleton, *ib.*　　　　[5]　Nicoll's *Diary*, 122.

who had hitherto held that post, raised no objection, but it was otherwise when he learnt that Sir George Monro, whose services in Scotland and Ireland had not been such as to inspire confidence, was to be second in command. An excuse for a quarrel was not likely to be long absent. At a dinner given by

March.
Quarrel
between
Glencairn
and
Monro.

Glencairn to Middleton and his officers, Glencairn boasted of his gallant army which, as he averred, he had raised out of nothing. " By God," cried Monro, starting from his seat with the jealousy of a professional soldier, " the men you speak of are no other than a pack of thieves and robbers. In a short time, I will show you other sort of men." Glencairn replied that his interrupter was ' a base liar,' after which Middleton did his best to reconcile the angry pair, and Glencairn, submissive in outward show, drank Monro's health, and accompanied Middleton a mile on his return home. The inevitable duel was introduced with all the stately politeness of a court. As the Earl was going to supper Sir George's brother appeared at the gate, when Glencairn asked him in and placed him at the head of the table next the daughter of the laird in whose house he had taken up his quarters. " Immediately after supper he told Monro that he would give him a spring if he could dance, which accordingly he did, the laird's daughter playing." Then, seizing a moment after the rest of the company had joined the dance, the two stepped aside, and in a dozen words arranged the time and place of meeting. When the disputants met the next morning, the Earl slashed Monro over the left hand and forehead, and but for the intervention of his own servant would have thrust his sword through his adversary's body.[1] A fortnight afterwards Glencairn left the camp in dudgeon with Middleton himself.

Such were the materials with which Middleton was ex- pected to reconquer Scotland. The fiery spirits were loyal

Further
disputes.

enough to their king, but they could not discipline themselves to forbear from personal attacks on one another. Not long before it had been Lorne and Glengarry,

---

[1] Peter Mews's Narrative, June 4, Firth's *Scotland and the Protectorate* ; Gwynn's *Military Memoirs*.

then it was Kenmure and Lorne,[1] now it was Glencairn and Monro. Not long afterwards Sutherland was complaining of Middleton himself, whilst Athol and Glengarry all but came to blows.[2] It had been part of Middleton's message to the chiefs that, if matters went well, Charles would follow to place himself at the head of the insurrection, but unless discipline could be restored, it was hardly likely that he would venture his person again in Scotland. Unluckily for the Royalist cause Middleton had none of that personal glamour which bowed all turbulent hearts in submission to Montrose.

Great as were the difficulties arising from the impossibility of taming the wild spirits of his nominal subordinates, there was looming in the future another scarcely less formidable. No Royalist movement would really be crowned with success unless it could win the Lowlands, and Montrose's failure had shown how hard it was to control the Lowlands without standing well with the clergy. Neither Middleton nor the noblemen who surrounded him were prepared to do more than flatter them. "It is strange," wrote an Englishman who accompanied the expedition, "to see how the rebels, by their favouring the people, had crept into their affections, they not being able to see to the bottom of the design. But I labour in all discourses to make them sensible of it, and press the ministers to instil the reasons of that smoothness from the pulpit, from whence it makes the greater impression ; and doubt not but I[3] shall prevail with some of them to set it on with all possible vehemency, which if they can once fancy they will need no spurs, for they are naturally good at that kind of oratory. . . . But, for your comfort, Mr. Presbyter is never like to put his oar in our boat ; at least, not to sit at the helm as formerly he hath done ; yet you must not expect that we should absolutely cashier him at the first dash."[4]

Middleton and the clergy.

---

[1] See p. 93.

[2] Lilburne to the Protector, April 11, 20, Firth's *Scotland and the Protectorate*.

[3] 'I' is omitted in the *MS*.

[4] Peter Mews's Narrative, Firth's *Scotland and the Protectorate*.

The eyes of 'Mr. Presbyter' were too widely open to be cajoled in such a fashion.

At last the weary Dutch war was ended, and on April 22 Monk arrived at Dalkeith to take in hand the military and civil government of Scotland. He at one recognised, as Lilburne had already recognised, that he had no mere insurrection of Highlanders to face, but an uprising extending sporadically over the Lowlands as well, wherever the English troops were not present to repress an actual outbreak. When he reached Dalkeith there was no more than 500*l.* in the treasury, and the soldiers' pay was sadly in arrear. By June 25, as he wrote, 33,000*l.* would be needed to make up this deficiency alone. If he was to answer for the consequences, money, men, and ships must be hastened up from England.[1] If Monk succeeded where Lilburne had failed, it was in part, at least, because his authoritative demands were attended to at Whitehall —slowly, indeed, as financial straits compelled, but still with something approaching regularity—whilst Lilburne's complaints had been ignored.

April 22.
Monk at
Dalkeith.

Demand
for money,
men, and
ships.

Yet, with all these advantages, Monk had no light work before him. "Hardly a younger brother," Lilburne had written in one of his last despatches, "but he's gone, and even from under the noses of our garrisons and quarters, do what we can to prevent them unless we should take all prisoners and then not know what to do with such a multitude. I hear they still break into Northumberland and steal horses, but some tell me the people there are confederates. I am doubtful the flame here may be far beyond what may be yet imagined by your Highness, or, indeed, by many that are here : the works of darkness are hard to be discerned. . . . Therefore, that it may not be at my door that a timely provision is not made even for the worst of evils that may arise here, I do in conscience and faithfulness declare my thoughts, and earnestly beg that though those in

April 1.
Lilburne's
gloomy
account
of the
situation.

[1] Monk to the Protector, April 22, 25; Monk to Lambert, April 22, Firth's *Scotland and the Protectorate.*

rebellion or that may join at this time may not prove so numerous or so dangerous as my apprehensions speak, yet considering the bloodiness, rebelliousness, and wretchedness of the spirits of the generality of this monstrous people who have not been sparing to shed the blood of many of their kings and rulers,[1] and upon private quarrels and feuds to murder one another, and who have, by the help of the hills to draw together in, become formidable, and then massacred and expelled the English armies several times, the memory of which is no little encouragement to these rebels." [There is every reason to fear the worst.] [2]

If Monk was secure of better financial support than had been given to Lilburne, he had also resources of his own in his

Monk's clear-sight-edness.

keener sense of the practical means needed to subdue resistance. It was useless indeed, as he well knew, to appeal to that spirit of patriotism which was heavily enlisted against him ; but he could at least show that civil order and individual well-being would find better security under his government than under any that was likely to be set up by the gay gallants of the north. On May 4, when

May 4. Proclamation of the Protectorate and of the Union.

he entered Edinburgh, after a great banquet given him by the town, he caused two proclamations to be read at the Market Cross in his own presence : the first announcing the establishment of the Protectorate ; the second, that according to an ordinance of the new ruler Scotland was now to form an integral part of the Commonwealth of England, Scotland, and Ireland, and that the authority of her ancient kings and her ancient parliaments having been abolished she was henceforth to send thirty members to sit in the Parliament at Westminster. Then followed a list of the boons which the larger and wealthier

---

[1] It cannot have entered into the mind of the writer of this phrase addressed to Cromwell that Charles I. had been put to death otherwise than after a fair trial.

[2] Lilburne to the Protector, April 1, Firth's *Scotland and the Protectorate*. The final clause having no principal verb it has been supplied by conjecture.

offered to the smaller and poorer nation. There was to be absolute freedom of trade on the borders ; no taxes were to be raised in Scotland which were not proportionable to those on the English side ; all tenures implying vassalage and servitude were to be swept away ; fines and other payments by tenants to be moderated and controlled by the State. Military services and heritable jurisdictions with all fees and casualties appertaining to the lords were abolished, whilst popular courts baron were set up in each locality, to be composed of the suitors of the manor court, with power to determine by the verdict of a jury all pleas arising out of contracts, debts, promises, and trespasses, where the amount sued for did not exceed the value of forty shillings.[1] To celebrate the munificence of the concession there was a great display of fireworks from the Market Cross.

The next day was reserved for the display of the sword which in the ordinance then proclaimed was suspended over the heads of the recalcitrant nobility. Pardon and grace in respect of all acts of hostility in time of war were indeed granted in general to the whole people of Scotland, but afterwards the names of twenty-four persons followed—all with three exceptions lords of Parliament or their heirs—whose estates, saving a provision to their wives and children, were wholly forfeited to the Commonwealth. On seventy-three persons fines varying from 14,000*l.* to 500*l.* were imposed. All persons who had taken arms against the Commonwealth since May 1, 1652, were excepted from the benefits of the ordinances,[2] whilst those who had connived at the rebellion of their brothers or wards and did not secure their surrender within twenty days were to be thrown into prison, and a fine imposed on every presbytery from which rebels had gone forth, as well as upon every parent whose son had taken part with the insurgents. A price of 200*l.* was set on the heads of Middleton, Seaforth, Kenmure and Dalziel.[3]

May 5.
Proclamation of pardon and of grace.

---

[1] *Scobell*, ii. 293, 295.   [2] *Ib.* ii. 288 ; Nicoll's *Diary*, 125.
[3] *Thurloe*, ii. 261.

Taking the two ordinances together the policy of the English Government was much the same as that which the French revolutionists were afterwards to display in more extravagant form upon their banners—War to the lordly house, Peace to the cottage ! If it were possible for any Scotsman to pass over the indignity of receiving grace and pardon from an alien government, there were two classes of persons to whom Monk might look for support : the traders who would have much to gain by the prospects opened to them by the suppression of the custom houses at Berwick and Carlisle, and the lawyers who favoured the extension of equal justice, and were hostile to the extreme claims lately put forward by the clergy. Of the towns, Monk was able to write after he had time to gain personal experience of their feelings, that they were 'generally the most faithful to us of any people in this nation.'[1] For the lawyers, we have the note of a patriotic diarist upon the death of Sir John Hope of Craighall, who had acted as one of the Parliamentary judges, that he held 'that few of the ministers of Scotland were honest, and that they, by bewraying the Scriptures, had raised errors ; giving out also that God had a great work to work by the English.'[2]

Import of the proclamations.

Feelings of the traders and lawyers.

Till Monk was ready to take the field, and as yet, in consequence of the dryness of the spring, there was no grass for his horses in the north, he applied himself to throwing obstacles in the way of the flocking of gentry to Middleton from the Lowlands. As a rule these men were younger sons who had nothing to lose, whilst their fathers and eldest brothers remained at home to avoid forfeiture of their estates. Monk had already suggested the imprisonment of fathers whose sons had taken the field,[3] but Oliver was loth to encourage a policy so violent, and measures of military watchfulness had to take its place. Monk's next thought was

Flocking of younger sons to Middleton.

---

[1] Monk to the Protector, Oct. 3, Firth's *Scotland and the Protectorate.*

[2] Nicoll's *Diary*, 124.

[3] Monk to the Protector, April 22, Firth's *Scotland and the Protectorate.*

to draw a virtually impassable line between Highlands and
Lowlands which no body of horse from the Lowlands could
overstep. Warned by the fate of Montrose, Middleton aimed
Middleton's at strengthening his cavalry, hoping to appear at the
plan. head of a body of horse composed of Lowlanders
collected in the Highlands, and not to be compelled to bring
down upon the Lowlands a force mainly composed of Highland
clansmen.

For the campaign now opening Monk could count on the
services of a highly intelligent staff of officers. Daniel com-
Monk's manded the garrison of Perth ; Hill was established
officers :
Daniel, Hill, at Ruthven in the heart of the wild country of
and Morgan. Badenoch ; and, above all, the active and skilful
Colonel Morgan, before whom Chepstow, Monmouth, and
Hereford had fallen in the latter days of the first civil war,[1] was
on the alert in the wide districts stretching to the hills from the
southern shore of the Moray Firth. It was Monk's own task
to seal up the accesses to the Highlands from the southern
Lowlands, thereby hindering Middleton from receiving the
accretions in men and horses upon which his calculations of
success depended.

With this object in view Monk left Dalkeith on May 10,
making for Stirling. Before going north, however, he turned
May 10. towards Cardross Castle, there to rest till the spring-
Monk breaks ing of the young grass in the hills afforded pasturage
up Middle-
ton's com- to his horse. As soon as he could move he made
munications his way by Kilsyth to Buchanan, where he super-
with Low-
lands. intended the destruction of the boats which had
conveyed passengers and horses to the northern glens. As he
established a strong party of horse at Glasgow, and as Dum-
barton was occupied by an English garrison, Monk was able to
assure himself before his return eastwards that this part of the
Highland frontier was secured, especially as Argyle was now
heartily co-operating with the English Government. With
a view to further operations, Monk established Colonel Brayne

[1] *Great Civil War*, ii. 376 ; iii. 21.

at Dunstaffnage with a detachment from Fleetwood's army in Ireland.[1]

Having thus secured the line of the Forth Monk proceeded to secure the line of the Tay. Marching from Perth on June 9,

June 9.
Monk on
the Tay.

with a force mainly composed of horse,[2] he reduced a small garrison on the Priory hill, near the foot of Loch Tay, leaving a few men in occupation of it, as well as of Weem Castle and Balloch.[3] After burning Garth Castle he made northwards for Strathspey, where he established himself at Ruthven Castle on the look-out for news.

The news of which Monk was in search was not long in reaching him. Hearing that Middleton was in Kintail, he

June 20.
Monk leaves
Ruthven
Castle.

marched to the foot of Loch Lochy, where, after full consultation with Argyle and Brayne, he formed the plan of action to which he subsequently adhered. Establishing Brayne with a strong force at Inverlochy, he himself plunged into the northern Highlands, resolved, as an apt pupil in the cruel school of Irish war, if—as might probably be the case—he failed to overtake the enemy, to make the country incapable of sustaining cavalry by burning and destroying every habitation of man, and every crop by which life might be supported. Beginning with the lands of the Camerons of Lochiel, he marched up Glenmoriston, raising fire in the homesteads of the Macdonalds of Glengarry. The work of destruction went on as he passed to Loch Alsh, through the country of Seaforth's Mackenzies.[4] "We have not found," writes a cornet who took part in the expedition, "man, woman, or child at their homes, all being in arms or in remote places with their cattle. At their return they will have new houses to build and

---

[1] J. Baynes to A. Baynes, May 11, *Letters from Roundhead Officers*, 69; Monk to the Protector, May 21, 28, 30, Firth's *Scotland and the Protectorate*.

[2] His force consisted of two regiments of horse and three and a half of foot.

[3] On the site of the present Taymouth Castle.

[4] Monk to Lambert, June 25, Monk's Narrative, Firth's *Scotland and the Protectorate*; Letter from Glenmoriston, June 25, *Merc. Pol.* E, 805, 5.

corn to seek, which will be a means to quiet them or nothing." [1]
Middleton had ferried his footmen over to Skye, and his horse
was not to be overtaken, but Morgan was despatched to Caithness, to take care that no provisions should be found there
when the winter came.   Monk himself, with his wearied troops,
made his way to seek repose at Inverness.[2]

News that Middleton had doubled back upon Blair Athol
induced Monk to recall Morgan, and to send him to Braemar to

July.
Middleton at
Blair Athol,
catch the enemy if he retreated in that direction.
For the present, however, there seemed little hope
that Middleton would fall into the trap.   By the
middle of July he had flung himself into the Campbell country,

and in the
Campbell
country.
marching along Loch Tay to Loch Awe, he too
burning the lands of his foemen as he passed.
Monk followed hard on his heels,[3] but though he
compelled Middleton to double back by way of Loch Rannoch
with his horse reduced from 3,000 to 1,200, he was himself too
exhausted by forced marches to do more than call a halt at

July 20.
Monk hears
news in Glen
Lyon.
Killin on the 19th, and to pursue his way into Glen
Lyon on the following day.   The news he received
there was such as to convince him that no further
pursuit was necessary.[4]

Even before this intelligence reached him Monk must have
known that there was no need of haste.   There was but one

[1] Cornet Baynes to A. Baynes, June 29, *Letters from Roundhead
Officers*, 78.

[2] Monk's Narrative, Firth's *Scotland and the Protectorate*.

[3] In a paper published in the *Highland Monthly* for May 1892, Mr.
W. Mackay inserts a map of Monk's marches, which I have made the
basis of my own map, though I have tested it throughout by the authorities.
In Monk's *Narrative* (p. 90) it is said that he marched on 'the 14th from
Glendowart (Glen Dochart) to Glen Lochee, about sixteen miles.'   The
latter glen cannot be, as Mr. Mackay holds, Glen Lochay, because Monk
tells us that in the evening some men were seen marching to Glen Strae,
which was quite invisible from any part of Glen Lochay.   It must have
been near Loch Awe.

[4] *Ib.*   Monk was on the 19th at Kinnell, close to Killin.   Clarke to
Errington, *Thurloe*, ii. 475.

route by which Middleton could reach the far north from Loch Rannoch, the route by the pass which connects the upper reaches of the Garry and the Spey, through which the Highland Railway at present runs. Either by his own intuition, or more likely by Monk's orders, Morgan had abandoned his eccentric march to Braemar, and posted himself at Ruthven on the Spey. Informed of Middleton's approach, Morgan crossed the watershed on July 19, and, posting himself at Dalnaspidal, where the stream brings down the waters of Loch Garry on the southern side of the pass,[1] made preparations to pass the night on a tolerably level piece of ground which had been used for generations as a camping-place by troops on the march. Before his men had alighted they perceived Middleton's forces on their way from Loch Rannoch approaching along the western side of the loch with the same object in view.[2] As Middleton debouched from the defile, with 800 horse and a larger number of unmounted men toiling after them at some distance, Morgan ordered his comparatively fresh cavalry to charge, and Middleton, recognising the hopelessness of the situation, gave directions to his worn followers to face round and retreat. An English party which had been in the van were thus brought into the rear. They acquitted themselves bravely for a short time, and then they too joined in the flight of their comrades, many of whom slipped off their horses and made for the bogs. Most of the men escaped, but of the horses—not easily replaced in the

Side notes: July 19. The fight at Dalnaspidal.

[1] " Since my last, the general resolved [on] easy motions after our hard marches, and to drive Middleton's almost tired forces on Colonel Morgan, who was fresh in Ruthven." Clarke to Errington, July 21, *Thurloe*, ii. 483. This disposes of the view that the two forces met in a casual encounter.

[2] Mr. J. T. Clark, the Librarian of the Advocates' Library, who knows the country well, tells me that the way over the hills from Loch Rannoch is passable in summer. Gwynn's Narrative (*Memorials*, 183) agrees with Morgan's despatch of July 22 (*Merc. Pol.* E, 806, 13) in placing the fight at the north end of Loch Garry, near which was the usual camping-ground for troops going in either direction over the pass now crossed by the Highland Railway.

Highlands—as many as three hundred were captured, and amongst them the general's sumpter-horse with his despatches and commission.[1]

With this the war, so far as fighting was concerned, virtually came to an end. Prisoners were shipped for Barbados,[2] and in August Monk turned upon Glencairn in the country about Aberfoyle, whilst Morgan was sent northwards to rouse Middleton from his lair in Caithness. It was a campaign of the torch, not of the sword. "Myself," wrote Monk on August 5, "am now destroying the country on this side the hills, where the enemy used to shelter themselves in winter."[3] Before this drastic treatment resistance withered away. By the end of August some of the noblemen who had supported the Royal cause were preparing to submit, and, as they were assured of easy terms, their example was before long readily followed.[4] Middleton himself, indeed, remained in the country till the following spring, but the rising had virtually come to an end long before. What had not come to an end was the bitterness with which the Scottish population regarded the masterful strangers who had planted the yoke of England upon their country's neck.

Aug.
Fire and destruction.

Aug.-Sept.
Submission of most of the nobility.

End of the rising.

[1] *Merc. Pol.* E, 806, 13.

[2] Monk to the Protector, Aug. 1, Firth's *Scotland and the Protectorate*.

[3] Monk to the Protector, Aug. 5 ; from the Camp at Lence (perhaps Lennox), *Thurloe*, ii. 526.

[4] Monk had some difficulty in dealing with persons sent up as hostages for the good behaviour of those who had submitted.   On Sept. 5 he writes to the Protector, asking whether he ' shall take Lowland security of very good bonds for them, two of them being young gentlemen students in the universities, and a third is so very fat that he could not come by land, but was sent by water.'   Firth's *Scotland and the Protectorate*.

CHAPTER XXXIII

A DOUBLE NEGOTIATION

THE mission of Joachim Hane to investigate the condition of the French sea-coast fortresses [1] may be taken as an indication that in October 1653 Oliver had still before his mind a possible intervention in favour of the French Protestants, which would bring with it a close alliance with Spain. In the course of November two reports were received from Hane. In the first he explained that Havre was unfortified, and that to place it in a state of defence would require 6,000*l*. In the second, dated from Rochelle, he announced that one of the two towers which guarded the town had been destroyed by fire, but that the other was being repaired by the King's Governor. [2] After his examination of Rochelle, Hane took passage in a vessel bound for Bordeaux, but having been recognised by a Scot, he was marked out by the authorities for the torture-chamber and the gallows, and it was only after a succession of hair-breadth escapes that some four months later he succeeded in reaching England. It is significant that in these regions which Cromwell anxiously desired to liberate from their oppressors, his agent failed to

Marginal notes:
1653. Oct. Hane's mission to France.
Oct. 25. His report on Havre,
Nov. 5. and on Rochelle.
His subsequent adventures.

---

[1] See p. 55.

[2] The two reports signed by Israel Bernard, and dated $\frac{Oct. 25}{Nov. 4}$, and Nov. $\frac{5}{15}$ (*Thurloe*, i. 553, 578), have been identified as Hane's by Mr. Firth, who published the Journal in 1896. I have no doubt that the place mentioned in the first letter is Havre, the only port passed by Hane on his voyage from Rye to Quillebœuf, where he landed.

meet with a single person to whose sympathies he could appeal.

It was, in fact, from the Huguenots of Languedoc rather than from those of Guienne that calls for English assistance were heard.   Early in November, Dr. More,[1] a Scot residing in Nîmes, arrived in London to plead their cause.[2]   About four weeks later it occurred to Barrière that a report on the position of the Protestants of the South from some one better known in England would receive greater attention, and for this employment he pitched upon Stouppe, the minister of the French congregation at the Savoy.   Having formerly acted as tutor to the children of a Protestant nobleman of Dauphiné, the Marquis of Montbrun,[3] he was peculiarly fitted to collect intelligence in the Rhone valley.   Stouppe, however, declared that he would not go without a direct authorisation from Condé, and it was some time before this authorisation was obtained. In the meanwhile he took an opportunity of conversing with influential personages in England, who assured him that if the Huguenots would commence a rising, a succour of 15,000 men would be sent to their aid.[4]

Nov.
Visit of Dr.
More.

Dec.
Barrière
proposes
to send
Stouppe into
France.

There had already been a talk of sending Sexby at the head of 6,000 men on the same service if Spain would undertake to pay them, but the design had been brought to an end by the news which reached England in November that the Spanish fleet, which had lingered in the Gironde since the fall of Bordeaux, had quitted its station and returned to its own country.[5]

---

[1] He is spoken of sometimes as a minister, sometimes as a physician.

[2] Bordeaux to Brienne, Nov. $\frac{14}{24}$; Bordeaux to Mazarin, Dec. $\frac{1}{11}$, *R.O. Transcripts.*

[3] Grandson of the Huguenot leader, whose title he inherited.   Garcel, *Bibliothèque Hist. et Literaire du Dauphiné*, iii. 442.   Compare the advice of Lamilitière, July $\frac{11}{21}$, *Guizot*, i. App. vi.

[4] Barrière to Condé, undated, but about Dec. $\frac{5}{15}$.   The writer says that Stouppe was ' un homme sans interest, et asseurément un homme d'honneur,' *Chantilly Transcripts.*   This appreciation is very different from that of Bishop Burnet.

[5] See Ellis Leighton's letter at p. 119, note 1.

It is probable that these projects were, to a great extent, the work of the men of the nominated Parliament, eager to support the Protestant cause, and not only dreaming of a complete toleration in England in which even Catholics were to share,[1] but expecting, it must be supposed, that a similar toleration would be accorded at least to Protestant Englishmen in Spain. To Oliver, on his accession to the Protectorate, the question must have appeared more complicated. It cannot be thought that a close connection with Spain attracted him greatly. There were, however, reasons weighing heavily with him in favour of a Spanish alliance. Not only was he personally disinclined to leave the French Protestants to their ruin, if it should appear that they really stood in need of his protection, but in this view of the situation he was pushed forward by the majority of the Council, and especially by Lambert, to whom he owed much and whose influence in the army was considerable. Nor were political arguments wanting to throw weight into the balance on the same side. It was a palpable danger to the Protectorate that the exiled Stuarts were still residing on French soil, and it was easy to draw the inference that Mazarin was only waiting his opportunity when at last Spain should have been beaten down in the field, to bend his energies to the restoration of his own master's cousin to the English throne, and thereby to bring England into subservience to the crown of France.

Policy of the nominated Parliament.

Hesitation of the Protector.

As a matter of fact Mazarin was far more inclined to smooth away the difficulties lying before his feet than to anticipate a distant future. He now set himself to meet Oliver's anxiety by the despatch of a special agent, the Baron de Baas,[2] who was to convey his personal assurances that a Stuart restoration would meet with no favour in France. When Baas reached England early in

Mazarin not really dangerous.

Mission of Baron de Baas.

---

[1] See *infra*, Ellis Leighton's letter at p. 119, note 1.

[2] Baas to Mazarin, Jan. $\frac{3}{13}$, *R.O. Transcripts*. Baas was the elder brother of D'Artagnan, whose name has acquired a greater celebrity in fiction than in history.

January, he found that though Bordeaux, who had not yet recognised the Protectorate,[1] was treated with the utmost
coolness, that coolness did not extend to himself.
He was well received, especially when it appeared
that his business was to give assurances that if the Protector
would ally himself with France, Charles Stuart would be prohibited from remaining on French soil.[2]   On the 26th
Baas took leave, bearing with him counter-propositions from Oliver, of the nature of which we have no
knowledge, but which may very well have stipulated for
guarantees for the good treatment of the Huguenots.[3]   Nothing
short of this, it may be believed, would satisfy the Council,[4] in
addition to the stoppage of the attacks on English commerce
by French privateers—especially by those in Charles's service
—of which Oliver complained openly to the envoy.[5]

*1654.
Jan.
Baas's pro-
position.*

*Jan. 26
Baas takes
leave.*

Pending Mazarin's reply, Oliver continued, as he had
hitherto done, to listen to Cardenas and Barrière.   Though
Cardenas fully understood that no positive decision
would be taken till the Dutch war was ended,[6] he
considered the prospect of an English diversion in
Guienne sufficiently hopeful.   Towards the end of
January Mazerolles, one of Condé's confidants,
landed in England, bringing with him that Conan
who had been employed more than two years before to solicit
English aid for Rochelle,[7] and who now returned to repeat his

*Negotia-
tion of
Cardenas
and
Barrière.*

*Mazerolles
and Conan
in England.*

---

[1] Bordeaux to Brienne, Jan. $\frac{19}{29}$, *R.O. Transcripts.*

[2] This does not appear from the despatches of Baas himself, but is
stated in a letter from Thurloe to Whitelocke, Feb. 24, Whitelocke's
Swedish Embassy, ii. 58.

[3] See p. 117, note 4.

[4] Pickering described Oliver to Baas as a man 'que ses amis avoient
presque chargé de la protection de l'Estat, et qui en toutes les grandes
affaires se soumet au Conseil d'Angleterre.'   Baas to Mazarin, Jan. $\frac{15}{25}$,
R.O. Transcripts.

[5] Bordeaux to Brienne, $\frac{\text{Jan. 26}}{\text{Feb. 5}}$, *ib.*

[6] Cardenas to Philip IV., Jan. $\frac{9}{19}$, *Simancas MSS.* 2,529.

[7] See vol. ii. p. 155.

request.[1] There can be no doubt that the pleading of these men made considerable impression on Oliver, as he sent for

Feb.
Stouppe
to report
on the
French
Protest-
ants. Stouppe, urging him to undertake the mission to the French Protestants for which he had been named by Barrière two months before.[2] He was to find out whether if they received help from England they would be ready to take arms, and whether Condé would help them in the enterprise. Either on this or on some

A Hugue-
not rising
suggested. subsequent occasion Oliver suggested that the command might be given to one of Condé's officers, the Prince of Tarente. England, he said, had ruined the party of the Huguenots, and it was for England to re-establish it.[3] Unwise as was the policy thus sketched out, the interest taken by Oliver in the fortunes of the Huguenots was at least founded on existing facts. Scarcely a post arrived from France without bringing news of some fresh attack upon them.[4] Whether the best way of assisting them was to stir them to resistance against their sovereign was another question.

It did not follow that because Oliver was making sympathetic inquiries into the situation and wishes of the Huguenots,

Discovery
of a
Royalist
conspiracy. he was prepared to engage himself to Spain before receiving the information he sought. To bring this about some occurrence was required which would have the effect of irritating him yet further against France. Such an occurrence was the discovery of a Royalist conspiracy

[1] Barrière to Condé, Jan. $\frac{18}{28}$, *Chantilly Transcripts* ; Bordeaux to Brienne, $\frac{\text{Jan. 30}}{\text{Feb. 9}}$, *R.O. Transcripts*.   [2] See p. 112.

[3] "Il l'entretient bien une heure et demie de l'estat des affaires de ceux de la religion de France, luy demanda fort s'il croioit que estant asseurez d'estre assistez par l'Angleterre ils voulussent prendre les armes, et si V. A. voudroit se joindre à eux. Il luy dit qu'il n'en doubtoit pas. Cromwel l'exhorta fort à faire le voyage et tesmoigna avoir passion pour cela, disant que l'Angleterre avoit ruiné le party, et qu'il falloit que l'Angleterre le restablît." Barrière to Condé, Feb. $\frac{10}{20}$, *Chantilly Transcripts*. On the choice of a commander see *Mémoires du Prince de Tarente*, 169–171.

[4] See Thurloe's French Intelligence of these months, and Benoît, *Hist. de l'Edit de Nantes*, 161–186

about a week after Stouppe's mission had been decided on. During the last two months of the preceding year a little group of Royalists had been accustomed to meet at various taverns in London, where they plotted over their cups a scheme for the overthrow of the existing government, and the restoration of the King.   One of their number, a Captain Dutton, rode about England to collect adherents who were to come up to London and join in seizing Whitehall, St. James's, the Tower, and the guards about the city.   A Colonel Whitely was to go to France to bring over commissions from Charles, but there was a difficulty about paying his expenses.   The conspirators were asked to contribute, but most of them declined to pay a farthing, and for a time the meetings came to an end.   Conspiracies of so loose a texture are apt to breed informers, and on February 16 one of the would-be insurgents, Roger Cotes,

Feb. 16.
Arrest
of the
plotters,

Feb. 17.
who are
committed
to the
Tower.

was telling all that he knew to the Council.   That night eleven of his companions were arrested at the Ship Tavern in the Old Bailey,[1] which they had probably visited at Cotes's invitation, and were on the following day committed to the Tower.   Cotes, who was amongst the number, was discharged on the 24th.[2]   This ridiculous conspiracy was not of a nature to call for severe punishment, and none of those concerned in it were even brought to trial.

Yet, ridiculous as the plot was, it had its serious side.   In the course of the examinations it came out that there existed a

A secret
Royalist
committee.

committee or council of Royalists authorised by Charles himself, and apparently consisting of Royalist noblemen and gentlemen preparing for an insur-

---

[1] Examination of R. Cotes, Feb. 16 ; examination of T. Smith, Feb. 24, *Thurloe*, ii. 75 ; *A Full and Perfect Relation of the Great Plot*, 130, 1.   A Roger Cotes was one of the destructive party in the nominated Parliament (see vol. ii. p. 309).   If he was the same man as the informer, the bitterness of that party against Cromwell must have procured his admission to a Royalist conspiracy even whilst the nominated Parliament was still in power.

[2] C. Order Book, *Interr.* I, 75, pp. 123, 127.

rection which would doubtless, when the time came, be conducted with far greater energy than had been shown by these poor tavern-haunters. The formation of such a committee had indeed been proposed to Charles as early as November 1649.[1] When it actually came into existence is unknown, but towards the end of 1653, or in the early part of the following year, its members declined to meddle further with the projects of the exiled court, and their place had been taken by a body of more energetic Royalists who styled themselves the 'Sealed Knot,' and at once entered on active preparations for a rising against the existing Government.[2]

The Sealed Knot.

It was already known to Thurloe that this committee was engaged in a design which was to be communicated to Charles as soon as it reached maturity,[3] and it can hardly be doubted that the knowledge that plots against himself were being hatched in France must have somewhat lessened Oliver's inclination to enter into an alliance with that power. Nor was it a hopeful sign that Baas, who had gone back as the bearer of Oliver's counter-propositions, had not yet returned, especially if, as was probably the case, he had carried with him a demand that the French Government should enter into some engagement to give to the Huguenots everything to which they were entitled by the Royal Edicts.[4] Taking these two facts together, there is enough to account for an irritation against France in

Delay in Baas's return.

Oliver irritated against France.

---

[1] Coventry to Nicholas, Nov. 12, 1649, *Nicholas Papers*, i. 154.

[2] The passage on which this statement is made veils the truth under commercial forms, as is usual in this correspondence. "Many of the principal old merchants in our parts had unhandsomely declined trusting. . . . 'Tis now settled in more hopeful hands." Sir M. Hobart to Charles, $\frac{Feb. 22}{March 4}$, *Clarendon MSS*. ii. No. 1,749.

[3] Intercepted Letters, Feb. 2, 6, *Thurloe*, ii. 64, 70.

[4] In his despatch of April $\frac{20}{30}$, Baas states that he had carried back proposals from the Protector, but does not say what they were. Considering that Oliver insisted for a long time on guarantees for the Huguenots, there is a strong probability that a part at least of his proposals referred to this subject.

Oliver's mind, of which Cardenas was not slow to take

Feb. 22.
Cardenas
proposes an
alliance
with Spain. advantage. On the 22nd he had a long audience, in the course of which he assured the Protector that he had received powers from his master to treat for an alliance. For some days Oliver kept back his

Feb. 28.
Oliver's
answer. answer, and it was not till the 28th, the day on which the Dutch ambassadors returned to England to settle the terms of peace,[1] and all danger of the prolongation of the naval war was virtually at an end, that he sent Thurloe with his reply.

In a proposal communicated to the representative of his Catholic Majesty, deep silence, if only for form's sake, was

He offers
an alliance
with Spain. preserved as to the woes of the French Protestants. Thurloe contented himself with the explanation that Oliver was, before all things, anxious to maintain his domestic position, apparently to countervail the machinations of the Stuart Princes who were under French protection. For this and other reasons discreetly veiled in silence he preferred alliance with Spain to one with France. Yet not only—as

Financial
objections to
a war with
France. Thurloe candidly admitted—was there no popular demand for a war of aggression, but the interruption of trade and the increased taxation to which it must lead would certainly give rise to the gravest discontent. What, therefore, was required was an inexpensive mode of carrying on war, and this could only be attained if Spain were willing to

Spain asked
to supply
the money. bear, if not the whole, at least the greater part of the expense. If that was admitted as the basis of the understanding, the Protector would be ready to declare war upon France, and to offer powerful assistance to Condé. Though Cardenas vainly urged Thurloe to name the sum he had in his mind, he forwarded the proposal to Madrid and Brussels, urging the importance of meeting Oliver's wishes as far as possible.[2]

A suggestion in itself so extraordinary, and still more extraordinary as emanating from the conqueror of Dunbar and

[1] See p. 67.
[2] Cardenas to Philip IV., March $\frac{3}{13}$, *Guizot*, ii. App. vi. *bis*, No. 1.

Worcester, undoubtedly calls for explanation, and that explanation can only be conjecturally supplied. There were at this time amongst the men who surrounded Oliver three different parties, as far as foreign policy was concerned. The first, that of Lambert and the officers supported by a majority of the Council, clamoured for a war with France ; the second, in a minority in the Council, was headed by Pickering and Strickland, and advocated a close alliance with France ; whilst a third, best represented by the sagacious Thurloe, was indeed desirous of coming to an understanding with France in order to put an end to the existing maritime warfare, but would have rested in the main on an alliance with the Protestant States, without taking part in the war raging between the two great continental powers.[1]

Differences of opinion on foreign policy.

[1] " Ad negotia Angliæ penitus dignoscenda, sciendum duas fore in Anglia factiones quæ Cromwellio adhuc adhærent et quibus ipse aurem præbet :—

" Una quæ illi suadet, ut ad sese stabiliendum fœdus ineat arctum cum Hispania et, si negotia intestina non impediant, Gallis bellum inferat, Principi Condæo suppetias ministret et urbes quasdam maritimas oræ Britannicæ oppositas occupare tentet. Et hæc fuit illa factio quæ apud eum prævalebat bellum facere contra Hollandos ut vires eorum minuerentur quominus possent Mazarino opitulari. Eo tempore misit Cromwellius emissarium primo ad Parisios qui postea ad Burdigalliam ibat, cui nomen et titulus Colonel Seikerby," *i.e.* Sexby, " vir obscuræ originis, sed acutissimi ingenii, et ejus persuasione et sociorum suorum in exercitu (quorum ille nunc apud Hispaniæ legatum agens est, utpote minoris auctoritatis homo) ita potuit apud Cromwellium ut, renitente et contra argumentante Thurleo (qui primi ferè ministri locum apud Cromwellium obtinet, et præcipuus est Angliæ Secretarius) concessum fuerit sex mille homines et naves quasdam ad auxilium Burdigallensium mittere, sed ea solummodo lege ut Rex Hispaniæ copias illas suo argento conduceret. Sed dum hoc agebatur Burdigala dedita est et classis Hispanica recedere coacta. Omnes illi qui ex hac parte stant volunt indulgentiam dare Catholicis et sæpius disputarunt tum in Parlamento tum in conciliis secretioribus ut libertas conscientiæ illis concederetur.

" Est alia pars quæ ex opposito Cromwellio suadent, ut se caput et ducem faciat fœderis Protestantis, et hi omnes, et præcipue secretarius Thurlæus, qui nunc unicus quasi est intimus Cromwellii consiliarius. Et hi volunt quod pacem paciscatur cum Hollandis, et ut potius Mazarino

Though the Dutch war was hastening to an end before the
end of February, the commotions in Scotland showed no signs

Oliver
hesitates.

of abating, and undoubtedly neither Oliver nor any
other sober person would decide for embarking at
the cost of the Commonwealth upon a war of which it was
impossible to see the end. Yet it was precisely this for which
the military party was heading, and those who are content to
refer the actions of public men to single motives will be ready
with the suggestion that Oliver, having no wish to contract an
alliance with Spain, merely intended to demonstrate to Lambert
and his fellows how hopeless it was to expect him to find the
supplies without which it would be unwise for England to

quam Hispanis adhæreat, licet suadent ut neutrisque fidat, sed conetur ut
Hollandi et Dani et Sueci (concurrente præcipue secretario Oxostirnio)
magis pendeant ab eo quam a Gallo vel Hispano, et instructio fuit in hunc
finem data legato extraordinario Whitlocki, et hoc novi ex uno qui
præsens erat quando Cromwellius illi valedicebat et dixit ' omnimodo
trahas Suecos ad fœdus Protestans de novo instaurandum.'

"Et ad hos nunc Cromwellius magis animum inclinat, et statuit apud
se, nisi intestinum cum Scotis bellum impediat eum, junctis copiis
maritimis ubique mercatura facienda legem imponere, et se pro Protes-
tantium protectore venditare, si aliquid ultro in Catholicos non moliatur,
quod timendum est.

"Verum est quod multum pendebit ex successu Scotorum Montanorum
quin si periculum Cromwellio de iis immineat pacem et neutralitatem
conabitur cum omnibus vicinis habere, sed si illis subactis per otium illi
licuerit extra Angliam arma proferre, consilia quæ pro præsente amplec-
titur omnia tendunt ad fœdus cum Protestantibus totius Europæ et ad
bellum interim per omnimoda artificia inter duas coronas alendum." Ellis
Leighton to —— ? March. *Vatican Archives, Nunziatura di Fiandra.*
Ellis Leighton, a son of Alexander Leighton, the Star Chamber martyr,
had become a Roman Catholic towards the end of 1652 (Hyde to
Nicholas, Dec. 20, 1652, *Clarendon MSS.* ii. No. 890). I imagine that
the plan of Sexby to land at Bordeaux at the head of 6,000 men was
stopped by the Spanish fleet leaving the Garonne, which was known in
England in Nov. 1653, rather than by the fall of Bordeaux in July, at
which time it was proposed to allow Cardenas to hire ships, but, as far as
we know, not to hire soldiers. Leighton, it will be observed, says
nothing of the French party in the Council of which there is frequent
mention in Bordeaux' despatches.

embark upon the war. Those who are acquainted with the involved character of Oliver's thought will hesitate before they accept so simple a solution of the problem. If he was dragged on by the military party in the direction of a war with France, there were hesitations enough in his own mind. He would doubtless have preferred to safeguard the position of the Huguenots with the help of France rather than of Spain ; but if this was not to be—and recent events had made him doubtful whether it would be—he had rather safeguard them with the help of Spain than not at all, to say nothing of his fear lest France should encourage the Stuart Pretenders. In the meanwhile he could patiently await the answer from Madrid, and even Lambert could hardly press him to hurry into a war before that answer was known.

If such thoughts as these were jostling together in Oliver's mind, it was hardly likely that he would refuse at least a hearing to a fresh overture brought by Baas from Mazarin on February 28, especially as it was accompanied by orders to Bordeaux to recognise the Protectorate. It may, indeed, be accepted as certain that Baas had no word to say about the Huguenots, but he offered in his master's name to assist the Protector with 4,000 horse in the event of his besieging Dunkirk, as well as to distract the Spanish army by simultaneously attacking some other town in the neighbourhood.[1] It was not, however, till March 5 that Baas was allowed to see the Protector, and shortly after that date Bordeaux was refused an audience on the ground that the Protector was unwell, though, as the ambassador bitterly complained, he was not only out walking two days before, but on the very evening of the day for which the audience had

Feb. 28. Overtures from Mazarin.

Coolness in the treatment of Bordeaux.

---

[1] These particulars are given in the instructions sent to Bordeaux on July $\frac{6}{16}$, *R.O. Transcripts*. The only question which arises is whether the offer was brought by Baas on his first or second visit. Considering that nothing of this sort was mentioned in Thurloe's letter to Whitelocke (see p. 114, note 2), and that Mazarin is not likely to have made two large offers at one time, I have no hesitation in connecting this one with the second visit.

been asked had publicly entertained one of the Dutch ambassadors. Meanwhile, the ears of the Frenchmen were filled with rumours of designs for the seizure of the Isle of Rhé and the despatch of thirty ships to occupy the Gironde. Sexby, it was said, was to raise two English regiments for a descent on Guienne, and three thousand Irishmen were to be levied for the same purpose.[1]

Alarmed by the turn of events in England, Mazarin did everything in his power to reassure the Protector on the points on which he was most sensitive. In a memorandum forwarded to his two representatives he informed them, with the evident intention of having his words repeated at Whitehall, that Cardenas had boasted of having cajoled Oliver by his flatteries. They were further to give assurances that if the Protector would join France rather than Spain, he might have an article in the treaty of alliance binding the King of France to give no assistance direct or indirect to any enemy of the present government—in other words binding him to refuse to countenance any designs of the House of Stuart to regain its position in England.[2]

March $\frac{1}{2}\frac{5}{5}$.
Mazarin reassures the Protector.

Scarcely had this memorandum been despatched than news reached Mazarin which convinced him that he must bid higher. The Archduke Leopold had advised Cardenas to offer 120,000l. a year without waiting for an answer from Madrid.[3] Mazarin at once instructed Baas to offer the same sum, and to go further if it proved necessary in order to clinch the bargain. He was also to remind Oliver that France invariably fulfilled her engagements, whereas Spain was seldom in case to perform hers. It was notorious that Condé, now that he was no longer necessary, had

Mazarin hears news from Brussels.
March $\frac{1}{2}\frac{1}{1}$.
The Archduke directs Cardenas to offer 120,000l. a year.
March $\frac{1}{2}\frac{7}{7}$.
Mazarin bids against him.

[1] Baas to Mazarin, March $\frac{2}{13}$, $\frac{6}{16}$, $\frac{13}{23}$; Bordeaux to Brienne, March $\frac{9}{19}$, $\frac{19}{22}$, *R.O. Transcripts.* The French ambassador had an informant amongst the deputies from Bordeaux.

[2] Memorandum, March $\frac{15}{25}$, *ib.*

[3] The Archduke to Cardenas, March $\frac{11}{21}$; Navarro to Cardenas, March $\frac{11}{21}$, *Guizot,* ii. App. vi. *bis,* Nos. 2, 3.

been left by the Spanish Government in a state of beggary.[1]
To the two continental powers it seemed that England was put
up to auction, and that Oliver was the salesman.

Of Oliver's power to damage that State against which he
turned his arms there could be no reasonable doubt.　In ad-

The fleet at
Ports-
mouth.

dition to the fleet which was confronting the Dutch
in the North Sea, another was gathering at Portsmouth.　An agent sent by Bordeaux to investigate
the condition of the latter reported that fifty-six ships had already arrived, that fifteen were at sea, and that fifty more were
expected before long.　If weight was to be given to the talk of
the officers, this powerful force was to be directed against the
coast of France, and most probably against the Isle of Rhé.　By
the time that this information reached Bordeaux, he learned that

March 18.
Boast of
Barrière.

Barrière, who had recently visited the Low Countries
to consult with Condé, had boasted after his return
that his master would soon be at the head of 14,000
men, and would be furnished in England with fifteen ships.
Mazerolles, it was added, was about to start for Spain to bring
back the money needed for the support of these armaments.[2]

Nevertheless the French envoys did not regard the situation
as in any way desperate.　Cromwell, it appears, had been

The
French
envoys
do not
despair.

greatly annoyed by the discovery that Mazarin had
so rapidly made himself acquainted with his negotiation with Spain, and was inclined to throw the
blame on Condé's indiscretion.[3]　Nor was he well
satisfied that, at the motion of the Archduke, Cardenas had
offered him a bare 120,000*l.* a year—far too little, as he plainly

---

[1] Mazarin to Baas, March $\frac{17}{27}$, *Guizot*, ii. App. vii. No. 6.　The French
offer was 1,200,000 livres, or 400,000 crowns.　The French livre was
worth 2*s.* and the crown 6*s.*　Malynes's *Lex Mercatoria* (ed. 1660),
Amphithalami, B. p. 32.

[2] Bordeaux to Mazarin, March $\frac{20}{30}$; Bordeaux to Brienne, March $\frac{20}{30}$,
$\frac{\text{March 23}}{\text{April 2}}$, *R.O. Transcripts*.

[3] Barrière to Condé, $\frac{\text{March 23}}{\text{April 3}}$, *Chantilly Transcripts*.　Burnet (i. 72)
states that Oliver afterwards characterised Condé thus: "Stultus est et
garrulus, et venditur a suis Cardinali."

told Barrière, to support a war.[1] The final answer from Spain had not yet been given, and it would be some weeks before it could be expected to arrive. Oliver, accordingly, was at some pains to show that he kept his ears open on both sides. On

April 4.
Commissioners appointed to treat with both ambassadors.

April 6.
Oliver asks Cardenas for more money.

April 4 the Council named two sets of commissioners, the one to treat with Cardenas, the other with Bordeaux.[2] On the 6th, Oliver informed Cardenas that he was ready to authorise the continuance of the negotiation on the understanding that the proposed Spanish subsidy should be increased. Cardenas, indeed, who well knew the poverty of his master, did not venture to speak hopefully on the subject, but it was probably at this time that he suggested that

Proposed siege of Calais.

the Spanish and English forces might engage in a joint siege of Calais, on the understanding that, after its surrender, the place should be given up to England.[3]

Now that the treaty with the Dutch was actually signed, it seemed hardly possible to postpone much longer a decision

Oliver said to wish to avoid war.

Talks of aiding Condé surreptitiously,

which, according to every indication, would be more or less favourable to Spain, though rumours were not wanting that Oliver, if he were free to follow his own inclination, would be glad to avoid war with either State.[4] At one time he talked of offering surreptitious aid to Condé, which, as he thought, would not entail a public breach with France, and justified the action by the precedent of the assistance given by France to the United Provinces after the Treaty of Vervins had been signed.[5] To Barrière, on the other hand, he talked as

---

[1] "M. le Protecteur nous dit que ce qui avoit empesché qu'il n'eust repondu à l'ambassadeur d'Espagne estoit que les offres qu'il luy avoit faict estoient si loin de ses pretentions." Barrière to Condé, April $\frac{7}{17}$, *Chantilly Transcripts*.

[2] C. Order Book, *Interr.* I, 75, p. 214.

[3] Barrière to Condé, April $\frac{7}{17}$, *Chantilly Transcripts*; Baas to Mazarin, April $\frac{20}{30}$, *R.O. Transcripts*.

[4] Bordeaux to Brienne, April $\frac{10}{20}$, *ib*.

[5] Baas to Mazarin, April $\frac{13}{23}$, *ib*.

if the question was merely one of money, and declared that
yet assures
Barrière
that he will
join Spain
if his
terms are
accepted. if Cardenas would satisfy his demands, the required
assistance would undoubtedly be given.[1] It was
probably with a view to keep open a door for a more
friendly understanding with France, in the event
of the Spanish negotiation breaking down, that he arranged for the presence of a gentleman belonging to the French
April 15.
A dinner
at Henry
Crom-
well's. embassy at a dinner given by Henry Cromwell to a
number of influential officers. The conversation
was likely to be extremely hostile to France, and
might, therefore, create an impression, not altogether
without foundation, that the Protector was being dragged
forward by the army further than he was himself inclined to go.
If this be the explanation, the exuberant speech of the officers
went a long way to answer Oliver's expectation. They talked
of the succour they were speedily to bear to their Protestant
brethren in France, of the impossibility of establishing a
durable peace with that country as long as a cardinal or any
other member of his profession was at the head of the
Government.[2]

At the French embassy little interest was taken in the
question whether Oliver was dragged on by his officers or not.[3]
Feeling
at the
French
embassy. Bordeaux had learnt that the design of an attack on
Guienne had reached an advanced stage, and the
language of Henry Cromwell's guests was not likely
to dissipate the belief that danger was at hand. Baas, whose
special mission it had been to reconcile the Protector to France,
Baas plots
for a
movement
in the army
against the
Protector. was irritated beyond measure, and within a day or two
after the banquet, he placed himself in communica-
tion with a French Anabaptist physician, named Naudin, either instigating him to stir up hostile action

---

[1] Barrière to Condé, April $\frac{14}{24}$, *Chantilly Transcripts.*

[2] Patt to Mazarin, April $\frac{17}{27}$, *Guizot*, ii. App. viii. No. 3.

[3] "Ce que je puis juger de toutes les diverses choses qui viennent à
ma cognoissance, est que M. le Protecteur incline assez à la paix, mais que
la plus grande partie des ministres y répugnent." Baas to Mazarin,
April $\frac{11}{21}$, *R.O. Transcripts.*

against the Protector amongst his Anabaptist friends in the army, or at all events listening complacently to the plan as it was unfolded by Naudin. Naudin applied to Colonel Buller, who was certainly in no hurry to betray the dangerous secret.[1]

On April 19, a day or two after his first interview with Naudin, Baas took the opportunity of an audience to vent his indignation on the Protector. Condé's agents, he told him, boasted that they were to be supplied with fifteen ships and 4,000 men for a descent on Guienne, whilst Cardenas had written to Brussels that the simultaneous appointment of commissioners to treat with France and Spain had been resolved on by his advice; that Whitelocke had proposed a triple alliance between England,

April 19.
Baas
reproaches
the
Protector.

---

[1] The date is approximately fixed by that of Naudin's interview with Buller, which took place on April 18 (*Thurloe*, ii. 352), and Naudin must have seen Baas on that day at the latest. Bordeaux gave, after the affair was discovered, the following account of it :— " Il sera sans doubte venu à vostre cognoissance que depuis deux mois un nommé Naudin, medecin François, avoit esté trouver ledit sieur de Baas, et s'estoit offert de gaigner quelques officiers de l'armée, mesme quelque place, et fomenter une division dans cet estat, si la France vouloit appuyer ce dessein, presupposant que nous ne debvions pas rejetter des propositions si advantagieux, puisque ce régime estoit entièrement porté à préferer l'amitié de l'Espagne à celle de la France. Quoique ceste ouverture, dans un temps auquel toutes nos instances pour l'accommodement ne produiroient aucun effect, pust estre escoultée, néantmoins le dict sieur de Baas ne se voulut point engager sur ce qu'il ne croyait pas que la Cour eust intention d'entrer dans de semblables entreprises tant qu'elle verroit jour à l'accommodement, le dict Naudin ne laissa pas de temps en temps de le revenir veoir, croyant sans doubte que sa Ma^te luy envoyeroit de nouveaux ordres. Ce commerce a continué sans ma participation jusques au jour que le dict Naudin a esté faict prisonnier." Bordeaux to Brienne, June $\frac{15}{25}$, *R.O. Transcripts*. The only point in dispute, therefore, is whether Baas invited Naudin to his house, or was visited without a previous invitation by Naudin. The latter always asserted that Baas began the intrigue (*Thurloe*, ii. 309, 351, 412), whilst Buller, on the other hand, agrees with Baas (*ib.* ii. 352) ; Buller, however, could only know what he was told by Naudin, and I suspect that Baas really invited Naudin, but that they agreed that the latter was to represent himself as the originator of the design. It is not, however, a point of much consequence.

Spain, and Sweden;[1] that the Protector himself had favourably received the Spanish offer to assist him in gaining Calais. After these revelations Baas ended by an ironical request that the Protector would extricate him with honour from this labyrinth, and would lighten up the darkness which, at present, clouded his sight.

Oliver had little expected to receive such full information on those schemes which he was most anxious to conceal. His countenance fell and his words dropped from his mouth more slowly than was his wont. Pickering, who, as was usual when the French language was employed, acted as interpreter, expounded the Protector's utterance as implying that he had no doubt listened to the proposals referred to, because the interest of the State required that he should hearken to every proposition brought before him, but that he had certainly not made them a subject of negotiation. Moreover, he could not hinder people from publishing any stories they pleased. After this halting explanation, Pickering conveniently remembered that his Highness had an engagement which made it impossible to prolong the conversation, though he would be glad to resume it on a more fitting occasion.

Yet, angry as the Frenchmen were, the information which they from time to time received led them to believe that Oliver had no personal grievance against France, and it is probable that if France would have yielded to his wishes he would at this time, in spite of Lambert and the officers, have dropped the negotiation with Spain. In fact, on April 20, the day after the Protector's stormy interview with Baas, there was a long discussion in the Council on the merits of the two policies, and though there was a pronounced difference on the subject, the general opinion, doubtless with the approval of the Protector, was on the side of a war against Spain in alliance with France. On that side the plea of the

A hesitating explanation.

Oliver unwilling to break with France.

---

[1] This was a mistake. Queen Christina had urged it—probably, as Whitelocke thought—at Pimentel's instigation; but Whitelocke had no authority to treat on the matter. Whitelocke's *Journal of the Swedish Embassy*, ii. 73.

necessity of either disarming or employing the 160 ships which were no longer needed against the Dutch, and the belief that an attack on the Spaniards in the Indies would be "the most profitable of any in the world," was strengthened by a call to uphold the standard of true religion. The Spaniard, it was said, "was the greatest enemy of the Protestant cause." On the other side, on which can be clearly distinguished the voice of Lambert, it was urged that the loss of the Spanish trade, through which there was an annual importation of no less than 150,000*l.* in bullion or in coined money, would more than counterbalance any gain that might be expected from a war of aggression. Evidently, however, this was but the view of the minority, and the Council was able calmly to consider what would be the best point of attack. On the whole they concluded it to be advisable to content themselves with the possession of Hispaniola and Havana in the first year, leaving the acquisition of the remainder of the Spanish West Indies to follow in its proper season.[1] It was, therefore, not without good ground that Colonel Dolman, who had done so much to bring about the peace with the United Provinces, informed Baas of his belief that the Protector had no wish to break with France, and almost at the same time a member of Oliver's family assured Bordeaux that, if the Protector had his will, he would remain at peace with all the world.[2] On one side and the other, however, the continuance of the conflicts at sea kept up the irritation. About the time when these consoling advices were received, three English men-of-war fell in with forty whalers from St. Malo, sank two and made prize of another. On the other side the Brest privateers ceaselessly made prey of English commerce. When the Protector brought the subject before the Council, one of its members—perhaps Lambert himself—asked if the wind were fair for Brest.[3]

Continuance of maritime warfare.

If Oliver was to break down this opposition—to say nothing

---

[1] Montague's Notes, April 20, *Clarke Papers*, iii. 203–206.
[2] Baas to Mazarin, April $\frac{20}{30}$, *R.O. Transcripts.*
[3] Bordeaux to Brienne, $\frac{\text{April 24}}{\text{May 4}}$, *ib.*

of his anxiety to satisfy his own mind—he must obtain from

Oliver
anxious to
obtain
assurances
from
Mazarin.

Mazarin some assurance that the edicts in favour of the Huguenots would be observed, and the English merchants compensated for their losses, which were reckoned in the City at what appeared in the eyes of Frenchmen to be the absurdly exaggerated sum of 2,000,000*l*.,[1] whilst little or no account was taken of losses inflicted on the

He knows
that
Cardenas
has received
a courier
from Spain.

French. Time pressed, as Oliver must have known that a courier from Madrid had brought despatches to Cardenas on or shortly before April 28 ;[2] and he cannot but have suspected that these despatches contained orders to give a definite answer respecting the subsidy which was to be paid as the price of the alliance with

May 1.
He offers
terms to
Baas.

England. Accordingly, on May 1, evidently with the hope of bending France to his terms, he sent for Baas, and after assuring him that though it was true that he had had communications with the enemies of France, he had as yet come to no understanding with them, or had any inclination to do so, he stated, on receiving a pledge of secrecy, the terms which would satisfy him. In the first place, no succour was to be given to any of the English Royal family except to the Queen-mother, who as a French princess might justly look to her nephew for support. In the second place he was ready to negotiate on propositions for a war against Spain, and particularly on a proposal for a joint attack on Dunkirk, which had been made by Mazarin earlier in the year,[3] but this was to be postponed till other questions had been settled. In the third place he asked that the liberties formerly conceded to the Huguenots might be confirmed, and that, if possible, Condé might be admitted to an accommodation. Finally the losses suffered by both sides might be referred to a commission, and in the meanwhile—Oliver apparently taking

---

[1] Baas, in his letter of May $\frac{4}{14}$, says that 20,000,000 was claimed. Evidently he reckons, as in other parts of his despatches, in livres.

[2] Barrière mentions the arrival of the courier in his letter to Condé of $\frac{\text{April 28}}{\text{May 8}}$, *Chantilly Transcripts*.

[3] See p. 121.

it for granted that those on the English side would be found to
outweigh those on the French—the King of France was to
deposit a sum, out of which the English merchants
might be satisfied. On the following day the sum
demanded was fixed at 200,000*l.*[1]

May 2.

After hearing these demands Baas spoke out. The French
Protestants, he said, were content with their lot. As for
Condé, he was now a mere burden upon the
Spanish treasury, and the King could listen to proposals for his return to France only if they came from one who
was already a friend or ally. He would never make it a condition of a treaty. It was impossible to say anything about the
deposit of 200,000*l.* till Bordeaux had been consulted. Then,
upon a request from Oliver that he would state the French
conditions, Baas replied that his master expected a league
against Spain. That, replied the Protector, would follow in
due course. The agreement with France would necessarily
lead to war with Spain, but it would be necessary to find
reasons for a breach, and such reasons would be sure to spring
up of themselves. If Baas were really desirous of concluding
the treaty, it could be finished in four days, before any one
knew that it was in hand.[2] The conference ended by a declaration from Baas that he had no power to treat without con-
sulting the ambassador. In rendering an account of this
conversation to Mazarin, the envoy recommended him, if he
wished to refuse payment, to place his refusal on the ground
that no security could be given by the present Government
until its title had been confirmed by a free Parliament.[3]

Baas's
defiance.

[1] Bordeaux to Brienne, May $\frac{4}{14}$; Baas to Mazarin, May $\frac{4}{14}$, *R.O.
Transcripts.*

[2] " Il me dit qu'infailliblement l'un seroit suivy de l'autre, et qu'il ne
pouvoit s'accommoder avec la France sans rompre avec l'Espagne, mais
qu'il falloit avoir des raisons, et qu'elles naistroient d'elles mesmes, et que
si je voulois, nostre traité seroit fait dans quatre jours, avant que personne
eust connoissance qu'il feust commencé." Baas to Mazarin, May $\frac{4}{14}$, *R.O.
Transcripts.*

[3] *Ib.*

In the taunting language he had used to the Protector Baas had perhaps been influenced by his conferences with Naudin, and by the confidence in the strength of the Levellers with which Naudin had inspired him.[1] It is clear that Oliver was seeking a plea to justify in his own eyes and in that of the Council the formation of an alliance with France. If Baas had had the diplomatic skill to recognise this fact, his mission would have been more successful than it was. His strong language must have angered Oliver past endurance, and as soon as the Frenchman's back was turned,[2] he sent Thurloe and two other councillors to Cardenas to inform him that he had resolved to employ against France 30 men-of-war, together with an army of 12,000 foot, and 7,000 horse and dragoons, with artillery in proportion. The annual cost of this would be 1,200,000*l.* He did not expect Spain to bear the whole burden, but he wished to know what was the highest offer she was prepared to make.

Result of Baas's strong language.

A message to Cardenas.

A military alliance offered to Spain.

This time the Spanish ambassador was prepared with a definite reply. On April 2, the Spanish Council of State had

---

[1] Baas probably also regarded the demand for 200,000*l.* as being on a piece with the venality which he found prevailing amongst part, at least, of the Protector's following. " L'argent," he writes, " est icy d'une force merveilleuse ; une humeur aisée et caressante est aussy fort nécessaire. Avec ces deux moyens on peut espérer de reussir dans les choses difficiles, mais sans cela asseurement, il n'y a pas grande chose à faire avec les particuliers." Baas to Mazarin, May $\frac{1}{11}$, *R.O. Transcripts.* In this conversation with Oliver, Baas seems to have forgotten to employ ' une humeur aisée et caressante.'

[2] I think we may assume this to have been the case, though we have only evidence that the two ambassadors were seen on the same day. It is obvious that the conversation with Cardenas must have been held later than that with Baas. Taking the whole story together, it is likely that the general course of the proceeding was arranged between Oliver and the majority of the Council beforehand. They might allow him to make the offers to France on condition that if they were rejected, he should proceed to bargain with Spain. The irritating nature of Baas's replies would not have been foreseen.

taken Oliver's previous offer into consideration. As might

April 3/13.
Resolutions
of the
Spanish
Council of
State.

have been expected, they regarded it as 'a plank of safety.' It was true, as they acknowledged, that it was the usual practice for each allied power to meet its own expenses, but, as matters were, it would be best to accept Oliver's aid on his own terms, even if he stood out for a few thousand crowns more than the 120,000*l.* which the Archduke had proposed to offer. An engagement might be given to pay the required sum as soon as the plate-fleet arrived—an event which usually occurred in June. It was, moreover, desirable that a small sum should be sent in advance to the ambassador, to enable him to secure the good will of influential personages ; in other words, to play once more the game of bribery which had been successful at the Court of James.[1]

Being thus in full possession of the wishes of the Council of State, Cardenas, on May 4, raised his former offer to

200,000*l.*[2] With this sum, amounting to no more than one-sixth of the expenses of the war, neither the Protector nor his Council was likely to be content,

and on the following day, Oliver sent three councillors to Bordeaux to suggest that a smaller payment than 200,000*l.* would suffice as a deposit, and to threaten that unless the ambassador would arrange for its payment there should be no further negotiation. Bordeaux replied proudly that reprisals must first be stopped, and that even then the damages suffered on both sides must be compared before a penny was paid. After this, Baas had a long talk with Pickering, who, well disposed as he was to France, could only say that, unless the money were paid, no understanding was possible. So strongly did the feeling of the Council run against France, that though the councillors agreed with the

[1] Consulta of the Council of State, April 2/12, *Guizot*, ii. App. vi. *bis*, No. 4.

[2] Barrière to Condé, May 5/15, *Chantilly Transcripts*. The sum named is 1,000,000 patagons, each, as we have from Barrière's letter of May 20/30, being worth 4*s.*

Protector in regretting the seizure of the St. Malo whalers,[1] a proposal to restore the prizes was cast out by a majority.[2]

On May 8 Cardenas, who must have been at least to some extent aware of what was passing, raised his offer to 300,000*l*.,

May 8. Cardenas raises his offer. of which two-thirds were to be paid at once.[3] To Oliver and his Council, it would be a serious matter to find the remaining 900,000*l*. which would be needed if the war was to be waged on the scale indicated to Cardenas less than a week before,[4] especially as at this time

Financial difficulties. Monk was daily calling out for money to enable him to subdue the insurgents in Scotland. No wonder that Oliver hesitated, and that Pickering was encouraged to

Hints thrown out by Pickering. throw out hints to Baas that, though Dunkirk could not be accepted by England for fear of creating jealousy in the minds of the Dutch, it might be possible for the French to suggest some more acceptable plan. On this, Baas recurred to the idea of carrying on war in the West Indies, of which it appears there had been frequent speech in the conversations between the two, but he was now informed that that would be equally unacceptable with the attack on Dunkirk. All that could be gained from Pickering was a dark suggestion, that after the money had been paid, the Protector would probably have a proposal to make. A decided refusal from Baas brought to an end an interview which had only served to bring into prominence the irresolution which at this time pervaded the Protector's mind.[5]

On the 18th, again Bordeaux had a somewhat stormy meeting with the commissioners appointed to treat with him,

May 18. A stormy discussion. the Protector himself being present. After the ambassador had refused point-blank to buy the friendship of England, and had declared it to be im-

---

[1] See p. 128.

[2] Bordeaux to Brienne, May $\frac{8}{18}$; Baas to Mazarin, May $\frac{8}{18}$, *R.O. Transcripts.*

[3] Barrière to Condé, undated, but before May $\frac{15}{25}$, *Chantilly Transcripts.*

[4] See p. 131.   [5] Baas to Mazarin, May $\frac{11}{21}$, *Chantilly Transcripts.*

possible for him to remain in the country to witness acts of
hostility against France, Oliver retorted that the French had
been the first to make prizes, and that even the King's ships
had joined in these hostile proceedings. Private wrongs might
be submitted to examination, but not those done by the vessels
of the State. Bordeaux, on his part, had a complaint to make :
some English sailors had landed at Cancale and had attempted
to carry off cattle. If so, replied Oliver, they had acted without
orders, whereas Englishmen had been mobbed at St. Malo.
Yes, said the ambassador, but the mob was goaded to violence
by the seizure of ships belonging to the port, and the Protector
ought rather to thank the governor for the protection he gave
to the sailors than condemn the justly aggrieved people of the
place.[1]

As might be expected, it was Cardenas who profited most
by this clash of words. On the 19th he received a message

May 19.
Cardenas
told that
war would
be declared
against
France.

that the Protector accepted his offer of 300,000*l.* a
year, and was ready to declare war against France.
It was however added that, in consequence of the
demands made on the army by the war in Scotland,
Oliver would be unable to make war by land in the
current year, though he was ready to make it by sea with thirty
ships. Cardenas would gladly have clinched the bargain without further delay, but the case which had arisen was not provided for in his instructions, and he referred to Brussels for the
authority he lacked. In the meanwhile he urged Oliver to lose

May 20.

no time in the issue of a manifesto declaring war against
France.[2] Oliver replied that it was not the custom
in England to declare war by manifesto. He was, however,
ready to increase the number of ships to forty, and with such
a force blockading the ports of France, there could be no
possible doubt that England was at war. Besides this, he was
ready to furnish vessels by means of which Condé could execute
his designs. Whether he could also allow Condé to employ

---

[1] Bordeaux to Brienne, $\frac{\text{May 22}}{\text{June 1}}$, *R.O. Transcripts.*

[2] Barrière to Condé, May $\frac{20}{30}$, *Chantilly Transcripts.*

3,000 English soldiers must for the present remain uncertain. Barrière attributed Oliver's refusal to issue a manifesto to his desire to obtain the sanction of Parliament to the war. Yet with all that he sounded a note of warning. It was a reason, he added, for accepting Oliver's proposal without delay that the Council was now in favour of an alliance with France, all England being passionately bent on an attack on the Indies.[1]

Barrière had put his finger on the weak point of what by this time appeared a triumphant cause. As in the negotiation Two policies. with the Dutch, two currents of opinion were contending for the mastery in England, and even in Oliver's own mind. That the material advantage of the nation lay in the plunder of treasure-ships and the conquest of the West India islands[2] was too tempting a belief to be easily rejected. Oliver and the Council agreed in upholding the succour of French Protestants as equally, if not as more worthy of the efforts of a Protestant nation. Of the genuineness of the belief in England that the French Protestants were in danger, the despatches of Bordeaux furnish incontrovertible evidence, whilst the letters of English agents in France during these months are full of the sufferings of the Huguenots.[3] No wonder Oliver was hopeful of combining both policies by an agreement with France. When this hope failed him, mainly, it must be acknowledged, in consequence of his own exorbitant demands, he decided with the approbation of his Council in favour of an agreement with Spain, hoping to save the Huguenots though

[1] " Les Espagnols doivent bien considérer cette affaire, car il est fort à craindre que s'ils ne traitent avec M. le Protecteur, il traitera avec la France, à quoy tout le conseil est fort incliné, et fort porté contre l'Espagne, comme l'ambassadeur sçait fort bien, toute l'Angleterre desirant avec passion que l'on attacque les Indes," &c. Barrière to Condé, $\frac{May 22}{June 1}$, *Chantilly Transcripts.*

[2] On April 26 W. Cooper sent Thurloe a book taken from a Dutchman about navigation in the West Indies, and recommends Capt. Shelley as knowing the American coasts, and Capt. Powel as well acquainted with the Gulf of Mexico. *Thurloe,* ii. 250.

[3] See Thurloe's collection from March to May. The date of a letter of intelligence from Paris, May $\frac{19}{29}$ (ii. 265) is misprinted May $\frac{19}{26}$.

he would have to leave the treasure fleets untouched.   It seems, however, that by the end of the third week in May the majority of the Council, hitherto standing firmly for the Spanish alliance, were coming over to the alternative policy, partly under the pressure of public opinion, partly perhaps in consequence of the acknowledged emptiness of the Spanish treasury.

On the 23rd all London was ringing with the news that a

A plot to murder the Protector.
May 23.
Baas's intrigue with Naudin discovered.

conspiracy to murder the Protector had been discovered, and that Naudin had testified to Baas's complicity in a scheme for debauching the army from its allegiance to the Protectorate.[1]   Not only the Protector but even the faithful Pickering complained that the plot had been hatched on French soil.[2]

[1] Naudin's confession, May 23, *Thurloe*, ii. 309.

[2] Bordeaux to Mazarin, $\frac{May\ 25}{June\ 4}$, $\frac{May\ 29}{June\ 8}$; Baas to Mazarin, $\frac{May\ 29}{June\ 8}$, *R.O. Transcripts.*

CHAPTER XXXIV

THE WESTERN DESIGN

SINCE his return from Worcester Charles had been living a disreputable life in Paris, consoling himself in low debauchery

*1652.
Dec.
Charles
looks for
help from
Germany.*

for the kingdoms he had lost. Yet from time to time he manifested a wish to achieve some enterprise worthy of his name, and in December 1652, after creating Wilmot Earl of Rochester, he despatched him to Germany to plead with the princes assembled at the Diet of Ratisbon for pecuniary aid.[1] Before the end of 1653

*1653.
Nov.
Money
granted to
him but not
paid.*

the Diet granted him a sum of 200,000 rix-dollars,[2] and with this money in hand Charles would have something to pass on to Middleton for the purchase of arms for Scotland, and possibly something left over for the prosecution of other designs. Month after month, however, passed away without a penny of the grant being actually paid,[3] and as Mazarin also omitted to pay Charles any part of

*1654.
Is supplied
by English
Royalists.*

the pension which had been granted him by the French Court, the exiled prince was reduced to depend for his own personal expenses—which, with his habits of life, cannot have been small—upon contributions surreptitiously despatched to him by the English Royalists.

At the exile's court the old factious spirit lessened all probability of harmonious action. Hyde, now warmly supported

---

[1] Charles to the Emperor and the German princes, $\frac{\text{Nov. 25}}{\text{Dec. 5}}$, Dec. $\frac{13}{23}$, 1652, *Clarendon MSS.* ii. No. 875.

[2] Extract of a letter from the Elector of Brandenburg, $\frac{\text{Oct. 23}}{\text{Nov. 2}}$, 1653, *ib.* ii. No. 1,473.

[3] *Clarendon,* xiv. 103.

by Ormond, argued that his master's only chance of success was to throw himself on the English Cavaliers, and it was with their

The Sealed Knot at work.

complete approbation that the Sealed Knot was organising an insurrection in England on a larger scale than that contemplated by the plotters arrested in February.   During the spring of 1654 communications were constantly passing between Charles and his supporters in England, and hopes were confidently entertained that with Middleton and Glencairn still in arms in the Highlands, a great rising in England would shake the Protectorate to the ground.[1]

In opposition to the idea of trusting to the English Cavaliers was the Queen's party, to which Jermyn and the Lord Keeper

The Queen's party.

Sir Edward Herbert were attached, who, so far as they were not instigated by mere personal dislike of Hyde and Ormond, appear to have wished to regain England mainly with Presbyterian help.   In the winter Herbert had egged on Lord Gerard, Sir John Berkeley, and the veteran intriguer Bamfield to a desperate attempt to ruin Hyde by an absurd accusation of corresponding with the Protector,[2] and though the charge absolutely broke down, its instigators continued in every possible way to discredit the policy to which

Rupert's demands.

Hyde was committed.   The appearance of Prince Rupert amongst them was by no means a source of strength, as Rupert was at that time engaged in a personal contest with the King, Charles having refused to allow his claim to retain not merely the whole of the prizes he had taken in the

Rupert's dispute with Charles.

course of his adventurous voyage, but also half the value of the cannon on board his own ship.   Some months later, indeed, Charles, with Mazarin's assistance, secured the price of the cannon,[3] but in the meanwhile,

---

[1] Charles to Loughborough, Feb. $\frac{11}{21}$; extract from Armorer's letter, $\frac{\text{March 24}}{\text{April 3}}$, *Clarendon MSS.* ii. Nos. 1,735, 1,833.

[2] Hatton to Nicholas, Dec. $\frac{20}{30}$, Jan. $\frac{6}{16}$, *Nicholas Papers*, ii. 37, 49.

[3] Statement by Rupert, undated; Hyde to Nicholas, March $\frac{3}{13}$, $\frac{\text{March 30}}{\text{April 10}}$; Hyde to Wentworth, $\frac{\text{April 21}}{\text{May 1}}$, *Clarendon MSS.* ii. Nos. 1,619, 1,771, 1,828, 1,868.

so long as the relations between France and England continued strained, Mazarin wished to detain Charles in Paris by keeping him short of money with the intention of launching him against England in the event of a rupture with the Protector. In consequence of this dispute, Rupert began to identify himself *He seeks support from the Queen's party.* with the Queen's party, though he had little in common with them, and had absolutely refused to associate himself with them in their false accusation against Hyde. Hyde, however, as the guardian of the King's well-nigh empty exchequer, was the firmest of the antagonists of Rupert's pretensions, and Rupert was therefore in a temper to welcome any plan of action which would be distasteful to the party of which Hyde was the acknowledged leader.

The opportunity, whether sought by Rupert or not, was not long in presenting itself. If the subsequent declarations of the *A previous assassination plot.* Government are to be trusted, there had been a design for the assassination of Oliver even before the dissolution of the Long Parliament. This design, whoever its authors may have been, had been betrayed by Fitzjames, who, though he had acted as a negotiator for the Commonwealth in the affair of Dunkirk in the early part of 1652,[1] still kept up his relations with the exiled court. Whatever may have been the truth in the matter of this early assassination *March. Henshaw in Paris.* plot, a certain Major Henshaw, one of those Royalists who kept themselves out of danger by occasionally rendering unimportant services to the Government, appeared in Paris about the end of February 1654,[2] accompanied by his half-brother, John Wiseman, both of whom had formerly served under Condé in Guienne, but had deserted *He proposes to assassinate the Protector.* their colours when royalism showed itself the winning cause.[3] Henshaw, having obtained an introduction to Rupert, now proposed to assassinate the Protector,

---

[1] *A True Account of the late . . . Conspiracy*, p. 6, E, 813, 22. This was published in Oct. 19, 1654, and should be supplemented by the *Declaration* (E, 857, 3) published on Oct. 31, 1655.

[2] *I.e.* the beginning of March, N.S. La Rivière to Desborough, $\frac{\text{May 31}}{\text{June 10}}$, *Thurloe*, ii. 336.   [3] *Ib.*

and Rupert asked Charles to see him. Charles, however,

Charles
refuses to
see him. refused to admit him to his presence on the ground that he was in relations with the English Government.

It is not unlikely that Charles had learnt that before the dissolution of the Long Parliament Henshaw had been sent as a spy into the Low Countries by Scot, though, as Scot complained that he received no information of importance from him, it is extremely probable that he regarded this employment as a mere blind to enable him to keep a footing in England.[1]

Yet there is reason to believe that Charles did not throw aside the idea of an assassination plot, a scheme which he would feel the less scruple in fostering, as the murders of Dorislaus and Ascham had been greeted with approval by such austere Royalists as Hyde and Nicholas. He accordingly—

Charles
invites
Fitzjames
to Paris. we have here again to rely on the statement of the English Government—invited Fitzjames to Paris, being in entire ignorance that he was in the service of the Protector.[2] When Fitzjames arrived he brought with

---

[1] That Henshaw was in heart a Royalist appears from Scot's complaint (Scot's Confession, *Hist. Rev.*, Jan. 1897, p. 116); the open denunciation of him as the chief contriver of the plot by the presiding judge at the trial of Gerard and Vowell, his escape to the Continent upon the discovery of the plot (see *infra*, p. 148, note 6), and his committal for high treason on Dec. 9, 1658. His connection with the story about Morland and Willis (Life of Thurloe, prefixed to *Thurloe*, i. xv.) is also good evidence for his reputation as a Royalist, though the date of his committal (*ib.* vii. 62), being subsequent to Oliver's death, shows that the story cannot be relied on. La Rivière states that Henshaw in Paris associated himself with Wilkenet, a Dutchman who had taken part in the murder of Rainsborough. See note at p. 142.

[2] As will be seen, Fitzjames was drowned on his return. Later in the year Hatton writes : " Bamfield is certainly very bad, as my informations out of England assure me ; and so was Fitzjames that was drowned, in whose pockets were found treacherous papers, and in particular some reflections upon Capt. Griffin, who lives near Dieppe, where Bamfield had certainly been, as well as in England." Hatton to Nicholas, $\frac{\text{Sept. 22}}{\text{Oct. 2}}$, *Nicholas Papers*, ii. 92. On Capt. Griffin, or Griffith, see *Hist. Rev.*, July 1896, pp. 483, 501, note 50. It was through him that Charles invited Fitzjames to Paris.

him John Gerard, who had been involved in the scuffle with
March.   Dom Pantaleon Sa. This youth was a cousin of
Fitzjames and Gerard in Paris.   Lord Gerard, and was consequently at once admitted
to the assemblies of the Queen's faction. It was
not long before he had an interview with Charles in his
cousin's chamber, at which Lord Gerard himself was present,
together with Fitzjames, Griffith, and the Colonel Whiteley who
had come over as the agent of the plotters who had been
arrested in February.[1] Charles, it appears, discouraged any
immediate attempt upon the Protector's life, apparently on the
ground that it would be useless as an isolated act, but was
favourably disposed to it if put in execution as a prelude to such
a rising of the Cavaliers as was impending under the orders
given to the Sealed Knot.[2]

[1] See p. 116.

[2] In the *Declaration* published in 1655 (E, 857, 3) the English
Government stated that Charles 'relied on Gerard and Fitzjames, to
whom he gave precise directions that they should not make their attempt
till all his friends were ready in England.' We have also, from the same
source, the information that Charles 'spake to both Fitzjames and Gerard
concerning it, and did not only approve thereof, but declared that he
looked upon it as a most necessary, if not the only, means to set all his
other designs in motion.' This is evidently based on Bamfield's statement
(*Thurloe*, ii. 510): " Henshaw came over before the other "—*i.e.* Gerard
—"applied himself to one Mons. Chockey "—*i.e.* Choqueux— "a
Frenchman, Prince Robert's agent, and by his means had access to the
Prince, proposed his désign to him with what he desired. The Prince
acquainted the King therewith, who approved his undertaking, was
resolved to speak with him about it, as soon as he could find a con-
veniency. In the interim advertisement came to the King out of England
that Henshaw was employed thence by his enemies, and that his undertakings were but to abuse him. Upon this the King gave the Prince
caution of him and my Lord Gerard his cousin but "—*i.e.* John Gerard—
"he justified him as a brave and honest man, and one who was real in
what he pretended. Upon this you may rely that the King both knew of
it and approved of it, and looked upon it as the only and most necessary
means to set all his other designs in motion." In a later letter (*ib.* ii.
533) Bamfield is somewhat more explicit : " Touching what you write
concerning the King of Scots . . . I assure you it's a matter of great
indifference to me whether he had been privy to it or not ; but since you

If this account be accepted, the most that can be said for
Charles is that his secret preparations compare not so very

desire my opinion of it, I shall tell you my certain knowledge, that he
was so far from not approving it, that long before either Gerard or Fitzjames came over, he endeavoured to engage another in it, as an essential
means to give motion to all his other designments ; but, failing of a
convenient person, he sent for Fitzjames, commanded Capt. Griffin to
write for him, engaged himself to give him a sum of money to defray his
charges, though he should not undertake what he had to propose to him :
Gerard and he came together to Paris, spake to the King together
upon Saturday night at ten of the clock in my Lord Gerard's chamber,
both together and apart ; was with them near two hours. There were
present my Lord Gerard, Col. Whiteley, Capt. Griffin, Fitzjames, and
Gerard. Jack Gerard had orders not to put the business in execution till
he had directions from the King for the serving of it. Henshaw the King
did not speak with, although he had promised it, by reason he received
advertisement he was employed out of England from his enemies to abuse
him, and that is still confidently believed." The question of Bamfield's
credibility at once arises. He was a Royalist who betrayed his master by
selling his secrets to his enemy, and is, therefore, to be regarded with suspicion. It must be remembered, however, that, except in exceptional cases,
it is in the interest of a spy to tell the truth, as his credit depends on his
doing so. This motive, too, must have been specially operative in a spy
of Oliver's, as it was notorious that he had many in his service, and was
specially well informed (compare the case of Henry Seymour, whom he
told as proof of his having seen Charles in France, 'when and where he
saw him, and in what rooms, and some things that were said' (*Nicholas
Papers*, ii. 99), so that it would be dangerous to attempt to deceive him.
The exceptional circumstances, where a spy says what his employer looks
for, and where he fears dismissal because he has nothing valuable to
report, were absent in Bamfield's case. It is evident that in the letter
just quoted Thurloe had expressed doubts of the truth of the charge
against Charles, and it is also evident, from the long paper from which
the first of the two quotations is taken, that there was no risk of his being
gravelled for lack of matter. On the other hand, that paper, dealing as
it does with many things, has all the appearance of being written with
great moderation by a man who is anxious not to pretend to greater
knowledge than he has. Moreover, Bamfield's account of the way in
which Henshaw's plot was introduced to Charles is corroborated by a letter
from Rivière—probably the La Rivière who, in 1651, brought a message
from Rochelle (see vol. ii. p. 155). " Thomas Henshaw," he says, " and
John Wiseman, with one Wilkenet, a Dutchman, who boasts to have helped

unfavourably with that of Monk who, a few weeks later, openly
set a price on the heads of the leaders of the rising
in the Highlands.[1] The general insurrection of
Royalists, to which Charles was looking forward,
would of necessity open with a surprisal of fortified posts and
the cutting down of the soldiers on guard. It might seem but
a short step in advance to begin the process with an attack
on the Protector, and to weaken the resistance of the army by the
destruction of its head. Yet it is hardly likely that such fine-
drawn arguments found any place in the exile's brain. That
no laws applicable to the ordinary relations of human society
had any value to protect the lives of the late King's murderers,
was the creed even of the stricter sect of Royalists.

Charles's conduct characterised.

Here, at all events, Charles's connection with the plot
appears to have come to an end. If the Gerards and their
allies of the Queen's party kept the scheme on foot
it was in opposition to the politicians to whom
Charles increasingly gave his confidence—the party
of insurrection under the control of the Sealed Knot. It is
certain that the members of the Queen's party were dissatisfied
with Charles on other grounds than the dispute with Rupert

His connection with the plot ceases.

to murder one Colonel Rainsborough near or at Doncaster, did propose unto
the King of Scots, with the assistance of one Walsingham, Mons. Digby's
secretary, who is a notable Jesuitical papist, and who hath great credit
amongst that generation, and of Mons. Montague's chaplain, a popish
priest, as also one named Choqueux, surgeon to Prince Robert, for to
murder the Protector Cromwell. As suddenly as Henshaw and Wiseman
had their answer, they returned into England to wait a time to execute
their damnable design." Rivière to Desborough, $\frac{\text{May 31}}{\text{June 10}}$, *Thurloe*, ii. 336.
The argument that Charles would not have countenanced a murder plot
because he was engaged in one for a general rising appears to me to be
worthless, and it is certainly no argument against his complicity that
Hyde did not believe it. *Clarendon MSS.* i. 1,937. A letter of intelli-
gence, written on $\frac{\text{June 24}}{\text{July 4}}$, probably hits the nail on the head : "R[ex]
C[arolus] confesses now he knew something of that plot ; but swears it
never began by him, nor from him, but by others which he will not name."
Thurloe, ii. 398.

[1] See p. 104.

about the cannon. We hear of Rupert, Gerard, and Herbert disparaging him in comparison with his brother James,[1] and finally persisting in the assassination plot after Charles had resolved to defer it.[2] Before the end of May Rupert found it advisable to betake himself to Germany, and Herbert, having tired out the patience of Charles, was driven to surrender the Great Seal.[3]

It is significant that when John Gerard, following Henshaw, returned to England, he travelled in company with Major Halsall, one of Ascham's murderers, 'with the intention,' it is said, 'to kill the Protector and divers others.'[4] If any further indication of the quarter in which the

*April.
Gerard goes
to England.*

---

[1] From a letter of intelligence from Paris of March $\frac{21}{31}$, we learn that the Queen wanted to send the Duke of York with Rupert, Lord Gerard, and Sir E. Herbert to Scotland, whilst Charles remained on the Continent, *Thurloe*, ii. 179. At Gerard's trial it was said that Rupert was to land in England with 10,000 men. As matters were, this looks like a ridiculous invention ; but it must be remembered that every one was speculating on a breach between France and England, and that Rupert may very well have asked for an army in case of Cromwell's allying himself with Spain. Considering the life that Charles was leading, it was natural enough for men like Rupert to think that the cause of Royalism would prosper better in more active hands, and also that the mother of the two young men should be of the same opinion.

[2] "I am told he"—*i.e.* Charles—"sharply reproved this mighty man at arms"—*i.e.* Lord Gerard—"for making use of his name, and meddling with his business without his allowance or knowledge." [D. O'Neill] to [W. Ashburnham], $\frac{\text{May } 27}{\text{June } 6}$, *Thurloe*, ii. 322.

[3] In an earlier letter, of $\frac{\text{May } 24}{\text{June } 3}$, the same writer says that Charles had had an altercation with his mother 'about Prince Rupert, Sir E. Herbert, and Sir J. Berkeley, in all which she had little satisfaction, for he said they had so behaved themselves to him that they should never more have his trust nor his company, if he could.' He then adds of Lord Gerard that he 'is upon as ticklish terms, and so will all those [be] that think to use this young man as they did his father ; for though in appearance he is gentle, familiar, and easy, yet he will not be gurmanded (*i.e.* gourmandé) nor governed by violent humours, such as these are.' *Thurloe*, ii. 312.

[4] —— to Scot $\frac{\text{April } 29}{\text{May } 9}$, *ib.* ii. 257. Gerard is here spoken of as having 'lately' gone. 'Lately' must have rather a wide interpretation if the following passage refers to him : "The last night Lord Gerard's cousin is

murder plot found its chief support is wanting, it would be seen

Alleged pro-
clamation
for the mur-
der of the
Protector. in a proclamation purporting to proceed from Charles himself, and offering a reward of 500*l*., a knighthood and a colonelcy, to any one who 'by pistol, sword or poison,' succeeded in killing 'a certain mechanic fellow, Oliver Cromwell.' If internal evidence be worth anything, that proclamation was never issued by Charles ; whilst the only man likely to have drawn it up was the ally of Rupert and the Gerards—Sir Edward Herbert.[1]

After their return to England Henshaw and Gerard devoted themselves to the accomplishment of their wild scheme. There

---

returned, because his brother dares not. By the next I shall know what trade he drives. If the King take not care such small factors will leave him in the lurch." Armorer to Nicholas, $\frac{\text{March 24}}{\text{April 3}}$, *Clarendon MSS*. ii. 1,833. Mr. Firth, however, tells me that the word here read as 'cousin' is almost undecipherable, and besides Lord Gerard had other cousins besides John. It seems, indeed, almost certain that John did not leave France till after the middle of April, as Halsall is probably one of the two persons referred to in a letter of $\frac{\text{April 21}}{\text{May 1}}$, in which Hyde tells Nicholas that he had written to him 'three days since by some honest gentlemen who pass by Calais ; . . . two of them are the brave fellows who spake with the rebel ambassador at Madrid, which for their safety I have advised them not to brag of.' *Clarendon State Papers*, iii. 235.

[1] Mr. Macray (*Preface to the Calendar of the Clarendon MSS*. iii. xi. note †) expresses a hope that it was only 'a proposed paper.' The basis of my argument that it did not emanate from Charles is to be found in the three names which were to be excepted from pardon after the murder of the Protector—those of Bradshaw, Lenthall, and Hazlerigg. The presence of Bradshaw's name is almost a matter of course, but it seems inconceivable that Charles should have been ready to pardon the other regicides, and it is difficult to find a reason why, if he was, he should except Lenthall and Hazlerigg from pardon. I can think of no one except Herbert who had a special grudge against these two. He had as the Attorney-General of Charles I. been foiled by the House of Commons in his attack on the five members, and may therefore have been quite ready to send to the gallows the Speaker of that House and one of the only two surviving members of the five, the other, Holles, as a Presbyterian who had been exiled for supporting a reconciliation with the King, being manifestly unfit for proscription.

were plenty of the King's old soldiers in London ready for
an attack on the authorities.   Yet the plot was not

Henshaw
and Gerard
active.

one that had any chance of success.   What was required was not merely to kill the Protector, but to
master the soldiers posted at Whitehall, St. James's, the Mews,
and other quarters.   How many men were listed for this latter
purpose it is impossible to say.   It was Henshaw's business to
multiply the number in order to give an impression of strength
to each new recruit.   At one time there was a talk of 700 ready
to take arms under himself, and some hundreds more under
other officers.   At another time the number swelled to three or
four thousand.   Amongst those gained over by Henshaw was
Gerard's kinsman, Somerset Fox, who undertook to make recruits amongst the City apprentices, and Peter Vowell, a
schoolmaster of Islington, who was ready to gain over his own
acquaintances.[1]

It is said that the first plan was to surprise the Protector on
May 14, after he had left Whitehall on his accustomed Saturday

May 14.
Failure of
an attempt
on the Pro-
tector.

visit to Hampton Court.   This time, however, Oliver
escaped by taking to the water as far as Chelsea,
instead of going by land after his usual habit.   The
fact was that the Government had for some time
been in possession of at least the outlines of the conspiracy.
Fitzjames, indeed, had been drowned in crossing the Channel on
his return home,[2] but before he left Paris another person, whose
name is unknown, had sent an information of Gerard's purpose

[1] Evidence given at the trial of Gerard and Vowell, *State Trials*, v.
524–530 ; examinations in *Thurloe*, ii. 334–355, *passim* ; and in *A True
Account*, E, 813, 22.   It must be remembered that a very small part of
the information in the hands of the Government has reached us.   The first
examination in Thurloe's collection is dated May 27, and is headed ' The
further examination of John Jones.'   Comparison of the documents officially
printed in the *True Account* with those in Thurloe's collection shows
that whilst the former are compressed by the omission of passages, they
were not being tampered with by the insertion of passages not in the
originals.

[2] *A True Account*, p. 8, E, 813, 22.

in a letter which must have been in the hands of the Government early in May.[1]

On the 18th the Council received more detailed intelligence from a Cavalier gentleman, who had been informed of the design, but had recoiled with abhorrence from assassination.[2]

---

[1] The letter, printed in *Thurloe*, ii. 257 (see p. 144, note 4), is unsigned. Mr. Firth, who has compared the handwriting with Henshaw's Vindication (*Clarendon MSS.* ii. No. 1,989) and with a tracing from Fitzjames's letter (*Add. MSS.* 32,093, fol. 185), informs me that there it has no resemblance with that of either of the two. The address to 'Mr. Thomas Scot' looks as if it came from one of the intelligencers employed by the Council of State of the Commonwealth, and not by the Protector.

[2] The story given in the official narrative, *A True Account*, is as follows : "Upon the 18th day of May last (though there had been some dark hints of the business before) there came to one related to his Highness and the public affairs a person of quality whose affections had always been on the other side, and told him that he had a matter of consequence to acquaint him with, which he said he did not as an Intelligencer, or out of a design to get any reward by it, but merely out of a sense he had of the bloodiness of the thing he had to discover ; and then declared there was a design to assassinate the Protector : that the persons who were to do it were agreed upon and listed, and had undertaken it : that their intent was to assault him as he should be going to Hampton Court, and, if they failed, then to attempt him sitting in Council ; or, if they could not have opportunity there, then to fall on him as he should be going to chapel ; that it was resolved the business should be executed suddenly : and he said it was to have been executed the Saturday before, and that which made it miss was because the Protector, contrary to his wonted course, had gone that day by water as far as Chelsea. He said also that two of the persons engaged in it were John Gerard and Tuder the Chirurgeon, neither of whose lodgings he knew, but affirmed that the thing was most real, and most earnestly desired the information might not be slighted, but that some speedy provision might be made against the danger, adding that, although he had been of the other side, yet he could not but perform his part in preventing so base and unworthy a design, and held himself bound in conscience to make this discovery.

"The same day there came another person of quality, and utterly unknown to the other, to a member of the Council, who, with some horror and amazement, told him that certainly there was a design to murder the Protector, and it was ripe and ready to be executed, concerning which he

On Sunday, May 21, probably after fresh details had become
known, the Council ordered the arrest of John Gerard, together
with five of his comrades.[1]   On the following day the number
Proclama- of prisoners was at least doubled.[2]   On the 23rd a
tion for the proclamation was issued directing the constables of
discovery of
lodgers.   London, Westminster, and Southwark to draw up a
list of all lodgers within their bounds, and to forbid such
lodgers to remove without special leave.[3]   The proclamation
and the sweeping arrests which followed were received with the
greatest indignation in the City, where placards were affixed
to the walls declaring the plot to be a mere invention of the
Government.[4]   Before long there were more than five hundred
persons in custody.[5]   The first suspicion, however had fallen on
Henshaw's Gerard rather than on Henshaw, and Henshaw took
escape.   the opportunity to escape to the Continent before any
attempt was made to arrest him.[6]   Some months later he drew
up a vindication of himself, asserting not only that he had had
no hand in the plot, but that there had never been a plot at all.

gave some reasons inducing a belief." It is easy to understand that the
Government, anxious to encourage Cavaliers of this type, should have
given prominence to their warning, and have thrust the earlier informants
into the background as authors of 'some dark hints.'

[1] Warrants, May 21, *Cal. S. P. Dom.* p. 436.
[2] Baas to Mazarin, $\frac{\text{May 22}}{\text{June 1}}$, *R.O. Transcripts*.
[3] Proclamation, *Interr.* I, 75, p. 320.
[4] Pauluzzi to Morosini, June $\frac{2}{12}$, *Letter Book R.O.*
[5] Pauluzzi to Morosini, June $\frac{16}{26}$, *ib.*
[6] Bordeaux, evidently alluding to Henshaw, writes on June $\frac{5}{15}$, that
the person who could throw most light on the matter had escaped. A
warrant was issued on June 6 (*Rawlinson MSS.* A, 328, fol. 80) for the
arrest of Henshaw and Col. Finch. Both were, however, still at large on
June 9 (*C. Order Book, Interr.* I, 75, p. 359). There is, indeed, an undated
list of conspirators printed in *Thurloe* (ii. 416), at the end of which is a
bracket, apparently including the whole number as 'examined.' Mr. Firth,
however, to whom I owe the reference to the Rawlinson MSS. in the
Bodleian Library, as given above, tells me that in the original MS. of
Thurloe's collection the bracket only includes the first twenty names,
Henshaw's being the first outside it. It may therefore be taken that
neither he nor Finch were captured.

It had been invented by a certain person who lived in the Mews, who had received 100*l.* and a yearly pension for his pains. As Henshaw's story was not even completed, it may be supposed that either the writer or those to whom it was communicated thought its falsehood too gross for publication.[1]

The Government had no wish to indulge in indiscriminate vengeance, and after a prolonged inquiry selected three of the prisoners for trial : Gerard and Vowell who had irritated their examiners by persistently declaring their entire innocence, and Somerset Fox, who, though acknowledging his guilt, had taken too conspicuous a part in the conspiracy as an organiser of the apprentices to be altogether passed over. Unfortunately for the Protector, it was as hopeless now as it had been in Lilburne's case in the preceding year to expect a condemnatory verdict from a London jury, and he was driven to reconstitute the High Court of Justice.[2] Nor could it be otherwise than damaging to the Government that a member of the court, Justice Atkins, refused to serve on the ground that no man ought to be tried for treason otherwise than by a jury. On June 30, however, the three prisoners, after an attempt to dispute the jurisdiction of the court had been overruled, were convicted of treason and condemned to death.[3] Gerard was beheaded and Vowell hanged on July 10, both of them protesting that they had had no hand whatever in the plot.[4] Fox, as having confessed his guilt, was reprieved, and in the following year, with a few of the other prisoners, was transported to Barbados.[5]

Gerard, Vowell, and Fox to be tried.

June 23. A High Court of Justice.

June 30. Trial of the prisoners.

July 10. Gerard and Vowell executed.

As the course of the plot was being unrolled, suspicion

---

[1] Henshaw's Vindication, Aug. ?, *Clarendon MSS.* ii. No. 1,989.

[2] E, 1,064, 15.

[3] *State Trials*, v. 518. Notes of Commissioner Lisle, *S. P. Dom.* lxxii. A.   [4] Dom Pantaleon Sa was beheaded on the same day.

[5] Warrant, May 18, 1655, *Thurloe*, iii. 453. It seems to have been a case of simple removal to the island ; there is nothing in the warrant about enforced service.

became in some way or another directed against the Catholics,[1]
either as taking an actual part in it or as being supposed to
look for their own advantage out of the turmoil which would

Position
of the
Catholics. follow its success.   Unluckily, just as the excitement
of the discovery was at its height, an old priest named
Southworth was captured and condemned to death.
Pressure was put upon Oliver by the ambassadors of Catholic
States to save his life, but he refused to intervene, and on

June 28.
Execution
of a priest. June 28 Southworth was done to death with the usual
barbarous accompaniments.[2]   It is possible that this
cruel refusal may be to some extent attributed to the
shock which the recent conspiracy had given to the Protector's
nerves.[3]   On the other hand, it may have been the result of
legal advice to the effect that the offence of being a priest was
treasonable by statute,[4] and therefore excepted by the Instrument from his power of pardon.[5]   Happily the penalty of death
merely for being a priest was, in this case, exacted for the last
time in English history.

As far as the Catholic laity was concerned, their position as
a body was less unenviable than it had been under the monarchy.

Condition
of the
recusants. It is true that the estates sequestered in the course
of the Civil War were kept in hand and the rents
gathered to the profit of the Exchequer, but no new
indictments for recusancy were allowed since the repeal of the
recusancy Acts in 1650,[6] and the Catholics as a whole had, therefore, no reason to regret the establishment of the Protectorate.[7]

---

[1] A ' papist ' woman is said to have introduced one of two soldiers to
Hudson, who is said to have been drawn into the plot by them.   Whether
this furnished the ground of suspicion or not, Pauluzzi at least connects
Southworth's execution with the conspiracy.

[2] Challoner's *Missionary Priests*, art. ' Southworth ' ; Pauluzzi to
Morosini, $\frac{\text{June 29}}{\text{July 9}}$, *Venetian Transcripts R.O.*

[3] In a despatch of $\frac{\text{June 29}}{\text{July 9}}$ Pauluzzi (*ib.*) writes that the Protector was
living ' con dupplicati risservi e timori, et vedendo malvolontieri appros-
simarsi a lui qualunque sorte di persona.'

[4] By 27 Eliz. cap. 2.   [5] See vol. ii. p. 334.   [6] See vol. ii. p. 3.

[7] That the sequestrated estates were retained appears from the title,

Though the discovery of the assassination plot may well have
led to some recrudescence of feeling against the Catholics, it
Feeling
against
France. was still more likely to stir up hostility against France,
especially in those who were aware of Baas's equivocal
June 8.
Arrest of
French-
men. proceedings.   On the night of June 8 a considerable
number of Frenchmen were arrested, and on the fol-
lowing day Baas was summoned before the Council
June 9.
Baas sent
for, to give an account of his intrigue with Naudin.   When
he made his appearance on the 12th he found himself in
June 12.
and ac-
cused by the
Protector. the presence of the Protector, as well as of five members of the Council and Secretary Thurloe.   To the
remonstrances addressed to him he replied that, if he
had done amiss it was for his own master to punish him.   The
'if' was too much for Oliver, who angrily asked whether it was
not amiss to instigate to rebellion and assassination, and to raise
factions in the army.   In reply to the production of Naudin's
confession Baas took a high tone.   He had himself been content, he said, to complain in private to his Highness when he
found him treating with the Spaniards contrary to the good words
he had given to France, sending messengers to turn the Huguenots from their allegiance, and engaging to favour Condé's rebellion.   If his Highness or Pickering had now been content
to remonstrate with him in private, he would not only have
satisfied their curiosity, but have obliged them to be grateful
for his conduct.   He refused, however, distinctly to submit to be
Baas
ordered
out of
England. interrogated by the Council, or to have his deposition
taken like an ordinary prisoner.   After some further
recrimination the Protector, having first consulted

'Delinquents and Papists,' which constantly appears in all manner of
financial summaries.   That there were no fresh indictments for recusancy
is shown by the Protector's declaration issued on April 26, 1655 (669, f.
19, No. 77), in which he declares that the laws have for some time been
executed with laxity, and then directs, not that 'the repealed recusancy
Acts' shall be enforced, but that an oath of abjuration of the Pope's
authority and the doctrine of transubstantiation, which had been enjoined
in an ordinance of Aug. 19, 1643 (*Husband's Collection*, 297), shall be
used as a test of 'Popery.'

his Council, ordered Baas to leave the country in three days.[1]

Nevertheless the Protector's wrath was vented on Baas alone. His relations with Spain had not of late been such as to inspire him with confidence in the resources of that monarchy. On May 25, indeed, he had consented, as far as ready money was concerned, to lower his terms to the payment of 100,000*l*.,[2] though he refused to abate anything of his whole demand. At Brussels, when Cardenas's despatch containing the Protector's offer arrived, the prospect of an alliance with England was received with exultation. Yet the Archduke knew full well how hard it would be for Spain to find even 100,000*l*. The treasure fleet was not due in Spain for some weeks, and its burden, rich as it was, was deeply pledged in advance. In his extremity the Archduke issued a proclamation, calling on all loyal subjects in the Low Countries who had money to spare to lend money or plate for the support of a war the only object of which was the re-establishment of peace. "God at last," he announced, "Who is accustomed to act by ways and means inscrutable to men, has raised up a human power that can make the scales incline to the side of peace by putting a finger ever so lightly upon them. This opportunity has now so suddenly presented itself that—it being impossible to give information to our Lord the King so speedily as the case requires, in order that he may embrace the offer without losing its essence and spirit through the unavoidable delay in sending the absolutely necessary contribution—we should consider that we had failed greatly in our duty if we did not invite all the good vassals and subjects of our Sovereign to provide for a few months by a singular effort as much as is needed for this

Marginal notes: May 25. Oliver's terms forwarded to Brussels.

Difficulty of raising 100,000*l*.

The Archduke calls for a loan.

[1] Baas to Mazarin, June $\frac{15}{25}$, *R.O. Transcripts.* On the same day Bordeaux wrote, admitting the intercourse between Baas and Naudin, but representing Naudin as having first asked for an interview, and Baas as waiting for further instructions before he replies.

[2] Navarro to Cardenas, June $\frac{3}{13}$, *Simancas MSS.* 2,083.

extraordinary supply, until his Majesty, when he has received information on the subject, can give the requisite orders to employ for this purpose the resources of his kingdoms." [1]

Personally the Archduke and his ministers were less confident of Oliver's sincerity than appeared on the face of this proclamation. In the letter in which Navarro, the Secretary of the Government at Brussels, gave an account to Cardenas of the efforts made to provide the sum required, he instructed him not only to take care that the Protector firmly bound himself to attack France by land in 1655, if he still refused to do more than to employ his fleet against her in the present year, but also informed him that a declaration of war either by proclamation or manifesto was indispensable. [2] Such a demand was not likely to be palatable to Oliver. Nor was the revelation of the desperate condition of the Spanish finances contained in the Archduke's proclamation otherwise than discouraging. If the government of the Low Countries was unable to raise 100,000*l.* without throwing itself on the benevolence of its subjects, what chance was there that either the Archduke or his master would be able to provide the far larger sums which would be eventually required of them? [3] The improbability was all the greater, because it became known

June 8/18.
The Archduke distrusts Oliver,

and demands further engagements.

Revelation of financial distress in the Low Countries.

---

[1] *Edict touchant le prest à faire pour les necessités de l'estat, et l'advancement de la paix*, June 1/11. The pressmark of the copy in the British Museum is 107, g. 5, No. 22.

[2] Navarro to Cardenas, June 3/13, *Simancas MSS.* 2,083.

[3] This feeling is attributed to Oliver in a despatch from the Nuncio at Brussels to Chigi, written on July 8/18, *Vatican Archives, Nunziatura di Fiandra*, vol. 38. Mazerolles expresses himself quite plainly on the subject: " Je me suis resolu à partir après avoir perdu l'esperance de pouvoir faire présentement icy quelque chose, fondé sur le peu de dispositions que j'ay veu à M. le Protecteur et sur l'impuissance de l'ambassadeur d'Espagne, qui n'a pas un sol, sans quoy on ne peut rien faire, cet imprimé faict en Flandres n'ayant si fort descrié les affaires des Espagnols et leur manière d'agir, qu'on ne traicteroit rien sur leur parole." Mazerolles to Condé, July 4/14, *Chantilly Transcripts.*

that the Genoese, who had long acted as the bankers of the King of Spain, had declined to advance him any further supplies of money.[1]

The financial helplessness of the Spanish monarchy provoked Oliver to fresh demands. He asked Cardenas how he

June 15. Oliver asks for Dunkirk as a pledge for the eventual delivery of Calais.

could be assured that the eventual payment of 200,000*l.* a year would in reality be made? Parliament was about to meet, and to it he was bound to render an account. On a request from the ambassador that he should himself specify the security, he replied that, in view of the projected siege of Calais and of its surrender to himself as soon as it was taken, he should expect Dunkirk to be placed in his hands at once. If that were done he would give his word to restore it as soon as Calais was taken and given to him in exchange.[2] Is it hazardous to conjecture that Oliver had little expectation of being taken at his word? For the present, at least, his attitude was far from friendly to Spain. To a request of Cardenas that he would at least allow his master to hire ships and men in England, Oliver appeared to listen favourably, but postponed his answer to the 19th.[3]

Oliver resolves to apply to Bordeaux.

What Oliver required was a respite to enable him to ascertain from Bordeaux the chance of a French alliance. On the 17th, but five days after his stern

---

[1] Consulta, $\frac{\text{June } 29}{\text{July } 9}$, *Simancas MSS.* 2,083. The Spanish Council of State acknowledges that it could send no money 'falta de medios.'

[2] He was to help to take Calais 'dandole alguna prenda de que en rindiendola se la pondriamos en sus manos, y que esta prenda seria entregarle Dunquerque con obligacion y palabra de que restituyria esta plaza en dandole a Cales si se ganasse.' Consulta in Cardenas's despatches of June $\frac{19}{29}$, $\frac{\text{June } 26}{\text{July } 6}$, *Simancas MSS.* 2,083. Barrière, writing to Condé on June $\frac{16}{26}$, speaks of Cardenas's audience being on June $\frac{15}{25}$, and says that Oliver told the ambassador that he could not declare war at the moment 'et que quand il voudroit la desclarer ce seroit avec l'appareil qu'il avoit propose et que pour cela les sommes qu'on luy avoit offertes n'estoyent suffisantes.' *Chantilly Transcripts.* Cardenas evidently did not inform Barrière about the demand for the surrender of Dunkirk.

[3] *Ib.*

dismissal of Baas, two of the commissioners appointed to treat on French affairs had an interview with the ambassador.

June 17.
Proposals
of two
commis-
sioners.

They told him that the interest of the Government might oblige the Protector to find occupation for his troops, which would lead to great expense. Yet the people of England were exhausted by heavy taxation, and it was therefore necessary to seek financial assistance outside the country. Spain, indeed, had offered a notable contribution, and though some considerations, especially those relating to religion, might give reason to prefer an alliance with France, nevertheless as his Highness was unable to do without a considerable subvention, it was to be feared that he would lean to the side of the enemies of France. Having thus done their best to show the danger of alienating the Protector, and having made some inquiries as to the amount which France was ready to contribute, the commissioners left on the understanding that the discussion should be resumed on the following day.

On the 18th the conversation turned on the siege of that very Dunkirk which Oliver had demanded from Cardenas only three days before. An English fleet, it was asked by the

June 18.
A talk
on the
siege of
Dunkirk.

English commissioners, should attack the place by sea and a French army by land. When captured it was to be placed in the hands of the Protector, not indeed absolutely, but as a security for the payment of the annual contributions which France was expected to make. At first the commissioners fixed the amount at 400,000*l.*, lowering their terms after a while to 150,000*l.* for the current season, and 200,000*l.* for each subsequent year. Bordeaux, on the other hand, offered 75,000*l.* for the first year, on account of the expense which would be entailed on his master by the siege, and an annual payment of 150,000*l.* in future. Nothing was at this time settled, but before the conference broke up the Englishmen added a demand for the exclusion of Charles and the Duke of York from French territory.

On the 19th Oliver addressed himself to the King of France,

announcing his resolution to continue the negotiation in spite of the misconduct of Baas,[1] and on the same day the English commissioners made fresh proposals. They asked that as long as Dunkirk remained untaken a French port should be placed in English hands by way of security, and gave Bordeaux to understand that the place aimed at was Brest. Some such acquisition, the commissioners explained, would be necessary to give popularity to a war with Spain. On the 22nd Bordeaux was admitted to a conference with the Protector himself. Beginning by magnifying the obedience of England and Ireland, and the submission of Scotland with the exception of a few malcontents, Oliver urged the ambassador to comply with the request of the commissioners ; and when Bordeaux rejected the idea of surrendering Brest, asked him what else he had to propose. Failing to extract an answer he put an end to the interview.[2]

June 19. Fresh proposals.

June 22. Oliver tries to win Bordeaux.

For some weeks the two negotiations hung in suspense, and the prospects of Spain were evidently sinking in the balance. It is true that no answer had yet been returned from Madrid on the proposal for a temporary cession of Dunkirk, as the Spanish Council of State did not reject it till August 14, but there could be little doubt what its decision would be, and long before it was given Oliver had thrown off even the pretence of sympathy with Spain. Early in July he declined to have anything to do with the loan of ships for Condé's service.[3] Yet in treating with France he remained anxious about the Huguenots, and pleaded with Bordeaux for the insertion in the treaty, of which a draft was now laid before the French ambassador, some engagement for their better treatment. Bordeaux peremptorily refused to bind his master by any such promise, and he equally took offence at a demand for a renunciation of the French doctrine, that

July. Oliver tending to an understanding with France.

---

[1] The Protector to Louis XIV., June $\frac{19}{29}$, *Guizot*, ii. App. i. 2.

[2] Bordeaux to Brienne, $\frac{\text{June } 22}{\text{July } 2}$, *R.O. Transcripts*.

[3] Barrière to Condé, July $\frac{7}{17}$, *Chantilly Transcripts*.

neutral ships carrying enemies' goods were lawfully subject to capture.[1]   So far as the Huguenots were concerned, it is

July 12.
Stouppe's
report.

probable that the return of Stouppe, who made his report to the Council on July 12,[2] helped to smooth difficulties away, as no hopes that the French Protestants of Languedoc would rise at the bidding of England could any longer be entertained.   For some weeks to come the nego-

Progress of
the negc-
tiation.

tiation slowly but satisfactorily advanced, especially as Bordeaux gave Oliver to understand that though his master would never bind himself to do anything for the Huguenots, any intercession addressed to him on their behalf would not fall upon deaf ears if only the treaty were signed.[3]   In that treaty, indeed, the proposed alliance against Spain found no place.   Oliver had at last made up his mind

The project
of a Euro-
pean war
against Spain
dropped.

to hold aloof from the contest in Europe, and to be content with a commercial and maritime understanding with France which would open French ports to English trade.   It was already resolved that Blake should take a considerable force into the Mediterranean, where his presence would shelter English shipping against attacks similar to those which had brought on the maritime troubles of the last few years.

Might it not have been possible to deal with the Spanish negotiation in the same way?   For some time the commis-

The com-
mercial
treaty with
Spain dis-
cussed.

sioners appointed to treat with Cardenas had been at work on a commercial treaty with the good wishes of the English mercantile community.   At the outset, however, two thorny questions presented them-

---

[1] Bordeaux to Mazarin, July $\frac{6}{16}$; Bordeaux to Brienne, July $\frac{6}{16}$; *R.O. Transcripts*.   This was the French law of prize, though it was seldom, if ever, put in force at this time.

[2] Bordeaux to Brienne, July $\frac{13}{23}$, *ib.*

[3] Bordeaux to Brienne, $\frac{\text{July 27}}{\text{Aug. 6}}$, *R.O. Transcripts*.   A draft treaty, dated $\frac{\text{July 26}}{\text{Aug. 5}}$, is printed in *Guizot*, ii. App. viii. 5.   As Article xxviii. establishes the French law of prize, it cannot possibly have come from an English source ; and as there is no hint in Bordeaux's despatches of his having prepared such a draft, it may be taken as a mere sketch prepared by one of Mazarin's secretaries.

selves for discussion. In the first place there was the difficulty
about the Inquisition. The English commissioners pressed for
that openly acknowledged liberty of worship in private
houses which had been vainly asked for by the
Long Parliament,[1] and had been now conceded by
the King of Portugal. On the other hand Cardenas was ready
to renew the article accorded to Charles I. in 1630,[2] exempting
Englishmen on Spanish soil from molestation by the Inquisition as long as they gave no scandal. Practically, for some
time past, the Inquisition had not meddled with a single
Englishman.[3] The second question related to traffic
in the West Indies. Though the treaty of 1630 had
proclaimed peace throughout all the dominions of
the two kings, and had ordained that neither party should in
any of those dominions do violence to the other,[4] it was
notorious that the Spanish authorities in the Indies had taken
the view that the whole of America was the property of their
master, and had not only made seizure of English ships trading
with English West India colonies, but had raided the colonies
themselves where the settlers were not sufficiently strong to offer
resistance. In or about 1650 a party of Spaniards from Porto
Rico surprised Santa Cruz, held by English conjointly with
Dutch settlers, and slew the governor and a hundred settlers.[5]
Between 1650 and 1653 four ships had been confiscated, and
the crews of two of them compelled to work as slaves on the
fortifications of Havanna.[6]

Question of liberty of worship.

Question of trade in the West Indies.

On July 20, with these material grievances before him,

---

[1] See vol. ii. p. 239.

[2] The secret articles of 1604, prolonged in 1630, are given in *Win-wood*, ii. 29.

[3] In his manifesto of October 1655, Oliver does not give a single
instance of persecution. All he says is: "De Inquisitione Hispanicâ
sanguinariâ nihil dicimus, inimicitiarum causâ universis Protestantibus
communi." *Scriptum Dom. Protectoris*, p. 38, E, 859, 2.

[4] Dumont, *Corps Universelle Diplomatique*, V. ii. 621.

[5] *Scriptum Dom. Protectoris*, p. 27, E, 829, 2.

[6] *Ib.* pp. 28-30. In 1634 the English in Tortuga had been treated
as those of Santa Cruz were sixteen years later.

Oliver made up his mind to bring the question of war or peace with Spain once more before the Council. Yet with characteristic impatience of material considerations, he opened the debate by an attempt to place the quarrel on the plane of religion. "We cannot," he cried, "have peace with Spain out of conscience to suffer our people to go thither and be idolaters. They have denied you commerce unless you be of their religion." On this enthusiastic and inaccurate view of the case Lambert proceeded to throw cold water. Success, he urged, was improbable, nor was it likely that even success would in any way advance the Protestant cause. Moreover, there was enough work at home to keep their hands full.

"God," replied the Protector, "had brought them where they were in order that they might consider the work they might do in the world as well as at home." As for the expense, 'it was told us that this design would cost little more than laying by the ships, and that with hope of great profit.' Lambert was naturally unable to recognise the force of this argument. The armies in Scotland and Ireland, he said, must forsake their posts, unless more treasure were found to support them, and this could not be done unless the West Indian design were dropped. Oliver's reply, as reported, was somewhat cryptic:—"The probability of the good of the design, both for the Protestants' cause and utility to the undertakers, and the cost no more for one twelve-month than would disband the ships." Yet his real meaning, as it can hardly be doubted, must have been that, as the pay of the men need not be found till after the return of the expedition, the immediate expense would be no greater than that of paying off the ships at once. Lambert's reply was at least worthy of attention from a financial point of view. He denied the feasibility of making war on such restricted terms. It was not to be supposed that the ships could be employed for twelve months without needing supplies. There were besides 'casualties of diseases and wars that men are subjected to.' Colonists would not settle in Hispaniola unless it could be held in secure peace, and the 'Spaniard will certainly struggle as much as he can to preserve it.' "Whenever," he said in conclusion, " you do lay down your ships, the charge will be much increased and must be paid." Oliver was sanguine even on this score. "It's hoped that the design will quit cost." Six nimble frigates should ' range up and down the Bay of Mexico to get prey.' [1]

The Protector's optimistic belief that the enterprise meditated by him in the service of God and of a larger world than that encompassed by the four seas which guarded the British Isles, was covered by divine protection, left no room in his mind for the prudential considerations which filled so large a space in Lambert's vision. At all events, it was he, and not Lambert, Oliver's who was the master of the hour, and he now resolved demands. to demand a redress of grievances from Cardenas. Two things, he told the ambassador, must be granted if there was to be friendship between Spain and England—liberty of conscience for Englishmen in the Spanish dominions, and freedom of trade in the West Indies. Cardenas would hear nothing of so rough a summons. " It is," he replied, " to ask my master's two eyes." [2]

---

[1] A debate in the Protector's Council, July 20, *Clarke Papers*, iii. 207.

[2] The story is told in Oliver's speech at the opening of his second Parliament (*Carlyle*, Speech V.), without any date. It was, however, partially told in a suppressed passage of the speech at the opening of the first Parliament on September 4, 1654, as we learn from Bordeaux's despatch dated Sept. $\frac{3}{13}$, in the transcript at the Record Office, but obviously not written earlier than Sept. $\frac{4}{14}$. The whole story is told by the same writer on $\frac{Sept. 21}{Oct. 1}$. Thurloe, in a paper on the foreign policy of the Protector (*Thurloe*, i. 759), puts it as the result of the negotiation on the commercial treaty, and it must almost certainly be dated before Aug 18, for reasons which will soon appear. Altogether the conversation may be placed, with a high degree of probability, either in the last fortnight of July or the first fortnight of August. "Then," writes Thurloe on another occasion, "it came into debate before Oliver and his Council, with which of these crowns an alliance was to be chosen. Oliver himself was for a war with Spain, at least in the West Indies, if satisfaction were not given for the past damages, and things well settled for the future." *Ib.* i. 761. [In the original preface to this volume Mr. Gardiner shows that this story is confirmed by the Genoese ambassador. ' In another despatch of August $\frac{14}{24}$, 1654, Bernardi refers to the story of the King of Spain's two eyes, thus

As far as Oliver himself was concerned the way was now cleared. If the Huguenots were safe and there was no call upon him to make war in France, a war with Spain confined to the West Indies would satisfy his own religious emotions, and would vindicate the claims of England to reparation for the slaughter of her colonists and the confiscation of her ships. If it brought treasure to a Protector in sore financial straits he would hardly think the worst of it for that. The long months of hesitation had come to an end at last. Yet the strangest side of the whole matter is that Oliver should have imagined it possible to confine the war to the Indies. The only possible explanation is that his mind was steeped in the Elizabethan tradition, and that he fancied that the fleet of an established government could repeat the exploits of the Drakes and Raleighs of former days. For him the doctrine that there was no peace beyond the line was still living, and he fancied that Philip would permit English merchants to enter Spanish harbours in all amity for purposes of trade, whilst an English fleet was capturing Spanish prizes and assailing Spanish ports in the Indies.

Project of a war confined to the West Indies.

For some little time, however, no effect was given to Oliver's resolution, probably because it was a work of some difficulty to bring the Council into line with himself. At last news arrived from the seat of war in the North of France which was enough to convince the waverers that Spain was on the losing side. During the last few weeks a duel between the two monarchies was being fought out on the Flemish frontier. On the French side was the genius of Turenne ; on the Spanish, Condé, the only general capable of making head against him, was subordinated to the inefficient Fuensaldaña, and to the still more inefficient Archduke Leopold who, on this occasion, took the field in person. At the opening of the campaign Turenne invested Stenay, whilst the Archduke invested Arras. Stenay capitulated to the French on July 17, setting

Aug. 18. News from Arras.

War on the Flemish frontier.

July 17. Capitulation of Stenay.

increasing the probability that Oliver's conversation with Cardenas took place in the first fortnight in August, probably in the second week.']

Turenne free to march to the deliverance of Arras. On

Aug. ¼.
Relief of
Arras.

August 14 he broke through the Spanish lines and put an end to the siege. But for the skill and vigour of Condé the Spanish army would hardly have escaped destruction.[1]

The effect of the blow was instantaneously felt at Westminster. On August 18, the very day on which the news arrived, a com-

Aug. 18.
Commis-
sioners ap-
pointed to
prepare an
attack on
the West
Indies.

mission was issued to certain persons, of whom Penn and Venables, who were marked out respectively for the naval and military commands of the projected expedition, were the first named, directing them to consult on the best means for assailing the Spanish power in the West Indies.[2] In the case of officials concerned in the matter there was to be no longer any concealment. In June the object of the fleet, of which Penn was ultimately appointed the commander, had been specified as ' The Western Design,'[3] a phrase equally applicable to an attack on Bordeaux or an attack on San Domingo. In August, at least in confidential documents, no ambiguity remained.

Whatever might be revealed to officials, every possible care was taken to shroud the project from the public gaze. No

The secret
to be kept.

means were neglected which might lull Spain into security, and rumours were designedly spread that Penn's squadron was intended to support Holland against the other six provinces which were enraged by her exclusion of the

---

[1] The Duke of Aumâle's *Hist. des Princes de Condé*, vi. 396–414.

[2] "Whereas we have, by advice of our Council, resolved, with all convenient speed, to send into America a squadron of ships of war, consisting of fourteen, and several other ships of burthen, to carry provisions and necessaries . . . and to send with the said ships three thousand soldiers in regiments and one hundred horse, and with the said forces to attack the Spanish both by sea and land in those parts ; who hath inhumanly murdered divers of our people there, taken away their possessions, and doth exercise all acts of hostility against them as open enemies, and hath several other ways given just cause to this State to take and prosecute the aforesaid resolutions," &c. Instructions to Penn and others, Aug. 18, *Stowe MSS.* 185, fol. 83.

[3] Proceedings in Council, June 5, *S. P. Dom.* lxxii. 10.

Prince of Orange.[1] War was to be made, not after the usual

A sorry
spectacle. methods of a great power openly seeking redress of grievances, but after the fashion of a midnight conspirator. No doubt Oliver might imagine that he was merely authorising reprisals for attacks on commerce, as the Commonwealth had authorised reprisals against France for injuries inflicted on English trade. Yet, after all is said, the deliberate concealment of warlike preparations against a State to which Oliver had but three months before proffered an active military alliance, an offer which had as yet never been retracted, was, at the best, a sorry spectacle.

Reticent as Oliver was with regard to the West Indian expedition, there was no reticence on the subject of the French

Progress
of the
French
treaty. negotiation. Parliament was to meet on September 3, and the Protector was anxious to announce to it the conclusion of the maritime strife. Now that he had ceased to ask for a formal guarantee for the toleration of the Huguenots or for an admission of the injustice of the French prize law, all that remained for consideration was the list of Englishmen to be expelled from France. As it had all along been taken for granted that Henrietta Maria, as the young king's aunt, should be unmolested, all else seemed easy

Difficulties
in the way. of adjustment. Yet at the last moment, on September 2, difficulties arose. Premising that his master would banish those whose names were agreed on as soon as the treaty had been signed, Bordeaux asked that none of the Queen's domestics should be dismissed, that the Duke of Gloucester might remain in France as being too young to be dangerous, and that no officer in the actual employment of the King of France should be sent across the frontiers. This the English commissioners demurred to on the ground that the Duke of York fell under the last category, and that they had no security against any obnoxious person being taken into the Queen's domestic service before the time arrived for the fulfilment of the engagement.[2] It was necessary for the am-

[1] Salvetti's Newsletter, Aug. $\frac{18}{28}$, *Add. MSS.* 27,962, O. fol. 304.
[2] Bordeaux to Brienne, Sept. $\frac{3}{13}$, *R.O. Transcripts.*

bassador to seek fresh instructions, and Oliver was therefore compelled to meet Parliament without any indication that the troubles with France had been brought to an end, whilst his attitude towards Spain, if touched on at all, must necessarily be veiled in a thick cloud of mystery.

Thus far a study of the foreign policy of the Protectorate reveals a distracting maze of fluctuations. Oliver is seen alternately courting France and Spain, constant only in inconstancy. It is, indeed, more than probable that, if the discussions at the Council table had been even partially handed down to us, we should be able to attribute some of these vacillations to the difficulty— far more real than modern writers imagine—of securing the support of that majority of the Councillors to whom *The Instrument of Government* gave the decisive voice. Yet, after all allowance made on this score, much remains which can only be accounted for by Oliver's own changeableness. He had embarked on foreign politics as upon an unknown sea, in which it was hard for him to find his bearings, and still harder to direct his course aright. In such case he was liable to be turned aside by sentiment or prejudice rather than to pursue a definite line of conduct from well-considered motives.

Oliver's vacilla- tions.

Nevertheless an attentive consideration of Oliver's variations leads to the conclusion that the desire to attack Spain was the dominant note in his mind. Towards the end of 1651 his leanings appeared in the negotiation he opened with France for the cession of Dunkirk. In the summer of 1653 he showed that he still retained the same feeling in the passionate outburst in which he pleaded with the Dutch ambassadors for their co-operation in the conquest of Spanish America. From time to time indeed he turned to Spain, but it was when he imagined himself to have reason to believe that the French Government was purposing to oppress the Huguenots, and to connive, if not to do more than connive, at a Stuart restoration in England. It was, indeed, a necessity of his nature to convince himself that whatever he did was done for the good of religion, and now that the danger of the

His mind set upon war with Spain.

French Protestants was seen to be imaginary, he was able to regard the attack on the Spanish West Indies as being in some way or other an attack on the Pope and the Inquisition.

For all that, it is not for any injury done to the Pope or the Inquisition that the Cromwellian maritime war owes its place in history. Later generations have seen in it no religious achievement—it is doubtful whether a single Protestant was the better for it—but the beginning of the prolonged effort by which England's empire beyond the seas was built up. The scattered colonies, the few West India Islands exposed to Spanish attack, and the few settlements along the Atlantic coast of the mainland, were to be bound together in a wider dominion by the acquisition of a mastery of the seas reaching far beyond that sovereignty hitherto claimed over the waters encircling our own island.

That the control of the sea should belong to England and not to Spain was the object for which these men of the seven-teenth century were in reality striving, and it was on this material side of the conflict that the eyes of those men were mainly fixed. To bring home treasure to England, and to extend the sway of their country over fertile islands was much more in their thoughts than the idea of extending orderly government or the virtues of freemen, to say nothing of the spiritual ecstasies of Puritanism.

Moral and material aims.

It is this predominance of material interest which made the resolution to send a fleet to the West Indies a turning point with Oliver, and even with the Commonwealth itself. In opposition to the futile oppression of Charles and Laud, the Puritan spirit had soared high. The in-evitable time of reaction arrived, and it came, as it ever does, with slow but increasingly emphatic steps. The return of the mundane spirit announced itself in the Dutch war, in the break-up of the nominated Parliament, and now—more distinctly still—in the attack on the West Indies. What is yet more noteworthy is that the attitude of Oliver himself towards these changes is gradually modified. He opposes the Dutch war, he accepts the abdication of the nominated Parliament, and

A turning point with Oliver and the Common-wealth.

he urges on the mission of the fleet. It cannot be denied without the gravest injustice that the Puritan spirit is still strong within him; but he has now given the first place to mundane endeavour. If the Restoration is to be regarded, not as a mere change of the forms of government, but as a return to a mode of thought anterior to Puritanism, it may fairly be said that the spirit of the Restoration had at last effected a lodgment within the bosom of Oliver himself.

CHAPTER XXXV

PROTECTOR AND PARLIAMENT

ON May 30, 1654, whilst the story of the assassination plot was circulating from mouth to mouth, Milton sent forth into the world his *Second Defence of the English People*. The coarse invective which deforms its pages concerns the modern reader merely as an illustration of the rude manners of the learned of the day. It is of more importance that the book gave voice to the opinions of those Englishmen to whom spiritual and intellectual liberty was of greater consequence than the independence of Parliament, and who were ready to turn their backs upon the representatives chosen by the constituencies if they threatened to erect a despotism over mental freedom. Yet, as a Parliament was soon to come into existence, Milton, unable to ignore the part it was called on to play in the new institutions, indirectly called on his countrymen to rally to the Protectorate by inserting in his pamphlet a series of laudatory comments not only on the lives and characters of Oliver and his principal supporters, but also on those of Bradshaw, the pronounced Republican, of Fairfax, the darling of the Presbyterians, and of Robert Overton, whose sympathies were enlisted on the side of the Levellers. Under these widely strewn panegyrics Milton undoubtedly concealed a call upon every Englishman possessed of any nobility of spirit to throw aside party feeling, and to serve under the standard of the great leader who stood foremost in the fight for those liberties of thought and action which claimed the lifelong devotion of the enthusiastic poet.[1]

Sidenote: 1654. May 30. Milton's Second Defence of the English People.

[1] I am here merely abbreviating the argument in **Masson's** *Life of Milton*, iv. 606.

To hold that standard upright—and, in Milton's eyes, this could hardly be done without a dissolution of such connection as still existed between Church and State—was, indeed, no easy task. Yet no practical consideration of the hopelessness of attempting to drag a nation into unaccustomed paths interfered for an instant with Milton's sublime optimism. If the people, he held, were disposed to evil, it was for the Government to educate them into the adoption of a nobler life. " To rule by your own counsel," he urged on the Protector, " three powerful nations ; to try to lead their peoples from bad habits to a better economy and discipline of life than any they have known hitherto ; to send your anxious thoughts all over the country to its most distant parts, to watch, to foresee, to refuse no labour, to spurn all blandishments of pleasure, to avoid the ostentation of wealth and power—these are difficulties in comparison with which war is but sport ; these will shake and winnow you ; these demand a man upheld by Divine aid, warned and instructed almost by direct intercourse with Heaven."

He pleads for liberty.

His conception of the functions of government.

Milton's exalted idealism forbade him to face without disgust the coarser realities of a Parliamentary career. " Unless," he urged upon his countrymen, " by true and sincere piety towards God and men, not vain and wordy, but efficacious and active, you drive from your souls all superstitions sprung from ignorance of true and solid religion, you will always have those who will make you their beasts of burden and sit upon your backs and necks ; they will put you up for sale as their easily-gotten booty, all your victories in war notwithstanding, and make a rich income out of your ignorance and superstition. Unless you expel avarice, ambition, luxury from your minds, aye, and luxurious living also from your families, then the tyrant you thought you had to seek externally and in the battlefield you will find in your own home, —you will find within yourselves a still harder taskmaster, nay there will sprout daily out of your own vitals a numerous brood of intolerable tyrants. . . . Were you fallen into such an abyss of easy self-corruption, no one—not even Cromwell himself, nor

He is doubtful about the Parliamentary system.

a whole host of Brutuses, if they could come to life again—could deliver you if they would, or would deliver you if they could. For why should anyone then assert for you the right of free suffrage, or the power of electing whom you will to the Parliament? Is it that you should be able, each of you, to elect in the cities men of your faction, or that person in the boroughs, however unworthy, who may have feasted yourselves most sumptuously or treated the country people and boors to the greatest quantity of drink? Then we should have our members of Parliament made for us, not by prudence and authority but by faction and feeding; we should have vintners and hucksters from city taverns, and graziers and cattle-men from the country districts. Should one entrust the Commonwealth to those to whom nobody would entrust a matter of private business? Know that, as to be free is the same thing exactly as to be pious, wise, just, temperate, self-providing, abstinent from the property of other people, and, in fine, magnanimous and brave, so to be the opposite of all that is the same thing as being a slave; and by the customary judgment of God, and a thoroughly just law of retribution, it comes to pass that a nation that cannot rule and govern itself, but has surrendered itself in slavery to its own lusts, is surrendered also to other masters whom it does not like, and made a slave not only with its will, but also against its will. It is a thing ratified by law and nature herself, that whosoever, through inbecility or frenzy of mind, cannot rightly administer his own affairs should not be in his own power, but should be given over as a minor to the government of others; and least of all should such a one be preferred to influence in other people's business or in the Commonwealth."[1]

In such words did the blind poet deliver to his contemporaries the highest message of political Puritanism—that the
Milton's
message to
his con-
tempo-
raries. good and wise were alone fit to bear the burden of the world. It was a view that was to a large extent shared by the Protector. Yet Oliver had failed

---

[1] Masson's *Life of Milton*, iv. 610.

signally in his attempt to carry it into practice in the Nominated Parliament, and, with all his spiritual exalta-
tion, he was sufficiently a man of the world to recognise the teaching of facts, and to seek thereby to
avoid a repetition of his mistake. It was certain that,
without abandoning his desire to thrust aside from the
high places of the State the ignorant and the profane, he would
do his best to come to an understanding with the new Parliament, without inquiring too closely whether the moral rectitude
of all its members reached the Miltonic standard. Yet it was no
less certain that, if he were driven to choose between
the two ideals which had inspired the Revolution—
the ideal of government by the best, and the ideal of government by the elected representatives of the nation—it would not
be on the side of the latter that his suffrage would be cast. It
has often been said—and that with truth—that the main problem before the Protectorate lay in the difficulty of reconciling
Parliament and Army. That problem, however, had its roots
in a still deeper controversy, in which the doctrine that the
people should be ruled for their own good, educated in moral
and religious principles, and preserved, so far as might be, from
contact with vice and falsehood, was opposed to the doctrine
that it is the first duty of a Government to conform its actions
to the national will. The first view was that taken by the most
prominent leaders of the Army ; the second by the Vanes, the
Bradshaws and the Lilburnes, though there might be considerable difference of opinion amongst them as to the manner
in which the representative body was to be constructed.

If those who sided with the Army could appeal to its
victorious career as evidence that it was an instrument of
Divine Providence, their opponents were able to
rely on memories to which few Englishmen could
be entirely deaf—to the struggle waged manfully
against absolute monarchy by Pym and Eliot, a struggle which
had the firmer hold on the imagination of Englishmen because
it was deeply rooted in the traditions of their race. Oliver
himself was not entirely uninfluenced by the reverence with

The Pro-
tector's
views
qualified
by practi-
cal con-
siderations.

Divergent
tendencies.

The Army
and Parlia-
mentarism.

which his countrymen regarded Parliaments. He had taken part, as Milton had not, in the political combat under Pym and Hampden, before he clove his way on the battlefield to the headship of the State, and he had, therefore, enough of the Parliamentary spirit to look hopefully on the experiment before him; though he was too good a judge of mankind to expect that men like Fairfax and Bradshaw would be found contending by his side. Yet, unless he could win over the leaders, it was hard for him to find capable assistants in his pacificatory work. At all events, when he added, as the Instrument permitted him, three members to his Council, the names of the personages selected were hardly such as to awaken widespread enthusiasm. The ablest of the three, Nathaniel Fiennes, was discredited, however unjustly, by the surrender of Bristol. Colonel Mackworth, who died within the year, had called attention to himself by his refusal to surrender Shrewsbury to Charles when he marched past on his way to Worcester; whilst the Earl of Mulgrave had no other recommendation than that he happened to be at the same time a peer, and, though he had refused to sit on the Council of State of the Commonwealth, a supporter of the existing Government.

Oliver hopeful of the success of the Parliamentary experiment.

Additions to the Council.

So far as the elections were concerned the framers of the Instrument had done their best to secure a favourable verdict. Resting, as they did, their hopes on the middle class, they had dealt roughly with the small boroughs, which fell naturally under the influence of the neighbouring gentry. Whereas the Long Parliament had contained 398 borough members, there were but 133 in the Parliament of 1654. The University representation sank at the same time from 4 to 2, whilst the number of county members was raised from 90 to 265. If the small boroughs were to be disfranchised, it was impossible to divide the representation in any other way. The great shifting of population which took place in the eighteenth century was still in the future, and when four new boroughs—Durham, Manchester, Leeds and Halifax

The constituencies.

—had been entitled to return members to Parliament the number of unrepresented towns containing any considerable population had been exhausted.

Partly, perhaps, with a view to the avoidance of opposition, but still more, it may be safely conjectured, in order to favour the middle class, the right of voting, so far as the boroughs were concerned, was left untouched. Except in a very few places, such as Preston and Westminster, that right had been either confined to the aldermen and common councillors, or expanded by the admission of the free burgesses. Even in this latter case the numbers of voters were comparatively scanty. In Colchester, for instance, where the free burgesses took part in the election, the entire number of those who voted in 1654 was but 200 ; in Leicester under similar conditions in 1656 it was but 59.[1] Newcastle on the other hand, being a populous place, counted over 600 voters.[2] In the counties more drastic measures had been taken. The time-honoured forty-shilling freeholder disappeared from political life, giving way to a new class of voters possessed of personal or real property valued at 200*l.* —equivalent to at least 800*l.* at the present day.

The franchise in towns,

and in the counties.

Other prescriptions of the Instrument were directed to the accomplishment of the same object. For the first time an elected Parliament was to contain representatives of Scotland and Ireland, to each of which thirty members had been allocated.[3] Later writers have pointed to this as a step towards the Parliamentary union of the three countries. If so, the step taken was of the shortest. Even in Scotland it was hardly probable that any considerable part of the population would take much interest in the elections, and the members returned were therefore likely to be selected from that little knot of men which had accepted the English Government. In Ireland, every Roman Catholic and every-

Representatives of Scotland and Ireland.

---

[1] *Hall Book of the Corporation of Leicester.*

[2] *Clarke Papers*, iii. 174.

[3] Scotland, indeed, had for a short time in the days of Edward I. been represented in the English Parliament.

one who had abetted the late rebellion being excluded from the franchise, the representation merely concerned the English and Scottish settlers.   Indeed, so great was the disturbance in that country that it appeared difficult to hold orderly elections at all, and the Government at Westminster actually proposed to take the nomination of the members into its own hands. Though this audacious pretension was abandoned,[1] the members returned were all supporters of the Government, the great majority of them being officers of the army.   The Irish representation, and to a great extent the Scottish, served the purpose of the Ministerial pocket-boroughs of the eighteenth century.   Nor did the precautions taken against the return of a too representative Parliament end here.   In accordance with the Instrument, not only were Royalists disqualified, but the indenture in which, under the old system, the returning officer joined with the principal electors in certifying that the persons named in it had been duly chosen was changed so as to include a declaration by them that the new members were debarred from altering the Government 'as now settled in à single person and Parliament.'[2]   By those who hold the franchise to be the right of all capable citizens, or who consider that form of government to be the best which rests on the widest possible basis, the restrictions of the Instrument need only to be mentioned to be condemned.   It is only fair to remember that the statesmen of the Protectorate held no such theories.   What they sought was to strengthen, by the help of a larger body than the Council, a system of government which in their eyes deserved to be maintained whether the nation approved of it or not.

Yet, in spite of all these precautions, when the English returns began to come in, it could hardly be concealed that the candidates supported by the Government had in many cases been unsuccessful, pronounced Re-

July.
Returns
come in.

---

[1] Ordinances, June 27, *Const. Documents*, 329, 332.   The Protector's correspondence with the Irish Government is printed by Mr. Firth in his edition of Ludlow's *Memoirs*, i. 387.

[2] A great number of the writs and returns are in the Record Office.

publicans, such as Bradshaw, Scot, and Hazlerigg, having been returned.   In a few districts—notably in the West—Royalists had been elected in the teeth of the Instrument, and in some places this result was ascribed to the influence or even to the violence of the returning officers.[1] Those who hurriedly drew up the Instrument in the midst of a political crisis had omitted to provide any machinery for the registration of voters, though such a provision had formed part of the *Agreement of the People*.   In old days, indeed, there had been little need of registration, as few persons can have held freehold land worth less than 40*s.* a year, and the names of those who held the status of a freeholder must have been perfectly well known to their neighbours. All this was now changed.   Even a voter himself must in many cases have been unable to say whether his real and personal property combined would fetch 200*l.* in the market, and it is hardly likely that the returning officer would be any better informed.   It is, therefore, no wonder that in the Wiltshire election—one of the very few concerning which details have been handed down—each party accused the other of deriving support from unqualified voters ;[2] and it is highly probable that what happened in one county happened also elsewhere.

In the boroughs, for which no rule had been laid down in the Instrument, there may in more than one case have been differences of opinion as to the precise method to be observed.   At Reading, for instance, a variety of practices had been followed.   In 1627 the corporation alone returned the members.   In 1645 the votes, not only of freemen, but even of householders who were not freemen, were held valid by the Long Parliament ; whilst in 1648 the same Parliament accepted an election made by the mayor, aldermen, and

A few Royalists returned.

No registration provided.

Difficulty of ascertaining whether a voter was qualified.

Case of Reading,

---

[1] These cases have been collected by Mrs. Everett Green in her preface to the Calendar of *S. P. Dom.* 1654.

[2] Mr. Firth has reprinted in his edition of Ludlow's *Memoirs*, i. 545. *A Copy of a Letter.* The retort from the other side will be found in *An Apology for the Ministers of the County of Wilts*, E, 808, 9.

burgesses alone.[1] Availing himself of this uncertainty, the mayor now announced that the corporation had elected Colonel Hammond, the late King's gaoler, though on a shout of protest from the crowd he allowed the townsmen to give their votes. It is said, however, that members of the corporation endeavoured to terrify the less wealthy of Hammond's opponents by threatening them with penalties for voting unless they possessed an estate worth 200*l.*, though they must have known perfectly well that this qualification had no application to the borough franchise.[2] In the end Hammond was returned, whether in consequence of these manœuvres, or because a supporter of the Protectorate was favoured even by the enlarged constituency, it is impossible to say.

At Southwark, on the other hand, the result of the election was less favourable to the Government. Highland and *and of* Warcup—the first-named having been one of the *Southwark.* advanced members of the Nominated Parliament— were the popular favourites, and the hall in which the election was held was crowded with their supporters. It happened, too, that, just as the friends of the Government were attempting to thrust themselves in, they were driven by a shower of rain to take shelter in the neighbouring houses. In their absence the returning officer, whose sympathies were on the other side, declared the poll closed and Highland and Warcup to be duly elected.[3]

It was probably injurious to the supporters of the Protectorate that the elections did not turn directly on the question *Questions* of the acceptance or rejection of the Instrument. So *at issue.* far as we are able to judge, the point which the electors had principally in mind was the acceptance or rejection of the subversive doctrines of the Nominees. On such an issue the result was a foregone conclusion. For that very reason many a candidate must have secured his election who, when

[1] Man's *Hist. of Reading*, 221–227 ; *C. J.* v. 631.

[2] *A Speech of the Mayor of Reading*, E, 745, 17.

[3] Petitions and arguments against the election of Highland and Warcup, *S. P. Dom.* lxxiv. 66, 67, 68.

once it came to be understood that ministry and magistracy were safe, would hardly be found on the side of the new Constitution.   As a political force, the Presbyterians were favourable to an enlargement of Parliamentary authority; and there was much in the present temper of the electors to favour the Presbyterian candidates, especially as the passive resistance of their congregations had baffled the attempts of the clergy to establish a rigid system of discipline,[1] and it was now understood that a Presbyterian layman was merely a Puritan of a somewhat conservative temper.   If society no longer stood in need of a saviour, the old arguments which had served against the Monarchy might be furbished up against Oliver without much alteration.   In Wiltshire the list of successful candidates was headed by Cooper, a local magnate who can hardly be classed as a Presbyterian; the unsuccessful list being headed by Ludlow, another native of the county, who, though his hostility to the Protectorate was well known, had little in common with the ecclesiastical innovators of the Nominated Parliament.   Ludlow's name, however, was followed by those of Baptists and Fifth-Monarchy men; that of Cooper by those of persons whose proclivities gained for them the support of Adoniram Byfield, the scribe of the Westminster Assembly, and led to their being taunted by their opponents with being the Scottish, or, in other words, the Presbyterian party.[2]

So far as the main issue was concerned the verdict of the constituencies was beyond dispute.   The party which had threatened law and property was wiped out of political existence.   Of the fifty-six who had given the last destructive vote in the Parliament of 1653, four only obtained seats in the Parliament of 1654.   It was made plain that England would not hear of a social revolution. Within these limits other forces than purely political ones had their weight, and it is usually difficult to judge whether the successful candidate owed his election to his political principles

The result of the elections.

[1] For the causes of the decay of the Presbyterian system see Shaw's *Church under the Commonwealth*, ii. 98–151.

[2] See p. 174, note 2.

or to his being favourably known as a neighbour. Goffe, for instance, may have been rejected at Colchester because, though warmly attached to the Protector, he was a stranger to the place, whilst his successful opponent, Maidstone, who was no less attached to the Protector, was an Essex man. On the other hand, Goffe may have failed because he was a soldier and his opponent a civilian; or, again, because his fervent religious sentiment rendered him unacceptable to the constituency. Local connection alone is hardly sufficient to account for the return of such men as Bradshaw, Scot and Hazlerigg. Whatever the cause may have been, the general result of the elections [1] made it necessary for the Protector to do his best to win the Presbyterians to his side; and he had sufficient confidence in his position to reject a proposal made in the Council to call on all members to accept personally the engagement taken for them by their constituencies, that they would do nothing to alter the Government as settled in a single person

[1] Foreign ambassadors concur in styling the majority a Presbyterian one, but they are seldom to be depended on for shades of ecclesiastical opinion. The situation is more fairly set out in a contemporary letter :—" One or more of the number," *i.e.* of the Anabaptists, " stood in most places, if not in all, and they had meetings so long since as June last (two or three hundred of them together in a market town) to provide votes aforehand against election day; and yet, notwithstanding their great preparation, packing and forestalling of votes in every market town, very few of them were elected. The country, in many elections, chose such as neither stood nor were upon the place; in most such as they knew opposite both to the new anabaptistical and levelling judgment; for they looked on this negative virtue as a prime qualification of a Parliament man, being mindful, it may seem, of the last Parliament, and fearing the effects their principles might produce should many of that constitution be admitted again to places of such eminent trust. . . . In this whole discourse the Presbyterian party is not once named, either amongst the known enemies or supposed malignants, because they are now fully reconciled to the Government," *i.e.* the Instrument, "greatly favoured by the Protector, walk hand in hand with the true-hearted Independents as to civil matters, and by this conjunction are become a great strength to the settlement." Greene to — ? Sept. 4, *Clarendon MSS.* xlix. fol. 56.

and Parliament, on pain of being excluded from the House.
Such a requirement would not only irritate hesitating members
but would assume, contrary to the fact, that the Instrument had
empowered the Council to make the demand.[1]

September 3, the day of Dunbar and Worcester, had been
selected for the meeting of Parliament, in spite of its falling in

Sept. 3.
The first
day of the
session.

1654 on a Sunday. It was not, therefore, till the
religious services of the day had been concluded that
the members took their places in the House. When
the summons to meet the Protector in the Painted Chamber was
delivered, Bradshaw, with ten or twelve others, cried out, 'Sit
still,' and refused to stir.[2] The attitude thus taken only served
to disclose the paucity of the numbers of the irreconcilable
party. They did not, however, lose much on this occasion.
All that Oliver had to say to those who made their appearance
in his presence was to exhort them to cultivate the spirit of
unity, and to invite them to listen on Monday morning, first to a
sermon in the Abbey, and afterwards to a speech from himself.

Much to the disgust of some of the members, the Protector,
when issuing from Whitehall on the following morning, assumed

Sept. 4.
The Pro-
tector in
the Painted
Chamber.

all but royal state. Around his coach as he passed
to the Painted Chamber a hundred officers and
soldiers marched with their heads uncovered.[3] The
tone of his speech was very different from the fervid
rhapsody with which he had greeted the Nominated

Tone of his
speech.

---

[1] By the Instrument the Council had the right of refusing leave to sit
to members who were disqualified as Royalists, &c., but not of demanding
a personal acceptance of the engagement taken for them at their election.
We owe to the Protector our knowledge of the fact that it had been proposed that the Council should exact such an acceptance. "This was
declined," he adds, "and hath not been done because I am persuaded
scarce any man could doubt you came with contrary minds." *Carlyle*,
Speech III.

[2] Goddard's notes in *Burton*, I. xviii. ; Bordeaux to Brienne, Sept. $\frac{7}{17}$,
French Transcripts, R.O. For convenience' sake the notes of Goddard
and others printed in the collection rightly, as Mrs. Lomas has shown,
ascribed to Thomas Burton will be referred to as *Burton*.

[3] Pauluzzi to Morosini, Sept. $\frac{10}{20}$, *Venetian Transcripts, R.O.*

Parliament. He had lost many illusions, and his own point of view had seriously changed. There was by this time in his mind a sympathy with the conservatism of the Presbyterians, which had no place in it when, more than a year before, he had invited the Nominees to show themselves worthy instruments of the actings of God. Nor can there be any reasonable doubt that he was animated by a conscious desire to win Presbyterian support, not, indeed, by misrepresenting his own views, but by placing in the foreground points of agreement, whilst leaving unnoticed those opinions of his hearers which differed from his own.[1]

Oliver accordingly began by reminding the House of the violent changes to which the nation had been subjected, though he avoided details which might have awakened bitter memories. He preferred to dwell on the hope, very *He hopes for union at home.* near to his heart, that the work of the present Parliament would be that of 'healing and settling,' of giving additional strength to a form of government adequate—as he firmly believed—to the national requirements. Singling *Speaks of the limits of toleration,* out the unpopular Levellers and Fifth Monarchists as the objects of attack, he held them up to scorn in language which—especially in the case of the Levellers—was distinctly unfair to the subjects of his vitupera-

[1] It may be a question how far the cramped and incoherent language of this speech is due to the reporter, and how far to the fact that Oliver knew himself to be addressing those who had still to be won, and therefore had to put a rein on his utterance. The *Clarke Papers* give equal incoherence to the speeches of others. But this speech, and also that of Sept. 12, were reported by a proficient shorthand writer, placed near the speaker, and a good deal of the confusion of which Carlyle complains must almost certainly have been Oliver's own. Perhaps a key to the riddle is found in an observation of Bonde, the Swedish Ambassador, who arrived in England in the summer of 1655. As the Protector, he says, 'piques himself on his good expression (*vältalighet*), he looks about for the most suitable English words.' If he stopped frequently in his speeches to pick out the best word it would account for his losing the thread of grammatical construction, as is so often the case when he was not carried away by his vehemency. Bonde to Charles X., Aug. 3, 1655, *Stockholm Transcripts.*

tion.[1]   After this, though he did not conceal his acceptance of
the principle of liberty of conscience, he preferred to dwell
persistently on the limitations with which it ought to be surrounded, and to vindicate for the magistrate the right of intervening whenever the pretext of religion was put forward as a
cloak for licentiousness.   From such utterances he must have
been glad to turn to the positive achievements of himself and
his Council.   Passing in review the more notable of the ordinances which he had issued in consequence of the legislative
power conferred on him by the Instrument, he turned with
satisfaction to the subject of foreign affairs.   Under
this head he could tell of peace made with the Dutch
and Danes, and of the treaty signed by the Portuguese Ambassador, albeit it was still unratified by his master.
In consequence of that treaty, he confidently assumed, Englishmen would be free to exercise their religion unhampered by
the terrors of the Inquisition.   Then followed a reference to
another sovereign whose ambassador had met a similar demand
with the answer that it was to ask his master's eye.[2]   This
reference to the Inquisition was received with loud applause.[3]

*and of
foreign
affairs.*

Once more Oliver called on his hearers to assist him in
healing the breaches of the Commonwealth.   "I have not
spoken these things," he told them, "as one who
assumes to himself dominion over you, but as one
who doth resolve to be a fellow-servant with you to
the interest of these great affairs and of the people of these
nations."   He trusted that, as soon as they had chosen a

*Oliver
appeals to
his hearers,*

---

[1] He made no distinction between the political Levellers who followed
Lilburne and the Socialists, of whom Winstanley was the most conspicuous example.   The Fifth Monarchists were defended by Spittle-
house : *An Answer to one part of the Lord Protector's Speech*, E, 813, 19.
Compare *A Declaration of several Churches of Christ*, E, 813, 15.

[2] We owe the knowledge of this to Bordeaux ; see p. 160, note 2.
This serious revelation was withdrawn from the printed speech.   Doubtless only one eye was mentioned because it would have been impolitic to
say anything of the demand for commerce in the West Indies, lest it
should be taken as evidence of the destination of Penn's fleet.

[3] Bordeaux to Brienne, Sept. $\frac{7}{17}$, *R.O. Transcripts*.

Speaker, they would take into consideration the Instrument
of Government.[1] It hardly admits of a doubt that
he expected the result of their consideration to be
its speedy acceptance, so little was he aware of the
objections likely to present themselves even to an unprejudiced
inquirer.

and asks them to examine the Instrument.

The first act of the House was to choose Lenthall Speaker.
As Bradshaw was suggested as a possible alternative,[2] the
selection of the man who had occupied the same
position in the Long Parliament can only be regarded
as a victory, if not for the Government, at least for
the peculiar combination between the Government and the
Presbyterians which Oliver hoped to call into existence. The
proceedings of the day ended with the appointment of a fast to
be held on September 13.

Lenthall chosen Speaker.

On the following morning the House addressed itself to
serious business. The appointment of a Committee on election
petitions[3] was followed by sharp speeches from the
Republicans. One complained of the more than
monarchical arrogance the Protector had shown by
summoning the House into his presence, whereas the
kings had met Parliament within its own doors.
Another asked his colleagues whether they were prepared to
leave the control over the law to the goodwill of a single man.[4]
Such an appeal to the desire, inherent in every assembly, to
magnify its powers was naturally received with applause. It
was reserved to Hazlerigg to touch the Presbyterians on a side

Sept. 5. Election petitions.

Constitutional claims.

[1] He added ' that the first deliberations were to this purpose, that in
the first place they should particularly examine the Government of the
Commonwealth concluded the sixteenth day of December last.' The
Dutch Ambassadors to the States General, Sept. $\frac{15}{25}$, *Thurloe*, ii. 606.
This sentence, too, was omitted from the published speech (*His Highness
the Lord Protector's Speeches*, E, 812, 1) after the experiment had turned
out badly. That the recommendation was really given is confirmed by
the proceedings in the first day's debate.

[2] *The Faithful Scout*, E, 233, 24.

[3] *C.J.* vii. 366 ; *Burton*, I. xxi.

[4] Pauluzzi to Morosini, Sept. $\frac{10}{20}$, *Venetian Transcripts, R.O.*

yet more tender. Let religion, he cried, be their first care.

Let them establish one good form, and suppress all the sects. At one bound, by this cynical proposal Hazlerigg had outbid the Protector. Independent and tolerationist as he had hitherto been, he was prepared to cast away his earlier political creed if only by this sop to their intolerance he could win over the Presbyterians to Republicanism. One of the Councillors in the House strove to avert the mischief by asking that no business should be done till the Instrument of Government had been taken into consideration.[1] Placed between the danger of too minute a discussion of the Instrument, and that of its being treated as absolutely of none effect, the Government chose the least of two evils.

When the House met again on the morning of the 6th the Councillors were made aware that they had to do with oppo-

---

[1] "Le mardi un d'entre eux qui estoit un des cinq que le Roy avoit voulu arrester proposa que le Parlement debvoit commencer ses deliberations sur la Religion, en fin d'en establir en Angleterre une bonne et supprimer toutes les sectes. Cet advis fut appuyé de quelques uns et contesté par la faction du Protecteur qui prétendirent que l'on debvoit auparavant que d'entrer en aucune matière reigler le Gouvernement." Bordeaux to Brienne, Sept. $\frac{7}{17}$, *French Transcripts, R.O.* "They therefore—from Court especially and from the soldiery and lawyers—pressed hard that the Government" (*i.e.* the Instrument of Government) "might be speedily taken into consideration, and some return made to my Lord Protector of thankfulness for his late speech." *Burton*, I. xvi. It is almost incredible that Oliver's supporters should have taken this line, unless they knew that the Protector was in favour of the submission of the Instrument to Parliament, especially if, as I suspect from the abuse which, according to Bordeaux, was levelled at Lawrence in the subsequent debate, the mover was the President of the Council himself. At all events, the incident strongly confirms the evidence of the Dutch Ambassadors as to the suppressed passages in the Protector's speech (see p. 181, note 1), and puts an end to the contention of Carlyle and his followers that Parliament entered on the discussion of the Instrument unasked by the Government. The member who moved for beginning with religion must have been Hazlerigg, as he and Holles were the only survivors of the five members. Holles did not sit in this Parliament.

nents who by long experience had become masters of Parlia-

Sept. 6.
Debate on
freedom of
speech.
mentary fence. The leaders of the opposition having discovered that Oliver's treason ordinance [1] prohibited any attack on his title, dilated on the danger to freedom of speech in Parliament if those members who assailed the foundations of the Protectorate were liable to be judicially questioned for their words. The Councillors on their part protested that no ordinance of this kind could possibly apply to words spoken in Parliament, and succeeded by a majority of 57 in rejecting as irrelevant a motion that no Act or ordinance could prejudice freedom of speech in Parliament. [2]

The claim of the Council, however, to regulate the admission of members by certificates of qualification was set at defiance

Uncertifi-
cated mem-
bers allowed
to sit.
by an order that the Earl of Stamford and his son should take their seats, though no such certificates had been issued to them—in all probability because they had not thought fit to demand them. [3] Either to cover its retreat, or to signify that it was not responsible for the omission, the Council sent the two members their certificates in the course of the day. [4] On the other hand the House concurred

---

[1] By this ordinance it was declared to be treason to assert that 'the Lord Protector and the people in Parliament assembled are not the supreme authority, or that the exercise of the chief magistracy and administration of the Government . . . is not in the Lord Protector, assisted with a Council,' or 'that the said authority or government is tyrannical, usurped, or unlawful.' E, 1063, 41.

[2] *C.J.* vii. 367. The supporters of the Government argued ' que le l'arlement estant naturellement libre, il n'estoit pas nécessaire d'agiter ceste question.' Bordeaux to Brienne, Sept. $\frac{7}{17}$, *French Transcripts, R.O.*

[3] It is not in the least likely that the Council should have interfered to stop their entrance, as they were under no disqualification as Royalists, the only question which, by the Instrument, the Council was empowered to decide.

[4] *Ib.* Bordeaux only gives Stamford's name ; but as we know from *The Perfect List of Members Returned and Approved* that Lord Grey had not been approved, there is no difficulty in filling in the second name. The B. M. press-mark of this list is 669, f. 19, No. 8.

with the Council in rejecting Aldermen Adams and Langham,

The House to be the judge of elections. who might be styled Royalists as having shared in the apprentices' attack on Parliament in 1647.[1]   Approving or disapproving, the House maintained against Oliver the claim of being the sole judge of electoral returns.

If the Government still entertained hopes that the Instrument would be accepted in its entirety by a single vote, they were soon disappointed.   On the 7th a resolution

Sept. 7. The Instrument referred to a Committee of the whole House. was passed to refer it to a Committee of the whole House, where details might be adequately discussed, though it is true that this decision was arrived at by a majority of no more than five.[2]   Yet in the debate which followed in Committee there were manifest

Constitutional divergencies. signs that parties were divided by more than a question of detail.   The supporters of the Protectorate asked for an affirmation of the words of the Instrument that the Government was settled in one single person and a Parliament.   Their more resolute opponents preferred to place it in Parliament alone.[3]   It was suggested as an

[1] *A Perfect Diurnal*, E, 233, 26.   [2] *C.J.* vii. 367.

[3] A paper of 'proposals made to the Parliament by a member thereof, 7' Sept., 1655' (*sic*), is amongst *Lord Braye's MSS*.   I take it to have been Bradshaw's, as it is suitable to his opinions, and also because at least one other paper connected with him is in the same collection.   It runs as follows :—

"That the proviso in the indentures of election for this present Parliament, purporting a limitation of the Parliament's power, is against the laws of the land, the fundamental liberties of the people, and of dangerous consequence.

" 1. That the supreme legislative power of this Commonwealth is and ought to be in the people assembled in Parliament.

" 2. That the administration of government be by such persons and in such manner as shall be by Parliament limited, expressed and declared.

" 3. That remonstration be made to the Lord Protector—who hath in the intervals of the late Parliament exercised another government—or these the people's rights, in order to the restitution and establishment of the same.

" 4. That in the settling hereof order be taken for the full indemnity

acceptable compromise that the Government might be placed 'in a Parliament . . . and a single person qualified with such instructions as the Parliament should think fit.' This last formula attracted considerable support amongst those who favoured the concentration of executive authority in a single hand, yet were as resolved as Bradshaw himself to maintain the absolute supremacy of Parliament. During the next two days the arguments necessarily turned on the relations between the legislative and executive powers. The former was pretty generally claimed for Parliament alone, freed not merely from the modest requirement of the Instrument that the Protector should be admitted to state his objections to any Bill accepted by the House, but also from the reservation of certain fundamental questions from Parliamentary legislation. The majority, in short, though ready to leave Oliver at the head of the executive, had made up its mind to impose restrictions on his independent action ; whilst the supporters of the Protectorate, now beginning to be known as the Court party, urged that it was no less necessary to place restrictions on the sovereignty of a single House. Whoever else might resist the House's claim, it had many of the London clergy on its side. On Sunday, the 10th, 'the parsons generally prayed for the Parliament . . . but not much concerning the single person.' [1]

> *Sept. 8, 9.*
> *Continuance of the discussion.*

> *Sept. 10.*
> *Clerical support.*

On the morning of the 11th the House voted for the con-

of all persons acting under the late Governments since the 20th of April, 1653, and all others concerned in the same.

" 5. That the members of this Commonwealth be enjoined to behave themselves quietly and peaceably in their several stations and places, expecting such further directions for their future deportment in relation to the Government as shall be hereafter given in that behalf ; the Parliament declaring their most earnest desires and intentions through God's assistance to heal breaches, and bring to a perfect and peaceable compromise, according to their duty, the disjointed and unsettled affairs of this Commonwealth.

" 6. That it be referred to a Committee to prepare a remonstrance upon these particulars."

[1] *Burton*, I. xxv.–xxvii.

stitution of an Assembly of Divines, nominated by itself, to
give advice on such matters as Parliament might lay
before them. The compact which Hazlerigg had
suggested was thus completed and the way cleared
for the establishment of an intolerant Church.[1]   On the political
ground, however, the advanced Republicans were powerless to
carry their whole programme.   In vain Bradshaw declared, as
Lilburne had declared formerly, that if he was to
have a master, he preferred Charles to Oliver.[2]   The
majority preferred Oliver, if only he would consent
to occupy the position assigned to him.   This party, in which
the more moderate opponents of the Protectorate were combined with some who had hitherto supported it, including, it
is said, a certain number of colonels, found a spokesman in
Matthew Hale.   From him had emanated the motion that the
Government should be 'in a Parliament and single person,
limited and restrained as the Parliament should think fit';
whilst either he or one of his supporters now suggested that, as
the best means of establishing Parliamentary control, the
members of the Council should be subject to re-election by the
House once in three years.[3]   Others talked of asking the
Protector to deliver up his commission as general and, restraining himself to his civil functions, to leave the command
of the army to an officer depending on Parliament.[4]   Those
who represented the Government, acting undoubtedly
with the approbation of Oliver himself,[5] asked that
the authority of the single person should at least be
such as to enable him to make it impossible for any

Sept. 11.
A vote for an Assembly of Divines.

A great central party formed.

The terms of the Government party.

[1] *Burton*, I. xxvii. ; *C.J.* vii. 367.

[2] See vol. i. 162.   In neither case can the words be taken as indicating
any active desire for a Stuart Restoration.   Neither Lilburne nor Bradshaw wished to have either Charles or Oliver as a master.

[3] Bordeaux to Brienne, Sept. $\frac{14}{24}$, *French Transcripts*, *R.O.*

[4] "Che . . . dovesse presentare il Protettore la commissione dell'
armi per altro generale d'esse, dipendente dell' auttorità dei Parlamento."
Pauluzzi to Morosini, Sept. $\frac{18}{28}$, *Venetian Transcripts*, *R.O.*

[5] We know this, as the three points reappear in his speech of
Sept. 12.

Parliament to perpetuate itself, that the power of the militia should be divided between the Protector and Parliament, and that religious freedom should be maintained.[1]

Evidently the Protector and Council had come to the resolution to accept from the House a constitution which might take the place of the Instrument, if only the House would agree to safeguard these three fundamental points. Oliver, as was his habit, had selected the points on which he was resolved to stand firm, whilst ready to throw over all minor claims. It was no merely personal question that was at issue. There are other conditions of good government than the direct rule of a Parliamentary majority, and the proposal made by Oliver through his representatives was virtually that, if these were secured, he was willing to consider all other changes in the Instrument.

A compromise offered.

In the meanwhile the question at issue pressed for a speedy solution. Only one day intervened between the last debate and the fast day which had been fixed for the 13th, and it was understood that the vote would be taken on the 12th. Nor was this all the danger against which Oliver had to provide. Taking advantage of the confusion prevailing in high quarters, Harrison had promised the Anabaptists to present to Parliament a petition calling on it to rise against tyranny, and had boasted that he would have 20,000 men at his back in its support. The Government, however, was not ignorant of his proceedings, and he was already placed under arrest and on his way to London to answer for sedition.[2]

Harrison's petition.

Sept. 9, His arrest.

---

[1] Bordeax to Brienne, Sept. $\frac{14}{24}$, *French Transcripts, R.O.* ; *Burton,* I. xxviii.–xxxii.

[2] The Dutch Ambassadors (*Thurloe,* ii. 606) speak of Harrison as having been secured in his house in the country. Greene, writing on Sept. 23 (*Clarendon MSS.* xlix. fol. 58), says he was confined about Sept. 9. *The Perfect Diurnal,* under date of Sept. 13 (E, 233, 32), says that he ' was secured yesterday by a party of horse,' and Goddard (*Burton,* xxxvii.) corroborates this statement. The 20,000 men are mentioned in Pauluzzi's despatch of $\frac{Sept. 24}{Oct. 4}$, who also says that Harrison was arrested in Parliament, which must be a mistake. Probably he was

Whatever might happen to Harrison, it was imperative on the Protector to devise some means to avert the risk of the despotism of a single House, unchecked by constitutional restrictions or by fear of the constituencies.[1] Accordingly,

Sept. 12.
Parlia-
ment sum-
moned
to the
Painted
Chamber.

when on Tuesday morning the members trooped together towards the entrance of the House, they found the doors locked and guarded by soldiers, who intimated to them that the Protector would meet them in the Painted Chamber. More than any other speech of his the words which Oliver now addressed to them revealed the inner workings of his mind. There was no longer necessity, as there had been a week before, to fit his language to the prejudices of his audience. There was no hesitation now, and the involved sayings of his former effort gave place to the majestic roll of his pleading or his indignation.

The Protector began by recalling to the memory of his hearers the words of his former speech, in which he had styled them

The Pro-
tector's
speech.

a free Parliament. He had not, he now assured them, changed his opinion, so long as they owned the authority which had brought them together. Leaving unnoticed the suggestion that the Instrument was the mere product of usurpation, he set forth emphatically his own claim to occupy the position he now held. " I see," he cried,

The basis
of autho-
rity.

" it will be necessary for me now a little to magnify my office, which I have not been apt to do. I have been of this mind since first I entered upon it that, if God will not bear it up, let it sink : but if a duty be incumbent upon me which in modesty I have hitherto forborne, I am in some measure now necessitated thereunto. . . . I called not

secured in Staffordshire about the 9th, and reached London on the 12th. The petition, of which an abstract is given in Greene's letter, appears to have attacked the Protectorate violently, and to have called on Parliament to extirpate its tyranny.

[1] Because a Parliament, the legislation of which was not subject to the Protector's veto, might have passed an Act declaring, as in 1641, that it could not be dissolved without its own consent.

myself to this place : of that God is witness ; and I have many witnesses who, I do believe, could readily lay down their lives to bear witness to the truth of that—that is to say, that I called not myself to this place ; and being in it, I bear not witness to myself, but God and the people of these nations have borne testimony to it also. If my calling be from God, and my testimony from the people, God and the people shall take it from me, else I will not part with it. I should be false to the trust that God hath placed upon me and to the interest of the people of these nations if I should."

In self-defence Oliver grew yet more personal. "I was," he continued, "by birth a gentleman, living neither in any con-
Personal justification. siderable height, nor yet in obscurity. I have been called to several employments in the nation. . . . and. . . . I did endeavour to discharge the duty of an honest man in those services to God and the people's interest. . . . having, when time was, a competent acceptation in the hearts of men and some evidences thereof." His own hope, he declared, had been that after the war had ended the nation would have been allowed to settle down in peace, and that he himself might have retired into private life. Then, after descanting on the misdeeds of the Long Parliament, and more especially on the arbitrariness by which it made 'men's estates liable to confiscation and their persons to imprisonment, sometimes by laws made after the fact committed, often by the Parliament's assuming to itself to give judgment both in capital and criminal things, which in former times was not known to exercise such a judicature,' he turned for an instant to justify his own part in the unhappy failure of the Nominees. Then, coming to the question immediately at issue, he spoke of the
The formation of the Instrument. position in which he found himself on their abdication. "We were," he said, "exceedingly to seek how to settle things for the future. My power again by this resignation was as boundless and unlimited as before, all things being subject to arbitrariness." On this certain gentlemen undertook to frame a constitution. "When they had finished their model in some measure, or made a very good

preparation of it, it became communicative.[1] They told me
that, except I would undertake the Government, they thought
things would hardly come to a composure and settlement, but
blood and confusion would break in upon us. I denied it
again and again, as God and those persons know, not compli-
mentingly, as they also know, and as God knows. I confess,
after many arguments, and after the letting of me know that I
did not receive anything that put me into a higher capacity
than I was in before, but that it limited me and bound my
hands to act nothing to the prejudice of the nations [2] without
consent of a Council until the Parliament, and then limited by
the Parliament as the Act of Government expresseth, I did
accept it."

Oliver had still to show that the Instrument approved itself
not merely to the handful of persons who had drawn it up, but
to the nation at large. To begin with, he averred it
'had the approbation of the officers of the army in
the three nations of England, Scotland, and Ireland.'
No one knew better than the speaker that, in the eyes of most
of those he was addressing, this was the very head and front of
his offending. " If," it had been said in the course
of debate, " titles be measured by the sword, the
Grand Turk may make a better title than any Christian
prince." [3] Nothing could be better than the spirit of Oliver's
reply : " Truly, until my hands were bound, and I limited, . .
when I had in my hands so great a power and arbitrariness, the
soldiery were a very considerable part of the nations, especially

National approval claimed.

Can an army found a Government?

---

[1] Carlyle here, as in so many other places, amends the text without
warning, and prints: "They became communicative." He has misled
Dr. Murray, who has quoted this phrase as the earliest instance of the
word in its modern sense. It should have been placed under the
obsolete sense of 'that which has the quality or habit of diffusing itself;
diffusive.'

[2] Carlyle boldly omits the words 'nothing to the prejudice of the
nations.' The sentence is not grammatically clear, but the meaning is
plain, that the necessity of obtaining the consent of the Council prevented
him from doing anything to the prejudice of the three nations.

[3] *Burton*, I. xxx.

all government being dissolved :—I say, when all government was thus dissolved, and nothing to keep things in order but the sword ; and yet they—which many histories will not parallel— even they were desirous that things might come to a consistency, and arbitrariness might be taken away, and the Government put into [1] a person limited and bounded as in the Act of Settlement,[2] whom they distrusted the least, and loved not the worst." In these words Oliver had touched on what, far more than any real or imaginary constitutional defects in the Instrument, was the vital point at issue—Could he succeed in changing a military into a civil State? It was much to show that the very soldiers were in favour of such a change. If he had succeeded in effecting it, the subsequent history of England would have been very different from what it became.

Then followed references to the civilian support accorded to the Instrument. Had he not been honourably entertained by

Civilian support claimed.

the City of London, and had not counties and cities —even the great county of York and the city of York —-approved of it? Had not the judges and all the justices of the peace acted under it ? Had not the members of Parliament themselves been elected in accordance with its provisions? Had not, he finally concluded, the electors signed the indenture depriving the members of the power of altering the Government, ' as it is now settled, in one single person and a Parliament ' ? [3]

The argument, it must be acknowledged, was by no means

Exceptions to the argument.

conclusive. It did not follow that, because the country had welcomed the Protectorate as a bulwark against fanaticism,[4] it therefore admired those clauses

[1] *I.e.* into ' the hands ' of a person, as Carlyle suggests.

[2] The use of this term is curious, as showing how Oliver's mind ran on ' settling.'

[3] The writs (see p. 173) require that the returning officer and some of the electors shall make this declaration under their hands and seals. The indentures contained in the returns insert the proviso that the elected shall have no power to make this change.

[4] It was argued on the 11th ' that the addresses and approbation of the country were not in reference to the present Government as formally

of the Instrument which exempted the executive from Parliamentary control; still less was there reason for surprise if those who could find their way into Parliament only by acceptance of the terms to which they were bound by their constituents discovered, when they arrived at Westminster, that their duty to their country demanded that they should cast them aside.[1]   All

Oliver ready for a compromise. such questions fall within the domain of theoretical politics. It was of practical importance that Oliver, whilst standing by the Instrument as in itself sufficient, announced his personal acceptance of the compromise proposed by his Councillors on the preceding day. " Some things," he said, "are fundamentals, about which I shall deal plainly with you. They may not be parted with, but will, I trust, be delivered over to posterity as being the fruits of our blood and

The four fundamentals. travail." First came the Government by a single person and a Parliament.[2]   Secondly, that Parliaments should not make themselves perpetual. Thirdly, that there should be liberty of conscience; fourthly, that neither Protector nor Parliament should have absolute power over the militia. It speaks volumes for Oliver's power of seeing into the heart of a situation that whilst the Instrument of Government, with its many artificial devices for stemming the tide of

established in a single person and a Parliament, but to congratulate the present deliverance out of those extremities and confusions which the little convention or assembly were putting upon us, as being sensible that any Government for the present were better, until it shall please God, in His due time, to bring us through many shakings to a steady foundation.' *Burton,* I. xxx.

[1] " For the indenture, that was calculated at Court; and, if it had not been sent down, it had never been sent up. Besides the clause itself was void, no restrictions being to be laid upon the supreme Government, which was supposed to be in Parliament; and the people when they had conferred their trust, could not limit their trustees, because they represented them; . . besides the legislative power was supposed to be a right so inherent in the people as they could not give it away, much less could their representatives." *Ib.*

[2] This was added to the three put forth in his name the day before. The addition was merely nominal, as this one was implied in the position taken by those who put forward the other three. See pp. 186, 187.

Parliamentary supremacy, perished without leaving its mark on the Constitution, his four fundamentals have been accepted by the nation, and are at this day as firmly rooted in its conscience as Parliamentary supremacy itself. In protesting against the bonds of a written constitution on which the nation had never been consulted the Bradshaws and Hazleriggs were doing, as Eliot would have said, the business of posterity. Oliver was no less serving the coming generations in insisting on conditions without which Parliamentary government is a vain show.

It was one thing for Oliver to point in the right direction: it was another thing to give effect to his desires. The real *The diffi-culty of re-conciling them with the claims of Parliament.* obstacle in his way, though he took little count of it, was that the nation, or even the intellectually active part of it, had not been educated in political thought. There were hundreds who could discourse on the true constitution of the Church, and who could expansively utter their opinions on the craggiest points of divinity, for one who could say anything worth listening to on the Constitution of the State. There had been a tide of reaction against the arbitrary government of Charles which had led men to place a Parliament on the throne of the ancient kings. More lately there had been another tide of reaction against the narrowness and self-seeking of the Long Parliament in its closing months, which had led other men to seek to bind such absoluteness in the toils of a written constitution. Yet to combine the two currents of opinion was, at all events for the present, an almost insuperable task. Oliver was at least justified in holding firmly *Oliver holds provisionally by the In-strument.* by the Instrument until some more serviceable arrangement could be placed in his hands. "Of what assurance," he asked, after speaking of the danger of Parliaments perpetuating themselves, "is a law to prevent so great an evil if it be in one and the same legislator to unlaw it again? . . . For the same men may unbuild what they have built." For this reason he was prepared to stand *Oliver's appeal.* by the Instrument, at least in its most important articles. "I say," he asseverated, as we may well believe with heightened voice and flashing eyes, "that the wilful throwing away of this Government, such as it is, so owned by God, so approved by men, so testified to—in the fundamentals of it—as is before mentioned, and that in relation to the good of these nations and posterity; I can sooner be willing to be rolled into my grave and buried with infamy than I can give my consent unto."

Yet Oliver, resolved as he was that, so far as he was concerned, the country should never again be bound under the yoke of one sovereign and uncontrolled House, was too much alive to the realities of the situation to expect members of Parliament to bind themselves to accept without discussion either the Instrument as a whole or even the four fundamentals on which he had laid stress. What he required was merely their signatures to the following Recognition as the condition of re-entering the House :—

He does not ask for assent to the four fundamentals.

" I do hereby freely promise and engage to be true and faithful to the Lord Protector and the Commonwealth of England, Scotland, and Ireland, and shall not, according to the tenor of the indentures whereby I am returned to serve in this present Parliament, propose or give my consent to alter the Government,[1] as it is settled in a single person and a Parliament." [2] All that was asked was that the representatives should take upon themselves personally the engagement which had been taken for them by their constituencies at the time of their election.

The Recognition.

---

[1] *I.e.* The Instrument.
[2] *C.J.* vii. 368 ; *Burton*, I. xxxiii.-xxxv. ; *Carlyle*, Speech III. ; *His Highness the Lord Protector's Speech*, E, 812, 11.

CHAPTER XXXVI

DRIFTING ASUNDER

So reasonable a requirement—amounting to no more than that the Instrument should be accepted as a basis of discussion,

1654.
Sept. 12.
A basis of
discussion. inviolable only on the point that government was to be divided between Parliament and a single person— was likely to conciliate all except the extreme Re-

The Re-
cognition
receives
signatures. publicans. Before the evening about a hundred members had signed the Recognition, and had been

Sept. 13.
A fast day. allowed by the guards stationed at the door to pass to their seats. On the following day, which had been set apart for a fast by the House itself,[1] Bradshaw and Hazlerigg attended the sermon in St. Margaret's in the places assigned to them as members; but they made no further attempt to press their claims, and after a brief delay retired from Westminster with the bulk of their followers. So secure did the Protector feel himself, that after his return from the

Sept. 12.
Harrison
liberated. Painted Chamber on the 12th he gave Harrison a good dinner at Whitehall, after which he assured him that his object in inviting him had been to discharge the office of a friend by admonishing him 'not to persist in those deceitful and slippery ways whose end is destruction.' Oliver then set his old comrade at liberty, dismissing him 'with much good counsel and more civility,' which profited neither the giver nor the receiver.[2] The fact that there was no longer any party sitting in the House likely to give a com-

[1] See p. 181
[2] Greene to --? Sept. 25, *Clarendon MSS.* xlix. fol. 59.

mission to Harrison to take up arms on its behalf doubtless formed the main consideration which influenced the Protector in dealing so leniently with one whom he had but recently regarded as dangerous to the State.

The number of members willing to sign the Recognition steadily increased. On the 14th they were reckoned as 140,

Sept. 14-21.
Increase of the numbers admitted to the House.

and no fewer than 190 were counted on the 21st.[1] Though the Government party must have occupied a strong position after the exclusion of their more pronounced adversaries, it took care to show that its object was to disarm, not to provoke, opposition. The Recognition itself, like the indenture prescribed by the Instrument upon which it had been modelled, was somewhat ambiguous, as it was not absolutely clear whether acknowledgment of ' the Government as settled in a single person and a Parliament' implied an acceptance of all the forty-one articles of the Instrument, or merely as was the better opinion, of the division of powers between Protector and Parliament. It was now voted by common consent that the Recognition did ' not

Sept. 14.
An explanation of the Recognition.

comprehend nor shall be construed to comprehend . . . . the whole of the ' Instrument of ' Government, . . . but that the same doth only include

Sept. 15.
The Instrument brought in.

what concerns the government of the Commonwealth by a single person and successive Parliaments.'[2] On the 15th the Instrument itself was

Sept. 18.
The Recognition acknowledged.

brought into the House, and the 18th was fixed for its discussion. When the 18th arrived Parliament asserted its independence by ordering the Recog-

Sept. 19.
The Instrument in Committee.

nition to be accepted by the members on the mere initiative of the House, thus entirely ignoring the Protector's action. On the following day it resolved itself into a Committee to debate the Instrument itself.

It is difficult to come to any other conclusion than that this line was taken with the tacit consent, if not with the ab-

---

[1] Bordeaux to Brienne, Sept. $\frac{14}{24}$, *French Transcripts, R.O.* ; *Burton*, I. xxxix.

[2] *C.J.* vii. 368.

solute approval, of the Protector. The essence of the under-

An understanding with the Protector probable.

standing he favoured was that the four fundamentals were in some way or other to be preserved, but that a Parliamentary constitution was to be substituted for the one drawn up by the Army. It was a settlement from which Oliver had everything to gain. Yet its adoption, even for a moment, implied the acceptance by both parties of some definite negotiator ; and though not a spark of evidence

Cooper's probable part in negotiating the understanding.

exists on the subject, every probability points to Cooper as the intermediary. All that is known of his future career shows him as a man who would be equally impatient of a military despotism and of the religious tyranny which a Government at the mercy of the popular will was likely to exercise. He had also—what Oliver had not—a constitutional mind, and he must fully have understood the advantage of securing a Parliamentary basis for the new settlement.

The discussion in Committee had not proceeded far when it became evident that a basis of agreement had been found.

Sept. 21. A basis of agreement found.

The fundamental provisions of the Constitution were not, as had been required in the Instrument, to be absolutely unalterable, but were only to be

A veto substituted for a prohibition.

alterable with difficulty ; and it was proposed that, to secure so desirable an object, they should not be changed by Parliament without the consent of the Protector for the time being. It probably cost Oliver somewhat even to contemplate the weakening of the rocky barrier he had opposed to the evils against which he was contending ; but, after all, there are no insuperable obstacles in political life, and it may well have been that the new arrangement, just because it was more flexible, would have been more serviceable than the scheme which had been imposed on him by Lambert and his confederates.

Discussion on the Constitution.

It remained to be seen whether Protector and Parliament could agree on the details of the proposed system. The first article of the Parliamentary constitution, giving supreme power to Protector and Parlia-

ment in the terms of the Instrument, was speedily adopted, and
provision was made against the danger of Parliament
perpetuating itself by a declaration in favour of
triennial elections; though, perhaps with the intention of showing its independence, the Committee resolved
that future sessions should extend to six instead of to five
months, and that beyond that period they should only be
lengthened by an Act of Parliament, on which, however, the
Protector was allowed to interpose his veto. Two out of the
four fundamentals having been thus disposed of, the Committee approached the third on the 22nd, voting that
'the Present Lord Protector during his life, the
Parliament sitting—with the consent of Parliament,
and not otherwise—shall dispose and employ the
forces both by sea and land, for the peace and good of the
three nations.' In this the House followed the lines of the
Instrument, except that nothing was settled as to the course
to be adopted after the Protector's death. Yet, in spite of
this omission, so pleased was Oliver with the progress made,
that he wrote to offer to the House an account of his naval
preparations. With equal courtesy the House replied that it
was willing to leave to His Highness the management of that
design.[1]

Two fundamentals accepted.

Sept. 22. The question of the armed forces.

The question of the armed forces, however, bristled with
difficulties. The Instrument had left their control in the intervals of Parliament to the Protector and Council, and when
this proposal was brought up for discussion, the
Committee, not unnaturally came to the conclusion
that before such extensive powers were granted to
the Council it would be well to determine what was to be the
composition and status of that body. By the Instrument its
members were appointed for life,[2] and, when removed by death
were replaced by a complicated process, in which the part of
Parliament was reduced to the presentation of six names for

Sept. 23. Attendant difficulties.

[1] *C.J.* vii. 369; *Burton*, I. xl., xli.

[2] Except when members were convicted of corruption or other abuse
of trust.

each vacancy, out of which two were to be selected by the Council, to be presented to the Protector in order that he might

Sept. 26.
The Coun-
cil to be
subject to
the ap-
proval of
Parlia-
ment make a final choice. By the 26th this scheme was definitely rejected, and it was proposed in its place that Councillors should be nominated by the Protector, subject to the approval of Parliament, but that not one of them should retain office more than forty days after the meeting of a new Parliament unless he secured the renewal of the vote of confidence which he had received on his appointment.

The position of the Council once settled, the question of the powers to be conceded to the Protector was next in order.

Sept. 27.
Question
of the Pro-
tectorate.

Sept. 29.
Oliver's
narrow
escape
from a
fatal
accident. The Committee, however, had not trenched far on this ground before it was reminded of the futility of building the foundations of government on the character or abilities of a single human being. On the 29th Oliver, accompanied by Thurloe, was in Hyde Park, taking the air in a coach drawn by six spirited horses recently presented to him by the Duke of Oldenburg, when he bethought himself of changing places with his coachman. Though he was no mean judge of horseflesh, he used the whip too freely, and in the rush which followed was jerked forward, first on the pole, and then on the ground. His foot catching in the reins, his life was for a moment in danger, especially as a pistol exploded in his pocket as he was being dragged along the ground. Contriving, however, to extricate himself from his dangerous position, he suffered no damage beyond a few scratches, though he was left in a state of nervous exhaustion. Thurloe, who had jumped out, was carried home with a dislocated ankle. Friends and foes agreed in celebrating the occurrence in prose and verse, though it is hard to say whether less of the poetic quality was shown by those who rejoiced in the Protector's marvellous escape, or by those who expressed a fervent hope that his next ride would be in a cart to Tyburn.[1]

[1] The story has been more fully told by Mr. Firth, in an article on Cromwell's views on sport, in *Macmillan's Magazine* for October 1894. To

During the following week the Committee busied itself with the powers to be accorded to the executive Government.   The

Sept. 30-
   Oct. 4.
The power
of war and
peace.

Instrument had granted the Protector and Council the right of making war and peace, merely insisting that, when once war had broken out, Parliament should be summoned to give ' advice concerning the same,' or, in other words, to provide money for carrying it on. The Committee on the other hand, in spite of the criticism of the Court party, voted without a division that, though the Protector might make peace with the consent of the Council alone when Parliament was not sitting, he must obtain the consent of Parliament to a declaration of war, even if it was necessary to hold a session specially convened for the purpose.[1] Other subjects then occupied the attention of the members for

Oct. 16-18.
Question of
the succes-
sion.

some days, and it was only on October 16 that the question of the succession was approached.   In the debate, which spread over three days, Lambert who, when the Instrument was being drawn up, had supported the proposal to give to Oliver the title of King, now urged that the Protectorate should be made hereditary.   The sense of the Committee was, however, against him, and it was resolved by the large majority of 200 to 65 that it should be elective.   It is almost certain that the majority comprised members of the Protector's own family,[2] who must have acted under the influence of Oliver himself, partly, perhaps, because he believed that government should be allotted to merit alone, and partly because he feared to irritate the generals who served under him, and who regarded the supreme magistracy as a prize to which

the evidence there collected may be added Bordeaux's account in his despatch of Oct. $\frac{2}{12}$.

[1] *Burton*, I. xliv.–xlvi.

[2] " D'abord son party parust le plus fort ; mesme le géneral Lambert fist harangue pour persuader le Parlement qu'il estoit nécessaire de rendre la charge de Protecteur héréditaire : mais lorsque l'on est venu à prendre les voix tous ses parens et amis ont été d'advis de la rendre eslective." Bordeaux to Brienne, Oct. $\frac{19}{29}$, *French Transcripts, R.O.*   Compare Beverning and Nieupoort to the States General, Oct. $\frac{20}{30}$.   *Add. MSS.* 17,677 U, fol. 433.   See also Burton's *Diary*, I. li.

all might aspire. Nor is it altogether impossible that the known incompetence of Richard had some effect in increasing the majority.[1]

The mode of election did not occupy the Committee long. On the 21st it was resolved that though the choice might be left to the Council during the intervals of Parliament, it should be made, if the House were in session at the time of a Protector's death, by Parliament itself. On the 24th it was resolved that the article in the Instrument which directed that officers of State appointed by the Protector should receive the approbation of Parliament was to remain unaltered.[2]

Oct. 21.
Mode of
electing a
Protector.

Oct. 24.
Officers of
State to be
approved by
Parliament.

Constitu-
tional im-
portance of
the mode in
which the
Council was
to be chosen.

By this time it was easy to see that though the Committee was inclined to push the pretensions of Parliament somewhat further than the Instrument allowed, it had as yet no wish, except on one point— that of the appointment of the Council—to make any violent changes, certainly not to revert to the system of Parliamentary omnipotence which Oliver had so lately deprecated. Yet the difference between the two modes of choosing Councillors was a radical one. Whenever a vacancy occurred in the Council the powers of Parliament, according to the Instrument, were limited to the sending in of a list of names, out of which a choice must

---

[1] The most convincing testimony to Richard's reputation at this time is given by a mistake of Pauluzzi, who forwarded to Venice a sketch of the characters of the brothers Richard and Henry, but took it for granted that Henry was the elder of the two. The same mistake was afterwards made by Bonde in the following summer. Probably Pauluzzi, to some extent, represents Oliver's own attitude. "S'accommoda il Protettore alla rissolutione, non havendo voluto insister nella successione de' figlioli, per non accrescersi maggiormente contrarii et odiosi i concetti che miri solo ad eternar in lui e nella discendenza il comando supremo di tutta l'Inghilterra." Pauluzzi to Morosini, $\frac{Oct. 28}{Nov. 7}$, *Venetian Transcripts*, *R.O.* A less generous view was taken by Bordeaux, who writes that the hereditary succession 'ne pouvoit qu'estre desagréable aux officiers de l'armée, dont le moindre prétend à son tour commander en Angleterre.' Bordeaux to Brienne, Oct. $\frac{19}{29}$, *French Transcripts*, *R.O.*

[2] *Burton*, I. lx.

be made by others. Though it is true that by this means it
could secure the exclusion of all candidates absolutely dis-
pleasing to itself, it could never hope to retain a hold upon the
political action of a Councillor to whom had been accorded a
seat for life, and who would come under the influence of
colleagues inured to the exercise of government and little
inclined to look with respect upon Parliamentary authority.
The new proposal, on the other hand, would make the Councillors anxious to secure the goodwill of future Parliaments, because
it was to Parliament alone they looked for the prolongation of
their office. The question, in short, was whether the main
executive authority was to be founded in confidence on Parliaments or not. Oliver would doubtless have preferred to retain

The Pro-
tector not
seriously
dissatisfied.
the Instrument as it originally stood, but there is no
indication that he was so dissatisfied as to desire to
set Parliament at defiance; though it is possible that
he was restrained from expressing what dissatisfaction he may
have entertained by the knowledge that the alterations effected
in Committee were to a large extent the work of his own supporters, some of them being even members of his Council.[1]

It was, in fact, impossible at this time to forecast the ultimate
attitude of the Protector to the new constitution, because

Oct. 5.
The two
outstanding
funda-
mentals.
The army.
much would depend on the attitude of Parliament to
the two fundamentals remaining to be discussed—
that of the management of the army, and that of
religious liberty. As yet the Committee had agreed
to nothing relating to the control of the army after
the death of the present Protector, having turned its attention
to a more immediately practical question — that of imposing some

[1] Foreign ambassadors during this period speak without hesitation of
Parliament as being subservient to the Protector, which is inconsistent
with the view that it was in revolt against him. An echo of this belief is
found in a letter written in Paris on Oct. $\frac{14}{24}$, in which the writer remarks
that the Protector 'had better have sat in his chair in the Painted
Chamber to govern the Parliament, which is more pliable to his pleasure,
than in the coach-box to govern his coach-horses, which have more
courage to put him out of the box than the three hundred members of
Parliament have to put him out of his chair.' *Thurloe*, ii. 674.

limitations on the existing superfluity of the land and sea forces. On October 5 the Protector, after conference with a Committee appointed to come to an understanding with him on the subject, had consented to reduce the fleet by twenty-eight ships.[1] The question of diminishing the army stood over for further consideration. As to religion, the House having dropped the proposal for gathering an Assembly of Divines, had appointed a

A religious settlement. Committee to consider the ecclesiastical arrangements of the country with the assistance of fifteen or twenty ministers,[2] and it was probable that these debates would

Nov. 4.
A conference
with the
Protector
asked for. occupy some considerable time. It is not unlikely that an experience of the difficulty of satisfying the combined theologians led on November 4 to the appointment of a sub-committee to confer with the

Nov. 7.
The reso-
lutions of
Committee
before the
House. Protector on the same subject. On November 7, in order to utilise the time needed for the consideration of these questions, the House[3] took up the

---

[1] *C.J.* vii. 373.   [2] *Burton*, I. xlvi.

[3] There is a difference of evidence as to the actual numbers who had by this time taken the Recognition. Under the date of Oct. 6 Whitelocke gives 300; but on Oct. $\frac{19}{29}$ Bordeaux (*French Transcripts*, *R.O.*) admits only 260, though this number may apply only to those present at an important vote. On Dec. 12 the House ordered 300 copies of a certain paper to be distributed amongst its members, and this number seems to have been generally accepted, though on $\frac{Oct. 27}{Nov. 6}$ Nieupoort (*Add. MSS.* 17,677, U. fol. 437) gives as many as 350, and Thurloe, writing to Pell on Oct. 24, informs him that there were 'not above 30 persons in the whole 460 that have refused to sign the Recognition.' (Vaughan's *Protectorate*, i. 71.) This must surely have been an exaggeration, unless Thurloe laid stress on the word 'refused,' excluding those who remained in the country without expressing an opinion. It may on the whole be assumed that by the end of October at least 300 had qualified for taking their seats. The highest number of voters, excluding tellers, in the two divisions taken before the enforcement of the Recognition was 317. In two divisions in October, both of them of a non-political character, the highest was 195. Of course, the numbers present on any given occasion were considerably less than 300. In fourteen divisions in November the number on one occasion reached 199. In fifteen in December the highest was 184. In twenty-eight in January the highest was 224, the highest mark of November being only exceeded in three

report of the Committee on so much of the new Constitution as had by this time been adopted.

It soon appeared that the members saw no reason to disagree with the conclusions which they had previously come to in Committee, though there were signs that the apparent harmony might change into discord when more exciting questions were reached. Speaking on behalf of the Court party on the disposal of the negative voice, Desborough expressed himself as if it had been a mere act of kindness in the Protector to divest himself in part of that absolute power which he had already in his hand. Parliament, he added, had not the opportunity to do anything it pleased ; its business was merely to amend the Instrument where the Protector gave it leave to do so. On the other side it was asserted that though Parliament had no intention of refusing the negative voice on the four fundamentals, it was for the House and not for the Protector, to impose such limitations on its inherent legislative power. Upon a division being taken it was decided by 109 to 85 that the right of passing Bills into law without the consent of the Protector should only extend to such as contained nothing contrary to matters wherein the Parliament should think fit to give a negative to the Lord Protector. Against this assumption that the House was a constituent body the whole Court party rose in revolt. " I could wish," cried Broghill, now one of the warmest of Oliver's adherents, " I could have redeemed that wound with a pound of the best blood in my body." [1]   In the

*Nov. 10.
A dispute on the negative voice*

The House claims to be a constituent body.

divisions, the first of which was taken on January 15. It may therefore be taken that there was no appreciable addition to the number of members actually sitting between October 25 and January 15. It follows from this calculation that any change in the attitude of Parliament towards the Protector between these two dates cannot have been caused by the influx of members hitherto keeping aloof from the House through hostility to the Protector.

[1] *Burton*, I. lxiii.–lxviii. The speaker is termed a person of honour and nobility. The name is suggested by the editor, and, indeed, Broghill was the only person amongst the Protector's partisans to whom this designation is applicable.

end, however, a compromise was accepted, the clause being

Nov. 15.
A com-
promise. toned down to a claim that the excepted Bills should 'contain nothing in them contrary to such matters wherein the said single person and the Parliament shall think fit to declare a negative to be in the said single person.'[1]

If, indeed, a breach was to come, it was far more likely to arise out of a difference of opinion on some concrete question,

Question
of the
disposal of
the army
and navy. such as the disposal of the army and navy, than out of a dispute on constitutional theory, the more so as, though the Instrument itself had laid down that a convenient number of ships for guarding the seas, together with 20,000 foot and 10,000 horse and dragoons, should be kept up by taxation agreed to by Protector and Council without recourse to Parliament, it had also declared that extraordinary forces rendered necessary by 'the present wars' should be supported by money raised 'by consent of Parliament and not otherwise.'[2] As matters now stood the whole of the two fleets under Blake and Penn, together with no less than 27,000 of an army which had been increased to 57,000 men,[3] were by the very terms of the Instrument dependent for support upon a Parliamentary grant. It was unavoidable that the additional burden should appear to Oliver to be, at least for the time, absolutely necessary, but should seem to members of Parliament to be capable of some alleviation. Yet there was no wish to

Nov. 15.
The Pro-
tector to
be asked
to reduce
military
expense. act in this matter apart from the Protector. A Committee which had been formerly directed to wait on him having reported that, at a conference with eight officers selected by the Protector, it had been informed that only six garrisons could prudently be

---

[1] *Burton*, I. lxx.

[2] Articles xxvii. and xxx.

[3] *Burton*, I. cviii., where it is stated that the number was over 57,000. An account printed in the *Antiquarian Repertory* (ed. 1808), ii. 12 gives the number as 52,965, 'according to the old former establishment.' Probably the army had been increased since that establishment was drawn up.

discharged, was now directed to return with a request for further reductions.[1]

It is likely enough that it was to a great extent mainly this persistency in diminishing what Oliver regarded as the necessary strength of the army which prompted the sharp reply given by him on the following day to a Committee which had come for his advice on some question relating to restrictions on toleration. He ' was,' he told them, ' wholly dissatisfied with the thing, and had no propensity nor inclination to it ; and that the Parliament had already taken the government abroad,[2] and had altered and changed it in the other articles as they pleased without his advice ; and therefore it would not become him to give any advice at all, singly and apart, as to this article.'[3] Yet, though Oliver's remarks applied in part to the constitutional amendments, they also struck at the attitude of the Committee in regard to toleration. For some time it had been listening to some fourteen divines, amongst whom Owen continued to press the adoption of the scheme requiring the acceptance of certain fundamentals of religious faith which had been originally promulgated in 1652 as a condition of toleration [4]—an attitude in which he was supported by all his colleagues, with the exception of Baxter and Vines. Yet, though Baxter proposed to content himself with setting up the Lord's Prayer, the Creed, and the Decalogue as the sole conditions of toleration, even this largeness of mind was insufficient for the Protector, who summoned Baxter before him, and, as the divine complained, smothered him in a torrent of words, to which he was not permitted to reply.[5]

Perhaps it was not only the contrariety of public affairs which had drawn from Oliver that sharp reply which he had

Marginal notes:

Nov. 16. A sharp reproof from the Protector.

The Committee on religion.

Owen and Baxter.

---

[1] *C.J.* vii. 385 ; *Burton*, I. lxxvii., lxxviii., note.

[2] *I.e.* ' in pieces.'

[3] *C.J.* vii. 385. This answer was reported to the House on the 17th, and therefore was almost certainly given on the 16th.

[4] See vol. ii. p. 101.

[5] *Reliquiæ Baxterianæ*, i. 197.

addressed to the Committee. On that day his aged mother,

Death of
Oliver's
mother.

now in her ninetieth year,[1] lay dying in that Whitehall to the splendours of which, it is said, she had never quite reconciled herself. That evening, when her harassed son visited her for the last time, she addressed him with words of heartfelt sympathy. "The Lord cause His face to shine upon you and comfort you in all your adversities, and enable you to do things for the glory of your Most High God and to be a relief unto His people. My dear son, I leave my heart with thee. A good night ! "[2]

Oliver had need of all his mother's confidence that his work was divinely righteous to hold up against the sea of

Fresh
troubles
impending.

Nov. 17.
The control
of the army
limited to
the present
Protector.

troubles to which he was exposed. A rift once established has a tendency to widen, and November 17, the day on which the Protector's scornful answer was reported, was marked in the House by the acceptance of the Committee's proposal limiting the control of the army to the lifetime of the present Protector.[3] The idea that the actual distribution of power was not to be permanent, but was merely a temporary concession to the necessity of a time when the country was sloughing off the revolutionary skin was one with which Parliament, in its present temper, was certain to familiarise itself, but was hardly likely to commend itself to the mind of Oliver. What followed must have strengthened his displeasure. On

Nov. 20.
Disposal of
the forces
after the
Protector's
death.

the 20th it was decided that, in the event of the death of the present Protector, the forces should be disposed of by the Council till Parliament could be assembled, and then by 'the Parliament, as they

---

[1] Thurloe (Vaughan's *Protectorate*, i. 81) makes her 94 ; but Chester's argument for the age given above (*Registers of Westminster Abbey*, 521, note 3) is confirmed by *An Epitaph on the late . . . Elizabeth Cromwell, who lived to the age of* 89. B. M. press-mark, 669, fol. 19, No. 41. Mr. Rye, in *The Genealogist* for 1884, has dispelled the unfounded belief that she was connected with the royal house of Scotland.

[2] Vaughan's *Protectorate*, i. 81.

[3] *C.J.* vii. 386.

shall think fit.' No division was taken, and the Court party, therefore, must have felt itself to be in a hopeless minority.

So far as it is possible to gather the intention of the majority from the speeches uttered, it would seem that the idea at the root of their conclusions was the necessity of providing for the rule of law, and the conviction that Parliaments were the best guardians of the law. To the argument 'that to strip the next Protector of the command of the standing forces were but to make him an insignificant nothing, a mere man of straw,' they replied 'that the standing forces were never meant to be in a single person, otherwise than by consent of Parliament. It was the manner and custom of this nation, and of our ancestors, not to put our king in the head of an army, especially of a standing army, but in the head of their laws.' " And certainly," the speaker—whoever he may have been—continued, " to place the command of the standing forces alone in a single person, or co-ordinately in him and the Parliament, would be to make the Parliament a mere Jack-a-Lent, and as insignificant a nothing as the single person, in case it should be placed wholly in the Parliament. For, give any single person in the world but power, and you give him a temptation to continue and engross that power wholly to himself and an opportunity to effect it. For, as, wheresoever there is a co-ordination of power, there is a right, mutually, on both sides to defend their interests, the one against the other ; so, whensoever any advantage offers itself, the one will usurp on the other, and, in fine, strive totally to subvert it." Parliament, in short, might impose limitations on its own authority : it could not admit that the power of the sword should be permanently in hands which might use it against the nation. Put in this form the argument carries conviction, at least to later generations. Oliver's main objection was doubtless conveyed by another speaker. It had been said, he declared, 'that to exclude the Protector from the command of the standing force would be to give up the cause, that eminent and glorious

Arguments on both sides.

<hr>

[1] *C.J.* vii. 387.

cause, which had been so much and so long contended ; for such Parliaments might hereafter be chosen as would betray the glorious cause of the people of God.'[1] In these last words

The difficulty of the Protectorate. we have the whole difficulty of establishing the Protectorate laid before us. Oliver, at least, had no love for government by the sword. Willingly, as he showed three years later, would he have exchanged a Constitution drawn up by officers and guaranteed by the army for a Constitution drawn up by Parliament and guaranteed by civil institutions. Yet in 1657, as well as in 1654, he was determined not to sacrifice 'the glorious cause of the people of God' to any institutions whatsoever. Convince him that this was safe and institutions might, with his goodwill, be shifted from one system to another. On the other hand, it must never be forgotten that he aimed at assuring the safety of the people of God, not by establishing them exclusively in the seats of power, but by securing them from persecution by the diffusion of liberty to all who were not blasphemers, if only they abstained from machinations against the existing Government.

Natural as was the desire of the House to assure its own supremacy in the future, its last step can hardly be qualified as

The last step of the House tends to a rupture. conciliatory. Yet it is scarcely likely that any circumspection would have induced the majority to act otherwise. Even if we credit them—as we almost certainly may—with a firm desire at the outset to establish a fair compromise which either side might accept without dishonour, the mere effluence of time must have made this achievement more difficult of attainment every day. Parliaments are as apt as Governments to stand upon their rights,

The struggle for the control over the army. and, however much both parties may have desired to divide the control of the army between them, the question which of the two was to predominate could not fail to thrust itself into the foreground ; and, when once discussion had begun upon those mysteries of sovereignty, no possible goodwill amongst the disputants could be trusted to

---

[1] *Burton*, I. lxxxiii.

bring about an amicable solution. Verbally, no doubt, the
Protector insisted, and would continue to insist, that he claimed
no exclusive power over the army. It was far easier to enun-
ciate such a proposition in general terms than to translate the
principle of divided authority into a detailed scheme. As a
matter of fact, the control must fall, in the last resort, either to
the Parliament or to the Protector, and it is not strange that
the members judged it best lodged in their own hands. Moreover, neither Parliament nor Protector was able to consider the
question of the army purely on its constitutional merits. That
army had too long been in the habit of intervening in politics
to make it easy for Parliament to regard it as a merely military
institution. To the Protector, on the other hand, Parliamentary
control over the army meant almost certain danger to the
religious liberty which lay nearest to his heart. Once more
the two ideals of the Revolution showed themselves to be
incompatible with one another.

Nor was it only by constitutional arrangements that Parliament sought to maintain its hold over the soldiery. Some of
its members, and not improbably the majority of the
House, contemplated a reversion—so far as might be
—to the military system which had prevailed before
the outbreak of the war.[1] The militia, it had been said on the
17th, was 'the intrinsic force of the nation.' The standing
forces were but such ' as, upon extraordinary emergencies, and
to supply the other, were raised, or to be raised, upon the
authority of Parliament, and to be maintained at the public
charge.'[2] Though, with the dangers which now threatened
the Commonwealth staring the members in the face, it was
obvious that the standing army could not immediately give
place to a militia, at no time during the session was any hint
given that the majority contemplated keeping on foot more than
the 30,000 regulars authorised by the Instrument, and there is
good reason to suppose that the thought which already pre-
dominated was that the place of the 27,000 who would be

Nov. 17.
Militia and
standing
army.

---

[1] Just as their successors did after the Peace of Ryswick.
[2] *Burton*, I. lxxix.

disbanded [1] must be filled by militia, the control of which would lie with the local authorities, and not with the central Government. [2]

The prospect of a disbandment could hardly fail to bring the officers into line against the Parliament. A few weeks Feeling in the army. before they had been less unanimous. Having been employed, as they had been, in combating the monarchy in the name of Parliament, it was inevitable that some of them would find the new Protectorate as obnoxious as the old kingship. Of these, one of the foremost was Colonel Alured, Saunders, and Okey. Alured, who, having been sent into Ireland in the spring to bring over reinforcements to Monk, used language about the evil designs of the Protector so offensive as to necessitate his recall. [3] On his return to Westminster, Alured found kindred spirits in two other colonels, Saunders and Okey, and not long after the meeting of Parliament these three entered into communication with Wildman, the Leveller. [4] The result was the preparation by Wildman The petition of the three colonels. of a petition to the Protector, which was at once adopted by the three colonels, and intended to be circulated for signature amongst other colonels whose approval might be expected. The petition was seized before It is seized, Oct. 18. but published. any further adhesions had been given in, and the three colonels placed under arrest. On October 18, [5] however, it was published in the form of a broadsheet, probably by Wildman, who is likely to have retained a copy.

---

[1] See p. 205. [2] See *infra*, p. 223.

[3] The Protector to Fleetwood, May 16; the Protector to Alured, May 16: *Carlyle*, Letters cxciii., cxciv. *The Case of Col. Alured*, E, 983, 25.

[4] Thurloe's Notes, *Thurloe*, iii. 147. Hacker is noted to have been present at the meeting where the petition was discussed. He was a strong Presbyterian, but remained constant to the Protector. Can he have informed the Government of what was going on?

[5] B. M. press-mark, 669, f. 19, No. 21, where the date of publication is given by Thomason. Mrs. Everett-Green wrongly gives it in her Calendar as Dec. 20, 1653.

Starting with a reference to the often-quoted Declarations of the Army, the petitioners assert that Charles I. had been

It recites the evils of monarchy.

brought to justice for opposing the supreme power of Parliament, 'the King's unaccountableness being the grand root of tyranny.' "We having, therefore," continue the three colonels, "seriously and sadly considered the present great transactions and the government in the settlement whereof our assistance is required, . . . declare to your Highness . . . that we sadly resent the dangerous consequences of establishing that supreme trust of the militia, at least for the space of two years and a half of every three years, in a single person and a council of his own, whom he may control by a negative voice at his pleasure." The army, too, might in the hands of some successor of the present Protector become 'wholly mercenary and be made use of to destroy at his pleasure the very being of Parliaments.' Moreover, though the Instrument enabled Parliament to pass ordinary Bills without the

Allegation that a negative voice is practically given to the Protector,

Protector's consent, it would always be open to a Protector to allege that any Bill to which he objected was contrary to some article of the Instrument, and so beyond the power of Parliament to insist on,[1] especially as it would be difficult to question the allegations of the master of 30,000 men. Nor, even if the Protector refrained from throwing his sword into the scale, was it easy to reconcile

as well as the right of raising supplies independently of Parliament.

with the ancient freedom of the country a Constitution which provided the Government with 200,000*l.* for the expenses of administration, as well as with sufficient means of keeping up an army of 30,000 men and a fleet sufficient to defend the coasts without any recourse to a Parliamentary grant.

On these premises the petitioners based no uncertain conclusion. "Now," they declared, " . . . finding in our apprehensions the public interest of right and freedom so far from

---

[1] This is, no doubt, an exaggerated statement, but it points to a real gap in the Instrument—its omission to provide a means of obtaining an authoritative decision as to what Bills were in accordance with the Instrument.

security that the first foundations thereof are unsettled, and the

What is the basis of the Protectorate?

gates are open that may lead us into endless troubles and hazards, the government not being clearly settled either upon the bottom of the people's consent, trust or contract, nor [upon] a right of conquest, . . . nor upon an immediate divine designation; and our ears being filled daily with the taunts, reproaches and scandals upon the profession of honesty, under colour that we have pretended the freedoms of our country, and made large professions against seeking our private interests, while we intended only to set up ourselves; these things thus meeting together do fill our hearts with trouble and sadness, and make us cautious of taking upon ourselves new engagements, although none shall more faithfully serve your Highness in all just designs; . . . and we are

An appeal to a free Parliament.

hereby enforced to . . . pray . . . that a full and free Parliament may, without any imposition upon their judgments and consciences, freely consider of those fundamental rights and freedoms of the Commonwealth that are the first subject of this great contest, which God hath decided on our side, according as the same have been proposed to the Parliament by the Grand Council of the Army in *the Agreement of the People*, which remains there upon record, that, by the assistance and direction of God, they may settle the Government of the Commonwealth and the ways of administration of justice, and secure our dearly-bought freedom of our consciences, persons and estates against all future attempts of tyranny; and such a settlement will stand upon a basis undoubtedly just by the laws of God and man—and therefore more likely to continue to us and our posterities—and in your Highness's prosecution of these great ends of the expense of all the blood and treasure in these three nations, your petitioners shall freely hazard their lives and estates in your just defence."

The appeal of the three colonels to a full and free Parliament

A constituent assembly demanded.

intended to act as a constituent assembly, in the hope that it would guarantee complete liberty of conscience, was astonishingly naïve. For that very reason it was likely to find an echo amongst those simple souls who had taken arms to regenerate their country, and who failed to see why salvation was so long on the way. Even in the navy—little given to idealisms as it was—the demands of the three colonels found transient favour. Blake's fleet had,

Oct. 8. Sailing of Blake's fleet.

indeed, sailed from Plymouth for the Mediterranean on October 8, but Penn's was still delayed at Portsmouth, and, almost at the same time that the

Discontent amongst Penn's crews.

petition of the colonels was discovered, a petition of his seamen was laid before the officers, with a request that it might be forwarded to the Protector. The prayer of the petitioners was that Parliament might be pleased to maintain and enlarge the liberties of the free people of England, whilst they reminded that body of the frequent declarations of the army in favour of political progress. Yet it

The seamen's petition.

soon appeared that the demands of the sailors did not exclusively relate to the constitutional requirements of the nation, as they proceeded to ask that impressment might be abandoned ;[1] that sailors might not be sent on foreign service without their own consent ; that, when that consent had been given, they might issue letters of attorney, enabling those dependent on them to draw their pay at least once in six months ; that in the event of their being themselves killed in the service these dependents might be entitled to such compensation as might be agreeable to justice ; and, finally, 'that all other liberties and privileges due to' the petitioners might ' be granted and secured.'[2]

Oct. 17. Approved by a Council of War.

On October 17 a council of war held on board Penn's ship, the 'Swiftsure,' was presided over, in his absence, by Vice-Admiral Lawson. It decided unanimously that it was 'lawful for seamen to tender

[1] They complained ' that your petitioners . . . continue under very great burdens, being imprested and haled on board the Commonwealth ships, turned over and confined there under a degree of thraldom and bondage, to the utter ruin of some of your petitioners' poor families.' This seems to dispose of the view that ' impresting ' or ' impressing ' was, at least in practice, a voluntary arrangement.

[2] *Petition to the Protector*, B. M. press-mark, 669, f. 19, No. 33.

their grievances by way of petition.' Descending to particulars, it decided, with only four dissentients, that the complaints were directed to real grievances, with the exception of the one relating to foreign service ; whilst the four who dissented objected only to the one relating to impressment.[1] With these remarks the petition was forwarded through the generals at sea to the Protector.[2]   Oliver was too well advised

Nov.
Desborough sent to inquire.

Money sent to the crews.

Nov.
Quiet restored.

to allow the fire to smoulder.   Sending Desborough to Portsmouth to inquire into the seamen's grievances,[3] he rightly judged that if the arrears of their pay were made up they would not persist in their other complaints.   There is every reason to believe that considerable sums were set aside for this purpose, and on November 6 Penn was able to write that by the blessing of God the fleet was in a quiet posture and without the least appearance of discontent.[4]

The petition not likely to have originated with the seamen.

For common seamen to send up, even through the hands of their officers, a semi-political petition was so completely at variance with established custom that it is in the highest degree improbable that the form taken by their complaints originated with themselves.

[1] Proceedings at a Council of War, Oct. 17 ; B. M. press-mark, 669, f. 19, No 32.

[2] The Council of War also voted, with two dissentients, that 'seamen petitioning their private commanders and delivering their fore-mentioned petition, with desires that they would please to move the generals and chief officers,' be owned, on the understanding that 'the Lord Protector is not immediately petitioned by the same.'   The court was composed of two admirals, eighteen captains, three lieutenants, and one master ; all of whom, except Lawson and two captains, went out under Penn.

[3] Pauluzzi, writing on Nov. $\frac{13}{23}$, states that one of the generals at sea had been sent.   Only Penn and Desborough were at that time available, and, if Pauluzzi had had Penn in his mind, he would almost certainly have referred to him as the Admiral of the fleet in question.

[4] Penn to the Admiralty Committee, Nov. 6, *Add. MSS.* 9304, fol. 97.   There is no direct evidence of the men being paid, but on Oct. 27 a patent directed the issue of 100,000*l.* to the Treasurer of the Navy (*R.O. Enrolment Book, Pells*, No. 12), and of this sum 55,000*l.* was paid to him on Nov. 1 (*R.O. Issue Book*, Mich. 1654–5).

If we cast about for its authorship, we can light on no
more probable draftsman than Lawson. A Baptist
by creed, he sympathised warmly with the Levellers,
and his name is to be found in a list, jotted down by
Thurloe for his own use, of those who had been present early
in September at a meeting between Wildman and the three
colonels.[1] Five months later his objections to the Protectoral
system were so well known that Charles attempted to enter into
communication with him.[2] Since the Protector, knowing as

Lawson its
probable
author.

---

[1] *Thurloe*, iii. 147.

[2] Charles to Lawson, Feb. $\frac{16}{26}$, 1655, *Clarendon MSS*. xlix. fol. 347.
The belief that Penn and Venables had offered their services to the King
is mainly founded on a passage in *Clarendon*, xv. 6 : " Both these
superior officers were well affected to the King's service, and were not
fond of the enterprise they were to conduct, the nature of which they yet
knew nothing of. They did, by several ways, without any communication
with each other—which they had not confidence to engage in—send to
the King that, if he were ready with any force from abroad, or secure of
possessing any port within, they would engage, with the power that was
under their charge, to declare for His Majesty ; . . . but neither of them
daring to trust the other, the King could not presume upon any port,
without which neither had promised to engage." Clarendon, in this later
part of his history, is not to be trusted implicitly, and his statement that
neither Penn nor Venables knew anything of the nature of the expedition
shows how little he was acquainted with the situation. Moreover, so far
as Venables was concerned, his regiments, brought from various quarters,
were never so much in hand as that he could presume on his authority
with them for such a purpose, though this is assumed in an improbable
story told in Barwick's *Vita J. Barwick*, p. 124. This book was published in 1721, though it was written some years before the publication of
Clarendon's *History*, and may therefore at least be taken as evidence of
an independent tradition among the Royalists. Granville Penn, indeed,
in his *Mem. of Penn*, ii. 14, attempts to bolster up Clarendon's statement
by a reference to a letter from Charles which he had seen in print in some
collection, the very title of which he had forgotten. As no such letter is
known to exist, this reference is of little weight. The only apparent
support Clarendon's statement finds is from a memorandum written by
Ormond for the Count Palatine of Neuburg, in which he says that :
" Besides the power the King hath in the navy and amongst the seamen,
and in this particular fleet under Penn, where—besides the common
soldiers and mariners—there are many principal officers who have served

much as he did, retained Lawson in command of the Channel Squadron, he must have had some strong reason for doing what was, on the face of it, an impolitic act—a reason which there would be no difficulty in specifying if Lawson had ingratiated himself with the seamen by giving voice to their inarticulate discontent.

The revelation of political discontent in the army was far more serious, and the three colonels had to suffer for their audacity. Saunders, indeed, had already made his submission and had been restored to his command; though afterwards he retracted his apology, and consequently lost his commission. Okey having been acquitted by a court-martial on a charge of treason, was allowed by the Protector to obtain his liberty on surrendering his commission. Alured's case was complicated by the charge against him of having attempted to stir up mutiny in the Irish army, and he was not only sentenced to be cashiered, but was detained in prison for more than a twelvemonth.[1]

Nov.-Dec. Fate of the three colonels.

It is not likely that the punishment inflicted on the colonels would, in itself, have affected the temper of a House which was hardly in sympathy with their demand for a free Parliament and unbounded liberty of conscience. Offence was, however, taken when it came to be understood that the chief officers of the army were

The army dissatisfied with Parliament.

His Majesty, and whose affections will dispose them to receive any orders from the King; all which will appear as soon as His Majesty hath the liberty of ports to encourage the resort of his ships and seamen to his service; which, whensoever he shall have, Cromwell will hardly adventure the setting forth of any great fleets, well knowing how ill-affected the seamen are to him." Memorandum, June $\frac{7}{17}$, 1655, Carte's *Orig. Letters*, ii. 54. It will be seen, however, that nothing is here said about Penn's personal fidelity to Charles, and that the ports to be opened are evidently not those on the English side of the Channel, but such as Dunkirk and Ostend, expected to be available on a breach between Spain and the Protector. If there was any expectation from the 'principal officers,' Lawson is likely to have been one of those referred to.

[1] Thurloe to Pell, Nov. 24, Dec. 1; Vaughan's *Protectorate*, i. 83, 87; Newsletter, Dec. 2, intercepted letter, Dec. 21, *Clarke Papers*, iii. 11, 15; *The Case of Colonel Alured*, E, 983, 25.

opposed not merely to these exaggerated demands, but to the attempt of the Parliament to supersede the Instrument, which they regarded as their own work, in favour of Parliamentary government. " I think I may tell you," wrote an onlooker as

Nov. 16.
Opinion of an onlooker.

early as November 16, "this Parliament will end without doing anything considerable—at least anything that should look like opposition to the Lord Protector ; and the officers of the army are, by his wisdom, taken off their discontents, which only would have given life to what cross votes could have passed ; and now the breath some of the House spend in opposing his greatness is little regarded ; the people's expectation of receiving relief from taxes, and for bringing the army from 56,000 [1] to 30,000, which is but according to the Instrument, is insensibly worn away, and very few care when or how they end." [2]

The officers were not slow in giving voice to their sentiments. On November 25, thirty or forty of them met at

Nov. 25.
A meeting of officers.

St. James's ; but though they adjourned in the hope of a fuller gathering, they had already allowed it to be understood that they were prepared to 'live and die to maintain the government as it is now settled.' To Thurloe this devotion to the unamended Instrument seemed hardly in place. " Possibly," he remarked, "they may be too severe upon that point, not being willing to part with a tittle of it."

Nov. 29.
A second meeting.

When the officers met again on the 29th they persisted in their resolution to live and die, not only with his Highness, but with 'the present Government,' or, in other words, to defend the Instrument against all opposers. [3]

In Parliament the intervention of the officers caused the

[1] The number appears to have been above 57,000. See *supra*, p. 205, note 3.

[2] Intercepted letter, Nov. 16, *Thurloe MSS.* xv. 173.

[3] Newsletters, Nov. 25, Nov. 30, *Clarke Papers*, iii. 10 ; Thurloe to Pell, Nov. 24, Dec. 1, Vaughan's *Protectorate*, i. 83, 87. As Thurloe's remark was made on the day before the first meeting, the officers must have taken care to allow their opinion to be known individually.

profoundest dissatisfaction. "The army," it was said, "has
Effect of the officers' intervention. shown its wish to take part in the government, as if
it had been a second House." [1]   The temper aroused
by what was naturally considered as unwarrantable
meddling could not fail to influence the deliberations of the
House. Yet for the time there was no definite rupture. On
Nov. 21. The assessment to be reduced. November 21, indeed, before the first meeting of the
officers, Parliament had resolved to reduce the
monthly assessment from 90,000*l.* to 30,000*l.*, but
Nov. 22. A Committee on finance. on the following day it referred the whole financial
question to a Committee, with a view to a more
complete settlement.[2]   After this a Committee which
Nov. 23. A conference with the Protector. had been appointed at an earlier stage to persuade
the Protector to reduce the army [3] reported that,
though he had expressed an opinion adverse to the
course on which Parliament was bent, he had concluded by
saying that he would not positively declare against the object
it had in view; upon which both sides had mutually agreed
that fresh conferences should be held to discuss the matter
Dec. 6. The debate on the army adjourned. further.[4]   Accordingly, on December 6, after the
officers' declaration was known, a debate on the
reduction of the army was adjourned on the express
ground that an understanding between Protector and Parliament was still to be expected.[5]

The removal of this question from immediate discussion
made room for another of an equally burning nature. On
Dec. 7. A vote for an Established Church. December 7, the day after the army debate was
adjourned, a vote that 'the true reformed Protestant
religion, as it is contained in the Holy Scriptures, . . . and no other, shall be asserted and maintained as
the public profession of these nations,' [6] was without difficulty
passed, the wording being somewhat more combative than that of
the Instrument.   On the 8th, when the question of tolerating

[1] Salvetti's Newsletter, Dec. $\frac{1}{11}$; *Add. MSS.* 27, 962 O, fol. 349.
[2] *C.J.* vii. 387.   [3] See *supra*, p. 205.
[4] *C.J.* vii. 388 ; *Burton*, I. xcii. xciii.
 Burton, I. cviii.   [6] *C.J.* vii. 397.

sectarian worship came up, difficulties began to arise. It is
true that the House voted that the Protector should
have a negative voice to any Bill compelling attendance on the services of the Established Church,
but it refused to allow him to exercise it in the case
of Bills enjoining attendance on religious ' duties in some
public church or chapel, or at some other congregational and
Christian meeting.' There was a warm discussion as to the
assertion that such meetings must be 'approved by the
magistrate according to law'; but though the Court party—in
this case the party of toleration—was beaten in a division by
79 to 62, it was strong enough to reopen the question, and the
words empowering the magistrate to decide what congregations
were to be suffered to meet were ultimately expunged.[1]   Though
it was agreed that the consent of the Protector would
be required to any Bill restraining persons of tender
consciences, unless they abused their liberty ' to the
civil liberty of others or the disturbance of the public
peace,' yet this offer was clogged by a proviso that Parliament
alone should pass Bills for the restraint of atheism, blasphemy,
damnable heresies, popery, prelacy, licentiousness and profaneness.   An attempt to except ' damnable heresies ' from the list
was defeated by 91 to 69.   On the 11th, however, the Court
party gained a victory, though by the barest possible majority,
carrying by 85 to 84 a vote that the ' damnable heresies '
excluding from toleration should be particularly enumerated in
the constitutional Act, instead of being left to the judgment of
future Parliaments, and still less to the judgment of individual
magistrates.[2]   In this frame of mind the House
politely waved aside a list of twenty fundamentals,[3]
though these had been accepted by the Committee
appointed to confer with the divines, who had contented themselves with reproducing the restrictive fundamentals
which Owen, that light of the Independents—now fallen under
the baleful influence of Cheynell—had attempted to press upon

Dec. 8.
Question
of the
toleration of
sectarian
worship.

Dec. 9-11.
Restricted
liberty for
tender con-
sciences.

Dec. 12
Twenty
funda-
mentals of
religion.

[1] *C.J.* vii. 398.   [2] *Ib.* vii. 399.   [3] *Ib.*

the Long Parliament in 1652. The Committee was, indeed, thanked for its services, but recommended to apply itself to the question of the fundamentals to be required not from tolerated congregations, but from the ministers who received public support within the limits of the Established Church.[1] It was about this time that some of the members, discontented with the concessions made by the House, applied themselves to the common councillors of the City, supporting them in the preparation of a petition intended 'to encourage Parliament in A City the settling of Church government,' evidently in the petition. old intolerant fashion. "When," sighed Oliver, "shall we have men of a universal spirit? Everyone desires to have liberty, but none will give it."[2]

Not unnaturally, what appeared in Parliament to be progress in the direction of toleration was, in the eyes of the military leaders, a mere reversion to the persecuting tyrannies of the past. About this time some of the officers presented a An army petition to the Protector asking, amongst other things, petition. 'that liberty of conscience be allowed, but not to papistry in public worship, that tithes be taken away,' and 'that a law be made for the righting persons wronged for liberty of Its effect conscience.'[3] The House had so much to gain by on the House. coming to terms with the Protector, in order to avert this renewed interference of the army, that it becomes easy

[1] See vol. ii. 101, and *supra*, p. 206. For the relation between Owen's fundamentals of 1652 and so much as is known of those of 1654, see Shaw's *Hist. of the . . . Church during the Civil Wars*, ii. 87.

[2] B. T. to ——? *Clarke Papers*, ii. Pref. xxxiv.–xxxvii. ; *Carlyle*, Speech IV.

[3] This petition is given in an undated letter, which, as it mentions the sailing of Penn's second squadron, must have been written about Dec. 25, but is inserted in the *Clarke Papers* (iii. 12–14) between other papers of the 16th and 19th. A despatch from Pauluzzi on the 12th (*Venetian Transcripts, R.O.*) speaks of a petition as having been already presented. Though the heads are not quite the same as those given in the Clarke letter, there is sufficient likeness to make it probable that the same petition is referred to The undated paper may easily have been displaced by a few days.

to account for the recent votes without having recourse to the supposition that the virtue of toleration was more appreciated than before.

Repressed feeling is sure to seek an outlet, and on the 13th the intolerant majority gave vent to its indignation in what

Dec. 13.
Biddle imprisoned.

might seem to be a safe direction by committing Biddle, the Socinian, to prison. For some time the House had been busy with his case, and his refusal to reply to such questions as "Whether Jesus Christ be God from everlasting to everlasting," and "Whether God have a bodily shape," brought matters to a crisis.[1] The next step taken by Parliament was likely to be attended by more serious

Dec. 15.
Parliament to enumerate heresies.

consequences. On the 15th the House reaffirmed the votes it had passed between the 9th and the 11th to the effect that the consent of the Protector should not be required to Bills in restraint of atheism, blasphemy, and damnable heresies, of which latter a list was to be drawn up by Parliament, if necessary without the Protector's consent.[2] Such a resolution was a distinct defiance of the army, and of Oliver himself.

All policies centre in finance, and though the question of the reduction of the army had made no further progress, it

Approaching expiration of the assessment.

could not possibly escape attention as soon as the expiration of the last assessment made it necessary to come to a decision on the public revenue and expenditure. For some time past a Committee had been occupied with the subject, and on November 29 a Bill granting the assessment at the rate of 60,000*l*. a month, in the place of the 90,000*l*. at which it now stood, had been read a second time.[3] For the Protector the reduction of the army involved in this change was a serious matter, and he took care to remind a deputation of members that the present assessment would expire on December 25, and that if no fresh taxation were

[1] *C.J.* vii. 400 ; see vol. ii. 98.

[2] *C.J.* vii. 401 ; see *supra*, p. 220.

[3] *Ib.* vii. 392. For a proposal to reduce it to 30,000*l*., see *supra*, p. 219.

provided the soldiers would be forced to live at free quarter.[1]
It is probable that the irritation of the House in consequence
of the inroad of the army into politics was the cause of a vote

Dec. 16.
A revenue
voted till
forty days
after
the next
meeting
of Parlia-
ment.

taken on the 16th, when it turned back from its
former intention of giving the control of the army to
the present Protector for life, and by the very large
majority of 90 to 56 granted a revenue for the support
of the army and navy merely till forty days had passed
after the next meeting of Parliament.[2]

Having thus gained the upper hand—so far as its own
resolutions could effect anything—the House sought to tighten its
hold on the army still further by limiting the supplies without
which the army could not be maintained. On December 18

Dec. 18.
A financial
debate.

the sub-Committee of Revenue, which had for some
time been active under the chairmanship of Colonel
Birch, was directed to make its report to the Committee of the whole House. In the debate which preceded
this order a member—perhaps Birch himself—argued that
'if we keep up our forces or our charge as high as now,
when we have voted but 60,000*l*., we must needs expect a vast

Proposal
to replace
regular
soldiers by
a militia.

debt, and an impossibility to discharge it ; but for the
proportion of 30,000 men it may well be that the
60,000*l. per mensem* may suffice ; and if that number
be not enough we can enlarge it when we fall on the
consideration of the militia.'[3]

There was little doubt that the solution of the military problem conveyed in these words would prove acceptable to the
Parliamentary majority. To reduce the standing forces to
30,000 and to disband the remaining 27,000, replacing them
by a local militia, which would fall under the power of the

---

[1] "Il . . . leur déclara, que si l'on n'augmentoit les impositions,
qu'il donneroit des quartiers aux troupes." Bordeaux to Brienne,
Dec. $\frac{11}{21}$, *French Transcripts, R.O.* So far as it goes, this seems to show
that the Protector was still unwilling to put forth his claims under the
Instrument, which undoubtedly gave the Protector and Council power
to levy money, at least for 30,000 men, without applying to Parliament.
[2] *C.J.* vii. 401.   [3] *Burton*, I. cxx.

Puritan country gentlemen who were preponderatingly represented in the House, was exactly the remedy which would
adapt itself to their interests and ideas. It was,
perhaps, a suspicion of the danger into which the
House was running that held it back from immediately acting on the suggestions now made. As if to show
its conciliatory intentions, it voted at once that 200,000*l*. should
be annually set aside for the expenses of the civil government
not only during the lifetime of the present Protector, but in
perpetuity.[1] The Assessment Bill passed its third
reading on the 20th.[2] On the following day it was
proposed to insert in this Bill a clause which had
been added to the Constitutional Bill on November 23[3] restricting in the terms of the Instrument the
right of levying taxation to Parliament, but omitting
the proviso of the Instrument which excepted the
supplies needed for the administration of government and for
the armed forces, an omission which in the case of the Constitutional Bill the House intended to supply by articles subsequently to be introduced. The Court party, apparently indignant at this attempt to settle a grave constitutional question in
connection with a money grant, carried Parliament with it in
refusing present consideration for the proviso by the considerable majority of 95 to 75, and the whole question of the assessment was then adjourned for eight days. Time would thus be
allowed for the House to consider the question more fully. On
December 23 the Court party gained another victory, carrying
by 111 to 73 a resolution that the various clauses of the Constitutional Bill should be referred once more to a
Committee of the whole House,[4] with the evident
hope that they might persuade it to adopt at least
a modification of the portions obnoxious to the
Government. There is strong reason to believe that at this
time neither Protector nor Parliament despaired of an under-

Hesitation of the House.

*Dec. 20.
Third reading of the Assess-ment Bill, Dec. 21.
The Court party in the ascen-dant.*

*Dec. 23.
The Con-stitutional Bill again in Committee.*

---

[1] *C.J.* vii. 403.

[2] *Ib.* vii. 405. After the third reading additional clauses and pro-
visoes might still be added.   [3] *C.J.* vii. 388.   [4] *Ib.* 408.

standing.[1] Some members, at least, hoped to find a different
basis of settlement. As soon as the House went into Com-

Garland's
motion for
offering the
kingship to
the Pro-
tector. mittee Augustine Garland, himself a regicide, proposed that the royal title should be offered to the
Protector. He was supported by Cooper and
Henry Cromwell, but it is probable that most, if not
all, of the soldiers in the House took part with the Parliamentarians against the proposal. At all events the motion was
withdrawn without a division.[2] The motives of those who
supported it must be left to conjecture, but it is probable that
they hoped that with the prestige of the old title Oliver would
be able to shake himself loose from military influence, and
would no longer be the object of those suspicions which had
induced Parliament to impose on his Government restrictions
to which he was hardly likely to submit. In supporting such a
scheme Cooper made his last effort to base the Constitution
on an understanding with the Protector rather than on an
absolute defiance of his wishes.

[1] "Hors la réduction des troupes à trente mille hommes, conforme à
l'instrument de l'armée, et celles des levées à proportion, il ne paroist rien
qui puisse exciter sujet de querelle, si ce n'est la religion, qui a esté réglée
sans laisser pouvoir au Protecteur de rien changer à vingt articles que l'on
a dressez." Bordeaux to Brienne, Dec. $\frac{20}{30}$, *French Transcripts, R.O.*
Bordeaux has not quite understood the involved vote of the 15th, but his
general impression that the points of difference were not many deserves
attention. Nieupoort states a few days later that 'den Heere Protecteur
twee puncten in het Gouvernement gaerne verandert sagh, en dievolgens
de eerste instellinge, by het Parlement soude vast gesteld wesen: Het
eerste is dat hy den Raedt soeckt vast to stellen sonder die limitatie, dat
haere Commissie soude duuren tot den veertigsten dagh in het aenstaende
Parlement: ende den tweeden dat de Electie van een Parlement ten
tyde van syn overleden als dan wude ordonneren; maer altyts absolutelyck
aen den Raedt werden gedefereert; aen welcke twee puncten veele
geloven, dat hy hem soo veel sal laeten gelegen wesen, dat hy niet sal
toegeven; eghter hoopen veele dat het nogh sal gevonden werden.'
Nieupoort to De Witt, $\frac{\text{Dec. 29}}{\text{Jan. 8}}$, De Witt's *Brieven*, iii. 8. The two
ambassadors do not agree as to the points in dispute, but both regard a
compromise as possible.

[2] Walker's Newsletter, Dec. 28, *Clarke Papers*, iii. 15. The exact
date is given by Bordeaux.

CHAPTER XXXVII

A SUMMARY DISSOLUTION

WHILST the tension between Parliament and army was becoming every day more strained, information was brought to Thurloe which laid bare the existence of a military plot far more dangerous than the constitutional effusions of the three colonels. A certain Dallington had been landed from the fleet with instructions to discover what support would be given in the country to the seamen's petition.[1] One William Prior, who had been in the forefront of the Levelling movement in 1649, met him some three or four weeks later,[2] and—apparently judging from his employment that he was discontented with the Government—produced from his pocket a declaration on behalf of several in the army that had resolved to stand to their first principles. Prior informed Dallington that this Declaration—which was, if not a copy of the petition of the three colonels, at least drawn up on the same lines[3]—was to be set up in every market-place. In January there would be meetings of the disaffected at various places, such as Marston Moor and Salisbury Plain. Though the conspirators could not count with certainty on Hazlerigg, they expected to be

margin notes: 1654. Dec. 21. Dallington's information.

A military plot.

---

[1] Prior to the Protector, *Thurloe*, iii. 146. I suppose that there can be no doubt that ‘Oakley's Papers’ means the Seamen's petition.

[2] For the time see Eyre's examination. *Ib*. iii. 126.

[3] The account given of it by Prior shows the similarity. It was to be printed and set up in every market-place. The petition of the three colonels was already printed.

supported by Lord Grey of Groby, one of those who had refused to sign the Recognition, as well as by Saunders and Okey. Agents, moreover, had been sent to Ireland and Scotland, and they hoped that many of the soldiers in those countries would join the movement. For further information

Eyre's part in the plot. Prior referred Dallington to Colonel Eyre, an officer who had been cashiered in 1647 for his attempt to stir up mutiny at Corkbush Field.[1] Eyre, however, received Dallington with suspicion, and, though he went so far as to say that ' he had fought for liberty, but had none, and that it was as good living in Turkey as here,' he showed no inclination

Eyre captured in Dublin. to disclose his secrets to his interrogator.[2] Eyre himself made his way to Dublin, where he was arrested and sent back a prisoner to England.[3]

So far as the attempt to spread the movement in the army in Scotland was concerned, Dallington's statement was con-

Sept.
Temper of the army in Scotland. firmed by information received from another quarter. That army, indeed, had as a whole shown itself inclined to support the Government, and in September Monk was able to report that he could not hear of any voice being raised in it against the exclusion of the members who had refused to take the Recognition.[4] There was, however, one officer holding a high command whose conduct was

Major-General Overton. naturally regarded as open to suspicion. Having done good service in the reduction of Scotland, Major-General Overton had returned in 1653 to his post as Governor of Hull. He approved of the dissolution of the Long Parliament,[5] but felt scruples as to the subsequent establishment of the Protectorate. He had, however, no

[1] *Great Civil War*, iv. 22.

[2] Dallington's examination, *Thurloe*, iii. 35. Prior afterwards said (*ib.* iii. 146) that he did not have the Declaration from Eyre, but from an unnamed ' black, fat man in Eyre's chamber.'

[3] Herbert to Thurloe, Jan. 27. Eyre's examination, Jan. 27. *Ib.* iii. 124, 126.

[4] Monk to the Protector, Sept. 28, Firth's *Scotland and the Protectorate*, 192.

[5] *More Hearts and Hands*, E, 699, 7.

intention of taking part in a conspiracy, and he travelled to London in search of more active employment.   Being admitted by the Protector to an audience, he engaged to inform him if at any time his conscience forbade him to render further service to him, adding that whenever he perceived that his Lordship ' did only design the setting up of himself, and not the good of those nations,' he ' would not set one foot before the other to serve him.'   " Thou wert a knave if thou wouldst," was Oliver's frank rejoinder.   On these terms Overton was sent back to Hull, and in the latter part of the summer was allowed to take over Morgan's command in the North of Scotland,[1] where he applied himself loyally and energetically to the task of winning over the discontented gentry.[2]

He receives a command in Scotland.

For all this Overton was in a thoroughly false position, a position which was inevitably rendered more difficult after the intervention of the Protector in Parliament on September 12.   The times were not such that military could be divorced from civil obligation.   Overton probably thought little of the fact that before leaving England he had held a conference with Wildman, at which they had confirmed one another in their dislike of the political situation.[3]   With the exclusion of the mem-

He is in a false position.

Is dissatisfied with the Government.

[1] Overton to a friend, Jan. 27, *Thurloe*, iii. 110.   On his arrival in Scotland he used much the same language to Monk.   Monk to the Protector, Sept. 28, Firth's *Scotland and the Protectorate*, 192.

[2] *Perf. Account*, E, 818, 21.

[3] Such jottings by a Minister as Thurloe's Notes on Wildman's plot (*Thurloe*, iii. 147) are of value only inferior to documentary evidence itself.   Being put down on paper merely for his own use, and without a view to publication, they show at least what he believes to be true, not what he wishes to be thought to believe true.   Unfortunately, these notes are in many places illegible, and in others were misread by the transcribers who prepared them for publication.   Mr. Firth has sent me several corrections, and the more important part of the paper may be taken to run as follows, conjectural words or parts of words being added in brackets :—

" That the first meeting was at Mr. Allen's house, a merchant in

bers from the House his dissatisfaction seems to have increased.

Birchen Lane, in the beginning of September, 1654.   Okey, Alured, Saunders, Hacker, Wildman, Lawson.

"Petition drawn by Wildman and . . . after Bishop had it, and showed it to Bradshaw.

"Meetings also were, at Blue Boar's Head, in King Street.   In Wildman's house, Dolphin Tavern in Tower Street, Derby House.

"Henry Marten, Lord Grey, Captain Bishop, Alexander Popham once, Anthony Pearson sometimes.

"The men they built upon was Sir G. Booth, Bradshaw, Hazlerigg, G. Fenwick, Birch, Her[bert] Morley, Wilmers, Pyne, Scot, Allen. Pearson went like Hazle[rigg] &c.   Bishop like Bradshaw, and their advices given by them.

"At the same time a petition from the City, where Bradshaw advised in, and several met at his house, especially one Eyre, Sir Ar[thur] H[azlerigg], Scot, Col. Sankey, Weaver, directed both the bringing on and the manner of p[romoting] it.

"Sankey at Bradshaw's often, where Bishop met him.

"Overton and Wildman spoke together before Overton going of their dislike of things, but no design laid thereon, the [General] of the army of Scotland not let know.

"But after he [went] he writ letters to let them know that there was a party that would stand right for a Commonwealth.   Then Br[ayman] sent to them.

"And a meeting of officers at Overton's quarters ; Oates much trusted and drew most of their papers.

"The regiments that they relied on : Rich's, Tomlinson's, Okey's, Pride's, Stirling Castle, Alured's, Overton's, some of the General's regiment.

"Begin with a mutiny, and then his person seized and put in Edinburgh Castle, which they were sure of, forced Overton to command.   He writ up hither and then declaration ready, which was drawn by the meeting here, and sent by Br[ayman] . . . and printed here.   Spoke as if they should have Berwick.

"Sure of Hull by Overton's means and the townsmen, and Overton's correspondence.   Leicestershire, Grey and Capt. Baliard.   Bed[ford-shire] Okey and Whitehead, and great dependence on Hacker, who at last declared, if any fighting for a Parliament, not meddle against them."

The remainder is concerned with movements in England.   It is much in favour of Thurloe's intention to be fair that he twice in the course of these notes exonerates Overton from the worst charges.

He not only wrote to the London conspirators, from whom the petition of the three colonels had proceeded, that there was in

Dabbles in conspiracy. Scotland 'a party that would stand right for a Commonwealth,' but he allowed disaffected officers to meet in his quarters without breathing to Monk a syllable of what was going on under his patronage. After his letter had been received a Lieutenant Brayman [1] was despatched to Scot-

Dec. 18.
A meeting at Aberdeen.

A seditious circular prepared. land to keep the agitation on foot. On December 18 the discontented officers met at Aberdeen and drew up a circular convening a meeting at Edinburgh on New Year's Day, with the intention, as they said, of considering whether they 'ought to sit down satisfied in the present state of affairs, and with a good conscience look the King of Terrors in the face,' the Most High God having called them forth ' to assert the freedoms of the people in the privileges of Parliament.' [2] Samuel Oates,[3] the chaplain of Pride's regiment, who was one of the signatories of the circular, asserted that nothing had been done without Overton's privity and consent ; whilst he also explained that no more was intended to be done than to offer a humble petition to the Protector and Parliament, and that only if Monk's leave had been previously obtained.[4] Overton, at all events, contented himself with sending to those engaged in it a warning ' to do everything in God's way,' and to 'acquaint the General herewith, and to do nothing without his consent ' ; [5] though he

---

[1] He and Prior were amongst the first agitators in 1647, *Clarke Papers*, i. 79, note.

[2] Circular by Hedworth and others, Dec. 18, *Thurloe*, iii. 29.

[3] Father of the notorious Titus.

[4] " I have done nothing of action without his privity and concession, nor of evil by that . . . We intended nothing but what was consonant to the ground and end of our wars and the honest declarations we have made and concluded. In fine to offer our service in this matter in a humble petition to the Protector and Parliament by the leave of General Monk, or to lay down and come peaceably home in case he would not have given us leave." Oates to —? *Thurloe*, iii. 241.

[5] Overton to a friend, Jan. 17, *ib.* iii. 110.

himself did not think fit to put pen to paper on the subject in any communication with Monk.[1]

Monk, who only learnt the truth from one of his own officers [2] to whom the circular had been sent, was hardly

Monk learns what is going on. likely to take a lenient view of the case, and at once directed his secretary, Clarke, to invite Overton's

Dec. 19. Monk sends for Overton. presence at his own headquarters at Dalkeith. Clarke, who apparently intended to apply to the General for a signed order, neglected either to obtain it or to enclose it, and Overton took advantage of this

1655. Jan. 4. Overton sent to London. forgetfulness to refuse to leave his post on a mere informal hint from Clarke. On this Monk at once ordered the arrest of the Major-General and shipped him off for England.[3]

It is probable that before Monk sent Overton on board he had received from London a copy of Dallington's information, and it did not require a tithe of his sagacity to connect the proposed meeting at Edinburgh on January 1 with Dallington's statement that troops were to enter England from Scotland to the support of the conspirators in the course of the same month. By that time, too,[4] Monk had received from one of his officers information that he had received proposals to take part in a

Discovery of a design to seize Monk and to send Overton to join the English conspirators. design for seizing on the person of the Commander-in-Chief; after which Overton was to have been placed in command of 3,000 foot, with an appropriate number of horse, that he might march into England, where he would be joined by considerable forces brought to him by Bradshaw and Hazlerigg.

Lawson, whose name is constantly appearing in connection with plots of this nature, was said to be engaged in the

---

[1] Monk to the Protector, Jan. 16; Bramston's examination, Jan. 22, Firth's *Scotland and the Protectorate*, 238, 241.

[2] Major Holms.

[3] Overton to Monk, Dec. 25; Monk to the Protector, Dec. 30, Jan 4; Overton to a friend, Jan. 27, *Thurloe*, iii. 46, 55, 76, 110.

[4] The information is referred to in a letter from Edinburgh of Jan. 4, *Merc. Pol.*, E, 825, 4.

design.[1] As the list of the officers expected to take part in it included the names of Pride and Wilks, devoted adherents of the Protector, it may be taken that the other pieces of information obtained from the same source represent rather the sanguine expectations of a conspirator than the evidence of a trustworthy witness. Thurloe, at least, whilst believing the project to have been really entertained, thought that Overton would have needed to be forced to take the part assigned to him.[2] It was this possibility which made Overton really dangerous. An efficient soldier, so infirm of purpose as to be the plaything of conspirators with whose general objects he sympathised, was scarcely the man to be left at large by a Government which counted those objects disastrous to the national welfare. On

Jan. 16.
He is committed to the Tower.
the day of his arrival[3] Overton was committed to the Tower, and he remained a prisoner there and elsewhere for more than five years. Possibly the Protector was not so ready as Thurloe to give him the benefit of the doubt ; and it must be acknowledged that, if Over-

Feb.
His supporters cashiered.
ton was no more than foolish, his folly was of that kind which borders closely on crime. His followers or supporters—whichever they are to be called—were brought before a court-martial in Scotland and cashiered.[4]

With the stamping out of the military conspiracy in Scotland the danger from the Levellers and Parliamentarians in the

1654.
Dec.
Royalist movements.
army was by no means at an end, especially if they should succeed in making common cause with the English Royalists. Much as the two parties differed from one another, they both agreed in crying out for a free Parliament, and, at all events, the information which reached the Government as to movements among the Levellers was accompanied by information as to movements

[1] A letter of information, *Thurloe*, iii. 185.

[2] See *supra*, p. 229, note.

[3] *The Weekly Intelligencer*, E, 826, 2.

[4] *Merc. Pol.*, E, 829, 16 ; Monk to the Protector, Feb. 17, 20, 27, Firth's *Scotland and the Protectorate*, 251–253.

among the Royalists as well. On December 20, partly, per-

Dec. 20–25.
The Tower
garrison
strength-
ened. haps, as a hint to Parliament, but partly, no doubt, to avert an actual danger, the Tower garrison was raised to 900, and on the 25th it was still further raised to 1,200.[1] Before long cannon were planted in front of Whitehall,[2] whilst every care was taken to secure the devotion of the soldiery which patrolled the streets by prompt payment

Transport
of powder
by
Royalists. of their wages.[3] Towards the end of the month suspicions had been aroused by the transport of powder from London into the country.[4] Inquiry into gun-shops showed that orders for muskets and pistols had

Dec. 31.
Orders for
the arrest
of those
concerned. been freely executed of late. On the last day of the year directions were given for the arrest of Sir Henry Little-ton, High Sheriff of Worcestershire, and of Sir John Packington, both of them being charged with receiving

1655.
Four
arrests
made. cases of arms.[5] A few days later Major Norwood, Rowland Thomas, and a merchant named Custice were imprisoned as having been cognisant of this secret traffic, and Walter Vernon, to whose house at Stokeley Park a consignment had been traced, was brought up to London together with his kinsman, Edward Vernon. Their arrest was followed by that of Nicholas Bagenal, an Anglesea landowner, who acknowledged having received from a Carnarvonshire gentleman named Bayly a commission to raise a regiment of horse ; whilst Bayly confessed to having another commission to raise a regiment of foot ; both commissions being traced to Colonel Stephens, one of Charles's most trusted agents.[6]

If any expectation was entertained by the Government that

---

[1] Warrants to Barkstead, Dec. 20, 25, *Thurloe*, iii. 56, 57.

[2] Pauluzzi to Morosini, Jan. $\frac{6}{16}$, *Venetian Transcripts*, *R.O.* ; *Clarke Papers*, iii. 16.

[3] Bordeaux to Mazarin, $\frac{\text{Dec. 24}}{\text{Jan. 4}}$, *French Transcripts*, *R.O.*

[4] Bordeaux to Brienne, $\frac{\text{Dec. 28}}{\text{Jan. 7}}$, *ib.*

[5] Hope to Thurloe, Jan. 5, *Thurloe*, iii. 76. Numerous other papers relating to the charge of moving arms and powder are to be found in the same volume.

[6] *Merc. Pol.*, E, 823, 5 ; *Thurloe*, iii. 125, 127.

the discovery of these dangers would moderate the resolution of the House, that expectation was disappointed.   It is possible that the increase of the Tower garrison on December 20 and 25 was taken by the House as a challenge.   Parliament on December 28 made an understanding almost impossible by resolving that Bills should pass without the consent of the Protector; 'except in such matters wherein the single person is hereby declared to have a negative.' By this vote the House threw over the compromise accepted on November 15,[1] by which the concurrent action of Protector and Parliament was required in the selection of subjects on which no laws could pass without the assent of the former. The House, which had already grasped at the control of the Executive by subjecting the members of the Council to rejection by itself at the commencement of each Parliament, now resolved to determine at its own pleasure what were points on which it would allow the Protector to throw constitutional impediments in the way of hasty legislation.

On another point not, indeed, directly aimed against the system of the Protectorate, but yet one in which the views of the principal officers were opposed to those of the House, Parliament was no less resolute.   On November 27 it had restored the county franchise to the forty-shilling freeholders, whilst leaving it to the new voters who, not being freeholders, were possessed of real or personal property to the value of 200*l.*[2] On January 1 it abolished the new qualification, leaving the old forty-shilling freeholders in unrivalled possession.[3]   An attempt to give the vote to 10*l.* copyholders was lost by 65 to 51; another attempt to give it to 20*l.* copyholders was lost only by the casting vote of the Speaker.   That Lenthall's voice should be given against the innovation may perhaps be accounted for by legal conservatism, but the rejection of the 200*l.*

1654.
Dec. 28.
Temper of the House.

1655.
Jan. 1.
Parliament declares against the new franchise.

---

[1] See *supra*, p. 205.

[2] As the current rate of interest was 8 per cent. personal property of 200*l.* represented—at least if held in cash—an income of 16*l.*

[3] *C.J.* vii. 391, 392, 410, 411.

voters must surely have been based on wider grounds. Its origin may, at least conjecturally, be traced to the jealousy of town-made fortunes in an assembly mainly consisting of landed proprietors.[1] At all events, the vote was a defiance to the army, which was particularly attached to the new mode of voting.

In thus lowering the franchise the House took care to fence it round with qualifications which would keep the voting

Disqualifi-
cations
extended. power not only, as the Instrument had done, out of the hands of Royalists and ' papists,' but should also shut out those immoral and irreligious persons who were detested by the staid Parliamentary puritans. Not only were all in holy orders to be excluded, but all who contravened the Act against atheistical, blasphemous, and execrable opinions derogatory to the honour of God and destructive of human society ; all common scoffers or revilers of religion or of its professors, as well as every one who had married a wife of the Popish religion, had trained up his children in it, or had allowed any of his children to marry one of that religion ; who denied ' the Scriptures to be the word of God, or the sacraments, prayer, magistracy, and ministry to be the ordinances of God.' Nor was any ' common profaner of the Lord's Day,' nor ' profane swearer nor curser, nor any drunkard or common haunter of taverns or ale-houses,' to find a seat in the House.[2] Such sweeping exclusions, of which the House was to be the sole judge, might easily become the weapons of personal or party jealousy.

Not but that there were in circulation opinions wild enough to irritate the soberest advocate of toleration. On December 30

1654.
Dec. 30.
Theauro-
John com-
mitted. Thomas Taney, a fanatic or madman, who called himself Theauro-John and inhabited a tent he had set up in Lambeth, lighted a bonfire, into which he threw a Bible, a saddle, a sword, and a pistol, telling those who crowded round the exhibition that these were the Gods of

---

[1] This view is supported by a vote taken on Nov. 27 that no 200*l.* voter should give his voice in a county election unless he had also a forty-shilling freehold in the county. *Ib.* vii. 392.

[2] *C. J.* vii. 410 ; *Const. Doc.* 436.

England. After this he proceeded to the door of Parliament, where he laid about him with a drawn sword. Happily he was arrested before he had done any damage, and was committed to prison by the House.[1]

On January 3, when the House took up once more the question of toleration, it was in no temper to relax its require-

1655.
Jan. 3.
The vote on
damnable
heresies
confirmed. ment that Bills against damnable heresies should become law even if the Protector refused his consent; and, indeed, it was only by a majority of 81 to 75 that the Government party secured the retention of the resolution that these heresies should previously be enumerated at all.[2] Yet the persistence of the House in claiming the exclusive right of enumerating heresies could hardly be taken as absolutely hostile to the Government till the actual enumeration had taken place; whereas on the financial question, which was brought up again on the 5th by

Jan. 5.
The
financial
question. an estimate presented by Colonel Birch's Committee,[3] the political discussion was put in such a form that the rudest soldier in the ranks would feel himself capable of forming a judgment upon it.

According to this report, the army being estimated at 30,000 and the fleet reduced to the Channel Squadron, the

Birch's
estimate. total expenditure, including the 200,000*l.* set apart for domestic government, would reach 1,340,000*l.* Birch proposed to reduce the pay of the private soldier in a cavalry regiment to 2*s.*, and that of a foot soldier to 8*d.*,[4] thus bringing the expenditure down to 1,202,000*l.*, a reduction

---

[1] *C. J.* vii. 410 ; *The Weekly Intelligencer*, E, 823, 2.

[2] *C. J.* vii. 412 ; see *supra*, p. 222.

[3] *Carte MSS.* lxxiv. fol. 108. Probably the report had been made on some former day to the Committee of the whole House, and Birch now brought it forward in the House itself.

[4] In lieu of 2*s.* 6*d.* and 10*d.* Even at the higher rate of 10*d.* the pay of a foot soldier compares disadvantageously with that of a ' hedger and ditcher, whose average pay in these years was 1*s.* a day.' Rogers, *History of Agriculture and Prices*, v. 669. The usual statement that men were attracted into the army by the high rate of pay will not bear examination. The pay was raised by an ' *Act for the more certain and constant supply*

which might be justified on the ground that the pay had been
raised in 1649 in consequence of the high rate of provisions in
that year, whereas prices had now fallen considerably. Omitting the assessment tax, which he apparently did not intend to
renew, he then estimated the revenue at 1,000,000*l.*, and proposed to fill up the deficit, not by re-imposing the assessment
in any form, but by re-admitting French wines, which he
expected to yield in Customs and Excise [1] 150,000*l.*, and by
imposing a new duty on French canvas and linen goods, which
he estimated at 60,000*l.* By these means the revenue would
be brought up to 1,210,000*l.*, affording a surplus of 8,000*l.*
That no element of finality might be wanting he proposed to
raise, for eighteen months only, a land tax of 50,000*l.* a month,
in order to provide a fund for the discharge of debt, which he
calculated to amount to 700,000*l.*, and also to provide 200,000*l.*
for the pay of the supernumerary forces before disbandment.[2]
The adoption of Birch's scheme would therefore imply the
diminution of the standing army by 27,000 men and the
disappearance of all resources wherewith to pay the two fleets
which had already sailed under Blake and Penn. For the
soldier it meant that his pay would be lowered, and that not far
short of half the army would be sent adrift to seek employment
as best it might.

With Birch's presentation of the subject the House was

---

of the soldiers,' May 12, 1649. B.M. press-mark 506, d. 9, No. 28. See
Firth, *Cromwell's Army*, p. 185.

[1] He must have meant this, though he only says ' by free trade in
wines.'

[2] The estimate abbreviated from that of Col. Birch is as follows :

Expenditure.	£	*Income.*	£
Navy	270,000	Excise and Customs . . .	840,000
Army	870,000	Irish and Scotch revenue . .	39,000
Civil government . .	200,000	Papists and delinquents . .	60,000
		Other revenues	61,000
	1,340,000		1,000,000
Reduction of soldiers' pay .	138,000	Wines	150,000
		Impositions on canvas, &c. .	60,000
	1,202,000		1,210,000

much impressed. On the other hand, the Government had
every cause for alarm. The estimate of revenue made by
its orders on October 3 had reached not 1,210,000*l*., but
2,250,000*l*., while their estimated expenditure stood at no less
than 2,611,000*l*.[1] In vain Montague, with all the weight of
his experience as a Treasury Commissioner, urged that Birch
had underestimated the outgoings, even on his own grounds,
by more than 153,000*l*. A vote was then taken for granting
to the Protector, not by a clause in the Constitutional Bill, but
by a temporary Act, no more than 1,000,000*l*. to meet the
whole expenditure, a grant which upon Birch's own showing
would undoubtedly be inadequate to the needs of the Government, unless Parliament was prepared to supplement it by
some additional supply.[2] The length of time during which

----

[1] The abstract in *Burton* (I. cxx., note) is mutilated, and is, perhaps,
wrongly placed under the date of Dec. 18.

In an abbreviated form the revenue on Oct. 3 (*Carte MSS*. lxxiv. fol.
64) was :—

	£
Excise and Customs	800,000
Assessments in the three nations	1,320,000
Post Office	10,000
Probate of wills	8,000
Exchequer and revenue	20,000
Papists and delinquents	70,000
Fines on alienations	20,000
Revenue from Jersey and Guernsey	2,000
	2,250,000

The last entry refers not to taxation, but to the income from confiscated
estates.

The expenditure may be estimated at :—

	£
Land forces	1,508,000
Sea forces	903,532
Civil expenditure	200,000
	2,611,532

Of the three items, the civil expenditure was a fixed one ; that for the
land forces is arrived at by multiplying by 13 the monthly pay given in
Burton, I. cxxi., note, which is the only entry I have found in which the
whole expenditure is given. That for the sea forces is derived from *Carte
MSS*. lxxiv. fol. 32.

[2] *Carte MSS*. lxxiv. fol. 113.

this insufficient grant was to continue was reserved for future discussion.[1]

It is not without significance that Birch, the prime mover in the financial scheme of the Parliament, whose prominence in
Birch's position. what was showing itself to be the crucial question of the hour almost placed him in that informal position of leadership which was all that was attainable in those days, was one of those who had been taken into counsel when the petition of the three colonels was in preparation. Soldier as he had been, he was now the incarnation of the anti-military spirit. Through finance the Protector's schemes of foreign [2] and domestic policy were to be held in check, whilst at the same time his authority would be weakened at home by restricting the numbers of the army and by opposing to it a militia having no dependence on the Governn.ent.

The vote of January 5, straitening the financial resources of the Government, followed closely on the other decision
The parting of the ways. taken on December 28, to leave the points on which the Protector might exercise a negative voice to the absolute discretion of Parliament, and on that other vote of January 3 which required that the limits of toleration should be settled by Parliament alone. These three resolutions, taken together, marked the parting of the ways. Oliver was tired of an intolerant Parliament which threatened to make itself supreme, if not directly by constitutional enactments indirectly by financial proposals. Parliament, on its part, was tired of a Government which, whether it desired it or not, was driven to throw the weight of the sword into the scales of Parliamentary debate. The struggle for the control of the army leapt to the eye as clearly as the struggle for the control of the militia in 1642. Behind the contention lay two constitutional ideas as opposed to one another as those which had divided

[1] *C.J.* vii. 413.
[2] The estimate for expenditure of the two fleets of Blake and Penn, only reckoning them to be provisioned to Oct. 1, was 1,022,737*l.*, no doubt including payments already made for stores and equipment. *Thurloe*, iii. 64. Not a penny of this was provided for in Birch's calculations.

Royalists and Parliamentarians at the opening of the Civil War.

Hints of an early disso- lution. It was significant of the belief prevailing amongst persons in Oliver's confidence, that compromise was no longer possible, that, on the day on which the financial vote was taken, newspapers under the influence of the Government for the first time threw out hints that the five months during which the sitting of Parliament was guaranteed by the Instrument might be calculated not by the calendar, but by the lunar months of the soldiers' pay, and that the session might therefore be brought to an end by January 22, instead of being prolonged to February 3.[1] Scarcely less significant was it that Cooper absented himself from the Council on January 5 —the day on which the financial vote was taken [2]—never again to return so long as the Protectorate lasted. Obviously his abstention must be accounted for by something which had taken place since the day on which, less than a fortnight before, he had urged that the crown should be placed on the Protector's head, and it is difficult to account for his conduct on any other ground than his conviction that the Government could no longer hope to rest on any foundation save that of the army.

On the other hand, it does not follow that Cooper accepted with pleasure all the decisions of the House, and it is at least not unlikely that the hand of the statesman who was afterwards likened to that Achitophel whose counsel was as the counsel of God, may be traced in a concession made by the House on the 12th, when it retraced its steps on the religious question

---

[1] Under the date of Jan. 5, *A Perfect Account* (E, 823, 4) informs its readers that if the Bill on Government be not approved Parliament 'will rise at the time appointed, either at the beginning of February or at the latter end of January.' Under the date of Jan. 6, *Mercurius Politicus* (E, 823, 5) is more explicit. If the Bill be not acceptable 'the time limited in the Almanack account is the 3rd of February next, or, by the month, the 20th of January instant.' The day is given in error for the 22nd, but the intention of the writer is obvious.

[2] Cooper's last appearance was on Dec. 28, but the Council did not sit after that date till Jan. 5, so that the latter day is the one of Cooper's disappearance.

by a vote that the 'damnable heresies' to be exempted from

Jan. 12.
'Damnable
heresies' to
be enume-
rated by
Protector
and Parlia-
ment. toleration should be enumerated not, as it had hitherto stubbornly maintained, by Parliament alone, but
by Parliament in conjunction with the Protector.[1]
The House, however, still claimed the sole right of
legislating against atheism, blasphemy, popery, prelacy, licentiousness and profaneness, and against those who
openly attacked by speech or print the doctrines set forth as the

Jan. 15.
A Com-
mittee to
prepare a
charge
against
Biddle. public profession.[2]   On the 15th it gave an example
of its views on blasphemy by appointing a committee
to prepare a charge against Biddle for having promulgated not merely ordinary Socinianism, but such
opinions as 'that God hath a bodily shape,' with a
left hand and a right, and is not devoid of passions, being neither

---

[1] *C.J.* vii. 414.

[2] *Ib.* vii. 416.   The 37th Clause of the Instrument was :—"That such as profess faith in God by Jesus Christ—though differing in judgment from the doctrine, worship, or discipline publicly held forth—shall not be restrained from, but shall be protected in, the profession of the faith and exercise of their religion ; so as they abuse not this liberty to the civil liberty of others and to the actual disturbance of the public peace on their parts ; provided this liberty be not extended to Popery or prelacy, nor to such as, under the profession of Christ, hold forth and practice licentious- ness."   The 23rd chapter of the Parliamentary constitution was :—"That without the consent of the Lord Protector and Parliament no law or statute be made for the restraining of such tender consciences as shall differ in doctrine, worship, or discipline from the public profession aforesaid, and shall not abuse their liberty to the civil injury of others, or the disturbance of the public peace ; provided that such Bills as shall be agreed upon by the Parliament for restraining of damnable heresies, particularly to be enumerated by the Lord Protector and Parliament, and also such Bills as shall be agreed upon by the Parliament for the restraining of atheism, blasphemy, popery, prelacy, licentiousness, and profaneness ; or such as shall preach, print, or publicly maintain anything contrary to the funda- mental principles of doctrines held within the public profession which shall be agreed upon by the Lord Protector and Parliament, or shall do any overt or public act to the disturbance thereof, shall pass into and become laws within twenty days after their presentation to the Lord Protector, although he shall not give his consent thereunto."   *Const. Doc. of the Puritan Revolution*, 324, 367.

omniscient nor immutable.   If only the House abstained from
inflicting savage and inhuman penalties, there was nothing in
this of which Oliver could seriously complain.[1]   It is, indeed,

Oliver's
position on
the tolera-
tion ques-
tion.

undeniable that his point of view was very different
from that of the Parliamentary majority, and that
whilst his mind was fixed on including as many
as possible within the limits of toleration, they
were thinking of making the exemptions as numerous as possible.   Yet, after all, considering how rapid progress in this
direction had been, and how little public opinion was prepared
to support a policy of extensive toleration, it may fairly be
argued that the Protector would have shown his prudence
in accepting the compromise.   Nor is it by any means impossible that he would have done so if other questions had
been settled to his mind.

Whether Oliver's third fundamental was sufficiently secured

The funda-
mental
concerning
the Militia.

or not was a matter on which it was possible honestly
to differ in opinion.   The problem of the militia
remained still unsolved, and the problem of the
militia lay at the foundation of all others.

The immediate danger was not to be found in the pre-
dominance of Protector over Parliament, or of Parliament over

The Parlia-
mentary
view.

Protector, but in the claim of the army to intervene
in political affairs.   This claim was no matter of
past history.   The very army which had dissolved
the Long Parliament, and had more recently dictated the
Constitution under which Englishmen were then living, was
at that very moment swaying at its pleasure the fortunes of the
nation.   It was no Parliamentary vote, it was a vote in the
Council of Officers, which had strengthened the arm of the
Protector in dealing with the three colonels and in weeding
out the Levellers from military command.   It was the army

---

[1] " As for profane persons," Oliver said in the speech in which he
dissolved Parliament, " blasphemers, such as preach sedition, the contentious railers, evil-speakers who seek by evil words to corrupt good
manners, persons of loose conversation—punishment from the civil
magistrate ought to meet with them."   *Carlyle*, Speech IV.

which had given Oliver confidence to insist on an extension
of toleration which was unpalatable to the men sitting upon the
benches at Westminster. On paper that army was the servant
of Protector and Parliament. In reality it was the master of
both.

To the Parliamentary majority this state of things was un-
endurable. Is it strange that the only remedy that commended
itself to their minds was an extension of their own
authority? Having already secured a Council responsible to themselves, they proceeded, so far as
mere voting could avail them, to secure an army which they
could control. Yet, with a skill which points to much ability
of leadership, they not only refrained from any rash demand, but
went to their uttermost tether in conceding everything not inconsistent with their main design. On the 15th a
combination between the Court party and the more
moderate members of the Opposition [1] raised the
grant to the Protector by 100,000l., giving him, in
addition to the 200,000l. assigned for domestic
government, 400,000l. for the navy and for the fortifications
needed for the safety of the country, both of which sums were
to be annually paid until Protector and Parliament agreed
to dispense with them. On the following day
700,000l. was voted to be expended on the army,
and though the Opposition urged that this grant
should terminate on December 25, 1656, at the expiration of
somewhat less than two years, the same coalition rejected the
proposal, and extended the term to December 25, 1659, thus
giving the Protector nearly five years of uninterrupted disposal
of the forces.[2]

Emboldened by success, the Court party audaciously proposed that if the Protector refused his consent to the new

Marginal notes:
Parliamentary strategy.

Jan. 15.
A coalition carries an increased grant to the Protector.

Jan. 16.
Provisions for the army.

[1] Birch and Worsley acted as tellers. The motion was carried by 121
to 84. This number, 205 in all, was higher than any that had appeared
since the enforcement of the Recognition on Sept. 12, showing that fresh
members came in when there was a chance of an agreement.

[2] *C.J.* vii. 417, 418.

Constitution the Instrument should remain in force.   The coali-

The coalition breaks up.

tion formed on the previous day was at once dissolved and the Opposition easily recovered its majority.

The House also rejected a proposal that the Constitutional Bill required the Protector's consent to give it validity, and another proposal that the Protector was to hold the command of the militia on the same terms as he held the

Jan. 17. An agreement with the Protector necessary to the passing of the Bill.

command of the army.   On the 17th, however, it recoiled from the former of these two decisions, voting that without an agreement with the Protector the Bill should be void and of none effect ; though, with a curious verbal prudery, it refused to admit that under these circumstances it ought not to be,

in part or in whole, made use of as a law.[1]   In the course of the debate Oliver's supporters had pleaded hard that the Bill, instead of being engrossed for presentation to the Protector, and therefore offered to him for acceptance or rejection as a whole, might first be subjected to a friendly discussion between him and some Committee representing the House, when the objections on either side might be taken into consideration.[2]

After the rejection of this proposal no hope of an understanding remained.   Step by step Parliament had come round

No more hope of an understanding.

to the position held, if not by Bradshaw and Hazlerigg, at least by Hale[3] before the exclusion of the members.   Parliament was not merely to hold the members of the Council responsible to itself, but was to keep the militia in its own hands, and to grant supplies for the standing army for no more than a specified time.   Moreover, whatever limitations were placed on its power, its own supreme authority in imposing them must be so unquestioned that a mere attempt to arrive at a friendly understanding with the Protector must be avoided.   About the disbandment of nearly

[1] *C.J.* vii. 418, 419.

[2] Bordeaux to Mazarin, Jan. $\frac{18}{28}$, *French Transcripts, R.O.*   Pauluzzi to Morosini, Jan. $\frac{21}{31}$, *Venetian Transcripts, R.O.*

[3] See p. 186.

half the existing army there was to be no further question.

Jan. 18.
A Committee of disbandment.

On the 18th a Committee was appointed to consider 'what moneys will be necessary for paying off the supernumerary forces, over and above the 30,000, until they be disbanded, and for their disbanding;

Jan. 20.
The militia to be controlled by Parliament.

and how moneys may be provided for the satisfaction and payment thereof,'[1] and on the 20th Parliament added to their Bill a final proviso declaring that 'whereas the militia of this Commonwealth ought not to be raised, formed and made use of but by common consent of the people assembled in Parliament, be it therefore enacted that the said militia, consisting of trained forces, shall be settled as the Lord Protector and Parliament shall hereafter agree, in order to the peace and safety of the Commonwealth, and not otherwise.'[2]

The proviso thus added to the Bill, though to all seeming indifferently framed, was in reality altogether favourable to the

Effect of this proviso.

pretensions of the House. If no single militiaman could be raised without its consent, the Protector would hardly be able to override its views when the question of the control of the force thus raised came up for settlement. Before the afternoon had passed the failure of the Court party to carry another proviso, 'that no future Lord Protector should consent to take away the negatives hereby declared to be in the Lord Protector,' only served to mark the tendencies now inherent in the Bill. The negatives, it appeared, were no bonds to bind permanently the Parliamentary Samson. They were but temporary concessions, which would be at the mercy of Parliament as soon as the five years for which supplies had been granted for the maintenance of the standing army had elapsed.

After this the Protector was not likely to agree to the prolongation of the sittings of the House an hour longer than was

Cause of the Protector's hostility.

warranted by the strictest interpretation of the Instrument. However much he may have objected to some of the provisions of the new Constitution,

[1] *C.J.* vii. 419.   [2] *Ib.* vii. 420, 421.

such as the responsibilty of the Councillors to Parliament, and the possible election of his successors by Parliament, it is almost incredible that he should have broken with the House on such grounds alone.[1]   It was only when Parliament insisted on using its financial control to place the armed force of the nation at its own disposal that he refused submission to what appeared to him an intolerable yoke.

To those who now resisted the Protector must be ascribed the merit of having fixed their eyes upon the one thing absolutely essential—the transference of the military into the civil State.   Yet it may fairly be doubted whether they were themselves entitled to stand forth as champions of this principle.   The civil State, if it is to be an object of desire, must not be another name for the uncontrolled absolutism of any single man or body of men standing apart from the nation itself.   "What signified," Oliver had said,[2] "a provision against perpetuating Parliaments if this power of the militia be solely in them?   Whether, without a check, Parliament have not liberty to alter the frame of government to democracy, to aristocracy, to anarchy, to anything, if this be fully in them—yea, into all confusion, and this without remedy?   And if this one thing be placed in one, that

The aims of the Parliamentary opposition.

[1] Bordeaux's testimony may be quoted against the view that the quarrel arose on merely constitutional points.   Writing after the dissolution, he says that ' il ne paroist point d'autre motif de ceste action que la réduction de l'armée, quoyque conforme à l'instrument de l'armée, et le refus qu'avoit fait le Parlement d'entrer en conférence devant que de grossoyer et rédiger en forme de loy son Acte concernant la forme du gouvernement de l'Angleterre.'   Bordeaux to Mazarin, $\frac{\text{Jan. 25}}{\text{Feb. 4}}$, *French Transcripts, R.O.*   It may be well also to clear up an error made at the time, as well as by modern writers, that unless the House had been dissolved the Bill would have become law within twenty days, even if the Protector had withheld his consent.   Not only was it excepted from this rule by the Instrument itself, as containing matter contrary to that Constitution, but even in the Parliamentary Bill there was a clause declaring it to be null and void unless it received the Protector's assent.

[2] *Carlyle*, Speech III.   I quote from the contemporary report, E, 812, 11, p. 32, without Carlyle's embellishments.

one, be it Parliament, be it supreme governor, they or he hath power to make what they please of all the rest." It was precisely the remedy for this evil that Parliament failed to provide. Posterity was to find one in the power of dissolution, by which the Government could appeal to the nation, or to what, for the time being, passed as the nation. In 1655 neither Protector nor Parliament was willing to accept the supreme verdict of that umpire. The Protector erected barriers against the popular will by the imposition of a fixed Constitution. Parliament erected them by the imposition of stringent disqualifications. By both an appeal to the free decision of the nation was regarded as beyond the pale of sane politics. Therefore it was that to neither party in the strife was it given to establish that civil State to which each was, with very real earnestness, devoted.

Great as was the difficulty in coming to an understanding, in consequence of the hopelessness of discovering a court of **Difficulty in sharing the control of the army.** appeal to which the two parties would be willing to submit their claims, there were even greater difficulties inherent in the subject-matter of the dispute. No one could be more explicit than Oliver in repudiating all desire of placing the control of the army in the hands of the Protector. He had repeatedly declared his view to be that it should in some way be shared between Protector and Parliament. Yet, excellent as his intentions were, he had never been able, and, we may safely say, never would have been able, to design any form of words which would carry them out in practice. By the very nature of things no laws can provide that an armed force shall be under the control of two constitutional bodies, so long as they are striving for the mastery. The device of accepting the orders of the king, signified by both Houses of Parliament, had not prevented the forces under Essex from being a purely Parliamentary army. Nor was it, in later and happier times, the mere wording of the Mutiny Act which prevented the army of the eighteenth century from deciding civil conflicts with the sword. Two reasons have combined to render our modern army innocuous to liberty.

In the first place, since the Revolution of 1688 our civil quarrels have never been sufficiently embittered to make our political parties desire an appeal to the arbitrament of the sword. In the second place, the army itself has been too homogeneous with the nation to have formed the wish to impose upon it a system of government other than that before which the nation itself willingly bowed. It was because both these conditions were wanting to the Protectorate that the task of healing and settling, to which Oliver from time to time so wistfully referred, was hopeless from the beginning.

There is no reason to suppose that Oliver grasped the whole of the insuperable problem. What was immediately before him he saw, and, seeing it, he prepared with a sad heart to face the inevitable conflict. "Truly," he wrote in answer to some friendly lines addressed to him by Colonel Wilks, "it was to me very seasonable, because, if I mistake not, my exercise of that little faith and patience I have was never greater; and, were it not that I know Whom I have believed, the comforts of all my friends would not support me, no, not one day. I can say this further to you, that if I looked for anything of help from men, or yet of kindness, it would be from such as fear the Lord, for whom I have been ready to lay down my life, and I hope still am, but I have not a few wounds from them ; nor are they, indeed, in this sad dispensation they are under—being divided in opinion and too much in affection ready to fall foul upon one another, whilst the enemy, to be sure, unite to good purpose to their common destruction—in a capacity to receive much good or to minister good one to another, through want of communion in love ; so that whosoever labours to walk with an even foot between the several interests of the people of God for healing and accommodating their differences is sure to have reproaches and anger from some of all sorts. And truly this is much of my portion at the present, so unwilling are men to be healed and atoned ; and although it be thus with me, yet the Lord will not let it be always so. If I have innocence and integrity, the Lord hath

Oliver's letter to Wilks.

mercy and truth, and will own it. If in these things I have made myself my aim, and desired to bring affairs to this issue for myself,[1] the Lord is engaged to disown me, but if the work be the Lord's, and that they are His purposes which He hath purposed in His own wisdom, He will make His own counsels stand ; and therefore let men take heed lest they be found fighters against Him, especially His own people." "The Cavalier party," he continued, "is so encouraged that they do account this spirit, principle and motions of these men as the likeliest way to bring them into their former interest that ever yet they had ; and of this we have a very full discovery."[2]

Obviously Oliver had failed to discern that this extraordinary phenomenon was to be explained not by the sinfulness of man-
Insuffi-ciency of its reasoning.
kind, but by a common detestation of a Government based on the power of the sword. In any case his
Jan. 22. Five lunar months at an end.
patience was rapidly becoming exhausted. When January 22 brought to an end the five lunar months by which he had decided to measure the span of the duration of Parliament, he once more summoned the members before him in the Painted Chamber. His failure to grasp the
The Pro-tector's speech.
situation as a whole renders the speech which he then delivered far less interesting than the one which he had addressed to the same House on September 12. Announcing his belief that the Protectorate was the outcome of the dispensations of God, he declared it to have been his hope that, after the signature of the Recognition, they would have left the Instrument as they found it, and have betaken themselves to useful legislation. Then he proceeded to complain as to the ignorance in which he had been left as to the

[1] Perhaps he was thinking of Overton's language to him at their parting.

[2] The Protector to Wilks, *Clarke Papers*, ii. 239. The letter is undated, but Mr. Firth informs me that 'from its position amongst the other letters it should be dated between 14 and 18 January.' Internal evidence points in the same direction. A breach is looked forward to as certain, but, if it had actually taken place there could hardly fail to have been some indication of the fact in the letter.

proceedings of the House.   "I do not know," he said, "whether you have been alive or dead.   I have not once heard from you all this time—I have not, and that you all know." [1]

From the refusal of Parliament to discuss the terms of the Bill with himself Oliver passed to the conspiracies which had sprung up during the session, the blame of which he threw entirely on the members.   "Dissettlement and division," he told his hearers, "discontent and dissatisfaction—together with real dangers to the whole—have been more multiplied within these five months of your sitting than in some years before ! Foundations have also been laid for the future renewing of the troubles of these nations by all the enemies of them abroad and at home. . . . I say the enemies of the peace of these nations abroad and at home—the discontented humours of these nations, which I think no man will grudge to call by that name of briars and thorns—they have nourished themselves under your shadow."   "I say unto you," he continued later on, "whilst you have been in the midst of these transactions that party, that Cavalier party. . . . have been designing and preparing to put this nation in blood again. . . .   They have been making great preparations of arms and, I do believe, it will be made evident to you that they have raked out many thousands of arms, even all that this city could afford, for divers months now past. . . . Banks of money have been framing for these and other such-like uses ; letters have been issued with Privy Seal to as great persons as most are in the nation for the advance of moneys, which have been discovered to us by the persons themselves; commissions for regiments of horse and foot, and command of castles, have been likewise given from Charles Stuart since your sitting, and what the general insolencies of that party have been the honest people have been sensible of, and can very well testify."

Such evil consequences, continued Oliver, had their root in

---

[1] This complaint was not strictly true, as he had received information from a Committee about the reduction of the army and other matters ; but the Protector seems to have been exclusively thinking about the refusal to enter into a discussion with him on the Constitutional Bill.

Parliament itself. "What," he argued, "if I am able to make it appear in fact that some amongst you have run into the City of London to persuade to petitions and addresses to you for reversing your own votes that you have passed.[1] . . . And whether debauching the army of England. . . . and starving it, and putting it upon free quarter, and occasioning and necessitating the greatest part thereof in Scotland to march into England, leaving the remainder thereof to have their throats cut there, and kindling by the rest a fire in our own bosoms, were for the advantage of our affairs here, let the world judge."[2] Then, adverting to the little care of the House to give 'just liberty to goodly men of different judgments,' Oliver protested that he had no desire to protect 'profane persons, blasphemers, such as preach sedition, the contentious railers, evil speakers, ... persons of loose conversation.'

Next, in the midst of an elaborate defence of the Instrument, he put his finger on the real ground of offence. "Although," he declared, "for the present the keeping up and having in his power the militia[3] seems the most hard, yet, if it should be yielded up at such a time as this, when there is as much need

---

[1] As might be expected, we have to depend on the Protector's own word for many of the charges he makes. It is, therefore, worth noting that the statement above would have been inexplicable but for the notice of a city petition for settling the Church, contained in one of the unpublished papers amongst the *Thurloe MSS.* printed by Mr. Firth. See *supra,* p. 221, note 2.

[2] This seems to point to a connection in Oliver's mind between the want of pay in the army in Scotland and the scheme of sending 3,000 men under Overton into England. With respect to the delay of voting supplies, the fact cannot be denied. The further question, whether Parliament held back supplies to assure the confirmation of its constitutional Bill, must be answered by those who have read the narrative above. For my own part, I believe that they intended to vote no supplies till their Bill had been accepted, and also that every member of the House was perfectly aware that the consequence would be—not surrender, but dissolution.

[3] In this case 'militia' means the whole of the armed forces. Some confusion is caused by the word being sometimes employed in this sense, and sometimes being applied only to the local forces, as distinct from the standing army.

to keep this cause by it—which is evidently at this time impugned by all the enemies of it—as there was to get it, what would become of all ? Or if it should not be equally placed in him and the Parliament, but yielded up at any time,[1] it determines the power either for doing the good he ought, or hindering Parliaments from perpetuating themselves, or from imposing what religion they please on the consciences of men or what government they please upon the nation, thereby subjecting us to dissettlement in every Parliament, and to the desperate consequences thereof ; and if the nation shall happen to fall into a blessed peace, how easily and certainly will their charge be taken off, and their forces disbanded ; and then where will the danger be to have the militia thus stated ? " It needs no further reading of the speech to understand why Oliver concluded with the words :—" I think myself bound, as in my duty to God, and to the people of these nations, for their safety and good in every respect,—I think it my duty to tell you that it is not for the profit of these nations, nor for common and public good, for you to continue here any longer, and therefore I do declare unto you that I do dissolve this Parliament." [2]

The Dissolution.

Was there, then, no place for repentance, or was it possible that a few words of mutual explanation might have cleared the air ? Such questionings, in truth, spring but from an idle fancy. It was no variance on details that separated Protector and Parliament. The disruption did not even spring from the claim of either party to the dispute to wield the sword for its own benefit. It arose rather from the resolution of both sides that the sword should not fall into the adverse possession of the other. On each side—on the Protector's as well as on the Parliament's—there was a statesmanlike perception of a danger to the Constitution from

The root of the misunderstanding.

---

[1] Referring to the determination of the grant of 700,000*l.* at the end of five years.

[2] *His Highness's Speech*, E, 826, 22 ; also in *Carlyle*, Speech IV., with alterations. The Parliamentary Constitution is printed as a whole in *Constitutional Documents*.

the victory of the other. Nor was the dispute one between military government and constitutional government. Army and Parliament were at one in desiring that the government should be constitutional, and not military. Dependent as he was on the army for support, Oliver carried the army with him in his constitutional views, and did not fall a victim to its insistence. Lambert was, no doubt, more ready than the Protector to draw a hard-and-fast line against the encroachments of Parliament, but in the main position assumed by the two men there was no difference between them.

Nor can it be said that the quarrel was one to be appeased by the exercise of greater wisdom and moderation on either side. Just as the strife between the King and Parliament in 1642 was not susceptible of arbitration till time and circumstances had spread abroad the perception of the virtue of toleration, so, too, the strife between the Protector and Parliament in 1655 was not susceptible of arbitration till time and circumstances had spread abroad the perception that adoption or acceptance by the nation itself is the only lasting test of the value of constitutional checks. The claim of the House to sovereignty expressed in terms of finance rested on the totally false assumption that it could justly qualify itself as 'the people assembled in Parliament.'[1] What Oliver, on the other hand, demanded was to hold posterity in mortmain. Special powers for a special crisis Parliament was willing to grant, and the extent of these might have been settled without difficulty at a friendly conference. Oliver, with a strong man's pertinacity, was resolved to raise barriers against the encroachments of Parliament not only for his own lifetime, but during that of his successors. Never till death put an end to his strivings did he relinquish that ground.

To speak of Oliver as an opportunist changing his political attitude from year to year, if not from day to day, is to misjudge his character. In truth he was the heir and successor of Strafford—like Strafford throwing himself open to the charge of apostasy, and like Strafford shifting his

The quarrel not susceptible of appeasement.

Oliver no opportunist.

[1] See p. 245.

instruments and his political combinations for the sake of the
people, whom he aimed at governing for their best advantage.
To him kingship, or Parliamentary authority, or the very Protectorate itself, were all one, if they conduced to that blessed
end. That democracy would conduce to it was beyond the
pale not only of Oliver's conceptions, but outside the region of
thought of every politician of the day, with the exception of the
Levellers. Always it had been authority which he sought to
found—it had been, during his past career, but a secondary
question in whose hands authority should be placed. That
was to be determined by the disqualifications of existing claim-
ants rather than by the ideal excellence of the one to whom he
had for the moment attached himself. The faults of the King
threw him on the side of Parliament ; the faults of Parliament
drove him to seek a solution of political difficulties in a violent
dissolution. In erecting the Nominated Parliament he had
been actuated mainly by his distrust of an assembly which
threatened to perpetuate itself ; his experience of the conduct
of the Nominees opened his eyes more widely than before to
the fact that an uncontrolled House might be dangerous even
if its duration were limited in point of time. Henceforth, indifferent as he was, and continued to be, to constitutional
details, he had made up his mind that good government—the
first object of which was to protect religious minorities willing
to submit to the existing authority in the State—was inconsistent with Parliamentary omnipotence.

Unfortunately, to check the Parliamentary assumption of
omnipotence, save by the intervention of the sword, was beyond
Oliver and   Oliver's power. Strong as was his desire to defend
William III. the Protectorate by laws rather than by arms, military
despotism was thrust upon him. It could not well be otherwise, unless he were prepared to acknowledge the sovereignty
of the nation over Protector and Parliament alike, and to allow
the nation, if it so pleased, to plant its heel on the newly won
liberties of ' the people of God.' To choose this path would be
to anticipate the policy of William III., and it would· be unreasonable to expect the child of a military revolution to be

able to adopt a course which proved comparatively easy to a crowned king, placed on the throne by the call of a wronged and indignant nation.

Some inkling of this had been at the bottom of Garland's proposal to confer the title of king upon Oliver under the new Constitution. That a mere change of name would have effected the purpose desired is most improbable. There is nothing to work miracles in the adoption of a style which has been appropriately used by others. What the nation sought restlessly for was such a recurrence to old use and wont as might enable it to consider reforms on their own merits, without the risk of being dashed violently out of its course by unsuspected currents. Oliver had destroyed, so far as acts can destroy, the superstition of a monarchy unaccountable for its deeds. He was not, nor could he be, in a position to build up the frame of the monarchy of the future—the monarchy strong in influence, because reflective of the mind and will of the nation as a whole.

The Royal title.

CHAPTER XXXVIII

A MOTLEY OPPOSITION

OLIVER lost no time in announcing to the world by actions rather than by words that, if his Government was not to be Parliamentary, it was to be—at least within the limits of practical politics—constitutional. The very postponement of the dissolution till the lapse of five months—lunar months though they were—showed this to be his aim ; and his position was made still more clear when, on February 8, he announced that the assessment would thenceforward be levied at the reduced rate which had been accepted by Parliament, that is to say, at 60,000*l.* a month from England, in lieu of the 90,000*l.* which had hitherto been received, and at 10,000*l.* a-piece from Scotland and Ireland.[1] To the same resolution must be attributed—what was at least a verbal homage to the Instrument—his abstention from issuing notifications of his will under the title of ordinances, thus avoiding the appearance of an assumption of legislative power to which he had no further claim after the day on which his first Parliament met.[2]

The reduction of the assessment was the more remarkable as, whilst showing a deference, not indeed to the Instrument,

1655.
An attempt at constitutional government.

Feb. 8.
The assessment lowered.

Oliver abstains from issuing ordinances.

---

[1] *Order for the Assessment*, Feb. 8, E, 1064, 47.

[2] " His Highness, by not making it an ordinance, hath modestly denied to assume the legislature of the nation ; though satisfied by many able judges and lawyers he may legally do it." — ? to Clarke, Feb. 13, *Clarke Papers*, iii. 22.

but to a mere resolution of the dissolved Parliament, the Government thereby became involved in a hopeless deficit,
unless both army and navy were reduced far below
the requirements of the time.   It was not in the
power of any man forthwith to recall Blake from the Mediterranean or Penn from the Indies, whither he had already sailed
in December.   Yet it was impossible to maintain their two
fleets without an annual expenditure of at least 461,000*l.*,[1] not
a penny of which could be derived from any existing source of
revenue.   Nor was it possible, so long as the country was
seething with sedition, suddenly to bring down the numbers of
the army from 57,000 to 30,000.   Yet, if none of these things
were done, a deficit of 721,000*l.* was the lowest that would
have to be faced.[2]   All that for the present could be accomplished was, whilst meeting declared opposition with firmness
and decision, to disarm, by wise and just administration, the
unpopularity which lay beneath the surface.   In such a process
it was hardly likely that the Protector could always keep within
the limits of the law.   He himself could hardly expect more than to avoid breaking out from those
limits in cases where the observance of the law did
not clash with his self-imposed duty of maintaining that Instrument of Government which he had bound himself to
defend.   Yet even those who accept this explanation of the
Protector's conduct as satisfactory can hardly deny that his
action was fraught with peril.   It was of the necessity of the
case that the determination of the points on which the Constitution could only be defended by breaking the law should
rest with the executive body—the Protector and Council—and

The financial situation.

Law and constitution.

---

[1] According to an estimate made on Oct. 3, 1654, the expense of
Blake's fleet would be 19,170*l.*, and that of Penn's 19,260*l.*, for a lunar
month, *Carte MSS.* lxxiv. fol. 32.   The annual expense of the two fleets
would, therefore, be 461,160*l.*   This estimate must be exclusive of the
money already paid for stores and equipment.   See *supra*, p. 239, note 2.

[2] Deducting 360,000*l.* for the remission on the assessment from the
estimate given at p. 238, note 1, we have a revenue of 1,890,000*l.* to meet
an estimated expenditure of 2,611,532*l.*, entailing a deficit of 721,532*l.*

not with the judges, if only because judges could not be trusted to advise the breach of the law in any case whatever. The position, therefore, was one temporarily defensible, at least from a political point of view, but it was one that would tend to prolong itself beyond the time during which it could be defended. It is certain that Oliver, above all men, would have welcomed the day when he could return to the fields of strict legality ; but, unhappily for the cause which he had so much at heart, he was likely to discover in practice the extreme difficulty of stiffening once more the legal rule which he had made flexible, even for the highest purposes.

Next to carrying conviction to the people at large that he had no purpose of increasing taxation, or even of maintaining it at its existing level, the Protector had most to gain by convincing them, so far as it was possible without violating his own principle of religious liberty, that he had no intention of casting his shield over those exorbitances of fanatical religion which had driven even men like Owen to urge that the time had come to narrow the limits of toleration. Following out the announcement made in his last speech, that he had no desire to protect extremists,[1] he now, though making no attempt to enumerate 'damnable heresies,' left Theauro-John and Biddle to the Court of Upper Bench, with the result that they were both admitted to bail and ultimately restored to liberty.[2] Nor did the Government interfere to decide the knotty point whether the so-styled 'Quakers'—and it must be remembered that the appellation was in those days conferred on many who were only loosely connected, or not connected at all with the Society of Friends [3]—were guilty of blasphemy or not. That the popular view was against these enthusiasts is, to some extent, shown by the fact that justices of the peace almost invariably held them to be blasphemers, whilst the

Question of the extent of toleration.

Cases of Theauro-John and Biddle, and of the 'Quakers.'

---

[1] See *supra*, p. 251.

[2] *Merc. Pol.* E, 826, 23 ; *Several Proceedings*, E, 479, 24.

[3] The list of doctrines ascribed to the 'Quakers' by Bunyan, in his *Grace Abounding*, would show this, even if there were not other evidence.

judges of the higher courts sometimes lent a favourable ear to their protestations.[1] Nor could there be much interference with the due process of law in favour of men who spoke rudely to magistrates and kept on their hats in the presence of those before whom it was customary to remove them ; still less when a more than usually unrestrained fanatic stripped himself to the skin, and walked about Smithfield in defiance of common decency.[2]

On one point especially Oliver's intervention was urgently demanded. Not only did the 'Quakers' scandalise the clergy by refusing, as Baxter put it, to 'have the Scriptures called the word of God,' but they railed at ministers 'as hirelings, deceivers, and false prophets,' bursting into congregations, and directing against the occupant of the pulpit such exclamations as "Come down, thou deceiver, thou hireling, thou dog!"[3] After this it was a little thing that they proceeded to argue with the preacher or criticised his right to occupy the position he filled. By the magistrates such acts were qualified as brawling, whilst they were defended by the intruders themselves as asserting the right of all religious persons to contribute to the edification of the assemblage. The Protector was within his rights in announcing his intention of enforcing the law as it was interpreted by legal authority, but it was not in his nature to touch even the apparent fringe of religious liberty without placing on record his conviction that religious liberty

They disturb congregations.

The Protector resolves to enforce the law.

---

[1] Chief Baron Wilde, for instance, refused to accept a verdict of guilty against a 'Quaker' under the Blasphemy Act. *Truth's Testimony*, E, 829, 8.

[2] *The Faithful Scout*, E, 481, 17. The story is told also by Nieupoort (*Add. MSS.* 17,677 W, fol. 40), as one of which he was credibly informed. A leading member of the Society, Richard Farnworth, in a pamphlet written in February on a very different subject, added before its issue on March 1 a postscript in defence of any person caused by the Lord to go naked as a sign, which he would hardly have done unless such a case had actually occurred. *The Pure Language*, E, 829, 5.

[3] *Reliquiæ Baxterianæ*, 77, 116.

itself, so far as he understood it, was in no danger in his hands.

Accordingly, on February 15 a proclamation appeared which may justly be regarded as the charter of religious freedom under the Protectorate. " It having pleased the Lord," it characteristically began, " by the manifest mercies and deliverances which He hath wrought in and for these nations of late years, and the blessings wherewith He hath blessed the endeavours of the good people thereof, in making them successful against His and their enemies, to crown us with this, as not the least token of His favour and goodwill to us, that there is a free and uninterrupted passage of the Gospel running through the midst of us, and liberty for all to hold forth and profess with sobriety their light and knowledge therein, according as the Lord in His rich grace and wisdom hath dispensed to every man, and with the same freedom to practise and exercise the faith of the Gospel, and to lead quiet and peaceable lives in all godliness and honesty, without any interruption from the powers God hath set over this Commonwealth ; nay, with all just and due encouragement thereto, and protection in so doing by the same : a mercy that is the price of much blood, and till of late years denied to this nation, as at this day it continues to be to most of the nations round about us, and which all that fear God amongst us ought duly to consider and be thankful for in this day wherein God hath so graciously visited and redeemed His people :—his Highness, as he reckons it a duty incumbent on him, and shall take all possible care to preserve and continue this freedom and liberty to all persons in this Commonwealth fearing God, though of differing judgments, by protecting them in the sober and quiet exercise and profession of religion and the sincere worship of God, against all such who shall, by imposing upon the consciences of their brethren, or offering violence to their persons, or any other way seek to hinder them therein ; so likewise doth he hold himself equally obliged to take care that on no pretence whatsoever such freedom given should be extended by any beyond those bounds which the royal law of love and Christian moderation have set us in our walking one towards another; or that thereby occasion should be taken by any to abuse this liberty to the disturbance or disquiet of any of their brethren in the same free exercise of their faith and worship which himself enjoys of his own. And his Highness cannot but sadly lament the woful distemper that is fallen upon the spirits of many professing religion and the fear of God in these days, who . . . do openly and avowedly, by rude and unchristian practices, disturb both the private and public meetings for preaching the word, and other religious exercises, and vilify, oppose, and interrupt the public preachers in their ministry, whereby the liberty of the Gospel, the profession of religion, and the name of God is much dishonoured and abused, and the spirits of all good men much grieved. His Highness, therefore, having information from divers parts of this Commonwealth of such practices by divers men lately risen up under the names of Quakers, Ranters, and others, who do daily both reproach and disturb the assemblies and congregations of Christians in their public and private meetings, and interrupt the preachers in dispensing the word, and others in their worship, contrary to just liberty, and to the disturbance of the public peace, doth hold himself obliged by his trust to declare his dislike of all such practices, as being contrary to the just freedom and liberties of the people, . . . and doth hereby strictly require that they forbear henceforth all such irregular and disorderly practices; and if in contempt hereof any persons shall presume to offend as aforesaid, we shall esteem them disturbers of the civil peace, and shall expect and do require all officers and ministers of justice to proceed against them accordingly."[1]

and against disturbing congregations.

It was hard for the Protector to keep his subordinates up to his high ideal. Colonel Hacker, whose own sympathies were with the Presbyterian clergy, had been so far able to assure the Protector of his devotion as to be entrusted with the duty of stamping out sedition

Hacker in Leicestershire.

[1] *Proclamation*, Feb. 15, B. M. press-mark, 669, f. 19, No. 71.

in Leicestershire.[1] In this capacity he chose to treat 'Quaker'
meetings as dangerous to the State, arresting many
persons who took part in them, and sending some
of them to Whitehall for judgment.[2] Amongst those
carried to London was Fox himself, who, being asked to sign
a paper engaging not to take arms against the Government,
replied that he was against taking arms in any case whatever.
Oliver, who seems to have known little of the 'Friends' except
by hostile report, admitted their leader into his
presence. Fox at once, after invoking peace upon
the House, opened an exhortation to the Protector
to 'keep in the fear of God, that he might receive wisdom
from Him, that by it he might be directed and order all things
under his hand to God's glory.' As soon as Oliver could get
in a word he asked the pertinent question why they quarrelled
with the ministers. Fox enlarged upon the duty of testifying
against those who preached for the sake of filthy lucre. With
Fox's spiritual instinct Oliver had a deep sympathy, even if he
was unable to concur in its practical application. "Come
again to my house," he said, as he dismissed his guest, "for
if thou and I were but an hour a day together we should be
nearer one to the other. I wish you no more ill than I do to
my own soul." Suiting the action to the word, he ordered
Fox to be set at liberty, and invited him to dine at the table
set for his own attendants. With sturdy independence Fox refused to eat of his bread or drink of his cup.[3] Not only did

Meetings broken up in Leicestershire.

Feb. 26. Fox before the Protector.

[1] Hacker, who had attended, at least at the outset, the meetings which
produced the petition of the three Colonels, perhaps approved of urging the
Protector, at the beginning of September, to accept the Parliamentary
system, but disapproved of the more violent opposition in which the
movement culminated. This is, however, no more than a conjecture.

[2] Nieupoort, in his despatch of Feb. $\frac{9}{19}$ (*Add. MSS.* 17,677 W, fol.
40), and therefore before the issue of the proclamation, writes of 'Quaker'
meetings broken up by order of the Government, and it is quite possible
that a dislike of such things led Oliver to consider the question.

[3] Fox, in his account of the matter, says that when this was reported
to the Protector, he said : "Now I see there is a people risen and come
up that I cannot win either with gifts, honours, offices or places; but

Fox go out a free man, but he was permitted to address meetings when he would, in London or elsewhere, though they had been closed by order of the Government not many days before.

all other sets and people I can." This is merely hearsay, and the latter part of the sentence is not only unlike any expression of Oliver's, but would be particularly absurd at the moment when he had failed, as will be seen, to win over several persons of other sects and parties.

¹ For the closing, see Nieupoort to the States General, Feb. $\frac{9}{19}$ (*Add. MSS.* 17,677 W, fol. 40). The date of Fox's interview with Cromwell, for which we depend on Fox's *Journal*, is assigned by Dr. Hodgkin (*George Fox*, 108) to the summer of 1654, apparently thinking that the plot referred to as being talked of at the time when Fox was taken was Gerard and Vowel's. Under the date of Feb. 26, however, *Merc. Pol.* (E, 829, 6) tells us that "Divers Quakers have been apprehended as they were roving about the country in Leicestershire, and among them one Fox, a principal leader of that frantic party; they are brought up hither and detained in custody." Moreover, it will be noticed that Oliver's first recorded words referred to the quarrelling with the ministers, which had been so much on his mind in issuing the proclamation of Feb. 15. Besides, Fox writes of Hacker as commanding in Leicestershire, and we have in *Thurloe* (iii. 148) a letter which shows he was in that position on Feb. 12. Moreover, we find Fox complaining of a minister who was an official news-writer—doubtless Henry Walker—that he put in his newspaper a statement that Fox wore ribbons. In *Perfect Proceedings* (E, 481, 9), under the date of Feb. 26, we find: "This afternoon Fox, the great Quaker, who is said to be one of the chief old ringleaders of them, was at Whitehall. He came out of Leicestershire—some say he was sent up from thence—and divers Quakers were at Whitehall following him. It is said that he, two years since, seduced Colonel Fell's wife, who, following him up and down the country, and still is (*sic*) of that gang, and divers others. And I heard a gentlewoman say this day at Whitehall, when he was there, that she heard him boast of his favours, showing bunches of ribbon in the country —about Lancashire—that he had from Colonel Fell's wife and others." As the statements in Fox's *Journal* are for the most part uncorroborated, it is worth while noting points in which they are borne out by contemporary evidence. Fox's complaint of being charged merely with wearing ribbons is now seen not to be the outburst of an ultra-puritanical mind, but the result of indignation against that charge brought against Mrs. Fell; though the word 'seduced' does not necessarily bear the meaning which it would have at the present day.

In dealing with 'Quakers' the Proctector had to do with men who were held to be blasphemers, and who were certainly not seldom disturbers of the general peace. The Fifth Monarchy men, whilst equally basing their conduct on religious grounds, directly attacked the existing Government, on the plea that earthly rule ought exclusively to be in the hands of the saints. Though this opinion was not likely to be very widely spread, it was not a time when Oliver could safely allow his authority to be openly challenged; though he can have found but little satisfaction in coercing men whose hearts were, as he believed, on the right side. In December, Simpson, who, together with Feake, had been confined at Windsor since the early days of the Protectorate,[1] broke prison, and reappeared on the 17th and 18th in his old pulpit at Allhallows, where he declaimed against the Triers, alleging their position to be 'absolute anti-Christian,' and declaring 'that he could with as good conscience go to the Pope and his cardinals for their approbation as to them.'[2] Being summoned before the Protector, he discussed the situation with him for the better part of a whole day, telling him, amongst other things, that he had broken his promise to abolish tithes. To this charge Oliver pleaded that he could not remember having given any engagement of the sort, but that, if he had, it was a sufficient excuse that his Council would not allow him to carry it out.[3] Turning to the constitutional question, Simpson reminded the Protector that he had formerly declared for a Commonwealth without king or House of Lords, and argued that by taking on himself his present title he had not only broken his vows, but had incurred the penal-

The Fifth Monarchy men.

1654 Dec. 17. Simpson's sermon.

Simpson's discussion with the Protector.

---

[1] See vol. iii. 7.

[2] ⸺ to Clarke, Dec. 19, *Clarke Papers*, iii. 14.

[3] See vol. ii. 102, note 2, and vol. iii. 20, note 2. Probably Oliver had promised to commute tithes by an ordinance before Parliament met, but the Council refused its consent. It can hardly be too often repeated that he was not an absolute ruler.

ties of high treason.[1] " Well said, Simpson !" was the half-amused reply. " Thou art plain indeed ; not only to tell me I have broken my vows, but that I am, in plain terms, a traitor." After this Oliver announced his intention not to abandon the position he occupied. " The Government," he said, " I have taken, and will stand to maintain it." The long conversation ended by the Protector's advice to Simpson to be more sober in his speech and conduct. The advice was thrown away. "We came away," wrote one of Simpson's followers who was present during this strange discussion, " very much dissatisfied

Simpson allowed to remain at liberty. with his spirit and his words." [2] In this case, at least, Oliver was determined to show that no harshness on his part should contribute to increase the irritation of these irritable Christians, and Simpson was allowed to remain

Dec. 23. Feake sent back to prison. at liberty. A discussion with Feake on the 23rd ended, on the other hand, by his being remanded to confinement at Windsor Castle. It is not unlikely that by this time some rumour that the Fifth Monarchists

Dec. 25. Arrest and release of Harrison. were engaged in one of the many plots of the day had reached the Protector's ears, as Harrison was re-arrested two days later ; though he was immediately released on giving an assurance to the Protector that, however much he disapproved of the existing form of government, he had no intention of conspiring for its overthrow.[3]

Another Fifth Monarchy preacher, John Rogers, had been John Rogers in prison. in custody at Lambeth for six months for asserting that God would pour forth His vials on ' the worldly

---

[1] The Act of March 17, 1649 (*Scobell*, ii. 7), declared that the office of king might not be exercised by any single person, and that it was treason to ' promote any person to the name, style, dignity, power, prerogative or authority of king.' Simpson would affirm, and Oliver deny, that the authority granted to a Protector by the Instrument was equivalent to that of a king.

[2] B. J. to ——? *Clarke Papers*, ii. pref. xxxiv.–xxxvii.

[3] ——? to Clarke, Dec. 23; *Clarke Papers*, iii. 15 ; *The Weekly Intelligencer*, E, 821, 13; Nieupoort to the States General, Jan. $\frac{5}{15}$, *Add. MSS.* 17,677 W, fol. 24.

powers, the powers of antichrist,' as well as for declaiming against the Protector. " Because," he had said, " he hath oppressed and forsaken the poor, because he hath violently taken away a house which he builded not, surely he shall not feel quietness in his belly ; he shall not save of that which he desired. O thou black Whitehall : Fah ! Fah ! it stinks of the brimstone of Sodom, and the smoke of the bottomless pit. The flying roll of God's curses shall overtake the family of that great thief there ; he that robbed us of the benefit of our prayers, of our tears, of our blood—the blood of my poor husband, will the widow say—the blood of my poor father, will the orphan say—the blood of my poor friend, will many say. These shed their blood for the cause cf Jesus Christ, and for the interest of His kingdom ; but that which they purchased at so dear a rate is taken from us by violence. We are robbed of it, and the cause of Christ is made the cause of a man.".[1]

Early in February twelve members of Rogers's congregation appeared before Oliver to ask for the liberation of their own pastor and of Feake, as sufferers for conscience' sake. To this Oliver replied that they suffered for their evil deeds; but he consented to discuss the question with Rogers, in the hope of convincing his advocates that their view of the case was false. The conference was fixed for the 6th, when the Protector maintained his position that attacks on the Government could not be allowed ; whilst Rogers stuck to the argument that if he had done wrong he ought to be brought to a lawful trial, and not forced to submit to an absolute or arbitrary power. The charge was too well founded to be otherwise than irritating to the Protector. " Where," he promptly asked, " is an arbitrary or absolute power ? " " Is not the long sword such ? " was the equally prompt reply. " By what law or power are we put into prison ? . . . And is not your power, with the army's, absolute to break up Parliament and do what you will ? " The Protector, on the other

Margin notes:
1655
Feb.
A demand for the release of Feake and Rogers.

Feb. 6.
Oliver's conference with Rogers.

[1] The information is dated May 8, obviously in 1654, but misplaced amongst the papers of 1655. *Thurloe*, iii. 483.

hand, had the advantage in setting forth the necessity of restraining Presbyterians, Independents, and Baptists from coming to blows. " His work," he said, " was to keep all the godly of several judgments in peace "—' He was as a constable,' he added, ' to part them and keep them in peace.' [1]

Oliver was no sooner[2] quit of Rogers than he was assailed by Harrison, who sought an interview with him at the head of Harrison and others support Rogers. a party comprising Colonel Rich, Quartermaster-General Courtney, together with Carew, Squib and Clement Ireton [3] —the first two having been members of the Nominated Parliament. As soon as they were admitted to Oliver's presence they urged him to release ' the prisoners of the Lord.' To this the Protector replied ' that if they were the prisoners of the Lord they should soon be set at liberty, but that he was sure there was nobody in England in prison for the Lord's sake or the Gospel's.' He subsequently sent for Feb. 16. Harrison, Rich, Carew, and Courtney before the Council. the four principal persons among them—Harrison, Carew, Courtney and Rich. As, however, they refused to obey either this message or a warrant which followed, and as information had been received that they had been stirring up resistance to the Government, they were fetched before the Protector and Council on the 16th.[4]

With one voice the four declared the Government to be anti-Christian and Babylonish, Carew adding that when the Protector dissolved the Nominated Parliament ' he took the crown off from the head of Christ and put it upon his own.' Against such a usurped authority these four concurred in holding it to be lawful to take up arms. Not that they had any sympathy either with the Levellers or with the majority in the late House.

---

[1] Rogers, *Life and Opinions of a Fifth Monarchy Man*, 173–224.

[2] ' The very same night,' *ib.* 220, marginal note.

[3] ' Mr. Ireton,' as given in a marginal note. Clement, a younger brother of the general, must, almost certainly, be intended.

[4] *Merc. Pol.*, E, 828, 7, where the date is given as Feb. 15. Thurloe's ' Friday in the afternoon '—*i.e.* the 16th—is more likely to be accurate.

Their greatest objection to the Protectorate was 'that it had a Parliament in it, whereby power is derived from the people, whereas all power belongs to Christ.' After this they were asked whether they would 'engage to live peaceably and not disturb the peace of the nation.' On their refusal [1] they were told 'that if they would retire into their own counties and promise not to come forth without leave' no harm should befall them. When even this kindly overture had been rejected the Protector lost all patience. Harrison, he said, 'had not only countenanced those who declaimed publicly against the Government, but had persuaded some of the lawfulness of taking arms against it'; Carew had not only joined Harrison in this, but had 'endeavoured to seduce some great officers from their trust'; Rich had opposed the levy of the assessment-tax; whilst Courtney had been in Norfolk persuading the churches to take up arms, and had said in the West that when he was in London he would "find both hands and hearts enough to overthrow this Government." To this charge they made no answer, and

Their committal. were thereupon committed to the custody of the Serjeant-at-Arms. A few days later three of them were despatched to separate prisons, Harrison to Portland, Carew to Pendennis, Courtney to Carisbrooke. Rich was allowed to remain at liberty for some time longer to attend on

Oliver's reluctance to imprison them. his dying wife. It was no pleasure to Oliver to deal harshly with men who did but exaggerate his own Puritanism. " I know," wrote Thurloe, "it is a trouble to my Lord Protector to have any one who is a saint in truth to be grieved or unsatisfied with him." Imprisonment had been inflicted on these men, according to the secretary, " in pity to them and some other people who are led by them, as well as for the sake of the nation, that they may not put things into blood and confusion, and be made use of by the Cavaliers and vile Levelling party to destroy and utterly root out all that are good and godly in the land." [2]

---

[1] Harrison in company with his three comrades was less compliant than he had been when he was alone. See *supra*, p. 265.

[2] Thurloe to Monk, Feb. ? *Clarke Papers*, ii. 242 ; —? to Clarke,

The contemptuous adjective applied by Thurloe to the Levelling party may doubtless be taken as the measure of his apprehension. Not only had the advocates of the sovereignty of a democratic Parliament bonds of union with a not insignificant party in the army itself, but they were able, at least so long as they confined themselves to criticism of the foundations of the existing Government, to attract to themselves Parliamentarians like Bradshaw, who had no aims in the direction of manhood suffrage, and even to find points of harmony with Royalists, who were as anxious to restore a free Parliament at Westminster as to replace the King at Whitehall. Consequently the Government resolved to do its best to arrest the leaders of that party for which Wildman and Sexby were the leading political agents, whilst Lord Grey of Groby was expected to stand forth as its military head.[1]   Of the three Wildman was seized at a village near Marlborough, by a party of horse under Major Butler on February 10, just as he was dictating a declaration inviting the people to take up arms against 'Oliver Cromwell, esquire,'[2] and was carried off for security to Chepstow Castle.   Grey was apprehended by Hacker, and though 'much distempered with the gout,' was carried to London and ultimately lodged as a prisoner in Windsor Castle,[3] where he remained till July, when he was liberated after making due submission.[4] Sexby—of whom it is not uncharitable to suppose that his political antagonism to the Protectorate was quickened into life by his disappointment of the com-

Case of the Levellers.

*Feb. 10.
Arrest of Wildman,*

*Feb. 12.
and of Grey.*

Sexby conceals himself.

Feb. 24, *Ib.* iii. 23; Nieupoort to the States General, March $\frac{2}{12}$, *Add. MSS.* 17,677 W, fol. 50.

[1] For a full account of the movements of these men see Dyer's information, *Thurloe,* vi. 829.   As this information was not given till Feb. 27, 165$\frac{7}{8}$, there was doubtless much in it not known to the Government three years earlier.

[2] Butler to the Protector, Feb. 10, *Thurloe,* iii. 147; *Merc. Pol.,* E, 826, 28.

[3] Hacker to the Protector, Feb. 12, *Thurloe,* iii. 148.

[4] Council Order Book, *Interr.* I, 76, p 178; *Merc. Pol.,* E.

mand which had been promised him in Guienne [1]—was more dangerous in consequence of his hold on the still numerous Levellers in the army. For some time he contrived to elude pursuit, but was at last tracked to Portland. His partisans in the island, however, were neither few nor without influence,

Feb. 20.
An attempt to seize him baffled.

and on February 20 a party of soldiers which arrived to arrest him was itself placed under arrest by the Mayor and the Governor of the Castle, on the ground that they were attempting to deprive an Englishman of his liberty without being able to show a written warrant ; though

He escapes to the Continent.

both the Mayor and the Governor were complaisant enough to express their belief that the new-comers had been deceived by representations made to

April 3.
Harrison moved to Carisbrooke.

them by others. In this way Sexby had time given him to effect his escape to the continent.[2] It was probably the knowledge thus gained of the disaffection prevailing at Portland which led to the removal of Harrison to securer quarters at Carisbrooke.[3]

Whatever may have been the exact plans of the Levellers, the importance of their movement was the greater in consequence of its concurrence, possibly only in point of time,

The Royalist plot.

though possibly also in something more, with those plans of the Royalists, a partial knowledge of which had led in January to the arrest of persons con-

1654.
July.
Activity of Colonel Stephens.

cerned in the transportation of arms. On that occasion the distribution of commissions from Charles had been traced to Colonel Stephens, who, after the

July 6.
Plans of the Royalists.

failure of Gerard's plot in the preceding July, had, in conjunction with another Royalist agent whose name

[1] See vol. iii. 112, 122.

[2] Council of State Order Book, *Interr.* I, 76a, p. 46.

[3] Narrative by Capt. Unton Croke, *Thurloe*, iii. 194. Captain Hurst, the Governor, related to Croke a conversation with Harrison, then a prisoner in the Castle, in which Harrison expressed an opinion that Sexby was a decoy for his Highness, though merely on the grounds that he had escaped arrest whilst his comrades had been caught. There was no connection between the politics of the two men : besides, Harrison thought Sexby 'a treacherous fellow,' which no doubt he was.

is unknown, laid before his master a statement of the hopes and fears of his party.[1] If only, they declared, Charles would no longer cast delays in the way of action, Tynemouth Castle could be secured in the North, and Sir Philip Musgrave would take the field at the head of 300 horse; the gentry of Surrey and Sussex could command 500, and Kent alone could provide a similar number. The Castles of Ludlow, Warwick and Denbigh might be secured. Sir Philip Musgrave, Sir John Grenville, Sir Humphrey Bennett, Lord Byron, Sir Thomas Peyton, Colonel Grey, Colonel Screven, respectively offered to get possession of Carlisle, Plymouth, Portsmouth, Nottingham, Sandwich, Tynemouth, and Shrewsbury. In Ireland, Carrickfergus, Galway, Londonderry, and probably Dublin and Athlone, might be gained without difficulty. All that Charles's English partisans demanded of him was that, after giving authority to their movements in writing, he would send Langdale to the North, offering pardon to certain persons they named; and would place either Ormond or the Duke of York by the water's side, with instructions to cross the Straits and head the insurgents in Kent and Surrey, where the store of arms provided at Sandwich for the use of the fleet could be easily secured. Charles at once wrote the required letters, copies of five of which are still extant in Hyde's handwriting.[2] In another, which some months later fell into the hands of the Protector, he endeavoured to explain his own previous hesitation and give encouragement to his partisans to act on his behalf as soon as possible. "You will easily believe," he wrote, "that I am very well pleased to hear how careful and solicitous you are for my concernments, and of the course you resolve to take. The truth is I have been so tender of my friends that I have deferred

Charles's letters.

His expectations of a rising.

---

[1] The statement (*Clarendon MSS.* xlviii. fol. 326) is said to have been drawn up by 'Col. Ste. and Fa.' Mr. Macray (*Clarendon*, xiv. 99, note) suggests that the latter may have been Fanshaw, but the account of his movements in Lady Fanshaw's *Memoirs* makes this improbable.

[2] *Clarendon MSS.* xlviii. fol. 328. See also Mr. Firth's references in the *Hist. Review* (April 1888), iii. 325.

to call upon them to appear till I could find myself able to give them good encouragement from abroad ; but since I find that comes on so slowly, I will no longer restrain those affections which I most desire to be beholden to ; and I have reason to believe that, if they who wish one and the same thing knew each other's mind, the work would be done without any difficulty, and if there was any handsome appearance in any one place, the rest would not sit still ; and I am persuaded I should then find supplies from those who are yet afraid to offer them. However, I am sure I would myself be with those who first wished for me, and to that purpose I will keep myself within a reasonable distance, consult with those you dare trust, and, if you are ready, agree upon a time ; and you cannot promise yourselves anything that you will be disappointed in and that is in the power of your affectionate friend—CHARLES R." [1] Charles, in fact, had given up all hope of receiving any considerable sum from the German princes, and was convinced of the necessity of relying entirely on his own subjects. This time, at least, it was an insurrection, not an assassination, that was in prospect.

The letters despatched to England were written at Mons, where Charles was on his way to visit his sister, the Princess of Orange, at Spa. His movements, however, were not guided by family affection alone. His position in France had been a strained one since Mazarin had avowed his eagerness to cultivate the friendship of the Protector. When he left Paris on June 30, it had been with a

June 30.
Charles
leaves
Paris,

---

[1] Charles to —? July $\frac{6}{18}$. *A Declaration of his Highness*, p. 26, E, 857, 3. This pamphlet was published by authority on Oct. 31, 1655. Mr. Firth, who reprinted the letter in the *Historical Review* (April 1888), iii. 324, urges in favour of its genuineness that 'it has never been denied to be really the King's.' To this argument it may be added, in the first place, that the date of July $\frac{6}{18}$ is a most likely one, as it is the day on which the statement by Stephens and his colleague was laid before Charles ; and, in the second place, that it corresponds in tone, and even in expression, with parts of the third and fifth of the five letters mentioned in the text, concerning which no doubt is possible.

determination to fix the seat of his exile outside the territory

and keeps
Court at
Spa. of France.[1]   At Spa he kept a gay and merry Court, spending the afternoon in dancing, and returning to the same amusement in the meadows after supper.[2] So far as he entertained any design of personally intervening in the impending struggle, it took the form of an intention to land in Scotland, where, the rout of Middleton at Dalnaspidal[3] being as yet unknown, the chances of the Royalists appeared far from desperate.[4]   Scared by an outbreak of small-pox in his sister's

Aug. 12.
Charles at
Aachen. household, Charles transferred his Court to Aachen, where he reinstated his father's secretary, Nicholas,

Nicholas
restored to
the secre-
taryship. in the office[5] in which he had served so faithfully, a promotion regarded by the English Cavaliers as assuring the triumph of their principles.[6]   It was, however, never safe to calculate upon Charles's devotion to a single party.   Nicholas and his allies can hardly have been well

Charles and
his sister at
vespers. pleased to hear that the King and his sister had enjoyed the music at vespers in a Roman Catholic church.   On the other hand, they can hardly have objected to his being taken to view the relics of Charles the Great.   The Princess kissed the skull and the hand of the restorer of the Empire, whilst her brother, in lighter mood, contented himself with kissing his sword and measuring its length against his own.[7]

The great Charles, it is true, was an emperor, not a saint. When, towards the end of September, his lesser namesake

---

[1] Nicholas to Middleton, July $\frac{11}{21}$, *Nicholas Papers*, ii. 78.

[2] Adams to Thurloe, $\frac{\text{July 31}}{\text{Aug. 10}}$, *Thurloe MSS.* xvi. 483.

[3] See *supra*, p. 109.

[4] A letter of Intelligence, $\frac{\text{July 31}}{\text{Aug. 10}}$, *Thurloe*, ii. 502 ; Nicholas to Norwich, $\frac{\text{Aug. 22}}{\text{Sept. 1}}$, *Nicholas Papers*, ii. 79.

[5] A letter of Intelligence, $\frac{\text{Aug. 22}}{\text{Sept. 1}}$. As Charles arrived at Aachen on Aug. $\frac{12}{22}$ (see a letter from the Nuncio at Cologne, Aug. $\frac{20}{30}$, *Roman Transcripts, R.O.*), Nicholas must have been placed in office between that date and $\frac{\text{Aug. 22}}{\text{Sept. 1}}$.

[6] Hatton to Nicholas, Sept. $\frac{15}{25}$, *Nicholas Papers*, ii. 88.

[7] Letters of Intelligence, $\frac{\text{Aug. 29}}{\text{Sept. 8}}$, *Thurloe*, ii. 567, 568.

moved on to Cologne, he at once sent a Jesuit and a friar of
his suite to the Papal Nuncio to beg for an interview.
The Nuncio, indeed, refused to receive in his own
house a king who declined to recognise the Pope, but
a meeting was arranged in the garden of a monas-
tery, where Charles professed his desire to allow the
English Catholics even to erect churches after he had succeeded,
with their assistance, in coming by his own. Not long afterwards an event occurred which forced Charles at least to
display his sentiments on the other side. His youngest
brother, the Duke of Gloucester, had been left with
his mother in France, under the charge of a tutor
named Lovell. Henrietta Maria had, indeed, promised that she would not tamper with her son's religion, but she thought it no shame to send him on a visit to
the Abbot of Pontoise—the Walter Montague of the Court of
Charles I.—in the hope that the boy would be induced by him to
change his creed, especially as Lovell was either too complaisant
or possessed too little authority to offer a stern resistance. At
once the colony of English Cavaliers in Paris appealed to Charles,
and Charles, who could do no otherwise than comply with
their wishes, despatched Ormond, not to argue with
the boy on points of faith, but to order him to leave
France, telling him at the same time that he owed a
higher duty to his King than to his mother. Ormond found
his task the easier as Gloucester, young as he was, clung to the
religion in which he had been educated, and, in spite of his
mother's angry protestations, expressed himself quite ready to
obey the orders conveyed to him, though he did not actually
leave Paris for Holland till December 8. On his
arrival he was taken in charge by the Princess of
Orange, who had by that time returned to her
adopted home.[1]

The recovery of the Duke from the influence of his mother
was a magnificent advertisement of Charles's claim to the

Marginal notes:

Sept. 29. Charles at Cologne.

Oct. 5. His meeting with the Nuncio.

Henrietta Maria tries to convert the Duke of Gloucester.

Nov. Ormond sent to fetch him away.

Dec. 8. The Duke leaves France.

[1] There are numerous letters on this matter in the *Nicholas Papers* and in the *Clarendon MSS.*

gratitude of the English Cavaliers. Some weeks before he had

Oct. 12.
Charles
writes to the
Scottish
ministers.

written to the Scottish ministers, appealing to the memory of his conversation and behaviour among them, and assuring them that he would never forget to walk always as in the sight of the Most High; though he could not but remind them how necessary it was to make

Dec.
A message to
the Nuncio.

friends of all sorts of men.[1] It was perhaps under the yoke of this necessity that, as soon as he heard of his brother's departure from France, he sent Lord Taaffe to the Nuncio with an assurance that he could not have acted otherwise without throwing out of gear his plans for the recovery of his kingdom; as, if he had been believed to be a consenting party to his brother's conversion, he would have been abandoned by the greater number of the English Royalists. If, on the other hand, the King could expect any advantage to his cause, he would be quite ready to change his own religion.[2] This cynical avowal only called from the Nuncio a protest against the supposition that the salvation of souls could be bargained for on temporal considerations. In reporting what had passed to Rome, he added that, from all he heard, Charles had not shown much personal anxiety to preserve the Duke from his mother's devices.[3] The calls of religion appealed in vain to his sensual nature. Like his grandfather, Henry IV., he cared for none of these things. If three kingdoms could be gained either by attendance on a Mass or by sitting under the most

---

[1] Charles to the Ministers of Scotland, Oct. $\frac{12}{22}$, *Clarendon MSS*. xlix. fol. 75.

[2] " Soggiungeva che quando potesse sperare qualche vantaggio nella sua causa dalla religione Cattolica l'haverebbe abbracciata S. M. istessa." Letter from the Nuncio, Dec. $\frac{10}{20}$, *Roman Transcripts, R.O.*

[3] " Confermano alcuni quel che mi fu supposto dal principio della poca premura del Rè in divertire il fratello; ma che il Marchese d'Ormond, il qual tien quasi sogetto lo spirito di S. M., habbia fatto lo sforzo per proprio istinto e per accreditarsi appresso gl'Eretici." Letter from the Nuncio, Dec. $\frac{10}{20}$, *Roman Transcripts, R.O.* Taaffe is not likely to have exceeded his instructions, as he must have known that Charles had had a friendly conference with the Nuncio, and might have another at any moment, when the truth could hardly fail to leak out.

long-drawn sermon, Charles would not hesitate to pay the price required.

It is hardly likely that this particular act of baseness was known to Oliver, but—well served as he was by spies in
Oliver and
Charles. Charles's Court—he cannot but have been aware that the character of his opponent was wanting in all those qualities which commended themselves to the Puritan mind.   Nor was he ignorant that Charles was putting forth all the skill he possessed to replace himself on the throne, therefrom to spread abroad those habits of self-indulgence which were most abhorrent to the strenuous Protector.

All through the second half of 1654 Charles was in constant communication with his English supporters, urging them, under
Charles
urges the
Royalists
to haste. the thin disguise of legal or mercantile jargon, to rise in insurrection with all possible speed.[1]   Scattered as were the English Royalists, it was not easy to bring them to a common action, and month after month passed away without any disturbance of the tranquillity which outwardly prevailed.   Nor was it only the difficulties of communication which hampered the movement.   The members of the
1655.
Jan.
The Sealed
Knot recom-
mends
patience. Sealed Knot,[2] Charles's accredited representatives in England, declared in the early part of the new year that the moment was not opportune for a rising.[3] The adhesion of the leaders of the army to the Protectorate in its conflict with Parliament must have carried conviction to the minds of those responsible for the success of the design that there was little hope of support amongst the soldiers; whilst the failure of the Levellers in Scotland, the arrest of Overton, and the restoration of discipline in Penn's fleet, must have strengthened their determination to avoid compromising themselves by isolated action.

[1] Many of these letters are amongst the *Clarendon MSS.*, as having been drafted or copied by Hyde, but it is most unlikely that the whole of them are to be found there.

[2] See *supra*, p. 138.

[3] Charles to Roles, $\frac{\text{Dec. 26}}{\text{Jan. 5}}$; Ormond to Hyde, $\frac{\text{Jan. 26}}{\text{Feb. 5}}$, Feb. $\frac{2}{12}$, *Clarendon MSS.* xlix. foll. 265, 321, 328.

It is, however, far from easy to arrest a movement once started on its course, and Cavaliers who had for months been warned to be ready whenever occasion called on them were indignant at the constant postponements of action,[1] and were not likely to be deterred by the arrest of some of their number or the seizure of a few cartloads of arms.[2] In the course of January the partisans of action despatched to Charles a messenger named Ross, with instructions to protest against further delays, and to ask that February 13 might be fixed as the date of the rising. Charles, with the sanguine impatience of an exile, welcomed the proposal ; but he was confronted by another messenger, sent off by James Halsall, who had been authorised by the Sealed Knot to warn him that the times were unpropitious. In spite of Ormond's advice to command his followers either to rise or to abstain from rising, he adopted a middle course, first expressing his approval of the resolution of the party of action, and subsequently sending Daniel O'Neill to England to mediate between the two factions, without issuing any direct orders, either commanding those who had entrusted their views to Ross to postpone the rising, or the Sealed Knot to abandon their opposition.[3]

Difficulty of arresting the movement.

Charles's indecision.

Feb. 8. Daniel O'Neill sent to mediate.

One result of the delay in Charles's answer was that the date of the rising was postponed. Another was that it gave the Protector time to strengthen his position. Knowing as well as any Royalist that the insurrection was intended to break out on the 13th, he employed his time in reducing its danger as far as possible by ordering the seizure of those whom he judged

The rising postponed.

Activity of the Protector.

[1] The story of insurrection has been told fully by Mr. Firth in the *Hist. Review*, iii. 323 ; iv. 313, 525. Unless for some special reason I shall refer my readers to the references there given.

[2] See *supra*, p. 233.

[3] Opton [or Roles] to Charles, Jan. ; Ormond to Hyde, Feb. $\frac{2}{12}$; Halsall to Charles, Feb. $\frac{2}{14}$; Charles to Roles, Feb. $\frac{8}{18}$, *Clarendon MSS.* xlix. foll. 315, 327, 340, 343. The important passages in these letters have been printed by Mr. Firth in the *Hist. Review* (Apr. 1888), iii. pp. 333–36.

likely to take part in it.[1] The most important of these arrests
was that of Read, who had formerly been a lieutenant in the

*Charles's
letter
found.*

Dutch service, and who had in his possession the
letter in Charles's own handwriting which placed
his encouragement of the insurrection beyond reasonable doubt. Fortified with this documentary evidence,

*Feb. 12.
Horses
seized.*

Oliver ordered that all horses in London and Westminster should be seized on the 12th, and on the
13th, the day on which the rising was expected to

*Feb. 13.
The letter
shown to
the
citizens.*

take place, he invited the Lord Mayor, the Aldermen, the Recorder, and sixty members of the
Common Council of the City to inspect the in-
criminating paper.[2] After they had satisfied themselves that
it was genuine, the Protector harangued them at some length,
urging on them the duty of looking to their own security and
of providing, at the same time, for the peace of the nation.
In the end he showed them the draft of a Commission which
he was about to issue for raising and bringing under discipline
the militia of the City of London.

The Commission was issued two days after it had thus been
announced. Once more the Protector showed his resolution

*Feb. 15.
A Militia
Commis-
sion for
London.*

to carry out in his own way the wishes of the dissolved Parliament. So far as the language used by
its members is to be trusted, that Parliament intended to call out a militia to bear the burden of
local defence. Oliver now appealed to the City to provide
him with a militia, to which he might reasonably look for support when the time arrived for that partial disbandment that
was inevitably impending. Yet it was not to be expected that
he should leave the armed force of the nation in the hands of
his opponents. The Commissioners named included, besides
the Lord Mayor and Aldermen, a considerable number of
officers, of whom Skippon was the most prominent. The
choice of the officers was left to the Protector, after consulta-

[1] *Merc. Pol.*, E, 826, 23; Salvetti's Newsletter, Feb. $\frac{9}{19}$, *Add. MSS.*
27,962 O, fol. 385.

[2] *Merc. Pol.*, E, 826, 28. For the letter see *supra*, p. 271.

tion with the Commissioners. The object of the new militia was declared to be the suppression of local disorders. It was specially announced that no citizen would be called on to serve outside the City or its liberties without his own consent.[1]

Oliver was aware that the danger had not passed away because the day of rising had been postponed. On February 24

Feb. 24.
A procla-
mation
against
horse
races. he issued a proclamation forbidding race-meetings for six months, on the ground that the concourse of people might be used to 'raise new troubles.'[2] As a matter of course orders had been

The ports
secured. given to secure the ports. At Dover, however, some of the officials were in collusion with the Royalist party. With their help Halsall and Ross had crossed to lay their messages before Charles, and the correspondence between the exiled Court at Cologne and its English supporters was kept briskly up. It was doubtless by the agency of these officials that Daniel O'Neill, who, travelling under the name of Bryan, had been arrested at Dover and confined in

Feb. 22.
O'Neill's
escape. the Castle, succeeded in making his escape and in pursuing his journey to London. Another notable Royalist agent, Nicholas Armorer, appearing under

Armorer
allowed to
pass. the name of Wright, was allowed to pass on the certificate of Day, the Clerk of the Passage. The result of this connivance with suspected persons was an order

Feb. 26.
Stricter
measures. to Captain Wilson, the Deputy Governor of Dover Castle, to hold himself personally responsible for the detention of all persons supposed to be travelling in Charles's interest.[3]

---

[1] Commission, Feb. 15, Council of State Order Book, *Interr*. I, 76a, p. 22.

[2] *Proclamation*, Feb. 24, B. M. press-mark, 669, f. 19, No. 69.

[3] The Princess of Orange to Hyde, $\frac{\text{Feb. 19}}{\text{March 1}}$; Charles to Hyde, March $\frac{3}{13}$, *Clarendon MSS*. xlix. foll. 367, 387. Wilson to Thurloe, Feb. 27, *Thurloe*, iii. 179. The intimation that Wright was probably Armorer was given by Sir R. Stone, *Thurloe MSS*. xxii. 107. Mr. Firth only allows the connivance of Day—the Clerk of the Passage—to be probable, the evidence against him not being conclusive (*Hist. Rev.* (April) iii. 1888,

O'Neill was not Charles's sole representative in England. On February 19 Rochester crossed from Dunkirk to Margate, in company with Sir Joseph Wagstaff, who had held a command under the late King in the Civil War.[1]   Both Rochester

Landing of Rochester and Wagstaff.

and Wagstaff succeeded in reaching London unobserved.   Rochester came, not like O'Neill, to mediate between the parties, but to put himself at the head of the one which had declared for immediate action. The longing for an opportunity of bringing his weary exile to an end had got the better of prudence in Charles's mind.[2]   Nor was he, to do him justice, desirous

Charles at Middelburg.

of sheltering his own person.   Slipping away from Cologne, he made his way through Düsseldorf to Middelburg, with the intention of crossing to England as

pp. 343, 344). He seems to have overlooked a passage in a letter from Manning, the spy, of May $\frac{11}{21}$: "At Dover all pass by the assistance of one And. Day, Fox, &c., searchers, and as long as they are there all will pass you . . . and Foster hath made O'Neill, Manning's, Armorer, Ross, Trelawny, Palmer, Halsall's, and the other Dover escapes, and many before," *Thurloe*, iii. 428. "And." may either stand for Andrew, a mistake for Robert, or be the first letters of some other name, such as Anderson.

Mr. Firth says that 'Cromwell does not appear to have dismissed Day from his post, probably because he did not regard the charges as proved ; but perhaps because he had already rendered Day harmless. At the end of February 1655, in consequence of the escape of several Royalist prisoners, the authority of the old Commissioners of the Passage was superseded, and the control of the police of the passage entrusted to the Deputy-Governor of Dover, Captain Wilson.' This argument requires, I think, to be supplemented by the consideration that to dismiss Day would give warning to Royalists that they must avoid Dover for the future, and so keep out of Wilson's hands. If this view be adopted, it will be unnecessary to consider the assumption that the Protector may not have regarded the charges as proved.

[1] Examination of F. Jones, April 4, *Thurloe*, iii. 344.

[2] Hyde's memoranda of the instructions to be given to Trelawny, *Clarendon MSS*. iii. 65. Clarendon's attempt to minimise Charles's decision long afterwards (*Clarendon*, xiv. 127) is of no importance beside the contemporary document.

soon as a reasonable prospect of success lay open before him.[1]

The information laid before Rochester on his arrival in London was such as might have discouraged a wiser man.

The situation in England. The Protector had been well enough served by his spies to lay hands on Sir Humphrey Bennett, who had engaged to secure Portsmouth ; Colonel Grey, a brother of Lord Grey of Wark, who had offered to make sure of Tynemouth Castle ; and Sir John Grenville, the former defender of the Scilly Isles, who had undertaken the surprise of Plymouth.[2] Small bodies which had gathered with the intention of seizing the cavalry posts at Taunton and Marlborough had been broken up, and some of their members arrested.[3] Yet neither O'Neill nor Rochester could perceive the symptoms of failure conveyed in these news. O'Neill's

O'Neill sanguine. communications with Charles were full of the most sanguine assurances. Sir George Booth, he wrote, would answer for Cheshire, and he even believed that Fairfax himself would carry Yorkshire with him to the Royal standard.[4]

---

[1] Charles's presence at Düsseldorf is attested by a letter from the Princess of Orange to Hyde, $\frac{\text{Feb. 26}}{\text{March 8}}$, *Clarendon MSS.* xlix. 373. A letter from Calais, of March $\frac{20}{30}$, affirms that he was at that time still at Middelburg, *Thurloe*, iii. 275.

[2] Robinson to Floyd, Feb. $\frac{8}{18}$, *Clarendon MSS.* xlix. fol. 373. *Perf. Diurnal*, E, 481, 13.

[3] Butler's letters of Feb. 26 and March 3, with the information of Gill and Stradling, *Thurloe*, iii. 176, 181, 191.

[4] The belief that Fairfax would be on their side was widely spread amongst the Royalists. On June 11 Percy Church informed Nicholas that he had heard that Buckingham had said ' that the Lord Fairfax promised to engage for his Majesty's interest, provided that the transactions between his Majesty and him might pass through the Duke's hands ; which request being refused, his Lordship quitted, and so his Majesty's design was frustrated.' " Opposite this passage," writes Mr. Warner in a note, " Nicholas has written in shorthand : ' I assure you I know not, nor by enquiry can find, that there was ever an offer or promise from the Lord Fairfax that he would engage for his Majesty's interest, so as the transactions between his Majesty and him might pass through the D. of B.'s hands ; but it's possible some third person might [have] proposed that the Duke

The West, it was confidently expected, would not be found wanting, and Shrewsbury, with the counties on the Welsh border, would follow the example. The night of March 8 was now fixed for a simultaneous rising of the Royalists. Wil-

Presbyterian support offered.

loughby of Parham engaged that the Presbyterians would stand by the Cavaliers, and promised the assistance of Waller and Major-General Browne.[1] Rochester himself set off for Yorkshire to conduct the negotiations with Fairfax, on which he had set his heart.[2]

It was one thing for a few returned exiles to conclude that the proposed insurrection was on a fair way to success ; it was

March 8. Chances of the rising.

another thing for them to induce hundreds of Royalist gentry to risk their lives and estates by flying in the face of an established Government, and, without adequate organisation and with spirits dulled by frequent postponement of action, to confront the strongest military force hitherto known in England. What really took place on the night of the 8th was the gathering of a few isolated bodies of enthusiasts at their allotted stations, whilst the great bulk of the Royalists, refusing to sacrifice life and

might be a fit man to treat between the King and that Lord, whereby to procure him to engage for the King. And this, I assure you, is the most that I know or can learn concerning that particular, and it's said by some that know Lord Fairfax very well that he had never any intention at all to engage for the King's interest ' " (*Nicholas Papers*, ii. 335). This seems to set the question at rest so far as Fairfax is concerned. Buckingham must, however, have conveyed the impression that Fairfax might be counted on, or O'Neill would have been less confident. As Fairfax had possession of Buckingham's estates, it would be to the interest of the latter that Fairfax should come to terms with himself before giving his support to a restoration.

[1] There is a curious story in Coyet's despatch of April 6 about a secret agent of the Government trying to trepan Browne into the Royalist plot to have an excuse for arresting him. If this is more than mere gossip, the Government can have merely wanted to get evidence, in an improper way, against a man of whom it entertained well-founded suspicions.

[2] O'Neill to Charles, March 8, *Nicholas Papers*, ii. 217. The uninterpreted name ' Mr. Humely,' ' whose consent was most necessary,' I take to be the town of Hull.

property in so harebrained an adventure, remained quietly at home.

Thus, at Duddoe, to the south of Morpeth, some eighty persons assembled in the hope of gaining admission into New-
Gathering at castle, were scared by the fortuitous approach of a
Duddoe, body of infantry on the march southwards from Berwick, and dispersed with all possible rapidity. The same ignominious fate befell a larger body, variously estimated at 100 and 300, which, being encouraged by the presence of Rochester
on Marston himself, collected on Marston Moor in the expectation
Moor that friendly hands would open to them the gates of York. Startled, according to one account, by the shouts of some travellers who had lost their way, they hurriedly escaped, leaving their arms behind them.[1] Nor was another party of
and at about 200 which gathered at Rufford, in Nottingham-
Rufford. shire, with the intention of marching northwards to join their comrades in York, any more persistent. So hurried had been their resolve that both Lord Byron, who had been marked out as their leader,[2] and the young owner of Rufford, Sir George Savile, who, as Earl and Marquis of Halifax, became pre-eminent as a statesman under the Government of the Restoration, were absent from home. Scarcely had the others met when the word that their secret had been betrayed spread consternation amongst them, and, throwing their arms into a pond, they fled without making an effort to carry out their purpose.[3]

---

[1] Thurloe to Pell, March 16, Vaughan's *Protectorate*, i. 146; Mews to Nicholas, $\frac{\text{May 25}}{\text{June 4}}$, *Nicholas Papers*, ii. 327; *Merc. Pol.*, E, 826, 11, 23; informations of W. Trumbel, E. Turner, M. Pratt, and W. Bell, *Thurloe*, iii. 216, 222, 228, 230.

[2] Manning to Thurloe, $\frac{\text{June 23}}{\text{July 3}}$, *S. P. Dom.* xciii. 45.

[3] Examination of Clayton and others, March 13; examination of Penniston Whalley and Baggelow, March 14; [Berry] to the Protector, undated; Berry to the Protector, March 17; information by Lockell, July 12, 1658, and by Cockhill, July 30, 1658, *Thurloe*, iii. 228, 241, 264, iv. 599, vii. 263, 301. The last two informers were Savile's servants. Penniston Whalley left his house at Screveton on the 8th, and took care

In Lancashire and Cheshire the failure of the Royalists was, if possible, still more complete. In the former county there was no movement whatever.[1] In the latter, Sir George Booth and Colonel Werden did no more than send two or three men to see whether sentinels were posted on the walls of Chester Castle, and finding them on the alert, at once abandoned all hope of capturing so strong a fortress.[2] Shrewsbury, from its proximity to the Welsh border, was of the greatest importance to the Government, and early in March the Protector, hearing of danger in that quarter, despatched a troop of horse to relieve the garrison, which at that time consisted of no more than seventy men under the Governor, Colonel Humphrey Mackworth.[3] On the 5th he empowered Colonel Crowne, Mackworth's uncle, to raise an infantry regiment in Shropshire.[4] On the 8th, however, before these orders had time to take effect, tidings which reached Mackworth induced him to send prompt notice of danger to Sir Thomas Middleton, who was also threatened in Chirk Castle. Then, seizing twenty horses in the town, he despatched as many men on them to Boreatton Park, the seat of Sir Thomas Harris, in which the rendezvous was to be held that night. The party, on its arrival, found twenty horses ready saddled in the stables,

Inaction in Lancashire and Cheshire.

Shrewsbury in danger.

The plot suppressed.

to be able to plead an *alibi* till the 9th. He was suspected of having betrayed the scheme, but may merely have wished to withdraw himself from a desperate cause.

[1] Mr. Firth (*Hist. Rev.* (Apr. 1888), iii. p. 342, and Apr. 1889, p. 324) ascribes this quiescence to the landing at Liverpool of some 3,000 men from the army in Ireland, quoting a letter of James Halsall to the effect that they would prevent the design of his brother to surprise that place. The landing, however, took place on Jan. 15, and the letter written abroad on Feb. $\frac{2}{12}$ (*Clarendon MSS.* xlix. fol. 343) might very well refer to such a difficulty at that time ; but there is no reason to suppose that these troops remained in Lancashire, and, indeed, nothing is heard of their being there in March.

[2] Examination of Pickering, July 20, *Thurloe*, iii. 677.

[3] The second son of the Colonel Mackworth, who died, in 1654, as a member of the Council. Blore's *Hist. of Rutland*, p. 129.

[4] The Protector to Crowne, March 5, *S. P. Dom.* xcix. 91, i.

many of them with charged pistols in the holsters, a barrel of powder and a suit of armour in the barn, and bullets newly cast in the study. The arrest of Sir Thomas followed as a matter of course. Subsequent examinations showed that the rendezvous was to have been held that night and an attempt made on Shrewsbury.[1] Had this failed the conspirators were to ride off to join any Royalist band which elsewhere had been more successful than they had been themselves.

[1] Mackworth to the Protector, March 8; Crowne to the Protector, March 10; examinations of Evanson and Bultry, March 21, *Thurloe*, iii. 208, 215, 288, 289. Mackworth makes Boreatton only five miles from Shrewsbury, whereas it is at least eight. I have said nothing of the confessions of Ralph Kynaston (*Thurloe*, iii. 209–211), who gave information that six soldiers, of whom two were to be disguised as women, were to procure an entrance into Shrewsbury Castle, at 4 P.M. on the 8th, on pretence of sight-seeing, and were to block the gate on leaving, giving opportunity to men concealed in alehouses near to rush the Castle, as it is not easy to understand why this attack should be made at 4 P.M., whilst the supporting force was not to rendezvous in Boreatton Park till 11 P.M. The following explanation may, however, be suggested. Prior to March 7 Mackworth had but twenty men at the most to garrison the Castle. This is shown by his own estimate of seventy foot and a troop of horse on the 10th (*Thurloe*, iii. 218). Fifty men had been put in by Crowne on the 7th (Crowne's Petition, *S. P. Dom.* xcix. 91), and the troop sent by the Protector had subsequently arrived. May we not, therefore, conjecture that the plan revealed by Kynaston was one made before the garrison was strengthened by Crowne, as the proposed scheme for overpowering the garrison would then appear feasible, and it would be unnecessary to bring up the horse from Boreatton to help in what could be done without them? As Kynaston's business was to raise a troop in Montgomery, it is not difficult to imagine that he had not heard that the reinforcement of the garrison had led to a change of plan.

CHAPTER XXXIX

PENRUDDOCK'S RISING

IN Wiltshire alone were the insurgents rewarded even by momentary success, and that merely because they contented themselves with attacking an unwalled and un-defended town. In spite of their failure in February the Royalists of that county continued hopeful, being encouraged by the presence of Sir Joseph Wagstaff, who had been sent from London to take command of the forces to be raised in the western counties. Of the local gentry, the most prominent were Colonel John Penruddock of Compton Chamberlayne, and Hugh Grove of Chisenbury. Penruddock's ancestors had emigrated from Cumberland ; and he himself, having served with his father in the King's army during the Civil War, had been driven to pay composition for his estates.[1] Of Grove's earlier life nothing appears to be known. It had been at first proposed to signalise the appointed 8th of March by an attack on the judges of assize at Winchester, a plan which was soon abandoned, in consequence of news that a troop of horse had appeared in that city.[2] The conspirators appear to have had a special grudge against the judges as the representatives of the Protector, and, as their commission was to be opened at Salisbury on the 12th, the night of the 11th was fixed

1655.
A movement in Wilt-shire.

Proposed attack on Winchester.

---

[1] Mr. Ravenhill, in the *Wiltshire Archæol. and Nat. Hist. Magazine*, xiii. 125, gives an entry written by Penruddock in his account-book of 1,300*l.* paid for composition. This includes his father's fine of 490*l.*

[2] Thurloe to Pell, March 16, Vaughan's *Protectorate*, i. 145.

for a rendezvous in Clarendon Park, about two miles from the city.

Accordingly, some sixty horsemen gathered on that historical site, where they were joined by forty more who came out of the city under John Mompesson, and later on by about eighty from Blandford.[1] Being thus some 180 strong, they entered Salisbury before dawn, placed guards at the inn-doors, seized the horses in the stables, flung open the doors of the gaol, and arrested in their beds the two judges, Chief Justice Rolle and Baron Nicholas, together with Dove, the High Sheriff of the county. When the three were brought out, the judges were forced to hand over their commission, and Wagstaff, rude soldier as he was, called out for the hanging of them all. This cruel counsel having been rejected at Penruddock's instance, Dove, who was especially obnoxious as a purchaser of Royalists' estates,[2] was asked to proclaim Charles II. On his refusal he was subjected to ill-treatment, receiving on his side a blow from a carbine. Ultimately the proclamation was made by one of the company, whilst the Sheriff himself was carried off as a hostage.[3] The insurgents, finding that the townsmen refused to join them, marched off to Blandford, where, finding the town-crier as obstinate as Dove, Penruddock was reduced to proclaim, with his own lips, Charles II.,

Mar. 11.
A gathering in Clarendon Park.

Mar. 12.
The Royalists in Salisbury.

---

[1] The examination of Arthur Collins, Wagstaff's servant (*The Perf. Diurnal*, E, 831, 1) begins by stating 'that on Sunday, being the 11th instant, the said Sir Joseph Wagstaff met at Clarendon Park, . . . where were mustered 60 horse, Mr. John Mompesson bringing from Salisbury to their aid 40 more, from whence they immediately marched towards Blandford, where about 80 more joined with them ; thence they marched to Salisbury.' From Clarendon Park to Blandford and back to Salisbury was about 46 miles, and it is incredible that the party, with all their work before them, should have added this to their toils. I suspect that they merely wheeled round Salisbury to the Blandford Road, and were there joined by the reinforcement.

[2] In the *Dictionary of Nat. Biog.* he is improperly styled a regicide. He sat only once on the court, and did not sign the death-warrant.

[3] *Clarendon*, xiv. 132 ; *Merc. Pol.*, E, 830, 11, 23.

the true Protestant religion, the liberty of the subject, and privilege of Parliament.[1] Then, sending out parties to right and left to sweep the country in search of recruits,[2] the main body pushed on hurriedly through Sherborne to Yeovil, where they halted till daylight on the morning of the 13th, having covered 47 miles since leaving Salisbury. By this time their hopes of gathering a large force had died away, and Dove was set free, perhaps as a mere incumbrance to a march which could hardly be distinguished from a flight.[3]

March 13. The insurgents at Yeovil.

It could not be long before the forces of the Government would be on the track of the fugitives. By the evening of the day on which they entered Salisbury, the Protector, alarmed at the news, appointed Desborough Major-General of the West, and despatched him to the scene of action.[4] On the evening of the 14th Desborough was at Newbury, intending to effect a junction at Amesbury with Major Butler, who, having half a cavalry regiment under his orders, had promptly marched to Salisbury, as well as with some troops which had been pushed forward from Chichester.[5] Long before this the supporters of the Government in the neighbouring counties were astir. At Bristol guards were enlisted and a troop of horse raised.[6] At Gloucester 400 of the citizens agreed to undertake the defence of the place, leaving the garrison free for service in the field.[7] In Somerset, which was more directly threatened, no less than 3,000 men rallied to the Government, and but for a dispute

March 12. Desborough Major-General of the West.

March 14. His arrival at Newbury.

Local offers of assistance.

---

[1] *Perf. Proceedings*, E, 831, 6 ; *State Trials*, v. 775.

[2] Bishop to Thurloe, March 14, *Thurloe*, iii. 242.

[3] Dove appeared at Salisbury on the morning of the 14th, which fixes the 13th as the day of his liberation at Yeovil.

[4] The Protector's instructions, March 12, *Thurloe*, iii. 221.

[5] Desborough to the Protector, March 15, *ib.* iii. 247.

[6] Aldworth and Powell to Thurloe, March 12, 15, *ib.* iii. 233, 248.

[7] Wade to Desborough, March 14, *ib.* iii. 239. Details are to be found in the *Gloucester Corporation Books*.

about the command would have taken the field at once.[1]
Colonel Copplestone, with a newly levied regiment quartered
in Devonshire,[2] was ready to bar the way of the retreating
Royalists.

It was, however, to none of these bodies that the overthrow
of the Royalists was due. On the morning of the day on which
the Royalists were hurrying out of Yeovil Captain Unton Croke,
the officer who had vainly attempted to arrest Sexby earlier in
the year,[3] started from Exeter with a party of soldiers in the
hope of being able to intercept the march of the insurgents.

Unton Croke misses the insurgents at Honiton.
When he reached Honiton he found that they had
already slipped past, and were pressing on in the
hope of reaching Cornwall, where there were Royal-

They push on to the West.
ists enough to welcome and assist them, and whence,
if their enterprise proved hopeless, escape to the
Continent was easy. Croke, indeed, had but sixty men under
his orders, whilst the enemy, in spite of having lost a considerable number by desertion, were reported to be two hundred. They were, however, depressed in mind, and both they
and their horses were weary from want of adequate rest.
Avoiding Exeter, lest they should fall into the hands of
Copplestone, they struggled on through Cullompton and
Tiverton, only drawing rein in the late evening at South
Molton. While the night was still young, Croke, who had not
slackened in pursuit, came up and surrounded them

The fight at South Molton.
in their quarters. The Royalists, surprised as they
were, defended themselves gallantly, firing out of the
windows at the troopers. Yet, perhaps because they had been
long unaccustomed to the use of arms, they did little execution,
not a man of Croke's little force being slain. Knowing that
their case was hopeless, some made their escape, Wagstaff
himself being one of the number. Others, like Penruddock
and Grove, together with Jones, who had been joined to the

---

[1] Thurloe to Pell, March 16, Vaughan's *Protectorate*, i. 151 ; Gough
to Malyn, March 14, *Thurloe*, iii. 237.

[2] Copplestone to the Protector, March 10, *ib*. iii. 219.

[3] See *supra*, p. 270.

other two in command, surrendered. Fifty or sixty prisoners were taken and lodged in Exeter Gaol.[1] Unfortunately, there is good reason to believe that a set of articles drawn

Probable
offer of
pardon. up by Penruddock, in which pardon for life and estate was offered to those who surrendered, had been agreed to by commissioners appointed by Croke.[2] Such terms Croke, as a mere military commander, had no power to grant, and it is hardly likely that he ever intended to grant them. At all events, they were tacitly repudiated by the Government as well as by himself.[3]

---

[1] Croke to the Protector, March 15, 16, *Merc. Pol.*, E, 830, 23.

[2] Penruddock and Jones drew up a petition to the Protector and Council in which, after recounting the circumstances of the fight, they say : "The Captain thought fit on this exigent to sound a parley and tender us conditions, whereupon hostages were delivered on both sides, and one Mr. Rogers, a corporal, and Mr. Lane, a gentleman of the troop, were sent in the behalf of Capt. Croke. Mr. Penruddock, having drawn the articles and read them distinctly to the said Rogers and Lane, th[ey in] the Capt.'s name signed the said articles, which were as followeth, or to this effect :—that the several persons therein comprised upon delivering up their several quarters should have their lives, liberties, and estates, and never be farther questioned by any power whatsoever, and were to have free quarter and a convoy to their several homes. The original thus signed we are able to produce and sufficiently prove " (*Wiltshire Archæol. and Nat. Hist. Magazine*, xiv. 39). Penruddock on his trial challenged Croke on the subject, who remained silent, and both he and Grove repeated this assertion in their dying speeches on the scaffold. On the other hand, the writer of one of the letters amongst the *Clarke Papers* (iii. 36) says that Croke said that 'they were no articles, but verbal conditions to this effect that they should have fair quarter, which they have had, and that he would earnestly intercede with my Lord Protector for their lives, liberties, and estates, which likewise he hath done.' Perhaps this was what Croke intended, though he may not have scrutinised closely the paper his commissioners signed.

[3] Croke, in his despatch written the next morning (*Merc. Pol.*, E, 830, 23), merely says 'some of them yielded to mercy. I promised them I would use my endeavours to intercede for their lives '; and this he afterwards did for five of them. The most probable explanation of the whole matter is that Croke urged the men firing from the house to sur-render, and, on their consent to negotiate, sent, as Penruddock states, a

With the capture and dispersal of the insurgents at South Molton the rash game played by Charles, at the hazard of his most devoted adherents, came to an end. No Government could pass over such a defiance, and after due deliberation a special Commission was issued for the western counties and another for the northern. The Government boasted that it was the first time since 1646 that treason had been submitted to juries. For all that, it was only by packing the juries with 'honest and well-affected' persons that a favourable verdict could be looked for.[1] Six of the prisoners put on their trial at Salisbury were found guilty of treason, one pleaded guilty, and three were acquitted; six others being found guilty of horse-stealing, probably, though not certainly, in connection with the insurrection.[2] Of those convicted of treason, only three were executed, one, a gentleman named Lucas, being beheaded, and the other two hanged; though in their case, as in other cases in the course of these assizes, the barbarous concomitants of hanging were remitted.[3] At Exeter, where the court opened on the 18th, twenty-six prisoners, including Penruddock and Grove, either pleaded guilty or were convicted, whilst three were acquitted and one had a No Bill found by the grand jury.[4] Of the whole number, seven only[5] were hanged, and two—Penruddock and

The insurrection at an end.

Apr. 11-12. Trials at Salisbury,

Apr. 18. at Exeter,

corporal and a trooper to treat. Penruddock, having drawn up these impossible articles, submits them to the two commissioners, who blindly accept them. Penruddock in his petition says nothing of Croke having given his personal word, but of course holds Croke responsible for his agents. That these articles, even if assented to by Croke, would be held to be quite worthless was shown by the similar case of Hamilton in 1649. See vol. i. 10.

[1] Thurloe to Pell, April 6, Vaughan's *Protectorate*, i. 162; Dove to Thurloe, March 29, *Thurloe*, iii. 318.

[2] *The Perf. Diurnal*, E, 833, 9.

[3] *The Faithful Scout*, E, 838, 5.   [4] *Thurloe*, iii. 394.

[5] *Perf. Proceedings*, E, 838, 3, gives only seven, but in the Protector's warrant, of which there is a facsimile in the *Wiltshire Arch. and Nat. Hist. Magazine*, xiv. 66, there are eight names. In a petition of the prisoners

Grove—beheaded.   At Chard, on April 25, the condemnations

were six.   As no executions are reported, it may be
presumed that none took place.

In the suppression of this rebellion the discipline
and fidelity of the soldiery had been placed beyond dispute.   The

attachment of the civilian population was more open
to question.   Before the defeat of the insurgents was
known in London, Thurloe assured a correspondent

'that all the counties in England would, instead of
rising for them, have risen against them ; and the
Protector could, if there had been need, have drawn into the
field, within fourteen days, 20,000 men, besides the standing
army.   So far are they mistaken who dream that the affections
of this people are towards the House of Stuart.'[1]   The Royalist

historian, writing long after the cause he favoured had
triumphed over its opponents, took a different view.
" There cannot," he declared, " be a greater manifestation of the
universal prejudice and aversion in the whole kingdom towards
Cromwell and his Government than that there could be so
many designs and conspiracies against him, which were communicated to so many men, and that such signal and notorious
persons could resort to London and remain there without any
such information or discovery as might enable him to cause
them to be apprehended." [2]

Clarendon, indeed, might have made out a yet stronger
case if he had noted the facility with which Royalist prisoners

succeeded in making their escape.   It is certain
that in one case, at least, it was not owing to the
lenity of the Government that the death sentences
at Chard were not followed by the usual result.   The most

(*Wiltshire Arch. and Nat. Hist. Magazine*, xiv. 65) only seven names are
marked with an asterisk as those of men afterwards hanged.   Amongst
those not so marked is John Harris, whereas in the Protector's death-warrant
is John Haynes.   If the clerk who drew up the warrant put in Haynes by
mistake for Harris, it would account for the escape of the eighth man.

[1] Thurloe to Pell, March 16, Vaughan's *Protectorate*, i. 151.
[2] *Clarendon*, xiv. 130.

important of the condemned was Major Thomas Hunt, who was
removed to Ilchester gaol, outside the walls of which a scaffold

May 15.
Escape of
Major
Hunt.

was erected on May 15, to serve for his execution on
the morrow. In the evening, however, he received
a visit from his two sisters, one of whom took his
place in bed, whilst, disguised in her clothes, he walked out in
company with the other, hiding his face as if to stifle his sobs,
and was no more heard of in England.[1] As the gaoler had
been ordered to place his prisoner in irons, and had neglected

Probable
connivance
of the
gaoler.

to do so, there is some reason to suppose that, like
the officials at Dover, he acted in opposition to the
Government in whose service he was. The two ladies
paid for their devotion by imprisonment for two years and
a half. It is difficult to resist the conclusion that similar assist-

March.
Escape of
Mauleverer
and Walter.

ance was given to two of the Yorkshire plotters, Sir
Richard Mauleverer and John Walter, who had been
captured near Chester. A guard was indeed placed
outside the door of the room in which they were confined, but
no notice was taken of a window in the room itself, through
which they dropped easily into the street and got safely away.[2]

Apr. 2.
Eyton's
escape,

Eyton, again, one of the Shrewsbury insurgents, was
allowed to let himself down from his window by tying
his sheets together. As strict orders given to the
marshal to put him in irons had been only so far complied with
that a single leg had been fettered, the evidence that the marshal
was in collusion with his prisoner appears to be complete.[3]

Outside the prison walls the absence of any desire to assist
the Government in arresting fugitives is even more significant.

Wagstaff's
escape,

Wagstaff and several of his comrades were able to
conceal themselves in the houses of western Royalists
till they found an opportunity to take shipping to the Conti-

---

[1] Cary and Barker to Desborough, May 18, *Thurloe*, iii. 453 ; *Merc.
Pol.*, E, 840, 7 ; Hunt's Petition, Aug. 1, 1660, *Hist. MSS. Com.*, Rep.
vii. 123.

[2] Griffith to Thurloe, March 19, 27, *Thurloe*, iii. 273, 304.

[3] Reynolds to Thurloe, April 2 ; Mackworth to the Protector, Aug. 11,
Thurloe, iii. 336, 706.

nent.[1]   Daniel O'Neill effected his escape in much the same

and
O'Neill's. manner.   Of all the conspirators, Rochester and Armorer were exposed to the greatest danger.   The pair,
making their way from Yorkshire, reached Aylesbury in the
company of the Earl's French servant, and of a countryman
whose services they had engaged on the way.[2]   At Aylesbury
they were arrested by a justice of the peace named Henn,[3]

March 20.
Arrest of
Rochester
and
Armorer. whose suspicions had been roused by the failure of
Rochester and his companion to give a satisfactory
account of their movements.   In the course of the
night, however, they bribed the innkeeper in whose
charge they had been left with a sum of money and a gold

March 21.
Their
escape. chain valued at 100*l*.   Abandoning their servants
and horses, they succeeded in slipping away to
London.   Rochester, after remaining there for some
time in the disguise of a Frenchman in a yellow periwig,[4]
reached Cologne about the end of May.[5]   Armorer was equally
successful in making his escape.

Yet, though all this makes for the acceptance of Clarendon's
view of the situation, there is something to be said on the

Support
given to the
Protector. other side.   If the Protector had been the object of
general aversion, he would hardly have raised the
4,000 men of the London militia so speedily as he
did, nor would 400 volunteers have risen to support him in
Gloucestershire, and still less 3,000 in Somerset even before
they received his summons.   Nor, it may be added, would the
insurgents have found so cold a welcome in every town through

---

[1] *Clarendon*, xiv. 134.

[2] Mews to Nicholas, $\frac{May\ 25}{June\ 4}$, *Nicholas Papers*, ii. 327.

[3] Well known to the readers of *The Verney Memoirs* as a sequestrator during the Civil War.

[4] Manning to Thurloe, April $\frac{3}{13}$, *Thurloe*, iii. 339.

[5] Henn's warrant, March 20; Henn to the Protector, April 2, *Thurloe*, iii. 281, 335.   Henn was to have met Ingoldsby on the 21st, who no doubt reported the affair at once to Whitehall.   On Rochester's final escape, and also on Armorer's, see Manning to Thurloe, May ?, *S. P. Dom.* xcvii. 109.

which they passed.[1]   On the whole, it is safest to conclude that both parties had a comparatively small number of devoted adherents, whilst the majority were more or less indifferent, and under the sway of two streams of feeling draw-ing them in opposite directions.   On the one hand was the dread of rekindling the embers of civil war by any challenge to existing authority.   On the other hand was a natural desire to save the life of a hunted fugitive, strengthened by a want of sympathy with the authorities who were seeking his death.

Probabilities of the case.

Of the composition of the Royalist group we have some means of judging from a list of prisoners confined in the gaols of Exeter, Taunton, and Ilchester.   Of 139 persons named, 43 were esquires, gentlemen,[2] or officers. There were 10 servants, 8 yeomen, 19 husbandmen, 2 innkeepers, and the remaining 56, except a few to whom no occupation is assigned, small traders or handicraftsmen mostly from villages.[3]   Evidently the rising had been one mainly of gentlemen and their dependents.   Of the partisans of the other side it is impossible to speak with equal certainty, and still less of the mass which took part with neither.   It is safe, however, to say that all the purchasers of confiscated lands supported the Protectorate, as well as that not inconsiderable class which was Puritan without being politically opinionative.

Composi-tion of the Royalist group.

At all events, there was sufficient evidence of support to justify the Protector in extending the system which he had already adopted in London.[4]   On March 14, two days after Desborough had been despatched to the west against the Salisbury insurgents, commissioners were appointed to organise the militia [5] in the twenty-

March 14. Appoint-ment of militia com-missioners.

---

[1] A few joined them in Salisbury, and a few in Blandford, but that is all.

[2] Including one described as ' of Gray's Inn.'

[3] *Thurloe*, iii. 306.   The most numerous of the last class were tailors, of whom there were six.   [4] See *supra*, p. 278.

[5] Under the monarchy the militia had been organised by the lords-lieutenant appointed by the Crown.   The innovation consisted merely in substituting bodies of commissioners for those functionaries.

one towns or rural districts in which danger was most to be
feared.   On the 20th, a few days after Croke's success at South

March 20.
A review in
London.

Molton was known, no less than 5,000 of the new
militia were mustered in London in the presence of
Richard and Henry Cromwell.   The Protector himself kept away, probably to emphasise the local and popular
nature of the display.[1]   For the present no more was needed.
The insurrection had been crushed, and on March 24 the

March 24
The militia
not to be
called out.

Protector announced to the militia commissioners,
appointed ten days before, that the danger was at an
end.   Thanking them for their zeal, he expressed
his resolution to avoid unnecessary expense, in the hope that
he would be thereby enabled to lighten the burdens on the
people, and directed that the militiamen should not be called
out unless some fresh danger made it needful to ask for their
services.[2]   The relief to the treasury brought about by the
dismissal of the militia must have been most welcome to the
Government.   A day or two later the financial strain upon
its insufficient resources was brought home to the Protector in
an unexpected way.   The soldiers of his lifeguard, finding that
their pay was left in arrear, broke into his kitchen at Whitehall,

The Pro-
tector's
dinner
seized.

and made their dinner off the dishes prepared for his
own table.   Oliver had too much sense to take
offence, and, coming down to the rioters, he assured
them that they should receive their pay before many days
were over, and directed his servants to furnish them with what
further provisions they needed.[3]

It would need more thoroughgoing measures to provide for
the whole army, and about the middle of April a committee of

April.
A committee
of officers re-
commends
the reduc-
tion of pay,

the leading officers was summoned to give advice on
the situation.   After some three weeks of deliberation they recommended a reduction in the pay of the
soldiers, following in this the example which had

[1] *Merc. Pol.*, E, 830, 23.

[2] Order Book of the Council of State, *Interr.* I, 76 a, pp. 26-34.
On the previous organisation of the militia, see vol. i. p. 267.

[3] Pauluzzi to Morosini, $\frac{\text{Mar. 31}}{\text{April 10}}$, *Venetian Transcripts, R.O.*

been set by Parliament; and though they appear not to have as yet drawn up any direct scheme for diminishing the numbers of the army, they reported that it was desirable to proceed with

and the
formation of
a militia. the organisation of a militia of horse to be kept in reserve, in which each man should receive 8*l.* a year on condition that he attended musters once in three months, and was prepared to be called out when needed for the defence of the country. When this plan had been carried into effect, the further question of reducing the numbers of the standing army would necessarily come up for consideration, as if it was impossible to find pay for 57,000 regular soldiers, it was still more impossible to provide for a militia as well, even if the militiamen were only to receive a small retaining fee in ordinary times.

Before the end of May the scheme for the militia was adopted by the Council, and officers were named to command

May.
A militia to
be raised. the troops about to be raised, whilst an announcement was made that whenever they were needed for service they would receive the same pay as was given to the cavalry of the standing army.[1] It was obviously necessary to connect these local forces with the general military organisation of the country, and on May 28—either by way of experiment

Desborough
to command
it in the
West. or because the Western counties had been the scene of the recent insurrection—Desborough, being already in command of the regular forces in the six Western counties, received a commission to command their

No per-
manent
militia
intended. militia as well.[2] Up to this point there was evidently no intention of creating a permanently embodied militia, and the Council therefore was able to discuss with the officers the question of reducing the army, hoping to bring the military expenditure within the limits laid down by Parliament as soon as this reduction had been carried out. In combining militia with regular troops the Government did but

[1] Downing to Clarke, April 24; —— to Clarke, May 13, *Clarke MSS.* xxvii. Nieupoort to the States General, *Add. MSS.* 17,677 W, fol. 82.

[2] *Thurloe*, iii. 486.

carry out the scheme of the dissolved Parliament. It was, however, one thing for the Protector and the officers to consent to reductions so planned as to leave the control over the militia in the hands of an elected House ; it was another thing to save themselves from financial ruin whilst keeping the whole of the forces under their own direction.

Had the opposition to the Protectorate been based solely on economical grounds, this programme would surely have been sufficient to ensure the support of the sober, hard-working classes. Unfortunately for Oliver, there were legal as well as religious and political susceptibilities to be taken into account, and he had already discovered that some at least of the judges

The judges and the In- strument. were unwilling to accept the Instrument as a final constitutional settlement which they had no more busi- ness to question than the Caroline judges had any business to question the basis of the monarchy. The first note of judicial resistance was sounded by two of the judges, Thorpe and Newdigate, who, with other commissioners, were sent to York to preside over the trials of the insurgents captured in the

Apr. 10. Legal difficulties. North. On April 10 the two judges, together with a fellow-commissioner, Serjeant Hutton, wrote to the Solicitor-General, bringing forward certain minor legal difficulties which stood in their way. Strickland, who, being himself a Yorkshire man, had influence in the North, was despatched to smooth these difficulties away, but he could only report that the root of the mischief lay deeper than had been imagined at Whitehall, and that the validity of the ordinance of treason was called in question.[1] As that ordinance had been

Apr. 17. The Instru- ment ques- tioned. issued, in full accordance with the provisions of the Instrument, before the meeting of Parliament, to throw doubts on its validity was tantamount to ques- tioning the Instrument itself. If Oliver had remained passive when the objection was raised he must have been content to see the whole edifice of his Government topple over. As it

[1] Thorpe, Newdigate, and Hutton to Ellis, April 10 ; Strickland to Thurloe, April 17, *Thurloe*, iii. 359, 385.

was, Thorpe and Newdigate were summoned before the Council
and dismissed from their posts.[1] Those who profited
most by the intervention of the Protector were the
Royalist prisoners in gaol. When, in course of time,
other judges arrived at York on circuit, they contented themselves with imposing fines for riot or
misdemeanour, and released those who were not
convicted on bail.[2]

May 3. Thorpe and Newdigate dismissed.

The prisoners released on bail.

The same question — that of the validity of the Instrument
— was at issue in a still more important case before the Upper
Bench at Westminster. In the preceding November
a city merchant named Cony had not only refused to
pay duty on a quantity of silk he had imported, but
had violently expelled from his house the deputies
of the Commissioners of Customs, in order to prevent them
from making seizure of his goods. Being summoned before a
committee of the Council for the preservation of the Customs,
which had been appointed for the protection of the Commissioners, he found his legal objections disregarded, and was
saddled with a fine of 500*l.* Refusing to pay, he
was committed to custody. On this he applied for
a writ of *habeas corpus* to the Upper Bench, where
his counsel prudently contented themselves with
urging that there were technical informalities in the
procedure against him. The mistake having been
acknowledged, he was imprisoned a second time upon
a fresh warrant, in which his offence was plainly
stated as arising out of a breach of an ordinance of December
29, 1653, whilst the powers of the Committee which had fined
him were based on another ordinance of September 2,
1654. A further effort of counsel to restrict the
question to technicalities having failed, the case came
up on May 28 to be tried on its merits.[3]

1654. Nov. 4. Cony refuses to pay Custom,

Nov. 16. and is fined

Dec. 12. and im-prisoned.

1655. Cony's case before the Upper Bench

May 28. is argued on its merits.

---

[1] *Merc. Pol.*, E, 838, 4.

[2] Nicholas to Jane, Sept. $\frac{7}{17}$, *S.P. Dom*, c. 99.

[3] A full account of these proceedings is given up to this point in
Selwood's *Narrative of the Proceedings . . . in the Case of Mr. Cony,*

Thus driven into a corner, the three counsel, Twysden, Maynard, and Windham, boldly attacked the two ordinances Arguments of counsel. as having no binding force whatever—Twysden particularly asserting that the fine imposed by the Committee of Council was condemned as illegal by the Star Chamber Act of 1651,[1] which had deprived the Privy Council of all jurisdiction over the property of the subject.[2] Maynard and Windham spoke to much the same effect.[3]

To question the validity of the Protector's power of taxation was, from a practical point of view, serious enough. It was The Instrument attacked. even more serious that the ordinances which the lawyers declared to be of no authority could not be assailed without assailing the Instrument on which they were based.[4] Accordingly, the three were summoned

E, 844, 4. The writer was evidently afraid of reporting the proceedings on May 28.

[1] 16 Car. I. cap. 10.

[2] "He also insisted much upon the Act for taking away the Star Chamber, whereof part was read, and from thence it was argued that the subjects were not to be imprisoned or their goods attached, but in a legal way, and on trial by jury, &c., and paralleled, as I conceive, the orders of the late Council"—*i.e.* the King's Privy Council—"with that ordinance whereby the Committee for preservation of Customs sat." Zanchy's statement, *S.P. Dom.* xcvii. 48.

[3] Nieuport to the States General, May $\frac{18}{28}$, *Add. MSS.* 17,677 W, fol. 95.

[4] If Article XXX. had stood alone, it might be possible to argue that it did not cover the case. It gave power to the Protector and Council to levy money for extraordinary forces till the meeting of Parliament, and empowered them 'to make laws and ordinances for the peace and welfare of these nations, . . . which shall be binding and in force until order shall be taken in Parliament concerning the same.' As no such order had been taken, the ordinances made prior to Sept. 3, 1654, were still binding; but it was perhaps possible to argue that this did not apply to ordinances enforcing taxation. Reference must be made to Art. XXVII., which settles a constant revenue to support 30,000 soldiers and 'a convenient number of ships for guarding the seas,' and other purposes, 'which revenue shall be raised by the Customs, and such other ways and means as shall be agreed upon by the Lord Protector and Council, and shall not be taken away or diminished, nor the way agreed upon for

before the Council, and on their refusal to retract their argument

Imprison-
ment of the
lawyers. were committed to prison, only obtaining freedom upon acknowledgment of their offence.[1] To the Protector the most dangerous feature in the situation

June 1.
Their
release. was that the Chief Justice shared in the scruples of the lawyers.[2] Rolle was therefore summoned before

May 18.
Chief Justice
Rolle before
the Council. the Council on the very day on which he allowed the offensive speeches of Cony's counsel to pass without interruption, and it was probably in consequence of an arrangement then made that he adjourned the case till

June 7.
He resigns
his office. the following term. Before its commencement he resigned his office, and was succeeded by the time-

Cony
submits. serving Glyn. Before Glyn took his seat Cony, aware that his case was now hopeless, submitted to necessity, and obtained his liberation on payment of his fine.[3]

July.
Wentworth
has the
collectors of
the assess-
ment
arrested, Later in the year Sir Peter Wentworth had the collectors of the assessment in Warwickshire arrested and prosecuted. His case differed from that of Cony in that he declared the exaction to be contrary not only to the law, but to the Instrument as well. Being summoned before the Council, Oliver asked him whether he

raising the same altered, but by the consent of the Lord Protector and the Parliament.' The Customs, therefore, were granted to the Protector by the Instrument itself.

[1] See *supra*, p. 16. Nieupoort to the States General, May $\frac{18}{28}$, June $\frac{8}{18}$, *Add. MSS.* 17,677 W, foll. 95, 110*b*. Compare *Perfect Proceedings*, E, 842, 6.

[2] At that time, at least, lawyers were occasionally governed by words. Rolle, who had scruples about the Instrument, had, together with the other judges of the Upper Bench, acknowledged the right of the Nominated Parliament to commit prisoners simply because that anomalous body chose to call itself a Parliament. See *supra*, p. 16.

[3] *Ludlow* (ed. Firth), i. 413. That Cony paid his fine is shown by Nieupoort's despatch of June $\frac{8}{18}$ (*Add. MSS.* 17,677 W, fol. 110*b*). His submission, therefore, took place on or before the 8th. A report of part of the case in one of its earlier stages adds : " Mes apres le matter fuit extrajudicialment determine perenter le Protector et luy, issint que le legality de dit imprisonment et le validity del ordinance fait per le Protector et son counsaile ne fuit adjudge." *Hargreave MSS.* 48, fol. 45.

would withdraw his action or no. "If you command me," re-

Aug. 20.
but submits. plied Wentworth, "I must submit." The command was given, and Wentworth was allowed to return home without further interference.[1]

That Oliver should have been driven to deprive no less than three judges of their posts because they refused to recognise Significance of the deprivation of the judges. the very basis of his Government was significant of the legal weakness of his position. It was hard to find independent lawyers to accept the doctrine that a few military officers were justified in giving a Constitution to the country. That a large body of opinion was on the side of the lawyers was indicated by the fact that, when once the constitutional question had been reached not a single newspaper stated the reasons for the dismissal of the three judges, and that even the Government did not venture to justify its case in public.

In the long run, however, a Government is never ruined by constitutional defects in the basis on which its authority is The need of law reform. founded, but by its failure to administer remedies to grievances generally felt. If one grievance more than another had been held up as crying for remedy, it had been that of law reform, especially in the Court of Chancery. Hitherto the Ordinance for the Reformation of Chancery had been in abeyance, in consequence of the resistance of the judges.

Apr. 23.
The Chancery judges asked to accept the Reform Ordinance. On April 23 the three Commissioners of the Great Seal—Lisle, Whitelocke and Widdrington—as well as Lenthall, the Master of the Rolls, were summoned before the Council, and ordered in the Protector's name to put the ordinance in execution. Lisle alone Their objections. declared his readiness to comply with the order. Lenthall characteristically led the chorus of objection by complaining that the new ordinance would reduce his income ; but both he and the other recalcitrant commissioners had more than their own interests to plead. Both on this occasion and on several others the arguments showed that, if the reluctance of the Chancery lawyers was to some extent founded on mere

---

[1] *Ludlow*, i. 413, 414 ; *S. P. Dom.* c. 44 ; Council Order Book, *Interr.* I, 76, p. 252.

official conservatism, it was also based on fear of the evil consequences likely to result if hard rules were substituted for a

June 6.
Resigna-
tion of
White-
locke and
Widdring-
ton.
more flexible system. It was not till June 6 that the
crisis came to a head. On that day Whitelocke and
Widdrington resigned office rather than give way.
Lenthall, who had boasted that he would be hanged
at the Rolls Gate before he would execute the

June 15.
Lisle and
Fiennes to
be Com-
missioners.
ordinance, shrank from the sacrifice and promised
compliance.[1] On June 15 Fiennes was given as a
colleague to Lisle, Whitelocke remarking that, of the
two Commissioners now presiding over the Court of Chancery,
one ' never had experience in matters of this nature, and the
other had as little knowledge of them till, by accompanying us,
he gained some.' Oliver, on the other hand, having no wish to
lose the services of men who had acted against their own

Whitelocke
and Wid-
drington
Commis-
sioners of the
Treasury.
interests from conscientious motives, named White-
locke and Widdrington Commissioners of the
Treasury, with Colonels Montague and Sydenham as
their colleagues.[2] From this secure retreat Whitelocke regarded the proceedings of his successors with a critical
eye, and took pleasure in recording that they failed either
wholly or partially in carrying out the ordinance which they
had undertaken to enforce.[3]

In the course of the discussion Whitelocke had thrown out
a suggestion which, if it had been accepted, might have paved

A suggestion
from White-
locke.
the way to better results. Might not the Commissioners ' have leave to offer regulations to my Lord
which shall be as effectual as those proposed in the
ordinance ? '[4] The Protector's reply is not recorded, but

---

[1] Arguments of the Commissioners, April 23, *Carte MSS.* lxxiv. 50 ;
Whitelocke, 621–27. See the remarks of Mr. Inderwick in *The Interregnum*, 224–29.

[2] *Whitelocke*, 627.

[3] *Ib.* 625. Whitelocke's expressions are somewhat obscure, but it
seems hardly likely that the ordinance should have been left wholly
unexecuted, though it may have proved impracticable in some of its
details.

[4] Arguments of the Commissioners, April 23, *Carte MSS.* xxiv. 50.

experience must have made him distrustful of any mere regulations of the court issued by lawyers so conservative as Whitelocke and Widdrington.

To those who had looked hopefully to the Protectorate as a centre of reforming energy, the discovery that its powers were spent must have been far from agreeable, and it can hardly be wondered at that a movement sprang up—not without consi-

Proposed
revival of the
kingship.

derable support outside Oliver's immediate surroundings—for the revival of the kingship in the person of the Protector, with the object of settling men's minds and assuring the permanence of civilian government.[1] By returning to the old Constitution the difficulties raised in the last Parliament would be laid aside, and, though Oliver's power would undoubtedly be diminished rather than increased, he might possibly think himself compensated by the growing number of adherents on whom he would be able to count. So widely spread was the expectation of an impending change that

June 1.
A crowd at
West-
minster.

on June 1 a large crowd assembled at Westminster, expecting to hear that the Protector would announce his purpose to assume the Crown, or at least that he would claim the right to exercise legislative power.[2] There can be little doubt that the first of these two proposals had been seriously discussed in the Council ; and there is good reason for believing that the preparation of the first great seal of the Protectorate was delayed because it was still uncertain whether the new title to be inserted in it was to be that of king or emperor.[3] It may fairly be assumed that the proposed

The assump-
tion of a new
title
favoured by
civilians.

assumption of the kingship was recommended by the civilian members of the Council ; whilst the officers advocated the title of emperor because, being unknown to the English constitution, its holder might

---

[1] Pauluzzi to Morosini, May $\frac{13}{23}$, $\frac{20}{30}$, *Venetian Transcripts*, *R.O.*

[2] Mabbott to Clarke, June 2, *Clarke Papers*, iii. 41 ; see *Perf. Proceedings*, E, 842, 6.

[3] Coyet to Charles X., June 1, 8, *Stockholm Transcripts*. The story about the great seal is to some extent borne out by the fact that the first seal of the Protectorate was not finished till some time after this date.

assume under it any power he chose, and especially that of issuing
ordinances, which, in accordance with the Instrument,
had lapsed at the meeting of the late Parliament.[1]   It
was understood that Oliver had, tentatively at least,
given his adhesion to the last-named plan, either with
or without a change of title, and that a council of
officers had been summoned to take the proposal
into consideration.[2]   The army had produced the
Instrument.   Why should it not amend a constitution which it had itself brought into existence?

The officers prefer a revival of the power to issue ordinances.

A council of officers summoned.

Difficulties in the way.

When, however, this council came together, further consideration only served to bring out the obstacles in the way—
obstacles which could only be increased by the formulation of
a definite plan for surrounding the Protector—by whatever title
he was thenceforward to be known—with a body composed
of the councillors, a certain number of officers, and twelve

---

[1] " His Highness, by not making it "—*i.e.* the declaration for collecting the assessment—" an ordinance, hath modestly denied to assume
the legislature of the nation, though satisfied by many able judges and
lawyers that he may legally do it." —? to Clarke, Feb. 13, *Clarke
Papers*, iii. 22.   I cannot imagine what the arguments of the judges and
lawyers can have been.

[2] " Di già s'intende che d' intelligenza con li capi et officiali principali
dell' armata habbi à seguire un gran consiglio di guerra in cui l' articolo
principale sarà quello d' invitare il medesimo Protettore à riasumere in se
il potere jurislativo, con il quale potrà riordinare questo punto importante
della confusa giustitia, formare, e riformare quelle leggi che piu li aggra-
dissero et in fine serrar la bocca à molti, e chiuder ad ogn' uno le speranze
de' nuovi Parlamenti in Inghilterra.   Questo ho inteso si progetti dalle
genti d'armi di concerto di quest' Altezza." Pauluzzi to Morosini,
June $\frac{4}{14}$, *Venetian Transcripts, R.O.* The words ' riasumere ' and
' riordinare ' bear out the supposition that no more was intended than the
revival of the lost power of issuing ordinances in the intervals of Parliament.   This is borne out by the language of a Royalist who writes on
June $\frac{7}{17}$: " We expect daily a declaration from the army where the
legislative power must reside in the vacancy of Parliament, which infalli-
bly will be in the Protector and Council " (*Nicholas Papers*, ii. 353).
The suggestion towards the end of Pauluzzi's letter may doubtless be
taken merely as an expression of opinion from one or two violent spirits.

lawyers, whose resolutions were to have the force of law.[1]   A
scheme so offensive to English feeling could never have been
made acceptable to the civilian members of the Council.   At
one time it had been hoped that the change might have been
announced and the disputed points of law settled before the
new term commenced on June 15,[2] but that hope had now to be
abandoned.

From soldiers Oliver turned to the lawyers.   If the army
had declared against the assumption of the kingly title,[3] the
lawyers no less decisively declared against any assumption of
legislative power without the authority of Parliament.[4]   Towards the end of June the idea sprang up of bringing
together in London a consultative body of civilian
officials gathered from every part of the country.[5]

A projected
assembly of
civilians.

---

[1] Coyet to Charles X., July 20, *Stockholm Transcripts.*

[2] "Con l' aviso de' principali capi et officiali dell' armata va il Protettore divisando e disponendo di rissolvere alcuna cosa per riddurre a
qualche buon stato l' ordine della giustitia nella confusione sua valevole a
partorire maggiori sconcerti, et a far pervenire all' orecchio dell' Altezza
sua sempre più vive le doglianze di popoli, et perciò tutto tende ai
concerti di riassumere in se tutto il potere jurislativo, che dall' armi
solamente li può esser conferito, et in occorenza vigorosamente sostenuto,
per l'abbolitione di quelle vecchie leggi, et institutione de nove che più
adequarsi potessero al particolare servizio dell' Altezza sua, onde quest' è
la materia che al presente più importa, parendo che senza vestirsi il
Protettore d' altro titolo, non possa aggiustatamente decretarsi et pur
questo, scuoprendosi molti e molti dell' Armata stessa con buone ragioni
più rennitenti che inclinati.   Resta incombenza del Protettore, il pensare
ai più proprii ispedienti per veder a qualche buon segno ridotto questo
importante articolo prima del maturar del termine giuditiario che sarà
fra pochi giorni."   Pauluzzi to Morosini, June $\frac{12}{22}$, *Venetian Transcripts,*
R.O.

[3] In a letter to Fleetwood on June 22 Oliver wrote that 'the noise of
my being crowned, &c., are . . . malicious figments,' *Carlyle,* Letter
cxcix.   Oliver, it will be observed, says nothing about the legislative
power.

[4] "La pluralità di quali"—*i.e.* of the lawyers—"accordono che
senza l'auttorità d' un Parlamento non possa ciò farsi."   Pauluzzi to Morosini, June $\frac{18}{28}$, *Venetian Transcripts,* *R.O.*

[5] "In questa settimana devono capitare qui in Londra tutti gli giudici,

No such assembly was, however, called into being, and the thought of making any further changes in the Constitution was dropped for some time to come. Dissatisfaction with

July 30.
A petition
for alteration
in the Instru-
ment.

the resourcelessness of the Government, however, appears still to have prevailed amongst some members of the Council, and it was probably their opinion which found expression in a petition drafted, but probably not originated, by a certain John Norbury,[1] and largely signed in the City. Those whose names were appended to it asked that the Protector should resume the legislative power in order to effect certain legal reforms, and especially to remove the injustice of the actual law of debtor and creditor. Taking a leaf from the authors of *The Agreement of the People*, the promoters of this petition proposed to obtain subscriptions in every county in sufficient numbers to give to their plan constitutional authority at least as good as that of the Instrument. After this had been done it was hoped that Oliver, having carried into effect the objects for which this new dictatorship was conferred on him, would consent to summon another Parliament. By this time, however, the Council, as a whole, was in no mood to run the Protectorate into danger by shifting the basis of the Government, and on August 10

Aug. 10.
The petition
suppressed.

strict orders were given for the suppression of Norbury's petition, on the distinct ground that it contained proposals incompatible with the Instrument.[2] This

commessarii e luogotenenti che siano nelle Provincie admessi dal medesimo Protettore." Pauluzzi to Morosini, $\frac{\text{June 24}}{\text{July 4}}$, *Venetian Transcripts, R.O.*

[1] On August 14 Norbury stated that he had only drawn up the petition as a lawyer for his clients. He was a small Chancery official who had complained of his loss of income by the Chancery reforms, and hardly the man to originate a scheme of this kind. See a petition signed by him on March 29, *S. P. Dom.* xcv. 80. The political petition is stated by Thomason as being 'cast about the streets in the night July 30.' Mrs. Everett Green incorrectly calendared it under August 10, the day on which Norbury appeared before the Council.

[2] Norbury's Petition, Aug. 10, *S. P. Dom.* c. 21. For the proceedings against Norbury see Council Order Book, *Interr.* I, 76, pp. 231, 233. "A petition," wrote Mabbott to Clarke on August 11, "is carrying on

step was taken at the instance of the officers, who though
The officers drop the plan of reviving the legislative power. they had originally suggested the project of reviving the legislative power, now dropped it in favour of the opposite plan of adhering literally to the pre-scriptions of the Instrument, as the sheet-anchor of the Protectorate.[1]

Since the officers had been caught by the notion of re-modelling the Instrument the fact had been brought home to
The officers alarmed. them, as well as to the Protector, that troublous times were still to be confronted, and that it would be in the highest degree dangerous for them to embark on fresh consti-
May 18. Five persons transported to Barbados. tutional experiments. It is true that on May 18, when the Royalist movement appeared to have been entirely suppressed, the Government had been so far satis-fied with the peacefulness of the outlook as to content itself with ordering the transportation to Barbados of no more than seven persons. Of these, one — Anthony Jackson — had proclaimed Charles as king of England before his defeat at Worcester. Three others—Somerset Fox, Francis Fox, and Thomas Saunders—had been implicated in the assassination plot of 1654, whilst Colonels Grey and Gardiner, together with Rowland Thomas, had taken a leading part in the recent conspiracy. An eighth, James Hodges, was charged, not with treason, but with 'high misdemeanours.' Two of the persons affected by this sentence—Grey and Jackson—were spared on account of the weakness of their health; and Hodges, too, appears to have been ultimately allowed to remain in England. If so, five only were forced to depart to what, at the best, was a cruel, though but a temporary, captivity.[2]   One of those

in several places here for his Highness to assume the title of emperor or king : the subscriptions will be many ; there is not any of them yet presented to his Highness," *Clarke Papers*, iii. 48. As no such title was suggested in Norbury's petition, which was, moreover, suppressed the day before these words were written, it looks as if other petitions were in circulation.

[1] Pauluzzi to Morosini, Sept. $\frac{7}{17}$, *Venetian Transcripts, R.O.*
[2] Warrant, May 18 ; Barkstead to Thurloe, March 25, 1660, *Thurloe,*

transported—Somerset Fox—had already been condemned to
death, and it was probably thought sufficient excuse for the
transportation of the others that the death sentence would
almost certainly have been passed upon them if they had been
sent before a jury.[1]

iii. 453 ; vii. 639.   In the last-named letter Hodges' name is not mentioned among those put on board ship.

[1] Prisoners and others sent to Barbados or elsewhere in America are
frequently spoken of as having been sent into slavery. If the word is
used rhetorically it may be true enough.   The petition of Marcellus
Rivers and Oxenbridge Foyle, after their return to England in 1659—
they having been among the prisoners charged with participation in
Penruddock's rising, and transported later in the year to Barbados—
shows their condition, even if allowance is made for exaggeration, to
have been deplorable enough.   " Being sadly arrived at Barbados," they
say, " the master of the ship sold your miserable petitioners and the
others, the generality of them to most inhuman and barbarous persons,
for 1,550 pounds weight of sugar apiece . . . as the goods and chattels
of Martin Noel and Major Thomas Alderne of London and Captain
Henry Hatsell of Plymouth, neither sparing the aged of threescore years
old, nor divines, nor officers, nor gentlemen, nor any age or condition of
men."   (*England's Slavery*, p. 4, E, 1,833, 3 ; see also p. 338, *post.*)
It is, however, certainly not the case that these men were condemned to
a lifelong servitude, though they were not allowed, after their time of
service had expired, to leave the island.   " The custom of all merchants
trading thither," writes F. Barrington, who visited Barbados in 1655, "is
to bring as many men and women as they can.   No sooner doth a ship
come to an anchor but presently the islanders go aboard her inquiring
what servants they can buy.   If they are above seventeen years of age,
they serve but four years, according to the law of the island ; but if under
seventeen, then left to the discretion of the merchant as he can agree
with the planter.   These servants planteth, weedeth, and manureth their
ground, all by hand. . . . The freemen . . . are such who served in
the country for their freedom, or paid their passage when transported from
England " (F. Barrington to Sir John Barrington, July 14, 1655, *Hist.
MSS. Com. Rep.* vii. App. 571).   Ligon, writing a little later, puts the
service at five years.   " The island is divided into three sorts of men, viz.
masters, servants, and slaves.   The slaves and their posterity, being
subject to their masters for ever, are kept and preserved with greater care
than the servants who are there but for five years, according to the law of
the island. . . . For the time the servants have the worse lives, for they

In any case, we have to do with an evasion of the law.
Three days later seven prisoners in the Tower—five Scots who

May 21.
Eight
prisoners
sent from
the Tower
into confine-
ment in the
country.

had been confined there since the battle of Worcester, Crawford, Lauderdale, Kellie, Sinclair, and David Leslie—were, together with three Englishmen —Grandison, and the two Ashburnhams—removed to various prisons in the country.[1] On the same day

Arrest of
Lord
Byron.

Lord Byron, who had been implicated in the late conspiracy, was arrested with a companion near

are put to very hard labour, ill lodging, and their diet very slight. . . . Truly I have seen such cruelty done to servants as I could not think one Christian could have done to another ; but as discreeter and better-natured have come to rule there, the servants' lives have been much bettered, for now most of the servants lie in hammocks and in warm rooms ; and, when they come in wet, have shift of shirts and drawers, which is all the clothes they wear, and are fed with bone meat twice or thrice a week " (Ligon's *Hist. of Barbados* (ed. 1657), pp. 43, 44). The early laws on the subject are not printed by Rawlins in the *Laws of Barbados*, probably because they were superseded by the law of 1661, by which seven years' service is appointed under the age of seventeen, and five years above that age (*ib.* p. 30). In answering Rivers' petition in 1659, Noel, the merchant who sent over Colonel Gardiner and the others, declared that 'indeed the work is hard, but none are sent without their consent.' It is, indeed, not unlikely that the form of asking consent was gone through to save appearance. Noel goes on to say : "They serve most commonly five years, and then have the yearly salary of the island. They have four times of refreshing, and work but from six to six ; so it is not so hard as is represented to you ; not so much as the common husbandman here " (Burton's *Diary*, iv. 258). This is, of course, an interested view of the situation. For an exhaustive study of the position of servants—as opposed to slaves—in Virginia, see Bruce's *Economic Hist. of Virginia*, i. 572-634, ii. 1-57.

[1] Nieupoort to the States General, $\frac{\text{May 25}}{\text{June 4}}$, *Add. MSS.* 17,677 W, fol. 100 ; *A Perfect Account*, E, 842, 4. There were rumours that they were to have been sent to the plantations. If this was contemplated, their imprisonment in England must be regarded as an act of clemency. Pauluzzi's statement on June $\frac{8}{18}$ (*Venetian Transcripts, R.O.*), that Grandison committed suicide on the way, is devoid of truth, as on August 30 he was in the Isle of Wight, and was soon afterwards liberated with the Earl of Kellie. Petition and order, August 30, *S.P. Dom.* c. 66 ; Council Order Book, *Interr.* I, 76, p. 259.

Covent Garden.[1] This arrest was probably made in consequence of a fresh search among the houses in London likely to harbour Royalists, a precaution adopted in consequence of information received from a young man named

March–May.
Manning's
reports.

Henry Manning, who had arrived at Charles's Court in the early part of the year. Finding himself, like many of his companions in misfortune, reduced to the direst straits, Manning resolved to ward off starvation by supplying intelligence to Thurloe. Since March 26[2] he had been writing diligently to the Secretary. Though not admitted to the secret counsels of the Court, he was able to pick up a considerable amount of information, which he committed to paper for Thurloe's benefit.[3] He had much to say on the movements of Royalists engaged against the Government, and the fictitious names by which some of them passed in England. In a letter written on May 11, which must have been in Thurloe's hands before orders were given for the search which resulted in Byron's capture, Manning, after imparting a considerable amount of information about the persons embarked in the late conspiracy, with details of persons and places which do not appear to have hitherto reached

He suggests
the existence
of a murder
plot.

the Government's ear, added that many Royalists had proposed to assassinate the Protector, though he acknowledged that Charles was 'not forward to have it done.'[4]

Whether Manning had or had not yielded to the temptation to exaggerate his knowledge of projects on which he can have

[1] Nieupoort to the States General, $\frac{May\ 25}{June\ 4}$, *Add. MSS.* 17,677 W, fol. 100 ; *Perf. Proceedings*, E, 840, 5.

[2] His first letter was written on March $\frac{3}{13}$, *Thurloe*, iii. 190 ; but for want of a cipher he sent no intelligence till the date named. Even then no cipher had been received, but he seems to have disregarded the difficulty in the hope of winning Thurloe's confidence ; see *Nicholas Papers*, iii. 149.

[3] Manning to Thurloe, $\frac{March\ 26}{April\ 5}$, April $\frac{3}{13}$, *Thurloe*, iii. 338 ; May [?], *S.P. Dom.* xcvii. 109.

[4] Manning to Thurloe, May $\frac{11}{21}$, *Thurloe*, iii. 428.

had no more than second-hand information,[1] his statements about persons were precise and definite. So far as appears

His informa-tion on persons in-volved in the last plot.

it was this part of the charge which took most hold of the Protector's mind. " We are able," he said in the following year, " to make it appear that persons who carried themselves the most demurely and fairly of any men in England were engaged in this business." [2] Unable to enter into the feelings which nestled in their aggrieved hearts, he ascribed their conduct to pure malignity, and came to the conclusion that, whether they were actively engaged in a new conspiracy or not, it was essential to deprive them of the means

June.
Royalists
arrested.

of doing harm. In the first week in June several prominent Royalists were arrested. On June 9 Lord Willoughby of Parham, Lord Newport [3] and his brother, with Geoffrey Palmer and Henry Seymour, were sent to the Tower. The Earl of Lindsey, Lord Lovelace, Lord Falkland, and many others had already been seized in Oxford-shire,[4] and the action of the agents of the Government in other counties was no less prompt. Before long Lambeth and St. James's were crowded with imprisoned Royalists, and when room failed in London, country prisons had to serve the turn. It is true that the confinement was made as easy as was com-patible with privation of liberty. "We are not kept close," wrote one of those under arrest at St. James's, "nor are our friends kept from us." [5] All through June the arrests were numerous,[6]

---

[1] It will, however, be seen that later in the year there was indubitably a plot to assassinate Oliver. It is clear from references in Manning's letters that others were written which have not reached us, so that we cannot tell how much more he disclosed.

[2] *Carlyle*, Speech V. Oliver directly attributed his information to Manning, who was then no longer alive.

[3] Lord Newport of High Ercall, not the Earl of Newport.

[4] Council Order Book, *Interr.* I, 76, p. 130 ; Croke and Smith to the Protector, June 6, *Thurloe*, iii. 521 ; Nieupoort to the States General, June $\frac{15}{25}$, *Add. MSS.* 17,677 W, fol. 113 ; *The Perf. Diurnal*, E, 843, 4.

[5] Sir R. Verney to E. Verney, June 22, *Verney MSS.*

[6] Nieupoort to the States General, $\frac{\text{June 29}}{\text{July 9}}$, *Add. MSS.* 17,677 W, fol. 121 ; *The Faithful Scout*, E, 845, 3 ; *Perfect Proceedings*, E, 845, 12.

Lords Coventry, Maynard, and Petre being amongst the victims. Before the end of the month no less than thirty-five Royalists were confined at Lynn alone.

Against these prisoners no definite charge was brought. They were, as the Protector afterwards allowed, arrested

The prisoners arrested on suspicion. merely on suspicion. If a new plot was in the air— and there can be little doubt that it was—it would be well to anticipate its outbreak by rendering innocuous all who were likely to take part in it. Before long Oliver's anxiety took a new turn. By the end of June Man-

Information that another rising is proposed, and of a murder plot. ning's letters began to point more clearly to a reso- lution of some, at least, of the Royalists abroad to resort to the murder of the Protector as a preliminary to another insurrection,[1] and it must have been to guard against such a contingency that orders were given on

July 6. Royalists banished from London. July 6 for the banishment from London and West- minster of all who had adhered to the Royal cause. Their enforced sojourn in the country was to last till October 20, when the commencement of Michaelmas Term would require the presence of many of them in the courts of law. It is hardly necessary to prove by evidence that the English Royalists [2] were quite ready to engage in a

[1] Manning to Thurloe, $\frac{\text{June } 23, 26}{\text{July } 3, 6}$, S.P. Dom. xcviii. 45, 52.

[2] A letter from Major Armorer does not go so far as to be quoted in evidence, but it shows what the temper of the Royalists was and, it may fairly be added, must have been. "Saturday last," he writes—Saturday was June 9, the day of the arrest of a large number of Royalists—"was a sore blow to your Majesty's good friends, who were both willing and able to serve you. . . . That sad misfortune has hindered me to make some propositions to your Majesty from some that I heard upon the way, as I left London, were amongst the number of those taken. . . . God has yet preserved some, that truly I hope cannot come under suspicion, who are both willing, and I hope will be able, to serve you. I am by their order to inform them, as soon as your Majesty thinks fit, which way your Majesty will be served by them. If it be the way my Lord Rochester proposed, they have promised to prepare their friends for it. If your Majesty resolve any other, they have appointed me a way how to let them know it when it shall be seasonable." Armorer to Charles, June 24, i.e. $\frac{14}{24}$, Thurloe, i. 695.

fresh insurrection if circumstances offered a chance of success, and it is now known[1] beyond dispute, not only that the murder-plot was no figment of Manning's brain, but that it had received the countenance of no less a personage than the Duke of York.

[1] "There is a proposition has been made to me which is too long to put into a letter, so that I will, as short as I can, let you know the heads of them. There are four Roman Catholics that have bound themselves in a solemn oath to kill Cromwell, and then to raise all the Catholics in the City and the army, which they pretend to be a number so considerable as may give a rise for your recovery, they being all warned to be ready for something that is to be done, without knowing what it is. They demand 10,000 livres in hand and, when the business is ended, some recompense for themselves, according to their several qualities, and the same liberty for Catholics in England as the Protestants have in France. I thought not fit to reject this proposition, but to acquaint you with it, because the first part of the design seems to me to be better laid and resolved on than any I have known of that kind ; and for the defects of the second, it may be supplied by some designs you may have to join to it. If you approve of it, one of the four, entrusted by the rest, will repair to you, his charges being borne, and give you a full account of the whole matter." The Duke of York to Charles, May $\frac{4}{14}$, *Thurloe*, i. 666. Though both this and the letter quoted in the last note are printed in the Thurloe collection, neither of them was ever in the hands of the Protector or his ministers, having been communicated to the editor by the Archbishop of Canterbury from the manuscript originals. These are now in the Lambeth Library (Vol. 645, No. 33), forming part of the Tenison collection.

CHAPTER XL

THE MAJOR-GENERALS

THE political situation had been much changed since the dissolution in January, when the Protector had set out with
the intention of governing in accordance with the
Instrument, so far as it was possible for him so to do.
Insurrectionary movements had followed closely on one another,
varied by an occasional plot for the assassination of the Chief
of the State. Fruitless as had been the discussions on a change
of the Constitution, it is not unlikely that they resulted in a
tacit understanding that, though there were no means of
changing the law, there should hereafter be less scruple in
breaking it wherever the safety of the existing Government was
concerned. In later times Parliament would have suspended
the action of the Habeas Corpus Act, and have thereby
empowered the Executive to take exceptional measures for the
safety of the State. Such a course being out of the question,
the Protector had no choice but to succumb to the
wave of conspiracy which beset him, or to resort to
measures which could not be justified by law. We
may blame him, if we will, for not having thrown down his
arms before a Parliament aiming, consciously or unconsciously,
at sovereignty, but our blame may well be moderated when we
remember that he was striving not for the gratification of
personal ambition, but for the maintenance of a Constitution
which, at least in its main provisions, he firmly believed to have
been framed in the best interests of the nation. It is usual to
compare the position thus assumed by the Protector with that

1655.
The political
situation.

The Pro-
tector and
the law.

which had been maintained by Charles I. Both were contending against the same antagonist—a Parliament resolved to subject all other institutions in the State
to its sole will and pleasure. Both set aside without
compunction the duty of subordinating their actions to the
nation's will, on the ground that the nation was ill-informed,
petulant, and hostile to its own surest friends. The difference
between the two men lay, in the first place, in the support
given by Charles to a system of external obedience and
conformity, whereas Oliver strove for a system of the utmost
practicable liberty in thought and belief ; and, in the second
place, in Charles's habit of clinging to formal legality, whilst
Oliver, having an army at his back, preferred to break openly
through the meshes of the law when they entangled his feet.
Charles, when necessity arose or appeared to arise, fumbled
over the knot of his destiny in his effort to unloose it ; Oliver
hacked at it with his sword. It may at least be set down to
the Protector's credit that, when he sinned, he sinned boldly.

Comparison between Oliver and Charles I.

Oliver's defence of his conduct in arresting Royalists and
keeping them in custody without legal warrant was plainspoken
enough. " If this be the case," he said, after setting
forth from his own point of view the history of the
late disturbances, " between us and the late King's
party—to wit that they have notoriously manifested it to the
consciences of all men that they do not only retain their old
principles, and still adhere to their former interest in direct
opposition to the Government established, but have been all
along hatching new disturbances and endeavouring, as well by
secret and bloody assassinations as by open force, to introduce
the one and overthrow and subvert the other, it will not be
thought strange upon any account whatsoever that we did lately
secure so many of the men of that interest, although they were
not visibly in arms upon the late insurrection." [1]

The Protector on his defence.

Yet, if the Protector and the army on which he based his
power were to maintain this defiant attitude, the financial

[1] *A Declaration of His Highness*, p. 13 : E, 857, 3.

necessities of the Government rendered it necessary not merely
to reduce the soldiers' pay, as had been proposed in April,[1]
but also to diminish the numbers under arms. With this
object in view a new establishment for the army in Great
Britain, bringing down the number of men in each regiment of
foot to 800, and in each regiment of horse to 300, was adopted

July 26.
The new
establish-
ment for the
army
    by the Council on July 26, and confirmed by the
Protector on the 31st.[2] England was to be guarded
by seven regiments of horse and five of foot;
Scotland by seven of horse and thirteen of foot.

July 31.
confirmed
by the
Protector.
    Including the soldiers in garrison, together with the
officers and non-combatants, such as chaplains and

The
numbers of
the army
reduced,
    surgeons, the whole force in the two countries
scarcely exceeded 21,000 men;[3] though unluckily,
it was impossible to effect a reduction on the same
scale in Ireland which would bring down the numbers of
the whole army to the 30,000 contemplated by the Instrument.
Secure of the support of the superior officers, the Council

and its pay.
    did not hesitate to cut down the pay of the cavalry
from 2s. 6d. to 2s. 3d. a day, and of the infantry
from 10d. to 9d., soldiers in garrison being even reduced
to 8d. The reduction was somewhat less than that contemplated by Birch,[4] and was justified for the same reasons as had
weighed with the Committee of which he was the chairman.
When this measure had been carried out it would be possible
to satisfy the claims of the army in Great Britain out of the
assessment, leaving 290,000l. a year to meet the wants of
the army in Ireland.[5]

[1] See *supra*, p. 296.

[2] Council Order Book, *Interr.* I, 76a, p. 107. In one case an
infantry regiment was allowed to contain 700 only.

[3] 14,780 foot, 4,245 horse, 1,944 officers. There were also a certain
number of soldiers of the train.

[4] According to Birch's report, the cavalry pay was to have been 2s.,
the infantry pay 8d. See *supra*, p. 236.

[5] The monthly pay of the army in England and Scotland was to be
50,486l. 11s. 4d., which, taking the year at thirteen lunar months, gives
an annual payment of 656,325l. 7s. 4d. Putting this at 670,000l. to

Such, at least, was the result on paper. Contingent expenses were, however, certain to arise unexpectedly, and amongst these the most burdensome was caused by the absolute necessity of providing some means of averting those Royalist plots and insurrections which had recently kept the Government continually on the alert. Always ready to carry out the ideas of the dissolved Parliament, so far as they could be made consistent with the strengthening of his own position, Oliver had already proposed to supplement the regular army by a local militia. For the attainment of this object he had already before the end of June actually embodied the new militia, instead of retaining the services of the men by a small payment, and leaving them to carry on their ordinary avocations at their homes in accordance with the scheme adopted by the Council in the preceding month.[1] This militia, consisting of volunteers who offered themselves from amongst the known supporters of the Government, was now raised in each county, numbering for the whole of England 6,220 horse and 200 foot. The annual expense of the new force was estimated at 80,067*l*.[2] Each of the troops into which this militia was divided was, as usual, commanded by its captain, but these troops were not formed into regiments. The purpose of the Government was to extend to the whole kingdom the system which prevailed in the West, where Desborough, with the style of major-general, would have commanded the militia of six counties whenever they were called out.

Fresh demands on the revenue.

A local militia to be raised.

Its numbers and organisation.

Accordingly, on August 9 ten officers were named to take the command, with the rank of Major-General, of the militia in the ten districts into which it was at this time proposed to divide England.[3] On August 22

Aug. 9. The militia placed under the command of ten Major-Generals.

allow for contingent expenditure, there remains 290,000*l*. for Ireland out of the 960,000*l*. which was the assessment of the three nations.

[1] See *supra*, p. 297.

[2] Council Order Book, *Interr.* I, 76, p. 861. The 200 foot were stationed at Norwich.

[3] *Ib.* p. 226. As the districts were subsequently changed, and their

Instructions were drawn up, the preamble to which plainly states the intentions of the Protector. "Whereas," it began, "we have—by the advice of our Council, for the preservation of the peace of the Commonwealth, and the preventing, obviating, and breaking the designs of the enemies thereof, who are still restless and unwearied in their endeavours to beget new troubles, and to put the nation into blood and confusion—thought fit to commissionate several persons of honour and approved integrity to raise, enlist, and command . . . troops of horse." The officer named in the Instructions was to take the command over these troops in the group of counties assigned to him, with the title of Major-General. With the authority thus conferred on him he was, in the first place, to attend to the discipline of the force under his orders, 'to suppress all tumults, insurrections, rebellion, and other unlawful assemblies,' and for that purpose to march at their head, not merely within his own district, but wherever he saw fit in England or Wales. Secondly, he was to see that the arms of all Papists and Royalists were taken from them. Thirdly, highways were to ·be made safe, and robbers and highwaymen secured and prosecuted according to law. Fourthly, a strict eye was to be kept on the carriage of the disaffected, and no 'horse-races, cock-fightings, bear-baitings, or any unlawful assemblies' permitted, on the ground that rebellion was usually hatched at such meetings. Fifthly, idlers and persons having no visible means of subsistence answerable to their expenditure were to be sent out of the Commonwealth, whilst the execution of the laws for the benefit of the poor was urged. Sixthly, the Major-Generals were, by their 'constant carriage and conversation, to encourage and promote godliness and virtue, and discourage and discountenance all profaneness and ungodliness,' and to 'endeavour—with the other justices of the peace and other ministers and officers who are entrusted with the care of those things—that the laws against drunkenness, profaneness, blaspheming, and taking of the name of God in

number increased to eleven, it is unnecessary to enter into particulars at present.

vain by swearing, cursing, and suchlike wickedness and abominations, be put in more effectual execution than they have been hitherto ; and such justices and others as you shall find remiss, and so unfit for their trusts, you shall certify us and the Council thereof, that we may make provision therein according to our duty and the trust reposed in us.'

In the draft presented to the Council a seventh and last clause informed the Major-Generals that, with the assistance of several other persons, they were to levy a tax on malignants for the support of the militia ; but this clause was withdrawn in favour of a colourless one requiring the Major-Generals to give notice to all persons concerned to meet them in their several counties.   It is not in the least likely that the change denoted any intention of abandoning the proposed tax ; but it may well have been thought undesirable to mention it till the subject had been more thoroughly considered, after which specific directions could be more fitly given.[1]

From these Instructions it may be gathered that, at least at this time, there was no intention of superseding the ordinary magistrates by the Major-Generals.   It was with the help of the justices of the peace that the law was to be put in force, and except that the expulsion of idle persons from the country was legally justifiable only on the double assumption that such persons might be dealt with as vagrants, and that the Government was permitted to change the penalties imposed by law on vagrancy into the punishment of banishment, there was nothing to give rise to the suggestion that the Major-Generals were intended to override the law.[2] Practically, their appointment would work an immense change.

Character of these Instructions.

----

[1] S. P. Dom. c. 42. Mrs. Everett Green, in calendaring this document, states, very properly, that the seventh clause was omitted and another added in its stead.   She has not, however, noticed that the new clause is to be found in No. 43, where it is expressly dated August 22. Under the date of August 24 she gives it as a preamble, which it certainly was not.

[2] This is on the supposition that the Protector's ordinances issued under the Instrument of Government had the force of law.

Remiss or timid justices of the peace would be encouraged or terrified into the exercise of the functions imposed on them. A police force would be constantly at hand, not merely to crush Royalist insurrections and to curb highwaymen and robbers, but also to support them in putting in force those unpopular statutes and ordinances which were directed against the spread of irreligion and vice. Those amongst the justices who continued to move in these matters with leaden steps would know that there was now a vigilant eye upon them, and that any neglect on their part would, without delay, be reported to headquarters.

Two days later a further Instruction was added directing
Aug. 24.
The ejection ordinance to be carried out.
the Major-Generals to report on the execution of the ordinance for the ejection of scandalous and inefficient ministers, which had hitherto been slackly carried out, and had probably not been carried out at all in many districts.[1] Evidently there was an increasing tendency to make use of the Major-Generals to quicken the zeal of the local authorities in miscellaneous directions.[2]

It was not till September 21 that, after the Coun-
Sept. 21.
A commission for the Major-Generals.

Orders for securing the peace of the Commonwealth.
cil, in the Protector's presence, had agreed to a form of commission for the Major-Generals,[3] a body of orders 'for securing the peace of the Commonwealth' was adopted to fill up in detail the requirements of the article which had been dropped on August 22. These orders were to be carried out, under the eye of the Major-Generals, by certain commissioners,[4] ultimately known as commissioners for

[1] This appears from the language of the reports of the Major-Generals. The ordinance had not, however, remained entirely a dead letter. The witnesses in the case of Pocock, the Orientalist, for instance, were examined by the ejectors at Abingdon on Feb. 12, 1655. Twells, *Life of Pocock*, prefixed to his *Theological Works*, i. 37. Other cases might be cited as well.

[2] *S. P. Dom.* c. 43.   [3] *Ib.* c. 133.

[4] On August 22 these had been styled vaguely as persons to assist the Major-Generals, but they were called Commissioners in an Order in Council

securing the peace of the country, who were named by the
County commissioners appointed. Government in each county. They were directed partly at weakening the Royalist party, and partly at securing from them a revenue which, following the precedent of the Elizabethan recusancy laws, might wring out of those who needed watching the financial resources required for the payment of the watchers. Royalists of property were dealt with in a drastic fashion. They were divided into three classes. The first, consisting of those who having, since the establishment of the Protectorate, taken part in any rebellion or in any plot against the person Exactions from the Royalists. of the Protector, were to be imprisoned or banished, their estates being sequestered for the payment of the newly raised militia, a third part being reserved for the wives and families of the offenders. The second, including those who, not having taken part in any rebellion or assassination plot, nevertheless appeared 'by their words or actions to adhere to the interests of the late King, or of Charles Stuart his son,' and to be dangerous enemies to the peace of the Commonwealth, were to be imprisoned or sent beyond the seas, though allowed to retain their estates. The third, comprising those who, not being active Royalists, had their estates sequestered for delinquency, or had in former times fought against Parliament, were to pay 10 per cent. on their rental from land if it amounted to 100*l.* and upwards, and 10*l.* on every 1,500*l.* of personal property in cases where there was

of the same date (Council Order Book, *Interr.* I, 76, p. 246). They are to be distinguished from the Militia Commissioners appointed in the spring, who are styled 'the former commissioners' in a letter from Lawrence to Desborough of Feb. 13, 1656 (*S. P. Dom.* cxxiv. 41). Though there is no evidence of the date on which these latter were suppressed, it is probable that their powers were recalled on Oct. 11, when the Major-Generals formally received their Commissions. It is impossible to write on the subject of the Major-Generals without expressing gratitude to Mr. D. W. Rannie, whose account of the matter in the *Hist Review* (July 1895), x. 471, did much to advance our knowledge. His occasional slips are for the most part owing to his confidence in defective calendars, which he did not test by the original documents.

no real estate worth 100*l.* a year, with the proviso that their annual payments under this head should never exceed 100*l.* As for persons who had no estate, they were only touched if they lived loosely and were unable to give an account of themselves ; in which case they were to ' be apprehended and transported into foreign parts, where they may earn their living by their labour,' a phrase which, differing as it does from the sentence of mere banishment pronounced on wealthier Royalists, is probably a euphemism for service in the colonies. No Royalist was, on pain of imprisonment, to keep arms in his house, and those who were banished—doubtless those under the second head alone are intended—were not to return without license, on pain of the sequestration of their estates.[1]

Of a different order are the rules laid down with the object of striking at the spiritual and intellectual root of Royalism,

The Royalist clergy silenced.

and which appear as a somewhat pale shadow of the statutes directed by Elizabethan Parliaments against Roman Catholic priests. After November 1 no Royalist was to be suffered to keep in his house any of the ejected clergy as a chaplain or a tutor for his children, under pain of having his fine doubled ; and no such clergyman was to keep a school, preach, or administer the sacraments, celebrate marriage, or use the Book of Common Prayer, on pain of three months' imprisonment for the first offence, of six months' for the second, and of banishment for the third.[2]

Every one of these orders frankly relinquished the domain of law. Political necessity alone could be pleaded in their

The orders do not pretend to legality.

favour. Their authors were, indeed, so anxious to cling to the skirts of legality wherever possible that, on the same day ' plays and interludes ' having been added to the list of malpractices against which the Major-

[1] Mrs. Everett Green gives it ' on pain of banishment,' which is not only improbable, but is not in the original. If the threat of sequestration had been meant to refer to the first class, it could only mean that the wife and family of the returning exile would lose the third assigned to them.

[2] *S. P. Dom.* c. 136.

Generals were to be on their guard, a reference to the Act
which declared them unlawful was added in the margin.[1] Of

Proclama-
tion
against the
election of
Royalists.

a proclamation issued on September 21 it may
fairly be said that, if it was illegal, it only escaped
legality by a hair's-breadth. In the counties the
executive authority was under the control of the
central authority, which appointed not merely special commissioners, but also the ordinary justices of the peace. In the
towns it was otherwise. Corporations chosen by election or
co-option formed the governing bodies, mayors and other
officials being elected in the manner indicated by the charter
of the place. The Long Parliament, anxious to prevent such
powers from falling into the hands of their opponents, had
passed an ordinance disabling delinquents from being placed
in office for the next five years.[2] This ordinance was renewed
as an Act in 1652, the term of its expiry being fixed at September 28, 1655.[3] When, therefore, the Protector issued a proclamation on the 21st, directing that this Act should be
punctually observed, his action was supported by the law[4] till
the week came to an end, but after that week had expired
obedience to his command rested on no foundation except his
own declared will.[5]

Much as had been done, the Government was not yet
prepared to set its instruments at work, as there were further

Further
Instructions
needed.

details to be considered before the Instructions to
the Major-Generals could be regarded as complete.

Oct. 4.
Lambert's
additional
Instructions

The result was that on October 4 Lambert, who had
taken a leading part in the committee of Council entrusted with this business, brought up a paper of

[1] *S. P. Dom.* c. 134. Mrs. Everett Green explains that these Instructions as accepted on Sept. 21 are the same as those calendared August 22
and 24. They, however, have the new clause (see p. 320) printed amongst
them, and several written amendments.

[2] *Scobell*, i. 135.   [3] *Ib.* ii. 209.

[4] That is to say, on the assumption that the Acts and ordinances of
the Long Parliament after the breach with the King were legal, an
assumption which was notoriously denied after the Restoration.

[5] Printed in *Hist. Rev.* (Oct. 1900) xv. 655.

additional Instructions, which was adopted, with amendments, by

Oct. 9.
adopted
with amend-
ments. Protector and Council on the 9th.[1] The Instructions thus added to the original seven were fourteen in number, of which the first nine were mere amplifica-

Points of
administra-
tive detail. tions of the former ones entering into questions of administrative detail. Royalist masters of families, after giving security that they would neither plot against the Government themselves, nor fail to reveal any such plot which came to their knowledge as having been entered on by others,[2] were to give bonds for the good behaviour of their servants, and a list of such bonds was to be kept by the Major-Generals, and by them forwarded to the office of a registrar to be established in London. No one was to land in England from beyond the sea, without informing the Major-General of his name, the place from which he came, and the place to which he was going, engaging himself at the same time that if he came to London he would give more specific information as to his movements and business. If he had taken the King's side in former times, he was to give similar information whenever he changed his place of abode, whether in London or the country. Further Instructions provided for the discovery of highwaymen and robbers, and directed that a more than ordinary regard should be had to the securing of the roads, chiefly about London.

The remaining five Instructions were of a different charac-ter, being almost entirely occupied with considerations which,

Moral or
social regu-
lations. though not without reference to the baffling of con-spirators, deal freely with questions connected with moral or social order. No house standing alone and out of a town was to 'sell ale, beer or wine, or to give enter-tainment.' No one was to be allowed to ride post without

---

[1] Council Order Book, *Interr.* I, 76, pp. 324, 327.

[2] This requirement is not to be found amongst the additional Instruc-tions, but the bond is set forth in *Merc. Pol.*, E, 491, 7. Most likely it was added as an additional order for securing the peace of the Common-wealth after Sept. 21, the date of the orders as they have reached us (*S. P. Dom.* c. 136).

previous notice being given to the nearest justice of the peace ; and the master of any inn, alehouse or tavern, who allowed his horses to be used for such a purpose was to forfeit his license. In London and Westminster all gaming-houses and houses of ill-fame were 'to be industriously sought out' and closed. All householders within the same limits who had no trade or calling, or did not labour in such trade or calling, or had no other visible estate, were to 'be bound to their good behaviour and compelled to work, and for want of good security to be sent to Bridewell.' Lastly, 'alehouses, taverns and victualling-houses towards the skirts of the said cities were to be suppressed, except such as were necessary to lodge travellers ; the number of alehouses in all other parts of the town to be abated, and none continued but such as could lodge strangers and were of good repute.' [1]

So far as a consideration of the order in which the various Instructions are placed may be allowed to influence our conclusions, it must be admitted that there is some indication—it would be impossible to style it evidence—of a twofold origin. The first six Instructions are, if not exclusively, yet to a great extent,[2] of a practical and administrative character ; and the same may be said of the first nine of the additional Instructions. To the first set was added, after an interval of two days, the Instruction to carry out the ordinance for the ejection of scandalous ministers ; to the second set are added the five Instructions which deal almost entirely with the repression of vice. From the position occupied by Lambert in the committee which prepared and amended these Instructions he may fairly be regarded as probably the originator, certainly the organiser, of the new police system, of which the Major-Generals were to be the official heads. If he were the same man as the Lambert who had withstood the Protector at the Council-table when the West Indian expedition was under

The Instructions fall under two heads.

Conjecture as to the part of Lambert.

[1] *Old Parliamentary History*, xx. 461–67.

[2] Some of these earliest Instructions may be the result of a compromise.

discussion,[1] and who before that had taken a leading part in framing the somewhat unimaginative Instrument of Government, we cannot but recognise his hand in the practical requirements of many of these Instructions. Is it wandering too far into the regions of conjecture to suggest that the readiness to add to the burdens originally laid on the shoulders of the Major-Generals the enormous task of encouraging virtue and discouraging vice must surely have proceeded from the

and of the Protector. Protector himself—the man who had so glorified a naval expedition sent forth to protect English commerce in the Indies that he saw in it nothing less than the avenging sword with which to strike down the enemies of God? Should this view of the case be accepted,[2] much that followed afterwards in the growing estrangement between Oliver and Lambert becomes easily intelligible without the necessity of having recourse to merely personal motives on one side or the other. For the time there was no breach. The Instruc-

Oct. 11. Commissions to the Major-Generals issued. tions were issued as a complete whole. On October 11 the commissions were formally distributed among the Major-Generals,[3] who were sent forth to work the will of the Protector and Council as best they could.

This view, that the morals and social aims of the Instructions were mainly inspired by the Protector himself, derives some corroboration from an attentive consideration of a Declaration issued by the Government on October 31. It is

Oct. 31. Declaration by the Protector and Council. true that till the end is approached this manifesto bears no trace of Oliver's own hand, and may very well have been the work of Fiennes, who by some

---

[1] See *supra*, pp. 128, 159.

[2] The length of time—from August 22 to Oct. 9—during which the Instructions were under discussion somewhat favours the view that there was some difference of opinion on the subject.

[3] Only the commission to Butler has been preserved, *R.O. Interr.* Box 2, No. 10. It may, however, be taken that the others bore the same date.

was believed to have been the author of the whole.[1] The
narrative of the conspiracies of 1654 and 1655, with which
the Declaration opens, and the assertion that a similar conspiracy was still cherished by the Royalists, may properly have
been left to a subordinate. Towards the close the reader
seems to catch the tones of Oliver himself. "It is plain," we
are told, "to everyone that is not blinded with prejudice that
these men are restless in their designs, and are the causes of
all our trouble and unsettlement, and will leave no stone un-
turned to render vain and fruitless all that blood which hath
been spilt to restore our liberties, and the hopes we have conceived of seeing this poor nation settled and reformed from
that spirit of profaneness which these men do keep up and
countenance, in contempt of all law and authority:—and therefore we thus argued, that unless we would give up the cause
so long contended for, and the lives, liberties and comforts of
all the well-affected of these three nations into their hands, or
leave them exposed to their continual attempts, the peace and
common concernments of this Commonwealth must be otherwise secured and provided for than at present they were ; that
this was not to be done without raising additional forces ; that
the charge of these forces ought not to be put upon the good
people who have borne the burden of the day, but upon those
who have been and are the occasion of all our danger."[2]

"Upon these grounds," he continued—if the voice was indeed the voice of Oliver—". . . we have thought fit to lay the
burden of maintaining these forces, and some other public
charges which are occasioned by them, upon those who have
been engaged in the late wars against the State, having respect
notwithstanding therein to such of them as are not able to
undergo that charge." To this followed an argument that
Charles's 'coming into the Low Countries[3] was sufficient

---

[1] *A Letter from a True and Lawful Member of Parliament*, p. 41,
E, 884, 2. On the authorship of this pamphlet, see *infra*, p. 330, note 1.

[2] It will be seen that the Protector did not in any way dissent from
Lambert's practical methods.

[3] To Middelburg ; see p. 280.

evidence that he had expected a general rising of his supporters in England, and that the collection of great sums for him was another proof that the design was favoured by many more than had actually risen in the spring.'[1]

Having enforced this view of the position by further reasoning, the writer proceeds to claim for the Supreme Magistrate that in such case he must not be 'tied up to the ordinary rules,' and to urge that it is justifiable to compel 'those of whom the people have reason to be afraid' to 'pay for securing the State against that danger which they are the authors of.' If, the author of this part of the Declaration argues, the Royalists are treated as a class apart, it is through their own determination to stand apart from the rest of the nation. "There is nothing," he writes, "they have more industriously laboured in than this —to keep themselves separated and distinguished from the well affected of this nation:—to which end they have kept their conversation apart, as if they would avoid the very beginnings of union; have bred and educated their children by the sequestered and ejected clergy, and very much confined their marriages and alliances within their own party, as if they meant to entail their quarrel and prevent the means to reconcile posterity; which, with the great pains they take upon all occasions to lessen and suppress the esteem and honour of the English nation in all their actions and undertakings abroad, striving withal to make other nations distinguish their interest from it, gives us ground to judge that they have separated themselves from the body of the nation; and therefore we leave it to all mankind to judge whether we ought not to be timely jealous of that separation, and to proceed so against them as they may be at the charge of those remedies which are required against the dangers they have bred."[2]

---

[1] It is not likely that much evidence as to the truth of this statement should be in existence. There are two accounts of Halsall's, dated June 23 and Nov. 25 respectively, showing that 3,390*l.* were sent over by him in the course of 1655, *Clarendon MSS.* l., fol. 72; *Thurloe,* iv. 245.

[2] *A Declaration of His Highness* (p. 38), E, 857, 3.

Some months later Hyde, assuming the character of a Presbyterian member of the Long Parliament, struck heavily
Hyde's reply. at the weakest point in this argument. " Let us revolve," he replied, " the vast treasure we have lost, and compare it with the nothing we possess. The law says, 'No man shall be punished if his offence be not proved by witnesses.' This Declaration says, ' Though we abstain from any unlawful action, we shall be punished for the malice and revenge in our hearts.' The law says 'that a conspiracy to levy war is no treason, except there be a levying war *in facto*.' Your Declaration says, ' If you have reason to believe that we have evil intention against the Government, we are without any right or title to anything we enjoy, and are at your mercy to dispose of as you please '—which is the lowest condition of traitors. If this be liberty, what nation in Europe lives in servitude ? " [1]

From the purely legal point of view Oliver had no defence to make. Like Strafford, when the Short Parliament threatened
Oliver does not defend himself on legal grounds. to overturn what, from his point of view, was the constitutional edifice under which the people were sheltered, the Protector held himself, so far as the enemies of the State were concerned, to be ' loose and absolved from all rules of government.' If the Constitution as settled by the Instrument was to be upheld, its enemies must, with or without the approval of the law, be rendered
His position as a constable. innocuous. In February he had explained that necessity had driven him to take upon himself the work of a constable to keep the peace between contending religious sects.[2] It now looked as if he would have to exercise the same office towards hostile political parties as well.

In treating Royalists as a class apart from the body of the nation the Protector did but follow in the lines laid down by the

[1] *A Letter from a True and Lawful Member of Parliament*, p. 45, E, 884, 2. Mr. Macray has identified the author with Hyde in the preface to the third volume of his *Calendar of the Clarendon MSS.*

[2] See *supra*, p. 267.

Long Parliament at the commencement of the Civil War. Yet

The Royalists treated as a class apart from the nation.

to do so was none the less a political error. The greater the determination of any single class to stand aside from the main current of national life, the greater is the interest, to say nothing of the duty, of every Government to close its eyes to the existence of the gulf which separates it from its compatriots, and to treat those who repudiate its authority, so long as they abstain from acts of resistance, as erring brethren, but as brethren still. The main question of interest, however, is whether Oliver's assumption that he had the national good will on his side was in accordance with facts or not. If it was, his system was likely to be permanent ; if not, it was doomed to speedy destruction.

If the experience of the late rising was to go for anything, it is impossible to regard the stricter Royalists otherwise than

Royalism not a preponderant force.

as a cultivated but comparatively small minority. No doubt their tenants and labourers looked up to them with respect, and, if circumstances were favourable, would have given them support. No doubt, too, there were in the towns a certain number of tradesmen and others who, though hostile to Royalty in 1642, would have been more or less willing to accept it in 1655. Of any burning zeal for the restoration of Stuart kingship, outside the Cavalier families, there is, however, no trace whatever. Thurloe's spies bring to him in abundance tales of the machinations of Levellers and Parliamentarians. Denunciations of any popular outcry in favour of the exiled Charles are few and far between. Even in their cups the men of the people do not cry out for their King.

It does not follow, however, that the masses were for Oliver because they were not for Charles. The more thinking

Divisions amongst the opponents of Royalism.

members of the anti-Royalist party were hopelessly divided, and the low social position of many of the officers went as far as any apprehension of constitutional danger to nourish disaffection to a Government resting on military support. " So strict a justice," wrote a foreign ambassador when the appointment of the Major-

Generals was still under discussion, "is held that the country hardly knows there is an army in it; but the meetings of its councils have caused an exceeding ill-will amongst all the inhabitants, the common folk being irritated at being ruled and commanded by those of their own class, and people of good birth despising the latter in their minds. One can therefore easily judge with what soreness of heart most persons see themselves placed at their mercy, and to have their own lot made lighter or heavier at their discretion." Such a state of feeling undoubtedly tended to a revival of Royalism. "There is no longer," writes the same ambassador, "a question whether they shall have a king, but who the king shall be, and so the former difference between the house of Stuart and all the inhabitants of the land is converted into a difference between the houses of Stuart and Cromwell."[1] These words were written at a time when the movement for offering the Crown to the Protector was in full swing, and the writer, in the reflections which follow, clearly anticipates that the successful candidate for the throne will be King Oliver rather than King Charles; but it is evident, even if we could close our eyes to the subsequent history of the nation, that there was growing up, even amongst those who were averse to Charles's restoration, a feeling, in some cases, of active hostility towards the Protectorate, and, in still more, of simmering dissatisfaction with the prevailing conditions of government.

The army not popular, (margin)

No doubt, so far as the decimation was concerned, Oliver had acted prudently in confining the infliction of special taxation to those who were possessed of what was in that age a substantial fortune. He was probably unaware of the extent to which he multiplied his enemies by his efforts to ensure the moral improvement of the people. Baxter, who, Puritan and controversialist as he was, at least kept his eyes open, characterised the 'Diocesan party' as consisting 'of some grave, learned, godly bishops, and some

nor the attempt to enforce morality. (margin)

[1] Bonde to Charles X., July 27, *Stockholm Transcripts.*

sober, godly people of their mind ; and withal of almost all
the carnal politicians, temporisers, profane, and haters of godliness in the land, and all the rabble of the ignorant, ungodly
vulgar.'[1] To struggle against ignorance and vice was a high
enterprise, worthy of the Protector's zeal. It was also an
enterprise calling for prudence and circumspection far above
the average. Was it so certain that by a wholesale closure of
alehouses and bear-gardens Oliver would really exalt the standard of morality in England ? No doubt he could plead that
these things were done for a political object, as depriving
Royalists of meeting-places where they might hatch their plots.
Those who had taken pleasure in watching the agonies of the
bear, and no less pleasure in fuddling themselves over their ale,
were only too likely to set down the new orders as the last
experiment of the virtuous to abolish cakes and ale in the land,
and, if they thought of politics at all, they would recall to mind
the times when the late King had left them to enjoy themselves
in their own fashion, and would long for the restoration of his
son, who, if all accounts were true, was not likely to enforce on
his subjects too high a standard of morality.

Such considerations were, however, far from the Protector's
mind. From the language in which he announced, on
November 21, the appointment of a day of humiliation it is evident that he looked on the quarrels
among Puritans with far greater apprehension than
on any imminent danger from the side of the Royalists.
Deploring 'the tares of division that had been sown by the
envious one, the abominable blasphemies vented, a spreading
of late through the apostacy of, and the abuse of liberty by

Nov. 21.
A day of
humiliation
appointed.

---

[1] *Reliquiæ Baxterianæ*, i. 145. When he comes to give his conjectural reasons for the adhesion of the last class, he suggests that one
may be 'because the worst and most do always fall in with the party that
is uppermost,' which cannot be applied to the times of the Protectorate.
The words were written long after those times, and no doubt Baxter
inadvertently gave expression to his judgment on what was passing before
his eyes, in forgetfulness that it did not apply to the subject of the preceding sentences.

many professing religion,' he complained of 'the continued
series of difficulties we have been and are exercised under by
the secret and open practices of those that, bearing evil will unto
Zion, have, Balaam-like, attempted all ways to frustrate our hopes
and endeavours of such a settlement and reformation as hath
been so long contended for; as also the weight of the work
of this generation.' On these grounds he called on the people
to unite in prayer that God would disappoint the designs of
all who set themselves 'against the interest of Christ and His
people.' He would then teach them to serve the Lord God
with one heart and one mind, and support those 'that are
more especially engaged in and entrusted with the great affairs
of this nation, by a spirit of counsel and wisdom to enable
them faithfully to discharge their weighty trust, and that they
may bear some proportion of serviceableness to the great
designs and promises of God concerning the kingdom of His
Son, our Blessed Lord, in these latter times, and may be used
as instruments in His hand for the continuance and increase of
the reformation and the security and settlement of these
nations.' [1]

This, then—the leading of the nation into paths of unity
and religious peace, not the establishment of protectoral

Oliver's main object. or parliamentary constitutions — was the object
nearest to Oliver's heart. Three days later he
announced by another Declaration that Royalists

Nov. 24. Declaration against keeping arms or maintaining ejected clergy. whose estates had been sequestered or who had
taken part in the war under the late King were to
refrain from keeping arms in their houses after
December 1, and from maintaining any of the
ejected clergy as chaplains or schoolmasters after
January 1—the date of November 1, previously fixed, having
proved too early, the organisation under the Major-Generals not
being capable of being put in operation so soon. The Declaration ended with a clause in which a ray of hope was permitted
to those at least of the ejected clergy who had given 'a real

---

[1] *A Declaration*, Nov. 21, B.M. press-mark 669, f. 20, No. 19.

testimony of their godliness and good affection to the present Government,' offering that to such 'so much tenderness shall be used as may consist with the safety and good of this nation.'[1] To a zealous Churchman like Evelyn, indeed, this last clause afforded no consolation. His occasional visits to London were made the opportunity of attending the ministrations of clergy who were not in the least likely to court a testimonial of good

Dec. 30.
A last
service.

affection to the present Government. To him the last Sunday in the year,[2] when he was present at the service held by Dr. Wilde at St. Gregory's—the only church in London in which the use of the Prayer Book had

Evelyn's
lament.

been hitherto connived at[3]—was as the closing scene of religion itself. "So this," he noted in his *Diary*, "was the mournfullest day that in my life I had seen in the Church of England herself since the Reformation, to the great rejoicing of both papist and presbyter. The Lord Jesus pity our distressed Church and bring back the captivity of Zion."[4] Yet the heart of Oliver was larger than his theories, and it was not long before the clouds began to break. In January the

1656.
Jan.
A petition
presented by
Ussher.

aged Ussher, trembling on the brink of the grave,[5] presented a petition on behalf of 'the poor outed clergy.' Not only was this petition left without a satisfactory answer, but, if a Royalist rumour may be accepted, the Archbishop was reduced to admit to the Protector that 'the Common Prayer was by the people made an idol, and therefore justly abolished.'[6] However this may have been, the

---

[1] *Declaration*, Nov. 24, B.M. press-mark 669, f. 20, No. 20.

[2] This service is usually assigned to Christmas Day, which is the date of the preceding entry ; but it is in the highest degree improbable that Dr. Wilde, on whose ministrations Evelyn attended, should have refrained from using the opportunity of meeting his congregation on the following Sunday, Dec. 30.

[3] Evelyn's *Diary*, ed. Bray, iv. 308.   [4] *Ib.* i. 311.

[5] He died on March 21, and was buried in Westminster Abbey, the Protector contributing 200*l.* to the expense.

[6] R. W[hitely] to Nicholas, Jan. $\frac{10}{20}$, $\frac{\text{Jan. 22}}{\text{Feb. 1}}$, *S. P. Dom.* cxxiii. 27 ; *Nicholas Papers*, iii. 261. [The rumour was subsequently denied by Ussher.]

old man's pleadings did not remain without effect.   On some

Feb.
A hopeful
answer to
the Epis-
copalian
clergy. day in February a few of the leading Episcopalian clergy were summoned to Whitehall, where Oliver assured them that, though he was well aware what was the drift of their teaching, he was neither ignorant nor unfeeling with regard to the condition into which they had fallen.   All that he asked was an engagement that if liberty were allowed them they would not make use of it to excite fresh disorders.[1]   On their assurance that the desired pledge would be forthcoming he promised to lay their case before the Council.   There can be little doubt that, though his reference to the Council was not made in a form that could be

The Decla-
ration not
executed
against the
clergy. placed on record, he fulfilled his promise.   The Declaration was not actually withdrawn or modified, but it was seldom, if ever, put in practice against the clergy.   Not a single one of the reports of the Major-Generals—so far as they have reached us—even alludes to the ejection of clergy from private houses.   The Royalist correspondents of Hyde and Nicholas have as little to say on a subject on which, if any evidence of facts came before them, they would gladly have dilated.   When, in the next generation, Walker collected all available information on the sufferings of the clergy of his Church, he did not succeed in producing a single instance of a chaplain or schoolmaster reduced to poverty by this action of the Protector.[2]

[1] Nieupoort to the States General, $\frac{\text{Feb. 22}}{\text{March 3}}$, *Add. MSS.*. 17,677 W, fol. 232.

[2] It may be well to note here that this affair affords evidence of un-blushing forgery on the part of Gauden.   Just before the Restoration, when bishoprics seemed likely to be offered, he published a Remonstrance (E, 765, 7) which, he said, he had presented to Oliver on behalf of the clergy suffering through the Declaration.   Unluckily for the truth of this allegation, he set down his words as pleading for those who had been condemned ' by your Highness's late edict of Jan. 1.'   In 1660 he might have forgotten that Jan. 1 was the date fixed for the expulsion, and not that of the edict, which was in reality issued on Nov. 24.   He could not have forgotten it in 1656.   The man capable of forging this Remonstrance was capable of forging the Eikon.

Having taken measures for assuring his military control over the Royalist gentry, Oliver was prepared to show that he no longer considered them personally dangerous.   On October 3

1655.
Oct. 3.
Release of
prisoners.

he resolved to throw open the prison-doors of the Royalists shut up as a precautionary measure, on condition of their giving security, not only to abstain from plotting against the Government, but also to give information against those who did.[1]   That the number of those set at liberty was large may be gathered from the fact that, out of four counties [2] alone, no fewer than seventy-two obtained their release.   A few had already been discharged on similar, or even on more onerous, conditions.[3]   It is, indeed, probable that this wholesale gaol-delivery was expedited by a suspicion that some of the prisoners might sue out a writ of *habeas corpus* when the new term enabled them to approach the courts—a move which would throw a fresh difficulty in the way of the adhesion of the

Oct. 25.
Royalists
expelled
from
London.

judges to the Protectorate.[4]   No one, least of all Oliver, would count on the gratitude of the liberated Royalists, and on October 25 a proclamation was issued to safeguard the Protector's life by renewing

[1] This security was subsequently demanded of all who had taken part in the Civil War.

[2] Essex, Suffolk, Norfolk, and Cambridge.

[3] "Divers gone off, but some on so hard, and others on so unhandsome conditions that I know not how to wish myself free on the same terms."   Sir R. Verney to Mrs. Sherard, August 27.   Sir Ralph had returned to England, thinking himself safe under the Protectorate, as his only offence had been a refusal to take the Covenant.   It is, however, easy to understand that, whilst a promise to betray any plots coming to his knowledge would be most repugnant to a man of his temperament, a refusal to give it might seem to the authorities an excellent test of Royalism.

[4] This is perhaps hinted at in the following extract from a set of Royalist verses printed in *Notes and Queries*, 7th series, x. 41, by Mr. Firth, who assigns them on good grounds to Denham :—

> "Though the governing part cannot find in their heart
>   To free the imprisoned throng,
> Yet I dare affirm next Michaelmas Term
>   We'll set them out in a song."

the order for the expulsion of all members of that party from London and Westminster.[1]

Before the end of November Exeter gaol was cleared after another fashion. For some months it had been crowded with

Nov. 30.
Transport-
ation of
the Exeter
prisoners.

prisoners committed for their participation in Penruddock's rising. Two of these having petitioned the Council for liberty as banished men, if permission to continue in England after liberation were refused them, advantage was taken of their request to order the transportation of the whole number to the Indies,[2] though one at least had had the bill against him thrown out by the grand jury,[3] and others had been acquitted by the petty jury. It was afterwards stated by an interested party that none of them were transported without their consent being first given ; but, if this was the case, the question must have been a pure formality, as there is nothing in the Order of the Council to suggest that any alternative was really offered.

The same partial witness, when called to account in 1659, not only stated, truly enough, that on their arrival in Barbados

Their treat-
ment in the
Indies.

they were to be retained in forced servitude for five years, after which they would receive payment for their work as free labourers, but did his best to represent their condition as an easier one than that of the husbandman at home.[4] Five of those who were the subjects of the experiment told a different story. On the outward voyage they were 'locked up under decks—and guards— amongst horses, that their souls through heat and steam, under the tropic, fainted in them.' On their arrival they were

[1] Proclamation, Oct. 25, B.M. press-mark 669, f. 20, No. 17.

[2] There was an order on Nov. 30 to transport some to the East Indies, and another on the same day to transport all to Barbados and other foreign plantations. Possibly the word ' East ' was miswritten for ' West,' or the second order may have been intended to cancel the first. Council Order Book, *Interr.* I, 76, p. 404 ; *S. P. Dom.* ci. 165.

[3] This, however, appears to have happened, not because the grand jury were convinced of his innocence, but because his indictment had been laid in a wrong county. Burton's *Diary*, iv. 258.

[4] Burton's *Diary*, iv. 258, 259.

enthralled 'in this most insupportable captivity, they now generally grinding at the mills, attending the furnaces, or digging in this scorching island ; having naught to feed on— notwithstanding their hard labour— but potato roots, nor to drink but water with such roots washed in it—besides the bread and tears of their own afflictions—being bought and sold still from one planter to another, or attached as horses and beasts for the debts of their masters, being whipped at their whipping-posts as rogues for their masters' pleasure, and sleeping in styes worse than hogs in England, and many other ways made miserable beyond expression or Christian imagination.'[1]

The practice of awarding transportation, even to unconvicted prisoners, at the mere pleasure of the executive Government had been growing from year to year. Coming into existence in the cases of the prisoners at Dunbar and Worcester, it had been extended in constantly increasing proportions to the Irish who were found to be incapable or undesirous of finding work, and the evil practice was now extending itself in England. Lilburne, uncondemned, had been sent to a prison in Jersey. After Penruddock's rising a few had been despatched to Barbados.[2] Now a larger number—about some seventy in all—were treated to the same measure. Very probably most of them, if they had been left to the severity of the law, would have met with a harder fate. For the community at large the danger lay in the growing habit of the executive, strong in the force of military support, to deal out penalties at its own will and pleasure, without definite rules laid down beforehand, and without adequate security for the release of the innocent.[3] Even Charles had better preserved the forms of legal justice.

By this time the new system was getting into working order.

Growth of the practice of transportation by executive order.

---

[1] Burton's *Diary*, iv. 256. Compare *England's Slavery*, E, 1833, 3.

[2] See *supra*, p. 309.

[3] Persons who had been engaged in rebellion were liable, by the first of the Orders for Securing the Peace of the Commonwealth (see p. 321), to be imprisoned or banished, but this does not imply transportation to the West Indies.

The proclamation of October 25, commanding the expulsion
of Royalists from London and Westminster, was
accompanied by a list of the Major-Generals—whose
number was now raised to eleven—in order that
those persons who had been sent back to their
homes in the country might know to whom they
must apply themselves with the bonds they were required to
offer for the good behaviour of themselves and their servants.
Of the eleven Major-Generals, Kelsey was to take charge of
Kent and Surrey; Goffe of Sussex, Hants, and Berkshire;
Desborough, as formerly, of the six counties of the West—
Gloucestershire, Wilts, Dorset, Somerset, Devon, and Cornwall; Fleetwood, who had by this time returned from Ireland,
of Oxfordshire, Bucks, Hertfordshire, Cambridgeshire, Essex,
Norfolk and Suffolk; Skippon of the City of London; Bark-
stead of the rest of Middlesex; Whalley of the shires of
Lincoln, Nottingham, Derby, Warwick, and Leicester; Butler
of those of Northampton, Bedford, Rutland, and Huntingdon;
Berry of Worcestershire, Herefordshire, Shropshire, and North
Wales; Worsley of Cheshire, Lancashire, and Staffordshire;
Lambert of Yorkshire, Durham, Cumberland, Westmoreland,
and Northumberland.[1]   Lambert and Fleetwood, whose
services were required at Whitehall as members of the Council,
were, however, allowed to appoint deputies, Cumberland,
Westmoreland, and Northumberland being assigned to Charles
Howard, and York and Durham to Robert Lilburne. In
Fleetwood's district, Norfolk, Suffolk, Essex, and Cambridgeshire were given to Hezekiah Haynes. The remainder of the
district was at first given to Tobias Bridge; but as, for some
unknown reason, he retired from the post, Packer was employed as deputy in Oxon and Herts, and also, in conjunction
with George Fleetwood, in Bucks.[2]   Monmouthshire and
South Wales remained for the present unallotted; but early in
January they were assigned to Berry, who, no doubt in conse-

Oct. 25.
Royalists ex-
pelled from
London.

A list of
the Major-
Generals.

---

[1] *The Public Intelligencer*, E, 489, 9.

[2] Council Order Book, *Interr.* I, 76, p. 343. This is not the brother
of the Lord Deputy.

quence of the enormous extent of his district, was permitted to name two deputies, Colonel Rowland Dawkins and Lieutenant-Colonel Nicholas.[1] So far as we know Whalley was the first Major-General to take up active work, as he met the county commissioners of Nottinghamshire at Newark on November 2.[2]

Nov. 2.
Whalley at Newark.

Between the Major-Generals and the Commissioners for securing the peace of the Commonwealth the utmost harmony prevailed ; and it would have been strange if it had been otherwise. Originally selected as devoted to the Protectorate, and reinforced by the Major-General with persons whom he selected after inquiry on the spot, they had the same friends and the same enemies as the Government itself. Being viewed with hostile eyes by the local magnates of their county, they were driven, in mere self-defence, to seek their own security in upholding the hand which brought them military support. If, on the other hand, as occasionally happened, one or other of the commissioners felt scruples at embarking on a service so unpopular amongst influential neighbours, it was easy to allow him to refrain from attending the meetings, and to drop out of sight without noise or scandal.[3] The first business of the Major-General on his arrival in the county was to hold a meeting of the commissioners, in whose ranks he was himself enrolled, and over whom he presided in the chair. The relation between them was by no means dissimilar from that which existed between the Protector and the Council. It was natural that in both cases attention should be called to the more active and showy element, and there can be no doubt that without the Protector at Whitehall, or his Major-General in the county, but little, if anything, would have been accomplished ; but it is not to be

The Major-Generals and the Commissioners.

---

[1] Council Order Book, *Interr.* I, 76, p. 457. The usual statement that Dawkins was a Major-General in his own right is a mere blunder.

[2] Whalley to Thurloe, Oct. 31, Nov. 2, *Thurloe,* iv. 125, 146.

[3] Goffe to Thurloe, Nov. 7, *Thurloe,* iv. 16. The relations between the Major-Generals and the Commissioners may be gathered from their correspondence at large.

imagined that Oliver had the intention to subject the country to a military despotism. What he aimed at was the establishment in the county and the nation of the rule—provisionally at least—of a Puritan oligarchy, with just so much of military strength behind it as was needed to make it effective for his purpose.

The exaction of the tax of 10 per cent. was troublesome enough, but presented no insuperable difficulty. The local knowledge of the commissioners, assisted by the lists of compounders kept in London at Goldsmiths' Hall, made it easy to ascertain, at least approximately, the income of each Royalist. As might have been expected, there were practical questions requiring to be referred from time to time to headquarters, as not a few of the Royalists did their utmost to produce reasons in favour of their personal exemption. There was, however, no attempt to resist openly, and the tax, once laid, was duly gathered in.[1] Nor were many obstacles laid in the way of the search for arms. Before long Royalists were deprived of their weapons from one end of the country to the other, and insurrection, save under the cover of a successful invasion by a foreign army, was rendered impossible in England. Other precautionary measures were enforced with equal rigour.

The Decimation.

Royalists disarmed.

Bonds for the quiet behaviour of those who had in any capacity sided with the late King or his son were demanded, even from persons whose property fell beneath the limit of decimation ; and there was an equally sweeping effort to obtain certainty as to the places of abode of those who might in any way be distinguished as Royalists.[2]

Enforcement of bonds.

---

[1] The details, taken from the *Thurloe Papers*, are given more fully by Mr. Rannie in the *Hist. Rev.* (July 1895), x. 484.

[2] In the British Museum there are three books (*Add. MSS.* 34,011-13) containing lists sent by the Major-Generals of every county except Middlesex. Taking so much of the list for Yorkshire as gives names beginning with the letter A, we find 113 entries. Two of these have no qualification appended. The remaining 111 show 13 esquires and gentlemen, the remaining 98 being tradesmen, artificers, farmers, yeomen,

There remained the cases of those Royalists who fell under the first order for the securing of the peace of the Commonwealth,

Persons
having
shared
in the late
conspiracy. as having taken part in rebellions or plots, and those who fell under the second, of being dangerous enemies to the peace.[1] Of the number of those falling under the first head, who were to be imprisoned or banished with the sequestration of their estates, it is impossible to speak with precision, as the reports of many of the Major-Generals have not been preserved. But, so far as we know, the only cases that occurred were those of the Northern conspirators who had been dealt with lightly at the last assizes.[2] Before the end

1656.
March.
Sentence
on Slingsby
and others. of March eight persons of quality, with Sir Henry Slingsby at their head, were imprisoned at Hull by Major-General Lilburne and the commissioners at York. In May fourteen others were sentenced to the

May.
Further
imprison-
ments. like punishment, the estates of those amongst them who were possessed of property being sequestered.[3]

One or two cases were heard elsewhere, but our information is insufficient to enable us to speak positively of the result.[4] Under any other Government these men would have fared as badly, if not worse. What is peculiar about their treatment is that they were sentenced without the intervention of a jury, because it was impossible to obtain a verdict against them in these Northern parts.

As to those who fell under the second head, who, without having taken part in any conspiracy, were dangerous on account of their avowed Royalism, and who were liable to imprisonment or to be sent beyond sea, the Major-Generals appear to have construed their orders somewhat liberally, holding themselves empowered to imprison on suspicion anyone known to entertain

husbandmen, labourers, &c. Such lists cannot have been drawn up with a view to decimation, but only to ascertain the abodes of persons who had given bonds.

[1] See p. 322.   [2] See p. 299.

[3] Lilburne to Thurloe, Jan. 22 ; Lilburne to the Protector, Jan. 25, Feb. 9, March 14, *Thurloe,* iv. 442, 468, 522, 614.

[4] Lilburne to the Protector, May 16, *ib.* v. 33.

Royalist opinions,[1] or who frequented the company of persons of the same way of thinking. They were especially hard on persons who appeared to be living beyond their means, thus affording evidence that they eked out their scanty income from some disreputable source. One of the first to suffer was the satirical poet, Cleveland, who was confined in Yarmouth by Haynes, on the ground that he had but 50*l*. a year, and could give no account of himself, except that he lived with Mr. Edward Coke, whom he helped in his studies. It was further noted against him that he seldom left Coke's house, that few resorted to him except Papists and Cavaliers, and that he was 'a person of great abilities, and so able to do greater disservice.'[2] Some three months later he petitioned Oliver for his release, professing that his fidelity to the King might be accepted as evidence that he would be faithful to the Protector, and complaining of being deprived of liberty merely for being poor;[3] an appeal which was followed by his prompt release.[4]

1656.
Cleveland imprisoned.

Feb.
His petition and release.

Cleveland had for a companion a Mr. Sherman, described by Haynes as 'a most malignant Episcopal minister who, though of sober life, yet of most destructive principles to the Government and good people, and professedly owned and held forth by him most seditiously in a sermon preached before the authority of Norwich.'[5] In other districts it was rather idleness and licentiousness that marked men out for imprisonment. The Bedfordshire commissioners, writes Butler, had assured him 'they would make it their business to find out and give me notice of all their profane and idle gentry, and others whose lives are a shame to' a 'Christian

1655.
Imprison-
ment of
Sherman.

Proceedings
of Butler,
Berry, and
Worsley.

---

[1] See the cases of John Goring in Sussex, and of Middleton and others in Lancashire, *Thurloe*, iv. 213, 733, 746.

[2] Haynes to Thurloe, Nov. 10, *ib.* iv. 185.

[3] Cleveland's petition was published on a broadsheet in Oct. 1657, B.M. press-mark 669, f. 20, No. 69.

[4] Wood's *Fast.* i. 499.

[5] Haynes to Thurloe, Nov. 19, *Thurloe*, iv. 216.

Commonwealth, and of all inferior persons that are dangerous and live without callings.' "We have secured," he adds, "in order to his Highness transporting him, one Pemberton, that was formerly in arms against the Parliament, a very desperate person, having no estate, and living after the rate of four or five hundred a year. . . . I do not think his Highness can be informed of a person more fit for banishment." [1] At Shrewsbury Berry imprisons 'divers lewd fellows, some for having a hand in the plot, others of dissolute life.' "If some of them were sent to the Indies," he adds, "it would do much good." [2] Worsley was no less active. "We . . . are now," he writes from Lancashire, "beginning to fill the prisons with suspicious fellows." "I have had many sad complaints," he writes a few days later, "against the attorneys of this county, and had against this meeting sent summons out to all attorneys that were delinquents or papists ; and they appearing yesterday, I have first taken the bonds ordered by the Council ; another bond, that they should never act any more as an attorney or solicitor in this Commonwealth, without special license from his Highness and his Council, or either of them, and the most of them have done this ; only one that did not appear, which we have sent to apprehend." In Cheshire he is no less thoroughgoing. "The Commissioners," he assures Thurloe, "some of them this day expressed that they could find near sixty gentlemen in this country, many of them younger sons, that were fit to be sent out of this Commonwealth, which done would much tend to the security thereof and terrify others. I light on [3] one Hugh Anderton, in Lancashire, one noted by all your friends to be one of the most wicked, dangerous men in this Commonwealth. I intend to send him to the castle of Chester to the rest." [4]

It is unnecessary to pursue the subject further in order to

---

[1] Butler to Thurloe, Nov. 19, *Thurloe*, iv. 218.
[2] Berry to Thurloe, Jan. 5, *ib.* iv. 393.
[3] 'Of' as printed.
[4] Worsley to Thurloe, Dec. 21, Feb. 1, Feb. 13, *Thurloe*, iv. 333, 495, 533.

discover the reasons why the conduct of the Major-Generals was far more offensive to Royalists and semi-Royalists than was warranted by their conduct as collectors of illegal taxation. In arresting loose-livers, and other persons whose expenditure was beyond their means, they were acting, no doubt, under the Instructions, but none the less without legal authority of any kind. Nor was this all. The arrests made by them, in this fashion, threw into their hands a power which, dependent as they were on the local knowledge of the commissioners, might easily be employed to give effect to private spite. Worsley's mode of dealing with the attorneys, again, may be taken as evidence of the way in which, when the mere enforcement of the law is entrusted to military men they are apt to step beyond the boundaries which would at once be recognised by a lawyer. So far as recusants were concerned [1]—and it is probable that, in such a county as Lancashire, a large proportion of the malignant attorneys were recusants—Worsley did no more than put in force against them a Statute of James I. The exclusion from practice of mere malignants, not being recusants, was absolutely illegal.[2] Such conduct, if followed—and it was likely enough that it would be followed by the other Major-Generals—could hardly fail to double the number of Royalists before the new system had been many months in operation.

[1] 3 Jac. I. c. 5, § 6.
[2] It could not be said, however, that the personal quarrels of the commissioners with their neighbours would in this matter weigh with the Major-General in picking out malignant attorneys, as he would depend on the sequestrators' certificates, and not on local gossip.

END OF THE THIRD VOLUME